BEARING WITNESS

ESSAYS IN HONOUR OF BRIJ V. LAL

BEARING WITNESS

ESSAYS IN HONOUR OF BRIJ V. LAL

EDITED BY DOUG MUNRO
AND JACK CORBETT

PRESS

STATE, SOCIETY AND GOVERNANCE IN MELANESIA SERIES

Published by ANU Press
The Australian National University
Acton ACT 2601, Australia
Email: anupress@anu.edu.au
This title is also available online at press.anu.edu.au

National Library of Australia Cataloguing-in-Publication entry

Title: Bearing witness : essays in honour of Brij V. Lal / editors : Doug Munro, Jack Corbett.

ISBN: 9781760461218 (paperback) 9781760461225 (ebook)

Subjects: Festschriften
 Indentured servants--Fiji--Biography.
 East Indians--Foreign countries--Intellectual life.
 Fiji--Politics and government
 Fiji--History.

Other Creators/Contributors:
 Lal Brij V. honouree.
 Munro Doug, editor.
 Corbett, Jack, editor.

All rights reserved. No part of this publication may be reproduced, stored in a retrieval system or transmitted in any form or by any means, electronic, mechanical, photocopying or otherwise, without the prior permission of the publisher.

Cover design and layout by ANU Press. Cover image: Oil painting by Jane Ricketts, Suva, 1996.

This edition © 2017 ANU Press

Contents

List of Illustrations... vii

Contributors.. ix

Acknowledgements xv

Brij Over Troubled Waters.. 1
Tessa Morris-Suzuki

Editors' Introduction... 3
Doug Munro and Jack Corbett

In His Own Words

1. Indenture and Contemporary Fiji........................... 13
   Doug Munro
2. From the Sidelines 29
   Vilsoni Hereniko
3. Curtain Call.. 47
   Jack Corbett

Indenture

4. Brij V. Lal: Rooting for History............................ 65
   Goolam Vahed
5. *Girmitiyas* and my Discovery of India 87
   Clem Seecharan
6. Reflections on Brij Lal's *Girmityas: The Origins
   of the Fiji Indians*.. 117
   Ralph Shlomowitz and Lance Brennan

Fiji Politics

7. A Political Paradox: The Common Franchise Question
   and Ethnic Conflict in Fiji's Decolonisation............... 129
   Robert Norton

8. Constituting Common Futures: Reflecting from Singapore about Decolonisation in Fiji 153
    Martha Kaplan and John D. Kelly

9. Ethnicity, Politics and Constitutions in Fiji 177
    Yash Pal Ghai

10. The Fiji Election of 2014: Rights, Representation and Legitimacy in Fiji Politics 207
    Stewart Firth

Family Album

Literature

11. Unfettering the Mind: Imagination, Creative Writing and the Art of the Historian. 231
    Tessa Morris-Suzuki

12. Autobiography and Faction. 247
    Doug Munro

Tributes

13. Aloha e Brij. 275
    David Hanlon

14. In the Shadow of the Master Carver 283
    Kate Fortune

15. Meetings with the Three Lals: That's Brij Lal, Professor Lal and Brij V. Lal 287
    Jack Corbett

16. The Boy from Labasa. 295
    Nicholas Halter

17. My Fijian *Wantok* 301
    Sam Alasia

He is the Very Model of a Pacific Historian .305
Robert Cribb

Bibliography of Brij V. Lal's Academic Writings 307
Compiled by Doug Munro

List of Illustrations

Figure 1. Cartoon of Brij and Padma Lal showing the confirmation of their life ban from travelling to Fiji by the Fijian government..........................xvi

Figure 2. Brij and Padma with granddaughter Maya Lal-Parks.....225

Figure 3. Three generations. From left to right – Brij Lal, Yogi Lal-Parks, Jayan Kenneth Lal-Parks (in front), Christopher Lal-Parks, Maya June Lal-Parks (in pram), Padma Lal, Niraj Lal, Sally Cunningham and Ash Arjun Lal Cunningham (in the baby wrap).....................226

Figure 4. Family group. Yogi, Jayan (in front), Brij, Padma, Niraj...227

Figure 5. Brij and Padma after the investiture..................228

Contributors

Sam Alasia is a private consultant, based in Honiara. From 1983 to 1988, he assisted Greg Denning and later Hugh Laracy in coordinating a Peoples' History project, which was published as *Ples blong Iumi: The Past Four Thousand Years* (1989). From 1989 to 1997, Alasia was a Member of the Solomon Islands Parliament and in 2000–01 he acted as a Special Adviser to the Prime Minister in brokering a peace deal between the warring militia groups of Malaita and Guadalcanal. His publications include a novel, *Fata'abu: The Voice of God* (2003), and a chapter entitled 'Rainbows across the mountains: The first post-RAMSI general elections', in *Politics and State Building in Solomon Islands* edited by Sinclair Dinnen and Stewart Firth (2008). Alasia is currently completing a book on the ethnic crisis in the Solomons within the broad framework of state- and nation-building in the Solomons.

Lance Brennan, having taught Indian History at Flinders University from 1973 to 1999, is now an adjunct Associate Professor. He has published on the agrarian and political history of Uttar Pradesh, famine and its relief, and—with Ralph Shlomowitz and John McDonald—has published *Well Being in India, Studies in Anthropometric History*.

Jack Corbett is Associate Professor in Politics at the University of Southampton; Honorary Associate Professor at the Coral Bell School of Asia Pacific Affairs, The Australian National University; and Adjunct Senior Research Fellow at the Centre for Governance and Public Policy, Griffith University. He is the author of *Being Political: Leadership and Democracy in the Pacific Islands* (2015), *Australia's Foreign Aid Dilemma: Humanitarian Aspirations Confront Democratic Legitimacy* (2017), and co-editor with Brij V. Lal of *Political Life Writing in the Pacific: Reflections on Practice* (2015). His current book project is entitled *Democracy in Small States: Why It Can Persist Against All Odds*.

Robert Cribb took his PhD from the School of Oriental and African Studies, University of London, with a thesis on Jakarta during the Indonesian revolution, 1945–49. He held research positions at The Australian National University, the Netherlands Institute for Advanced Study and the Nordic Institute of Asian Studies, where he was also director for two years. He rejoined The Australian National University at the beginning of 2003. His research deals with national identity, mass violence, historical geography and environmental politics, especially in Indonesia. His books include *Historical Atlas of Northeast Asia 1590–2010: Korea, Manchuria, Mongolia, Eastern Siberia* (2014, with Li Narangoa), *Wild Man from Borneo: A Cultural History of the Orangutan* (2014, with Helen Gilbert and Helen Tiffin) and *Japanese War Criminals: The Politics of Justice after the Second World War* (2017, with Sandra Wilson, Beatrice Trefalt and Dean Aszkielowicz).

Stewart Firth is a Research Fellow at the State, Society and Governance in Melanesia Program, ANU College of Asia and the Pacific. He was Professor of Politics at the University of the South Pacific, Suva, Fiji, 1998–2004. He co-edited *From Election to Coup in Fiji: The 2006 Campaign and its Aftermath* (2007), *Politics and State-Building in Solomon Islands* (2008) and *The 2006 Military Takeover in Fiji: A Coup to End All Coups?* (2009), all published by ANU E Press. His most recent book is *Australia in International Politics: An Introduction to Australian Foreign Policy*, 3rd ed., Allen & Unwin, Sydney, 2011. He is chair of the Pacific Editorial Board for ANU Press, and he teaches an ANU undergraduate course on Pacific Politics.

Kate Fortune has been involved in various aspects of the book trade throughout her working life, and has been employed as an editor in Australia, New Zealand and Switzerland. After becoming administrator at the NZ Book Council (1977–80), she was Director of Booksellers NZ (1980–87) and later worked for Allen & Unwin and Bridget Williams Books. She was Publications Coordinator, National Library of Australia (1994–96) and was co-editor (with Brij Lal) of *The Pacific Islands: An Encyclopedia* (2000). Now in retirement in Wellington, she is a board member of the Peppercorn Press (publisher of *New Zealand Books Pukapuka Aotearoa*) and of the *Turnbull Library Record*.

Yash Pal Ghai has taught at several universities in different parts of the world, with long spells at the University of East Africa at Dar es Salaam, Warwick University and the University of Hong Kong. He was visiting professor at a number of universities including Harvard, Yale and Cape Town, as well as the University of the South Pacific and the National University of Singapore. His primary area of interest is public law, particularly in multiethnic countries. He has written or edited over 20 books and over 150 articles in world's leading journals. He has also written or helped to write a number of constitutions, including that of his own country Kenya, as well as Papua New Guinea, Solomon Islands, Vanuatu, Fiji, Afghanistan, Iraq, Nepal and Somalia.

Nicholas Halter is a history lecturer at the University of the South Pacific in Suva, Fiji. He completed his PhD in 2015, under the supervision of Brij Lal, on Australian travel writing about the Pacific Islands, and is currently working on a history of tourism in Fiji.

David Hanlon first came to the Pacific in 1970 with the Peace Corps. He holds an MA degree in international relations from the Johns Hopkins University's School of Advanced International Studies and a doctorate in Pacific Islands history from the University of Hawai'i at Mānoa. David is the author of the award-winning book *Upon a Stone Altar: A History of the Island of Pohnpei to 1890* (1988) and the more recent *Making Micronesia: A Political Biography of Tosiwo Nakayama* (2014). He is also co-editor with Geoffrey M. White of *Voyaging Through the Contemporary Pacific* (2000). He was one of the founders of *The Contemporary Pacific: A Journal of Island Affairs* and served as its editor for seven years before becoming editor of the *Pacific Islands Monograph Series*. He also sits on the editorial board of the University of Hawai'i Press.

Vilsoni Hereniko Vilsoni Hereniko was born in Rotuma, Fiji. He is a playwright, screenwriter, stage and film director, and Professor of Creative Media at the University of Hawai'i at Mānoa. He has a PhD in Language and Literature from the University of the South Pacific in Fiji. He is a former director of the Center for Pacific Islands Studies at the University of Hawai'i at Mānoa as well as the Oceania Center for Arts, Culture and Pacific Studies at the University of the South Pacific. He is also a former editor of the award-winning journal *The Contemporary Pacific* and is author of *Woven Gods: Female Clowns and Power in Rotuma* (1995). After *The Land Has Eyes*, his second feature film is called *Until the Dolphin Flies,* and is slated for production in 2018.

Martha Kaplan is Professor of Anthropology, Vassar College. A cultural and historical anthropologist who studies meaning in colonial and postcolonial situations, she has pursued research in Fiji, India, upper New York State and Singapore. She is author of *Neither Cargo Nor Cult: Ritual Politics and the Colonial Imagination in Fiji* (1995), co-author (with John Kelly) of *Represented Communities: Fiji and World Decolonization* (2001), editor of *Outside Gods and Foreign Powers: Making Local History with Global Means in the Pacific* (*Ethnohistory* special issue 2005) and co-editor (with John Kelly and Bernard Bate) of *Ethnographic Notes on the Funeral Rituals for Lee Kuan Yew*, special section of *JMBRAS* (2016). Her current research and publications on the cultural politics of water, supported by the Wenner Gren Foundation, the National Science Foundation and a Fulbright Fellowship, focus comparatively on drinking water and environmental imagination in Fiji, the United States and Singapore.

John D. Kelly, Professor of Anthropology, University of Chicago, works on capitalism, colonialism, decolonisation and Pax Americana in the Pacific, especially Fiji and Singapore, and in India and Highland Asia. His books include *A Politics of Virtue: Hinduism, Sexuality, and Countercolonial Discourse in Fiji* (1991), a translation (with Uttra Singh) of *My Twenty-One Years in the Fiji Islands* by Totaram Sanadhya (published in Fiji in 1991), *Represented Communities: Fiji and World Decolonization* (2001) (with Martha Kaplan), *The American Game: Capitalism, Decolonization, World Domination and Baseball* (2006), *Anthropology and Global Counterinsurgency* (co-editor, 2010), *The Ontological Turn in French Philosophical Anthropology* (2014) (editor), *Corporate Social Responsibility? Human Rights in the New Global Economy* (co-editor, 2015) and *A Practice of Anthropology: The Thought and Influence of Marshall Sahlins* (co-editor, 2016). His next book, on the Asian Highlands, concerns decolonisation, the Bandung Conference, ongoing counterinsurgencies, and the paradoxes of actual self-determination.

Doug Munro is a Wellington-based biographer and historian who has taught at universities in Queensland and Fiji. He is now an Adjunct Professor of History at the University of Queensland. His publications include *The Ivory Tower and Beyond: Participant Historians of the Pacific* (2009), *J.C. Beaglehole: Public Intellectual, Critical Conscience* (2012) and co-authorship of *Crisis: The Collapse of the National Bank of Fiji* (2002). In the 2000s he was involved in a major project on suicide in twentieth-century New Zealand, under the direction of John C. Weaver

(McMaster University). Doug is currently working on a history of the New Zealand Opera Company (which his father founded) with the aid of a research grant from the Friends of the Turnbull Library.

Robert Norton has researched on political development in Fiji since 1966. His *Race and Politics in Fiji*, the first book-length study of the development of national politics in Fiji, was published by the University of Queensland Press and St Martin's Press in 1977. An extensively revised edition, now available online, was published by University of Queensland Press in 1990. He has published numerous journal articles and book chapters on various aspects of Fiji's politics; his article 'Averting irresponsible nationalism: Political origins of Ratu Sukuna's Fijian Administration' was awarded the prize for the best research paper published in the *Journal of Pacific History* in 2013. He has also researched village politics and social change in Western Samoa, and social aspects of industrial wage employment in the Kingdom of Tonga. He was a foundation member of the Department of Anthropology at Macquarie University in Sydney and lectured there from 1969 until 2004.

Clem Seecharan studied at McMaster University in Canada, and taught Caribbean Studies at the University of Guyana before completing his doctorate in History at the University of Warwick in 1990. He joined the staff of the University of North London (now London Metropolitan University) and was Head of Caribbean Studies for 20 years. In 2002, he was awarded a Professorship in History at London Metropolitan University, where he is now Emeritus Professor of History. Among his many publications are *Bechu: 'Bound Coolie' Radical in British Guiana* (1999); *Sweetening Bitter Sugar: Jock Campbell, the Booker Reformer in British Guiana* (2005) which was awarded the Elsa Goveia Prize by the Association of Caribbean Historians; and *Finding Myself: Essays in Race, Politics and Culture*. He is writing a three-volume history of cricket in Guyana, the first of which is published.

Ralph Shlomowitz is an economic historian who taught at Flinders University from 1975 to 2007. In 2004, he was elected a Fellow of the Academy of the Social Sciences in Australia. His research concentrated on the economics of coercive labour systems, anthropometric history and the link between mortality and migration.

Tessa Morris-Suzuki is Distinguished Professor of Japanese History and Australian Research Council Laureate Fellow in the College of Asia and the Pacific at The Australian National University. Her publications include *Re-inventing Japan: Time, Space, Nation* (1997), *Exodus to North Korea: Shadows from Japan's Cold War* (2007), *Borderline Japan: Foreigners and Frontier Controls in the Postwar Era* (2010) and *East Asia Beyond the History Wars: Confronting the Ghosts of Violence* (co-authored, 2013). She is currently engaged in an ARC Laureate project on 'informal life politics' in Northeast Asia, looking at self-help grassroots schemes to address social and political problems in six countries of the region, including Japan, China and Korea. An outcome of this research is *New Worlds From Below: Informal Life Politics and Grassroots Action in Twenty-First Century Northeast Asia* (co-edited, 2017).

Goolam Vahed is a Professor of History at the University of KwaZulu Natal. He received his PhD from Indiana University, Bloomington, USA, and has worked on identity formation, citizenship, ethnicity, migration and transnationalism among Indian South Africans, as well as the role of sport and culture in South African society. He has published widely in peer-reviewed journals and his recent co-authored books include *Schooling Muslims in Natal: Identity, State and the Orient Islamic Educational Institute* (2015) and *The South African Gandhi. Stretcher-Bearer of Empire* (2016). He is currently working on a project on migration from Porbandar in Gujarat, India, to Durban, South Africa, entitled *A Small Ocean: Family, Religion and Trade between Porbander and Durban, c. 1870–1920s*.

Acknowledgements

Our gratitude goes to *Itinerario: European Journal of Overseas History*, the *Contemporary Pacific: A Journal of Island Affairs* and *The Round Table: The Commonwealth Journal of International Affairs*, for their kind permission to republish Chapters 1, 2 and 10, respectively. Clem Seecheran permitted the republication of his chapter in this volume. Tessa Morris-Suzuki and Robert Cribb kindly allowed the publication of their poems.

We are also grateful to the State, Society and Governance in Melanesia program at The Australian National University for the funding that enabled Carolyn Brewer's exemplary copyediting; and to Stewart Firth for his support throughout the life cycle of this project.

We also wish to thank the staff at Special Collections, Barr Smith Library, University of Adelaide, and Sandra Tarte of the University of the South Pacific for assistance of various sorts.

Not least we thank the contributors for making this volume possible and for their patience and cooperation along the way.

Doug Munro and Jack Corbett
March 2017

Figure 1. Cartoon of Brij and Padma Lal showing the confirmation of their life ban from travelling to Fiji by the Fijian government

Source: *Truth for Fiji* website, March/April 2015. Anonymous cartoonist. Online: truthforfiji.com/jan---mar-2015.html. Used with the permission of *Truth*.

Brij Over Troubled Waters

Tessa Morris-Suzuki

Read out in February 2013, at the function to thank Brij Lal when he stepped down from his role as Acting Director of CHL.

> In 2012 we were sorely perplexed:
> our Director was gone; we awaited the next.
> Ken George was appointed, but till he was here
> how would we survive a long leaderless year?
> Then, when all was confusion, and none could find peace
> an intrepid captain stepped up at the crease.
> He could bat like Tendulkar and out-bowl Patel
> when it came to defending our Team CHL.
> He dealt with our crises with patience and humour
> (assisted of course by the wisdom of Huma).
> He knew about budgets, RTS and RIBG
> and could argue our case with the powers that be,
> But even more crucial (I know you'll agree)
> was the way he promoted the School Morning Tea.
> His burden was heavy and painful at times
> (almost as painful as some of these rhymes)
> but we're endlessly grateful for all that he's done,
> for (if you will forgive the obvious pun)
> he's served as our bridge over wild stormy seas
> with his warm human touch and his calm expertise.
> So lift up your glasses and give a big cheer
> For a match-winning innings throughout the past year.
> From Suva to Seoul to the Suez Canal
> there's no leader like our own captain, Brij Lal.

Glossary

CHL — School of Culture, History and Language, College of Asia and the Pacific, The Australian National University

RTS — Research Training Scheme. A grant given to domestic students undertaking a higher degree at an Australian university

RIBG — A Research Infrastructure Block Grant is described, in the weasel words of the funding body, as being dispensed 'on a calendar year basis, to eligible Australian higher education providers (HEP) to maintain and strengthen Australia's knowledge base and research capabilities by developing an effective research and research training system' (Australian Government Department of Education and Training, 'Research Infrastructure Block Grants.' Online: education.gov.au/research-infrastructure-block-grants (accessed 13 December 2016)).

Editors' Introduction

Doug Munro and Jack Corbett

Brij V. Lal (b. 1952) has always had both of his historian-trained eyes on the present. His unabashed emphasis on the here and now—what he calls 'bearing witness'—makes him inimitable among his discipline. It also made compiling this Festschrift a challenge. A Festschrift is many things: part intellectual biography, part book review, part memoir, part reflection, part tribute. This book is all of those. It also fundamentally marks the passing of time in a way that both defines and transcends its subject. Brij's work, always contemporary in its outlook, always pungent with political overtones, captured the ideas, individuals and events who were at the heart of a particular postcolonial moment. That moment is passing. In reflecting on Brij's contribution, this volume offers the opportunity to consider what it meant.

Reading across each of the contributions collected here, we are struck by the fact that Brij's life and work embodies a particular postcolonial paradox; his achievements are laudable but his writing is forever tinged with regret for the opportunities lost and chances squandered. These themes emerge most clearly in the present volume in the three republished interviews about contemporary Fiji. The first, conducted in 1996 when Brij was one of the three Constitution Review Commissioners, exudes a cautious confidence that a better future was possible. The second was conducted four months after George Speight's coup in May 2000 and Brij dispassionately analyses the unfolding situation. The third interview, in 2015, is more the voice of despair that the situation is probably beyond reprieve for the foreseeable future. He also expresses disquiet at the state of the discipline of Pacific History and of academic life generally. Combined, this genealogy speaks to the intersection of both achievement and regret that in retrospect seems an inevitable consequence of Brij's steadfast desire to 'bear witness'.

Brij is what the English would call a 'scholarship boy', one of those lads from the provinces who would not have received a tertiary education but for their fees and allowances having been met through the award of a competitive scholarship (Harrison 1995: 65–82). It started with a Canadian Third Country Scholarship, in 1971, to study at the recently founded University of the South Pacific. Thus did the boy from the back blocks of Labasa, whose parents were illiterate, start on the journey that would lead to a stellar career as an historian of the Pacific Islands and especially of Fiji. He is not simply the most distinguished graduate of the University of the South Pacific but would grace the roll of graduates of any university in the world. For over 30 years, Brij has moved purposefully through the major periods of Fiji's history. As well as having 10 academic monographs to his name, he has been involved with some 30 edited collections, including *The Pacific Islands: An Encyclopaedia* (Lal and Fortune 2000), *The Encyclopaedia of the Indian Diaspora* (Lal, Reeves and Rai 2006) and *British Documents on the End of Empire, Series B, Volume 10: Fiji* (Lal 2006). As well as guest editing three special issues of journals—*Contemporary Pacific* (Lal 1990), *South Asia* (Brennan and Lal 1998), and *The Round Table* (Lal 2012)—he has published five volumes of his collected essays. The academic monographs alone exceed 3,000 pages, all-up.

It is an extraordinary output. His first book was the revision of his PhD thesis (*Girmitiyas: The Origins of the Fiji Indians*, 1983a, reissued 2004), but the emphasis thereafter has increasingly focused on the political history of twentieth-century Fiji, including political biographies of A.D. Patel and Jai Ram Reddy. His first journal article appeared in 1977 and in the ensuing decades his productivity has not slackened, as demonstrated by the chronologically organised bibliography that is appended to the present volume. In addition to his own work, Brij was the founding editor of both the *Contemporary Pacific* and *Conversations*, the series editor of the University of Hawai'i Press's Topics in the Contemporary Pacific Series, review editor of the *Journal of Pacific Studies*, and a long-term member of the *Journal of Pacific History's* Editorial Board, which included several terms as a joint editor. Then there is the supervision of postgraduate theses and his involvement in rejuvenating the Pacific Manuscripts Bureau. Suffice to say, his influence over a generation of scholarship has been enormous.

Brij is fond of quoting the great Australian historian Ken Inglis to the effect that 'A lot of history is concealed autobiography' (Inglis 1983: 1). The description exactly captures the extent to which his own writings are forged through a specific mind intersecting with particular experiences. This conjunction of mind and matters means that History, for Brij, is not so many dispassionate words on paper but the recounting of real and lived experience. Brij, moreover, needs a sense of involvement and attachment before he can warm to a subject. In his earlier work on the indenture system in Fiji he found a topic where the heart and the head came together: his choice of subject stemmed from relevance and a sense of rendezvous with his own roots. As Brij explains in the 2000 interview (republished in the present volume), he has 'to be emotionally engaged with something to be intellectually engaged with it'. There is more to it. His writings on indenture contain a strong argumentative line, often accompanied by a moral stance: the labourers *were* exploited and women labourers especially so; labourers soon learned *not* to engage in confrontational resistance to the plantation system; women were *not* the major cause of the high suicide rates on the plantations (Lal 2000: 167–238).

The nexus between manner and matter applies to Brij's work on the contemporary history of Fiji in particular. He started writing on the subject well before the 1987 coups. But the coups did impart a sense of urgency and fuel the moral dimension of his work. He said in his 1996 interview, 'there is something fundamentally wrong and immoral about deposing a duly elected democratic government through a military coup', and he has not deviated from that position from that day to this. When *Broken Waves*, his history of twentieth-century Fiji, appeared in 1992 as a volume in the Pacific Islands Monograph Series, the series editor pointed out that it:

> is a history with a point of view; it is neither impartial nor ambiguous and may well provoke controversy. Lal's own perspectives and value judgments are explicit, and he does not conceal his disappointment and even anguish over the failure to create a truly democratic multi-racial society (Kiste 1992: viii).

So, Brij's readers can be assured that what they see is what they get. There is no question of his flying in under false colours.

The section in this book on 'Fiji Politics' contains four substantial chapters—by Robert Norton, Martha Kaplan and John Kelly, Yash Pal Ghai, and Stewart Firth—and the underlying motif of each is that public and political affairs are largely mediated through the prism of race, whether the issues at stake are decolonisation, the electoral system or constitutions. Or, as Brij has said elsewhere, 'Fiji is an ethnically divided society where public memory has long been racially archived' (Lal 2015: 59). There are reminders in the chapters on 'Fiji Politics' of Brij's role as observer, commentator and participant in the political affairs of the country. What started as an interest in the 1982 election (Lal 1983b) intensified with the 1987 coups. His deepest immersion was his role as one of the three members of the Reeves Commission to review the 1990 Fiji constitution. For the most part, however, Brij's role has been that of chronicler of contemporary Fiji. Although he feels uneasy at being labelled a public intellectual (Lal 2011: 4), that is what he is: he has recognised expertise and an acknowledged reputation (or cultural authority), he is willing to express his views in a variety of media, and he has a constituency (Collini 2006: 52). 'Scholarship', he writes, 'should, as a matter of moral duty, speak truth to power; silence can never be an option' (Lal 2011: 138). But speaking truth to power can be a dangerous thing; as Stewart Firth points out (in this volume), the Bainimarama regime has 'created a new and unprecedented political atmosphere, in which criticism of the government became treasonous'. In 2009, Brij was detained, roughed up and given 24 hours to leave the country (Lal 2011: 303–06).

In effect, he had been 'grounded'—unable to return to the country of his birth and where his academic interests lay. Prior to this event, however, Brij commonly used the metaphors of travel to denote both historical processes and individual experiences—'journey', 'odyssey', 'voyage', 'banishment', 'sojourn'. Journeys usually involve changes of direction, hence one of Brij's 'faction' books was entitled *Turnings* (2008). More recently, the term 'intersections' has been added to his lexicon—those often happenstance criss-crossings between life and events—or as Brij puts more precisely, the 'series of haphazard intersections between the primitive and the modern, colonial and postcolonial, past and present, and scholarship and political activism' (Lal 2011: 321). It is the thematic range of his interest, both historical and literary, that drives the present volume.

Echoing this, quite by chance, three contributions focus on Brij's first book, *Girmitiyas: The Origins of the Fiji Indians*, a quantitative analysis of the 60,965 Indian indentured labourers who left for Fiji. Goolam Vahed and Clem Seecharan both recount the personal and professional impact the book has had on them, whilst Ralph Shlomowitz and Lance Brennan reflect on the influence of *Girmitiyas* on their own work and on wider scholarship. It is extraordinary that a young man's book can have such an effect on seasoned scholars. The irony is that Brij turned his back on the methodology upon which his start to fame rests; at the first opportunity he escaped the world of quantification and returned to the documentary and humanistic research from which he had started.

Thus, the two essays in the section on 'Literature' reflect Brij's preoccupation with the authenticity and beauty of good fictional writing. His own forays into creative writing have attempted 'to capture the inner truth rather than the factual accuracy of an experience' (Lal 2011: 119). For this reason, he insists that his quasi-fictional writing still involves his skills as an historian; and 'art of the historian' in fictional writing is the subject of a reflective tribute by close comrade-in-arms Tessa Morris-Suzuki. The other chapter in the section on 'Literature' by Doug Munro moves from the general to the particular in surveying Brij's autobiographical and creative writing and tracing his attraction to these genres.

The final section of this volume contains a selection of tributes from friends and colleagues, which reveal a many many-faceted life. These chapters are too diffuse to even think about summarising, and neither is there any need for summary; they are there for the reader to savour. In the spirit of a Festschrift we conclude our Editors' Introduction by quoting the final sentence of the final chapter, by Brij's student Sam Alasia, who writes: 'Enjoy your well-earned retirement with your family and *tagio tu mas* [thank you very much]'. Those sentiments are shared by us all. The contributors, and many more besides, will join in thanking you, Brij, for your massive contribution to scholarship, for your friendship, and for the memories.

References

Brennan, Lance and Brij V. Lal (eds). 1998. *Across the Kala Pani: Indian Overseas Migration and Settlement*. Special issue of *South Asia: A Journal of South Asian Studies*, 21:(sup. 001): 1–237.

Collini, Stefan. 2006. *Absent Minds: Intellectuals in Britain*. Oxford: Oxford University Press.

Corbett, Jack and Brij V. Lal (eds). 2015. *Political Life Writing in the Pacific: Reflections on Practice*. Canberra: ANU Press. Online: press.anu.edu.au?p=319171 (accessed 12 December 2016).

Harrison, J.C.F. (John Fletcher Clews). 1995. *Scholarship Boy: A Personal History of the Mid-Twentieth Century*. London: Rivers Oram Press.

Inglis, K.S. (Kenneth Stanley), assisted by Jan Brazier. 1983. *This is the ABC: The Australian Broadcasting Corporation, 1932–1983*. Melbourne: Melbourne University Press.

Kiste, Robert C. 1992. 'Editor's notes'. In *Broken Waves: A History of the Fiji Islands in the Twentieth Century*, edited by Brij V. Lal, 1–27. Honolulu: University of Hawaii Press.

Lal, Brij V. 1983a. *Girmitiyas: The Origins of the Fiji Indians*. Canberra: The Journal of Pacific History.

——.1983b. 'The Fiji general election of 1982: The tidal wave that never came'. *Journal of Pacific History*, 18(2): 134–57.

——. 2000. *Chalo Jahagi: On a Journey through Indenture in Fiji*, with a preface by Brisnley Simaroo. Canberra: Division of Pacific & Asian History, The Australian National University; and Suva: Fiji Museum.

——. 2008. *Turnings: Fiji Factions*. Lautoka: Fiji Institute of Applied Studies.

——. 2011. *Intersections: History, Memory, Discipline*, with a 'Foreword' by Doug Munro. Lautoka: Fiji Institute of Applied Studies; and Sydney: Asia Pacific Publications.

——. 2015. '"End of a phase of history": Writing the life of a reluctant politician'. In *Political Life Writing in the Pacific: Reflections on Practice*, edited by Jack Corbett and Brij V. Lal, 59–74. Canberra: ANU Press. Online: press-files.anu.edu.au/downloads/press/p319171/pdf/ch053.pdf (accessed 12 December 2016).

Lal, Brij V. (ed.). 1990. *As the Dust Settles: Impact and Implications of the Fiji Crisis*. Special issue, *Contemporary Pacific: A Journal of Island Affairs*, 2(1): 1–230.

——. (ed.). 1992. *Broken Waves: A History of the Fiji Islands in the Twentieth Century*, with 'Preface' by Robert C. Kiste. Honolulu: University of Hawaii Press.

——. (ed.). 2006. *British Documents on the End of Empire, Series B, Volume 10: Fiji*. London: The Stationery Office.

——. (ed.). 2012. *Fiji and the Coup Syndrome*. Special issue *The Round Table: The Commonwealth Journal of International Affairs*, 101(6): 489–601.

Lal, Brij V. and Kate Fortune (eds). 2000. *The Pacific Islands: An Encyclopaedia*. Honolulu: University of Hawaii Press.

Lal, Brij V., Peter Reeves and Rajesh Rai (eds). 2006. *The Encyclopaedia of the Indian Diaspora*. Singapore: Editions Didier Millet in association National University of Singapore; and Delhi: Oxford University Press; Honolulu: University of Hawaii Press.

In His Own Words

1
Indenture and Contemporary Fiji

Doug Munro

This interview was conducted by Doug Munro on 9 October 1995 at the University of the South Pacific. At the time Brij Lal was one of three members of Fiji's Constitutional Review Commission, and he was completing his biography of A.D. Patel.[1]

DM: I would like to start off by noting that you are the grandson of one of the 60,000 Indian indentured labourers on Fiji. How would you describe your background?

BVL: My grandfather came to Fiji in 1908. After serving his five-year term of indenture he leased some native land and started his family there. My parents grew up in Labasa and I was born in Tabia village where the family farm still exists. Like most Indian people of that generation, my parents were illiterate although my mother somehow learned how to sign her name. But always at the back of their minds was the memory of indenture—the poverty, the petty humiliations—and my parents did not want to see their children go through a similar experience. Moreover, there was the insecurity of land tenure. We could only lease land for short periods; we could not own land. We were a large family of eight people so there was no way in which our parents could provide for all of us a future on the land, so economic insecurity played a part. Also, education was culturally valued by our community. Most primary schools were started

---

1 Republished with permission from *Itinerario: European Journal of Overseas History*, 21(1) (1997): 16–27.

by our parents and grandparents amidst great difficulties. I went to the local primary school (which in fact is celebrating its 50th anniversary this year) and then to Labasa College for my high school education and from there to university here and elsewhere. But it was that experience of growing up on the farm that I think has been very important in shaping my imagination, helping me understand certain things. My interest in history really starts there.

DM: It is fair enough to say that you come from an improving class that was intent on upward social and economic mobility for subsequent generations. But you come from a fairly disadvantaged background and also an improbable background for someone who has since become one of the two foremost historians of Fiji and also an authority on the history of indentured servitude. So, interest aside, what made you become an historian and not something else? You did say that your background gave you a sense of a past that had to be rectified. But what about the opportunities that came your way and the people who helped to make it possible?

BVL: Growing up on a small farm in an isolated part of Fiji where a week old *Fiji Times* or *Shanti Dut* was the only interesting reading material available, I felt the need to know about the outside world beyond the village. My grandfather was alive when I was a child. I used to sleep in his bed and he used to tell me stories about India, about his growing up in a village, about why he came. When I was a child I used to see these funny looking people, the surviving *girmitiyas*, wearing turbans and *dhoti*, congregating in the evenings under a mango tree or in a small shed, smoking *hukka* and talking in a strange language. They used to sing *bhajan* together. This intrigued me, and I suppose it is not altogether surprising that my first book deals with the background and identity of these people, a kind of collective biography (Lal 1983a). My high school teachers played an important role, too. I wanted to do English literature and history. Both these subjects really interested me and I had some fantastic teachers who asked us to read writers like W.B. Yeats, T.S. Eliot, Tolstoy, Dostoyevsky, the Bronte sisters, Shakespeare, the American classics of John Steinbeck and F. Scott Fitzgerald, and Australian authors like Patrick White. We read many of the great classics of English literature. And we had a history teacher—who later became a labour politician—who one day turned up for class with a placard around his neck bearing the opening words of *The Communist Manifesto*. They were people who took their profession seriously, were interested and interesting, and who encouraged us to go on. I got the sense when I was at high school that knowledge was fun and that passion to understand has continued. I chose history but to this day I have an abiding love of good literature.

DM: As you said earlier, you found your niche, initially, in the history of the *girmitiyas*. I take it that your own background provided you with some advantage, if only a sense of commitment.

BVL: Yes, it was a project in which the heart and the head came together. I was writing about my own people, about myself really. So there was a sense of immediacy, emotional attachment. I had the language, I had contacts. I was making discoveries which had a direct social and personal interest. I have since discovered—no doubt my early exposure to great literature played a part here—that I am not very good at things abstract, remote. A subject has to appeal to me emotionally, has to have some personal relevance, for me to be intellectually engaged with it. The great Australian historian, Ken Inglis, once said that history is largely concealed autobiography (Inglis 1983: 1). I think there is much truth in that.

Take my eventual choice of a thesis topic. At first I wrote to The Australian National University saying that I wanted to do a PhD in historical demography. But they had no one to supervise me and also thought that I had insufficient background in mathematics. So they shifted me into history, and there was Ken Gillion, the distinguished scholar of Indian migration and of indenture (Gillion 1962). Ken told me that there was the topic of the Fiji Indians and he also mentioned that I could work on Sikhs on Fiji, because my Master's thesis was on Sikhs in Vancouver. There was this larger Sikh diaspora which Ken thought I could explore. But I found after a month or so of reading that I could not become enthused with the subject, so Ken said: the Fiji aspect of indenture is covered (and there might have been a territorial element there) so why not look at the background of these people in India—why they came? who they were? and the whole process of recruitment and migration. He had in mind the idea that I might be able to provide some insights into the whole process of migration and social change in one part of India. So that is how I started.

DM: Soon after we first met as postgraduate students in 1979 you presented a seminar paper on your PhD work that challenged the notion that *girmitiyas* were deceived into signing on for service on Fiji. It struck me at the time as rather too assiduous an application of the type of history that was around the Department of Pacific History at ANU at the time—the Davidson tradition, if you like—where Pacific Islanders (and indentured Asians for that matter) were accorded a proactive role in the shaping of events and their outcomes (Davidson 1966). Afterwards, by contrast, when you followed the *girmitiyas* onto the plantations, and published a series of articles in the mid-1980s, a very indignant tone enters your writing, and you stress the exploitative and oppressive lives led by the *girmitiyas* (esp. Lal 1986a). Put it this way: I noticed the contrast.

BVL: I am not sure that when I went to do my PhD I had read what Davidson had written about agency and the role Pacific Islanders themselves had played in the making of their own histories. The book on Pacific history that most impressed me initially was Peter Corris's work on the Solomon Island labour recruitment and migration (Corris 1973). Also, a highly influential work came out in 1974 and that was Hugh Tinker's *A New System of Slavery*—a very emotional work whose thesis is explicit in the title (Tinker 1974). I began to wonder as I read more about the tremendous changes taking part in nineteenth-century India, and the enormous migration from the Indo-Gangetic plain to different parts of the world, whether it could be that millions of people would leave their homes because they were deceived. It just did not sound right to me. Also, I realised that people over a 40-year period, even more in some cases, were leaving India for other colonies, coming back, and so there were communication links. So I was not convinced that deception was as important a factor in inducing people to leave. I do not discount that fraud and deceit were important factors in inducing people to move. But its extent seemed to be exaggerated. After all, migration to Fiji and other colonies was but a very small part of a larger process of migration to, say, the Assam gardens, to the Calcutta jute mills, to the coal mines in Bihar, to the Bombay textile mills—and there was a very lively debate going on at that time about the role that the British had played in undermining the handicraft industry and to what extent poverty in India was caused by British colonial policies (e.g. Morris 1968a, 1968b). Given the context of what was taking place in India at the time, my emphasis was on agency and participation by the subjects themselves.

Now, if there is a shift in tone when I write about indenture on Fiji, I would say that it is not as marked as you suggest. It is all a matter of perspective. I do not discount the oppressive consequences of the plantation system, and the terrible conditions under which *girmitiyas* lived and worked and survived. But I have also emphasised the role of individuals themselves in making their own history. You will note the emphasis I have placed on *sirdars* or Indian foremen—their collaborative role with the overseers and the plantation management. In my article on women and suicide—the social history of indenture—I look at the role of sexism and racism (Lal 1985). I look at the role that the patriarchal values played in marginalising women from the social processes (Lal 1986b). So there is some continuity. I look at the role of individuals in making their own history. When I talk about recruitment I look at the reasons why they left. And when I look at the experience on plantations, I try to understand why things happened the way they did, and in that context I emphasise individual agency.

DM: Those articles in the mid-'80s were highly revisionary. Where do you think that your work goes beyond your predecessors? I mean, Ken Gillion must have been a hard act to follow.

BVL: Ken Gillion's book *Fiji's Indian Migrants* is still a standard starting point, but it is a product of its time. I think what Gillion was trying to do was to maintain 'balance'. I have looked at the same records that he looked at, and many more. I have the sense that he did not mine as much out of the historical evidence as he might have. He was loath to upset the balance of perspective, so everyone gets their share of his attention. As an historian, Ken was making an evaluation of the total system and he attempts to provide a complete picture of the entire experience. I admire his work to that extent. It is what helps to make it an invaluable point of reference. But when you go beyond that framework, I think you begin to realise that things are more complex.

DM: Such as the question of women and suicide?

BVL: Exactly. Not only Gillion but others who have written about the very high suicide rate among the *girmitiyas* always held the 'immoral character' of women as the major factor. But I cannot expect them to anticipate the thinking and research of a generation later. I respect and admire the work that has been accomplished and I am mindful of the context in which it was written, the paradigms used. But I think that we have moved on in pushing the frontiers of indenture historiography.

DM: In what ways do you feel, then, that your work has advanced on your predecessors'?

BVL: I suppose my contribution would be in enlarging our understanding of the everyday life on plantations—through the exploration of specific issues, such as the treatment of women, such as social problems of suicide, such as workers' actual experiences on plantations, and the methods that they used to accommodate and resist the demands made on them. That is where I have tried to link the Indo-Fijian experience with experiences elsewhere. I have tried to be broader than the very Fiji-focused work of my predecessors and not only relate it to the Indians' indenture experiences elsewhere but to work into Pacific Islands history generally. I think, if I can be so bold as to say so, that my contribution is to locate Fiji Indian history in the indenture experience in this larger context. I think I have also used more cultural evidence, such as in my work on Totaram Sanadhaya (Lal and Yadav 1994), and the kind of work I now propose to do, looking at representing the human reality of the experience.

DM: Both of us take an explicitly comparative perspective. Where we broadly differ is that I am concerned with the more conventional questions of power relations in the plantations, resistance and accommodation. You are concerned with that too but go further because you are interested in the hidden world of the worker—on questions of evolving identity, individual and group.

BVL: Well I think that the work that you have done on power relations is vital. That sets the framework and the parameter. Without that groundbreaking work it would be very difficult to do the work that we are thinking of doing now. I do not think that one is necessarily better than the other. I think it is very important—and this is in line with developments in historiography—to look at the experience of workers, the unwritten history of people, deciphering their texts. That is interesting, that is useful. I believe I have access to certain sources and that I have certain skills by virtue of who I am—a member of the community that I am writing about—access to information, and to that extent I am privileged. I find it interesting, this history of the subaltern strata. It fascinates me and how to incorporate their experiences, their vision, their hopes into the larger text is what historians have done for other parts of the world for slavery, indenture, peasants. So this approach is informed by developments elsewhere, which try to represent the experience of the ordinary people.

DM: If you had to make a statement on the nature of indenture, at least with respect to the Indian diaspora, what would it be?

1. INDENTURE AND CONTEMPORARY FIJI

BVL: Leaving aside the questions of exploitation, racism and the institutional aspects of indenture, I think that the indenture experience is an extremely important, formative and defining period in the history of overseas Indian communities, particularly in the Caribbean, Mauritius, South Africa and Fiji, because that is the site of the initial social transformation. It is fundamental. When the Old World meets the New, then old ways of doing things, old values, institutions, and practices start to change. We begin to confront the reality of a completely different order when former ways of doing things, the world view, seem to lose their relevance. The caste system breaks down, and along with that a host of social conventions and practices. Everyone is a 'coolie', huddled together on estate lines in cramped quarters. In that sense, everyone is equal in the denial of their individual humanity. The indenture experience was a great leveller of hierarchy and status. So I see the indenture process as the death of one world and the beginning of another. The details vary from colony to colony, but the process is the same everywhere.

DM: A feature of your work is that you have moved purposefully through the major divisions of not just indenture history but Fiji history—from your Master's thesis on the Sikhs through to the origins and plantation experiences of Indo-Fijians. That done, you have written extensively on contemporary Fijian political history, most recently a biography of the great Indian leader A.D. Patel. Now you are looking at indenture in a far more comparative perspective. There does seem to be a rhythm and a pattern that your work has gone through. Was this planned or semi-planned, or was it the way that things simply panned out?

BVL: Simply the way things panned out. I had absolutely no idea when I finished my PhD that I would go on and do work on Fijian indenture. When I went to Hawai'i I thought I had done enough on indenture on Fiji and I expected to move on to other things. For a while I contemplated writing a history of indenture in Hawai'i.

DM: But that was exactly the time that you were writing all those articles on indenture on Fiji.

BVL: If in hindsight there is a pattern, it was not carefully designed. My journey into various things has basically come from the quest to understand myself. Indenture provided an understanding of my origins, my social identity, my beginnings. Then I wanted to look at my place in the wider society of Fiji and that is why I began to think more systematically about the larger social environment which also informed my identity and where I was. As for contemporary political history, I have certainly had a very keen desire to understand the present. For me, history provides a tool and a method to understand the contemporary world. And I have always found myself, as one reviewer put it, an interested spectator of the history of Fiji. My work, when I was at the University of the South Pacific and then at Hawai'i, deals with contemporary issues—beginning with my research into the 1982 Fiji elections (Lal 1983b)—partly because I was living in separate environments where I was constantly called upon to comment on social problems and social issues—and more so on Fiji as a member of a small educated elite. I could not have neglected that responsibility, and the more I was asked to comment about politics, about contemporary developments, the more I began to move closer to the recent period. The past and present, to me, are not discrete entities, they are two sides of the same coin, and I enjoy living and working at the interface between the two.

DM: And then, I guess, Fijian history thrust itself upon you with the coups in 1987 and that was something you could not have avoided even if you had wanted to. You have made the point that your approach to political history, and especially writing the contemporary history of this country, is one of '[c]ritical attachment rather than cool detachment' (Lal 1992: xvii). Could you elaborate?

BVL: Yes, I was here during that critical period in 1987. I care deeply about this country, about its people, about its future. I cannot be indifferent to it. Cool detachment, in my view, comes from someone who assumes an air of dispassionate objectivity, distance and a certain coolness—the sense that one can stand outside time and space and history and judge things impartially, which is certainly not for me. One cannot be neutral about the coup. One can try and understand but one cannot claim complete detachment. So in that sense when I talk about critical attachment I write with affection, I write with a certain concern and commitment. I just cannot be indifferent to what happens in this country where I was born.

DM: I remember you telling me that you wrote your book on the Fiji coups (Lal 1988) in a matter of weeks, this outpouring of words with papers and research notes lying all over the living room floor, totally absorbed in your work, your family life on hold. I got the impression that this writing performance was a matter of release, almost as though the exorcist had walked through the door. What is it like, to work under that sort of impetus?

BVL: A month after the coup I went back to Honolulu where I was teaching and where I had my regular job. I had just experienced a major event in the life of one Pacific Island nation, but on Hawai'i, except for very brief and rather ill-informed commentary, there was absolutely no awareness of the depth of the tragedy and its implications for the Pacific Islands region as a whole. There were colleagues who were sympathetic but they lacked even the most basic understanding of Fijian politics and social dynamics. I found myself talking to myself. I could not communicate my experiences to people under these circumstances, so I turned to writing. I found that words just came tumbling out. I sat there and wrote and wrote and wrote, and at the end of it I felt exhausted and relieved. I also desperately wanted to contribute an alternative explanation about the causes of the coup, contrary to what was portrayed in the media. There was that additional pressure, self-imposed I suppose.

You see, there is something fundamentally wrong and immoral about deposing a duly democratically elected government through a military coup, a government that had been in office less than a month. Most people in this country regret that the Labour government was not given sufficient time to prove itself. Given its inexperience and the nature of the coalition agreement they may or may not have succeeded. But I think that denying them the opportunity was wrong. Fiji faced the first test of democracy— respecting the electorate's verdict on a change of government—and it failed the test.

DM: I guess that you find the writing about recent events a very different type of exercise than writing about the more distant past.

BVL: No.

DM: Could you comment, then, upon the possibility and the desirability of writing about the very recent past, particularly when you do not know what is going to happen next, such as a coup just around the corner?

BVL: I would disagree with you about the differences between writing about the distant past and more recent times. I would argue that the processes of investigation are the same. The critical approach to one's sources, the evaluation of evidence, rigour, rules of verification—all these apply as much to ancient history as to modern history. I think there are distinct advantages in writing about more recent times, in terms of evidence and more varied opportunities to cross-check it. Oral evidence has an extremely vital role to play. It is a source, when properly used, that can enrich and deepen a study in ways that archival documents cannot. So I feel that in that sense there are opportunities.

DM: But there are certain opportunities that you will not get in dealing with the more distant past, apart from the advantage of oral evidence and of course there is more evidence as time moves on. I am not questioning the points you made about the need for the critical approach, methodology and rigour. But often the documents are not available to you, and in your book *Broken Waves* you could only use documents up to 1959. And also perhaps the constraints of common decency will not allow you to talk about certain things within the lifetime of individuals, in much the same way as Jim Davidson, when writing his book on Samoa, imposed a self-denying ordinance by declining to identify those people, especially close colleagues, when he had something wholly derogatory to say about them (Davidson 1969: 37–38).

BVL: Yes, certainly the points you make about the unavailability of certain kinds of documents can be a problem. But when I researched the more recent period, from the 1960s, I found that a lot of confidential material found its way into the media, into the Hansard of the Legislative Council and the House of Representatives, private papers and tapes of the meetings in the possession of individuals. Information is available in different ways and I think that I was not unduly disadvantaged. And then of course you have the vernacular and English-language newspapers, which report meetings, issues and events of substance. While you do not know exactly what the governors said to London, for example, you do know broadly speaking what happened. For an historian it is not so much these facts but explaining them and providing the context that is important. The other point you raised, about people talking to you in confidence, is one we have to grapple with. It does raise the ethical problem of how to use that evidence. The approach that I have taken is not to mention names, who said what to whom, but if I found the evidence credible, and was able to verify it independently, I would state the substance of their view without breaching confidentially, real or implied. I am not being dishonest with the evidence given to me but at the same time I am concerned not to divulge the source, unless the person said otherwise.

Of course, when you talk to people and get to know them, socialise with them, it does become rather difficult to write critically about them and there is always the risk of compromising yourself. For that reason I have deliberately kept myself away from the powers that be. I always want to maintain my distance and my independence. There is nothing more satisfying than writing the truth as you see it, unaffected by social obligations and unfettered by the potential consequences of your work.

DM: Writers of contemporary history, more so than so-called 'conventional' historians, are at risk of being overtaken by events. If you had to write your book on the Fiji coup now, rather than in 1988, in what ways would it be the same or different?

BVL: This is a very important question. Since writing the book I have read what other people have written, I have talked to many people very close to the action, and I can say truthfully that nothing I have heard since I wrote my account causes me to change my mind. On the contrary, if I can say so, I am comforted, reassured by what has happened since the coups, that my analysis is correct. A few details here and there may vary, but the foundations remain unshaken. I argued then, and I believe even more strongly now, that the coup was not so much about race as it was a deliberate act of contrivance by vested interests bent on recapturing power they had lost at the polls. There was nothing inevitable about the coup. Coups do not solve problems, they compound them.

DM: In what ways do you apply your training as an historian to your work on the Constitutional Review Commission? Does it give access to insights and understandings that would not be possible otherwise?

BVL: Yes. I think I have a fairly good understanding of the dynamics of Fijian history. I am aware of previous attempts at constitution-making, and I have read very carefully and closely the Hansard; the transcripts of the Constitutional Conferences in 1965 and 1970; the records of the Street Commission in 1975; and the various commissions in and attempts at constitution-making since 1987. When you see the kinds of issues that were raised, the kinds of solutions that were devised or proposed, you notice that the basic issues have not changed very much. The same issues are repeated in various forms at various times. So it is an awareness of the historical dimension that I bring to my present work on the Commission. I suppose I also bring the ability and the training of the historian to read critically, to make an evaluation of an enormous amount of evidence that comes your way through public submissions. Reading, analysis, synthesis: these are part and parcel of our trade. Also, a certain humanistic perspective, as I believe that constitution-making is not simply a legal task; it involves people, it involves the hopes and aspirations of people, and in that sense the background and broadening experience in the humanities helps me understand better the large issues.

DM: You have written prolifically but you have also confined yourself largely to Fiji and the Indian diaspora. I make this observation in the light of Oskar Spate's call, back in the late 1970s, that historians from the Pacific Islands should tackle European themes 'in their own right', and that we should have as 'our ideal, a community of scholars drawn from both cultures, each of whom can move in either with reasonable, even if not quite equal, assurance' (Spate 1978: 44). Even after all these years it has not reached the stage where historians indigenous to the region have moved outside their own cultures and backgrounds. Do you have any comment on this state of affairs?

BVL: Yes, it is a pattern; but I am not sure that it is a bad one, actually, because we are able to offer a particular perspective, borne out of lifelong experience. We have access to certain resources—language, people, data, evidence—that may not be easily available to others. And once you begin writing you tend to stick to a particular course, and unless there is a major shift in your life from one university to another, or some other circumstance, you tend to keep generally in the same broad field. It is natural and pretty universal, I think. The other thing that is important for me is the commitment I talked about earlier. I have a commitment to my discipline and profession, but my greater commitment is to the subjects that I write about. I am very deeply committed to the history and politics of the country of my birth, as I am also to the broader Indian diaspora of which I am a fragment. I have not ventured further afield because there is so much that keeps me occupied. Unlike international relations experts, sociologists, and such, for whom the concepts and theories matter more than particular geographic regions or topics as such, historians tend to learn the language, immerse themselves in the culture, and that gives their work a certain depth and enduring quality. They make a longer-term commitment to their particular subject.

DM: There is also another point and that is the Pacific Islands of the 1990s reminds me very much of New Zealand in the 1950s. I grew up in a place where there were very limited opportunities for artists and writers, many of whom took off for greener overseas pastures. Is it not necessary, in much the same way, for historians from within the region to get out in order to get on, and often just to do worthwhile things?

BVL: I think that is absolutely vital. I do not at all accept the idea that to write sympathetically and knowledgably about the Islands you have to live in the Islands. Certainly you have to immerse yourself in the culture and learn the language, but the place where you work and write is irrelevant. In fact, it is very important for Island scholars to spend time outside the region, to reacquaint themselves with the latest developments in their fields. I would take Oskar Spate's point further and say that it is invaluable for Island scholars to spend time at metropolitan universities, and for people from those areas to spend time in the Islands. I am a strong believer in collaboration, in doing things together, helping each other out and sharing information, experiences, and, in the process, enriching ourselves and our discipline as well.

DM: Finally, could you provide a preview of your forthcoming book on A.D. Patel (Lal 1997).

BVL: A.D. Patel was politically active in Fiji from the late 1920s to the late 1960s. Fine mind, fine intellect, who believed in democracy, liberty, equality, justice; who fought against colonialism and the mighty Colonial Sugar Refining (CSR) Company on behalf of the cane growers. He was a man of wide reading and great learning. Edmund Burke was regular fare, Tolstoy, Thomas Hardy, Gerard Manly Hopkins, great Indian classics of Kalidas and Kautilya and, most important of all, the Bhagvat Gita. He spoke several languages and was the leading criminal lawyer in this country. Lord Denning, the Master of the Rolls, described him as one of the most outstanding advocates he had ever met. So I found him fascinating. I empathise with his vision of Fiji as an inclusive, democratic, non-racial society. These are things I find attractive, but I feel that he has not been given enough credit in the history of Fiji. He was the one, more than anyone else, who agitated for independence, and was responsible for the departure of the CSR Company in 1973, three years after independence. But you find his name omitted from the gallery of people who have had a hand in making the history of the country.

I have never written a biography before and what I am trying to do in this work is to present an alternative vision for Fiji, and I have let Patel speak as much as I can. I am not being judgemental. I just say: this is what he was saying, and the context in which he was saying these things. I place on record his thoughts, ideas and experiences, and create a text that others will hopefully find interesting and useful.

DM: And after Patel?

BVL: Let me finish this constitutional work first.

References

Corris, Peter. 1973. *Passage, Port and Plantation: A History of Solomon Islands Labour Migration, 1870–1914*. Melbourne: Melbourne University Press.

Davidson, J.W. 1966. 'Problems of Pacific history'. *Journal of Pacific History*, 1: 5–21.

———. 1969. 'Understanding Pacific history: The participant as historian'. In *The Feel of Truth: Essays in New Zealand and Pacific History*, edited by Peter Munz, pp. 27–42. Wellington: A.W. & A.H. Reed.

Gillion, K.L. 1962. *Fiji's Indian Migrants: A History to the End of Indenture in 1920*. Melbourne: Oxford University Press.

Gunson, Niel (ed.). 1978. *The Changing Pacific: Essays in Honour of H.E. Maude*. Melbourne: Oxford University Press.

Inglis, K.S., assisted by Jan Brazier. 1983. *This is the ABC: The Australian Broadcasting Corporation, 1932–1983*. Melbourne: Melbourne University Press.

Lal, Brij V. 1983a. *Girmitiyas: The Origins of the Fiji Indians*. Canberra: The Journal of Pacific History.

———. 1983b. 'The Fiji general elections of 1982: The tidal wave that never came'. *Journal of Pacific History*, 18(2): 134–57.

———. 1985. 'Veil of dishonour: Sexual jealousy and suicide on Fiji plantations'. *Journal of Pacific History*, 20(3): 135–55.

———. 1986a. 'Murmurs of dissent: Nonresistance on Fiji plantations'. *Hawaiian Journal of History*, 20: 188–214.

———. 1986b. 'Kunti's cry: Indentured women on Fiji plantations'. *Indian Economic and Social History Review* 22(1): 55–71.

———. 1988. *Power and Prejudice: The Making of the Fiji Coups*. Wellington: New Zealand Institute of International Affairs.

———. 1992. *Broken Waves: A History of the Fiji Islands in the Twentieth Century*. Honolulu: University of Hawai'i Press.

———. 1997. *A Vision for Change: AD Patel and the Politics of Fiji*. Canberra: National Centre for Development Studies, The Australian National University.

Lal, Brij V. and Yogendra Yadav. 1994. *Bhut Len Ki Kalha: Totaram Sanadhaya's Fiji*. New Delhi: Saraswati Press (in Hindi).

Morris, David Morris. 1968a. 'Towards a reinterpretation of nineteenth century Indian economic history'. *Indian Economic and Social History Review*, 5(1): 1–15.

———. 1968b. 'Trends and tendencies in Indian economic history'. *Indian Economic and Social History Review*, 5(4): 319–88.

Munz, Peter (ed.). 1969. *The Feel of Truth: Essays in New Zealand and Pacific History*. Wellington: A.W. & A.H. Reed.

Spate, O.H.K. 1978. 'The Pacific as an artefact'. In *The Changing Pacific: Essays in Honour of H.E. Maude*, edited by Niel Gunson, pp. 32–45. Melbourne: Oxford University Press.

Tinker, Hugh. 1974. *A New System of Slavery: The Export of Indian Labour Overseas, 1830–1920*. London: Oxford University Press.

2

From the Sidelines[1]

Vilsoni Hereniko

This interview was conducted by Vilsoni Hereniko at The Australian National University on 21 September 2000. Much had changed in the four years since the previous interview, and Lal now reflects on Fiji and legacy of the Constitution Review Commission (CRC) in the immediate aftermath of George Speight's coup. On this occasion, he is able to discuss matters relating to the CRC that were off-limits when talking about events in late 1995.

VH: How long have you been here at The Australian National University (ANU) and why are you here instead of Fiji?

BVL: I've been here since 1990. Before that, I was at the University of Hawai'i (UH). I left Fiji in 1983. The reason why I am at ANU and not at the University of Hawai'i has nothing to do with professional satisfaction, because UH was intellectually stimulating, with wonderful colleagues, especially at the Center for Pacific Islands Studies. But I came here in 1990 to write a book and my family decided that this is where they wanted to be. All of a sudden I discovered the joys of discovering the familiar contours of Anglo-Australasian culture with which I had grown up—the kind of texts we had read, the kind of people we had met. So this was a more familiar cultural surrounding to me than the States was. And the family liked it. Also, of course, Australia has cricket and rugby,

---

1 Republished with permission from *Contemporary Pacific: A Journal of Island Affairs*, 14(1) (2002): 168–84.

and those things began to matter. Why not Fiji? I've always wanted to go back to Fiji, but the opportunity never came. Certainly if the Rabuka–Reddy coalition had won the elections, I would have been there and given up an academic career. From time to time, I've also wanted to return to the University of the South Pacific, but the continued political upheaval in Fiji and all that it entails for academic freedom dissuades me from going back to Fiji immediately.

VH: Let's go way back to your childhood. Tell me, where did you grow up, what school did you go to, and what inspired you to be the kind of person you are today?

BVL: I grew up on a small cane farm, 10 acres of cane farm on leased native land. Both my parents were unlettered. We came from a big family of six boys and two girls. From very early on, it was very clear to us that there was no future on the farm for all six of us; our parents said, well you'd better get educated and become a clerk or cash earner in some capacity. The incentive to do well was always there, propelled by economic circumstances. My interest in history started very early. My grandfather was an indentured labourer and it just happened I was his favourite grandson. I used to sleep in his bed and take him around to do his ablutions, and so on. I heard stories about India, about his experiences on the plantations. Many of these were romanticised, but reinforced by the kind of cultural environment in which I was growing up: essentially Indian, Hindu and all of that. My curiosity about distant people and distant places started very early on. I was curious about these people; who they were, how did they come to Fiji? They spoke a funny language, they dressed differently. And then at primary school, I did reasonably well. I went to secondary school, had some very fine teachers. All of them have done very, very well indeed: Vijay Mishra, professor of literature in Perth; Subramani, a professor at the university in Fiji; Krishna Dutt, my history teacher, who is a prominent public figure in Fiji; all of these people freshly graduated had a kind of dynamism. They took teaching seriously, they took you seriously, because in a sense your success reflected their own success as teachers or mentors. So early on my parents were supportive, partly out of necessity, economic necessity. My teachers were encouraging, interesting, interested. I suppose I had a natural curiosity; I mean, I wanted to become an English teacher. In high school we had novels I've mentioned in my books, English texts—Dickens, Bronte, Hardy and so on. That imaginative world appealed to me. I suppose it was a form of escapism, from the dreary realities of poor life in the rural countryside. Then at university I met people who were extremely encouraging. One, whose political views I have always disagreed with, is Ron Crocombe. But Ron was a very stimulating kind of person. He provoked you, but he took you seriously as a scholar. My favourite teacher was a lady by the name of June Cook, a chain-smoking Englishwoman who came to Fiji after being at the United Nations. She was a professional historian. She read her lectures as a don would read a lecture at Oxford or Cambridge, and we took her seriously. I think the University of the South Pacific (USP) in the early days, let's say until about from the early to mid-'70s, was an interesting place to be because we were experimenting with a regional project. There was also a deep concern among both staff and students to prove ourselves, that we were a first-rate academic institution. Just because we happened to be in the third world didn't mean that we were third rate. So this eagerness to prove our intellectual prowess, if you will, made a very exciting atmosphere and after USP I knew that I was hooked on the humanities and I haven't looked back.

VH: So where did you go after USP?

BVL: I finished my USP degree in 1974, curiously before my three years. Then I applied to Walter Johnson, who was from the University of Hawai'i but teaching at USP, a very distinguished professor of history, former chairman at the University of Chicago. He taught a course on recent American history. He saw some potential in me and asked me to apply to go to UH to become his teaching assistant in the World Civilizations program. But UH rejected me. They rejected me because they said you only have a three-year degree and we have four years; we don't know about the calibre of teaching at USP. Besides, English is your second or third language, and so they rejected me for a teaching assistant. As it happened, the chairman of the history department of the University of British Columbia (UBC), Margaret Prang, was visiting USP. Ron Crocombe talked to her about me, and Margaret Prang said we'd like to have him and flew me over to UBC as a teaching assistant. Within about three weeks they gave me a graduate fellowship to complete my Master's, which was in Asian history. As it happened, at the end of my MA, when I graduated they gave me a prize for the most outstanding student in history. I remember very distinctly people at USP elated with my success because this was proof that the kind of graduates they were producing locally could do well outside. After that I went back to Fiji in 1976 and taught there for two years and then applied to get a scholarship to come to ANU, which I did. I arrived here in 1977 and finished my PhD in 1980, on the history of indenture, and then I went back to Fiji for a couple of years. For six months I was unemployed because there was no job for me at USP. But after that I decided I wanted to leave Fiji because I was not happy with the intellectual atmosphere there. I mean, having done a PhD at a university like ANU, which is rigorous and intellectually exciting, I felt that I was called on to play the role of a public figure, as one of the few doctorate locals at USP. I found that socially satisfying, but intellectually very, very arid. I felt that if I wanted to make a success of myself as an academic, I'd have to get away from USP. Maybe it was narrow-minded thinking on my part at that time, but I felt I needed to prove myself somewhere else. And so I went to Hawai'i, and after that I came to ANU.

VH: You say you joined the history departments in Hawai'i and ANU? When did your interest in politics begin?

BVL: When I went back to Fiji after finishing my PhD in the year 1982, when Fiji had its general election; it was a very tense period. There was a real possibility of a change of government because the Western United Front with Ratu Osea Gavidi had joined up with the National Federation Party. They were looking for someone to chair a radio broadcast, but no one would touch it, because it was so sensitive, and Fiji is such a small place. So they asked me. At first I hesitated, but I accepted the responsibility and I chaired those sessions, the panel discussions. I commented on the elections—my interest in electoral politics started from there. But at the same time, I suppose, living in my own country, I couldn't really escape my responsibility to understand what was happening. I was an historian working on the nineteenth century, but I was living in the present. There was a need there for me to understand what was happening and also a responsibility and obligation to articulate it as I saw it. I think there's a tension in my life: I inhabit the interface between scholarship and practical action. I have to be emotionally engaged with something to be intellectually engaged with it. Those are the two things I have been doing. After I did the elections, a book came of out of it, and I began to do both history and politics. I suppose living in Hawai'i meant that I could write without looking over my shoulder to see who was approving or disapproving of what I was writing. There was no internal censorship. I wrote honestly and as objectively as I could, without any fear of persecution. I suppose if I was living in Fiji, subconsciously I would be aware of what I was writing. Being away from Fiji meant I was not aligned to any faction within different political parties. I suppose over time people began to read what I wrote. Some agreed, some disagreed, but at least they didn't question my integrity or my credibility. Then in 1995 the constitution review exercise came. I think that was partly out of respect for what I was doing.

VH: Who approached you?

BVL: I was approached by Mr Jai Ram Reddy, leader of the opposition, whom I had known a little bit. I later found out that he asked a number of people who might be the best candidate to represent the opposition. I understand that my name was mentioned by many people, but they felt that while I had the intellectual strength and the ability and experience, I wasn't political enough. I didn't understand politics. Mr Reddy's position was that this was precisely the kind of person they wanted, who could at least try to understand things from the other side as well. To give us some fresh ideas; we don't want a puppet there. We want somebody who would be critical of what we are, what we have done, as well as understand and engage with issues of concern to other communities. It's a fact that a number of my former colleagues advised me against taking up the appointment because they said it was a farce, that nothing was going to come of it. 'Do you think that the man who had done the coup would turn around and change the constitution?' So, there was cynicism, there was doubt, and good reason for it, given what had happened in the past. But I thought it was a challenge that I had to take up. I'm glad I agreed because five years later I have no regrets about what I did, or the recommendations we made.

VH: It was a huge responsibility put on your shoulders to be one of the architects of this constitution. Did you find that daunting at all?

BVL: Yes! I was overwhelmed at times. The fact that I lived by myself for 16 months, cooped up in a small apartment, simply intensified the pressure. I could not talk to anybody because the protocol required I keep my distance. I deliberately kept away. I never talked to any political leaders because it was not the right thing; I couldn't have done it anyway. So I knew the history, I knew something about the task, but I wasn't fully aware of the enormity of what was there and the huge expectations. Everyone expected me to fail. Also there were many new areas I had to read about that I had never read before. International conventions, couched in legalistic kinds of terms about indigenous rights, political rights and civil rights. Sometimes my interpretation of a document conflicted with somebody else's interpretation. The enormous amount of reading was exhausting. But I think the good thing about that exercise was that there were only three of us. There was no fallback. Sir Paul said to us that if you two agree among yourselves I won't stand in your way, and this is what happened. Mr Vakatora and I agreed on many things. We had to talk to each other, get to know each other, explore each other's fears and concerns with communities and the groups we represented. I think that promoted intense dialogue; if it had been a larger committee, people could have passed the buck. In this case there was no passing the buck, there were just two of us.

VH: Tell us very briefly about the other two on the committee, Mr Vakatora and Sir Paul Reeves.

BVL: Mr Vakatora was a former speaker of the house, a cabinet minister, and a very senior public servant during the time of independence. A very, very hard politician, highly intelligent, he had been involved in the cabinet's draft, which laid the basis for the 1990 constitution. So he had been involved in this process beforehand. A lot of people told me that with him on the Commission it was a sure sign that we would fail—because of his undeserved reputation for being very hard, an obstructionist. In the end, we worked very hard and we became lifelong friends. I have the deepest admiration for him as a man, his intellect, and his integrity. Sir Paul didn't know Fiji, but he brought with him a wealth of goodwill, and his public persona was reassuring. He was a very good leader in the sense of not being frightened of receiving ideas from others. The fact that he was part Māori, the fact that he was a man of the cloth, the fact that he was a governor-general, all of that and the fact that he had the confidence of both sides of politics certainly helped the process. Of course we had our legal counsel, who basically translated our thoughts into acceptable legalistic terms.

VH: During this time of working on the constitution, what would you say were the most important insights that you gained?

BVL: There are many things. I think that one insight I gained was that people are not as far apart as was often made out. When we went to rural areas, right across Viti Levu from Sigatoka to Rakiraki, and other places in Vanua Levu as well, we many times heard Fijians and Indians telling us that at the village level we get along very well. We've lived together for 100 years. We know each other, we speak each other's languages. A number of times Indo-Fijians came to us and wanted to make a submission in their own Fijian dialect. The problem, they said, was that in Suva politicians stand up and, for whatever reasons, espouse all kinds of extremist rhetoric and that filters down to the grassroots level. So honestly I believe that with proper leadership, people at the grassroots level work together very well. I wish there was some kind of administrative mechanism to bring them together instead of having a provincial council for Fijians and advisory councils for Indo-Fijians. That's the first insight. The second insight I got was that there is a deep respect for certain Fijian institutions among Indo-Fijians. The Great Council of Chiefs is one. Many people asked, 'What's wrong with having a Fijian as a president?' Nothing. We celebrate that. A lot of people said we wouldn't be able to sell that to the Indian community, but I was able to because that's something that I support. I'm quite content with the Fijian side of my heritage and I think, as you can see, everyone else approves of that in parliament. The third insight came from what people said in private, not necessarily in public. From the prime minister down, including the Methodist Church in its formal presentation, people said that elections shouldn't take place from provincial boundaries because this accentuates provincialism. It's destructive, it's divisive, and it's counterproductive as far as Fijians are concerned. They want to go back to the constituency-based system of the 1970 constitution, because that provided more unity of focus and activity and so on. The impression I got was that there's a fear of provincialism resurfacing and increasing the fragmentation of Fijian society, which is what happened in the 1999 election. So many Fijian political parties, and now with confederacy politics, have accepted provincial representation, so we are going that route. There was a great deal of understanding and tolerance, whether it was what people were just saying to us I don't know, but the sense I got was that with proper leadership we could have crossed the bridge.

VH: It seems to me that one of the main problems with the present situation is this crisis in leadership. One of the things you touched on is the separation between the chiefs and the common people. I think what has happened over the years is that the Fijian chiefs, many of them, have lost touch with the common people. At present in Fiji, there's no one person who stands out as being capable of leading the country, navigating the canoe through treacherous waters at this point in time. Would you say that is the problem?

BVL: That is definitely a major problem. There are two problems here. Let's talk for the moment about the Fijian community. The Fijian community is far more complex and divided now than it was in the past. Some 40–45 per cent of the Fijian people are living in urban or peri-urban areas, where their interests and concerns and aspirations are different from those of their counterparts in rural areas. There's a sizable Fijian middle class, particularly after 1987, that has its own needs and agendas. The rural chiefs are unable to come to terms with this new reality caused by urbanisation, migration, modern education, travel—the new horizons opening— and also interactions with the multiracial world of other communities. So you're talking about a complex, fluid society that's changing very, very rapidly. An institution that filled a particular need at a particular point in time, is finding it very difficult now. But something else, which you touched on, which I think is very important about leadership: among Fijians, all the way through the twentieth century, you had Ratu Joni Madraiwiwi, then you had Ratu Sir Lala Sukuna, then you had the four greats—Ratu Penaia Ganilau, Ratu George Cakobau, Ratu Edward Cakobau, Ratu Sir Kamisese Mara—people who were tutored to take over national leadership in the course of time, when Fiji became independent. These were chiefs who had an overarching kind of mana and influence right across the Fijian community and nationally. Even though Ratu Mara came from Lau, he was seen as a national leader. With his departure, we see the end of an era in Fijian leadership. What you'll find is that now people will gain their influence, their authority and their mana from the provinces. Because of the resurgence of provincialism and confederacy politics, their larger influences seem to me to be more circumscribed. You may have a paramount chief from this area, a paramount chief from that area, but I don't see anyone on the horizon who has the makings of a national leader.

The second thing is, you have commoners, not necessarily high chiefs, who will rise to the top. Their success in politics—Rabuka, Qarase, Filipe Bole, Kamikamica, whoever it is—will also bring a new dynamic to Fijian leadership. The question is not whether it's Fijians who are at the helm, but which Fijian, what kind of Fijian. These questions will be asked more and more now than in the past. In the past, the Fijian interest was very clear. We knew who the Fijian leaders were. But not today. I think more questions are being asked and the answers contested, more so than in the past. On the Indo-Fijian side, there's also a dearth of leadership. From 1929 to 1969 we had A.D. Patel, S.M. Koya, and a few others.

After the mid-1970s to 1999 we had Jai Ram Reddy and also Mahendra Chaudhry. But these are people in their 60s, and they are on their way out, eventually, in the next four, five, 10 years. The best and the brightest of the Indo-Fijian community are leaving in the thousands. They're migrating. So what you have in Fiji is basically people who can't migrate, won't go, and that affects the kind of people who are thrown up as leaders. I think as far as leadership is concerned this is going to be an issue that people of Fiji will have to grapple with in the future.

VH: What is the ideal profile for a new leader for Fiji, one that may be able to grapple with the realities and the complexities of the present situation? What should be the characteristics of this leader?

BVL: That's a question that's almost impossible to answer. I suppose one would need to have somebody who has the confidence of his or her own community, but has a larger vision that encompasses others. One who is inclusive. But maybe time has moved on for one person as a single leader. Maybe time is now opportune for a collective kind of leadership—people with strengths in different areas. I don't think you're likely to see another Ratu Mara in your lifetime, that kind of experience and background. I don't know, the situation is so politicised, so fraught. The logic of politics in an ethnically divided society dictates that to win votes you have to take an extreme position, which is what happened in 1999. Rabuka and Reddy were seen to be trying to move to the centre. They were outflanked on the one hand by other Fijian parties, and on the other, by Chaudhry. In an ethnically divided society, when you have moderate leaders coming together to forge a common ground, they will always be outflanked by racial extremists. That is a real challenge for leadership. People need to understand that in a society like Fiji we have to make progress cautiously. We must always be sensitive to many divergent interests and needs and different forms of discourse. The Fijian form of political discourse is indirect, allusive; the Indo-Fijian's based on a long tradition of robust democratic debate. And the two clash. What we need is a leader who understands some of the inner logic and inner dynamics of the other community, as well as his or her own.

VH: I think it was Rabuka who said that democracy is a foreign flower. It seems to me that the democratic process is one that doesn't suit Fiji. Thus, it's not very productive when everyone focuses on democratic principles. History seems to have shown us that if democracy is to work something has to be modified, to take into account the Fijian chiefly system, its hierarchical nature. For example, supposing there's a council of leaders consisting of conflicting factions, including members of the Indian community—something that seems rather attractive in the present situation. Is anyone considering alternatives?

BVL: I think we need to have some kind of dialogue between representatives of the different communities. I think the Great Council of Chiefs missed a golden opportunity. For the first time, in the 1997 constitution the Great Council of Chiefs was constitutionally recognised. The expectation was that it would be representative not only of indigenous Fijian interests but also of national interests. That was our idea—a council of chiefs for Fiji. But not all Fijian chiefs were interested. So when the test came they failed. When George Speight's coup took place, they listened to Speight and his demands for political control and supremacy, but there was no place at their table for any representative of the democratic voice. At the least, they should have said, we want to hear the other side as well before we make a decision. I think that's one thing that's disappointing. The other thing is, of course, that the Great Council of Chiefs was in some senses hijacked by younger chiefs and others with private political agendas and motivations. Some of the chiefs from rural areas did not have a full understanding of the complexities of what was happening. In a way, George Speight put a gun at the head of the Great Council of Chiefs. 'You'll decide this, you'll appoint this person as the vice president and this person as the president.' Then, when appointing the president, they were told, now you must appoint so and so as the prime minister. That, I think, undermined in some serious way the sanctity of the Great Council of Chiefs. I think they haven't come out of this crisis very well. I certainly hope that the Indo-Fijians will be able to get together and form a group of elders who are above party politics, to be able to deliberate on issues at the national level and in some sense create a liaison with the Great Council of Chiefs at an informal level. I think that's important, that kind of dialogue, regular dialogue at the grassroots level, the provincial level, and the national level, outside the political arena. That's very important. When you talk about democracy as a foreign flower, several things I would say: one is that Fiji never had democracy, in the sense that we understand the term. There are many models of democracy. For example, in Fiji the president is nominated by the Great Council of Chiefs. Half the senate is nominated by the Great Council of Chiefs. So many other things—land ownership and so on—these things are outside the arena of politics. So Fiji's democracy has always grappled with and tried to accommodate special interests within a broadly overarching democratic polity. So democracy has many models. If democracy is a foreign flower, then there are many other foreign flowers as well. For example, Christianity is a foreign flower. In Fiji it is now a part of the indigenous culture. The truth is that democracy was fine as long as they were winning—1966 to 1987. It failed when they failed to win. That's the second thing. The third thing is: What would you put in place of democracy? Theocracy? Ethnocracy? I think that the way forward for Fiji is to do two things. One is to acknowledge the sanctity, the authority, and the power of certain indigenous Fijian things. That's absolutely vital, and that's what we did in our report. We have got to acknowledge that. Sometimes it comes very close to breaching international conventions, but we said no, the president should be a Fijian, and everyone should accept that. This is an explicit acknowledgment of Fijians' special place and control over those institutions by Fijians. All of this should happen within the broadly overarching framework of equal citizenship. There must be respect for individual rights. You see, I come back to the point that indigenous Fijians are divided and diverse in their lifestyles, their orientations, their ideologies, and their values. In the long run, democracy will be good for them. Democracy here means the right to exercise individual choice to vote. Given the enormous diversity, and given increasing urbanisation and other factors, the Indo-Fijian population is likely to decline significantly. Already we are in the 40 per cent range; in the next 10 years we are likely to be in the 30s. So the Indo-Fijian presence wouldn't be a big factor in the way it was in Fiji politics for much of the twentieth century. While we must have institutions and organisations at different levels to facilitate discourse outside the arena of active politics, at the same time, I don't know what would be a better alternative to democracy, the ballot box, the parliament, and all of that.

VH: We have to take into account that people like Rabuka or George Speight, acting on their own accord or as pawns of other interests, were able to walk into parliament and wrest control of power. On the other hand, the majority of people appear happy to deal with their own grievances within the constitution, but once you've got someone like Rabuka or George Speight taking over parliament, then all the repressed or suppressed feelings of people come to the surface and the response becomes a very emotional rather than a rational one. So yes, I think the democratic process can work for most people, but how do we take care of people like Rabuka or Speight? How do we prevent anything like that ever happening again?

BVL: No constitution can prevent a coup. That's a given. I think there's no guarantee that coups won't take place in Fiji or elsewhere. What's happened in Fiji, and this is my judgement, is that there was dissatisfaction right across the country, especially among the Fijians, with the style of Chaudhry's administration. It was seen as confrontational; it was seen as doing too many things too quickly. People felt rushed; Chaudhry was in a rush to deliver, having made those costly promises during the campaign. Chaudhry is a strong trade union leader, and a trade union has its own culture of dealing with problems. For instance, the end is really the important thing, the means is neither here nor there. Dissatisfaction was widespread. I also have the sense that many people were saying, well let's give him a chance and see. Some people were unwilling to wait, including a number of groups—one is diehard nationalists who basically believed that Fiji should always be run by Fijians, the Butadroka group. Another group is people who were defeated at the polls, who sought revenge. They will use any excuse—I am thinking of Apisai Tora, for example; he will support any cause that will support Tora. So there's a politics of revenge. There are also people who missed out under the policies of globalisation. In that category are also people who were fast-tracked to promotion, or benefited from racially accommodated action programs, and they wanted to reach the top right away. There were well-connected businessmen and others who felt their ambitions thwarted by this new government with its own network and its own clientele. All of these people supported the coups, but at the end of the day I have a sense that they had their own agendas and they exploited the confused and innocent emotions of people. There was already a kind of substratum of dissatisfaction—somehow things were not right—and they tapped into that.

VH: Do you think there's something that's very particular or specific to Fijian culture that makes it seem so easy, during times of tension in Fiji, not to follow the rule of law, but somehow resort to something very primal?

BVL: We are a multiethnic society. We've practised the politics of communalism for nearly a century. So we've always practised compartmentalised communal politics—our group first and the nation second. That reinforces feelings of primordiality and all of that and suspicion of the other group. Way back in the 1960s you always had the cry, 'If Fijians don't unite, Indians will take their land away', and that was enough of a rallying cry for people to come together. Race was always used as a political mobilising tool, so when this kind of thing happens—a new government comes into power that is perceived to be anti-Fijian—they go back and say, Fijians have had it again; this is our country. Yet these people don't realise that Rabuka was in power in 1990 and the same people threw him out. There is now a reservoir of suspicion and mutual hostility that can be tapped into for any particular purpose. In that context the appeal for support is achieved most successfully.

VH: One of the things that amazed me was the initial reaction from the Fijian community once Speight had taken over parliament. You would think that the leadership would be against it immediately and denounce it. By not doing that they seemed to be endorsing Speight's actions. One way of reading that would be to say, well the majority of Fijians approve, even though they may tell us in public that they don't.

BVL: I agree that what began as an individual action of a group of people carrying out this coup later on, through propaganda and through the media, became part of the larger rhetoric of 'This is for the Fijian interest, for the land', and so on. I think over time it developed a momentum of its own. I mentioned the Great Council of Chiefs, who, in my judgement, failed to exercise the leadership that was expected of them and that they wanted themselves. I think that the army certainly was divided. They dithered, and the Fijian people will pay a huge price for this in the future, because Fijians have shown that when push comes to shove, their loyalty is to the *vanua*, to the chiefs, not to the institution of the army. I think that is a very dangerous thing. That is why I've argued that the army needs more outsiders to act as a buffer, more Rotumans, maybe more Indo-Fijians in the army. It's an important fact. I think security forces show that they did not really live up to expectations. The judiciary caved in, abolishing the Supreme Court by decree. I myself think the president failed in his leadership by tinkering with the constitution when he had no authority to do so, giving George Speight and the Great Council of Chiefs 'his personal guarantee that things would be done to their satisfaction' when he, as president, had no legal authority to do that. So the institutions collapsed, or were compromised. Maybe deep down they sided with Mr Speight and what he stood for. Which leads me to my next point: the very same people who dithered and silently supported Speight now single him out as a traitor. They want him tried for treason. My argument always has been that while Speight must face up to the consequences of his actions, he's not the only one. Other institutions and individuals, for whom Speight was a front man, should also be held accountable. The very same people who are benefiting from what Speight did are now turning on him saying he is the culprit; just as in 1987, they expected Rabuka to do the deed and move out. Of course he didn't. In this case, Speight has done the deed and he's now being tried by the very same people who are benefiting from his actions. There's an element of hypocrisy, an element of trying to show the world that things are returning to normal, but of course, they're not, because singling Speight out, scapegoating and brushing things under the carpet will not work.

VH: Are you suggesting then that these people should not have benefited at all, or that George Speight should not be tried? What is a better way of responding to the situation?

BVL: I think he should be tried; there's no question in my mind about that. Rabuka went free and then we had Speight; if he goes free, there'll be somebody else. That's the lesson of our recent history. What I am suggesting is there ought to be a deep and sincere investigation, something like a truth commission. What happened? Why didn't things work out? Did the 1997 constitution fail? What did we do wrong? What do we need to do now to prevent such acts from happening in the future? That kind of soul-searching. Where have the Indians fallen short? What should they do? What more should they do to become fully accepted as part of society? Are there shortcomings within Fijian society that prevent it from dealing with the demands and realities of a modern, commercial, globalised world? Rather than focusing on simply another affirmative action policy here, more seats there, we need to grapple with those real questions. The 1997 constitution was widely approved after thorough consultation, blessed by the Great Council of Chiefs, and approved unanimously by the parliament. What went wrong? Do we need to throw the rule book out just because a team loses the game? What kinds of rules are necessary for the questions you were asking early on? Maybe we should look at alternative models. What alternative models, that our commission didn't look at, might they look at? That kind of thing is very important, but I honestly believe Mr Speight should be tried. I'm just saying that he's not the only one, and people need to understand that there's a wider network. One doesn't necessarily have to be accusatory and vindictive, but the need to understand is absolutely vital.

VH: Do you think there are people in Fiji who can be objective or neutral, or do you think these people will have to come from outside?

BVL: I think there'll be resistance to outsiders. It's a natural reaction to outsiders who judge us by other standards. So if there's consensus you could get some distinguished person from the region who understands the Pacific region and its cultures, one who is trusted by the people, to be a part of this exercise. I have noticed that we don't use our own people often enough. What about someone like Michael Somare from Papua New Guinea or Ieremia Tabai from Kiribati?

VH: I find it interesting that both those two you mention are not Fijians. Are you including them as insiders?

BVL: What I'm saying is that if you're going to have outsiders, then get people from the region who have long experience, understand the situation, and can lend a helping hand. But as members of this commission or this group, the majority will have to come from Fiji itself. They must not be tokens. They must be representatives chosen by the different communities, and they must rise above politics. Look at where we went wrong, tell us. Go and look at other experiences, if you want to. This is what happened with our commission. We were put there by two different groups and yet we were able to rise above politics, the kind of groups that supported us. It is possible. I really do think that there are people in the community, people of goodwill and foresight.

VH: Do you think this is being done or going to be done?

BVL: I hope the government will do it. There is a ministry for reconciliation headed by the interim prime minister himself. I hope he will have the foresight and vision to appoint people who may not necessarily agree with him but will have the courage and independence to say what they think. I think that kind of soul-searching, that kind of talking through these things is very important. The atmosphere is extremely polarised in Fiji right now. People are hurt, and the anguish is there, but I think it is important to now start the process of reconciliation. The best way to go about it is to choose respected citizens, who have the confidence of the people. Where did we go wrong and how can we prevent future actions like this?

VH: So when you review the constitution and the work that the three of you accomplished, how do you feel about the constitution now? If you could make changes, what would you change, if anything?

BVL: The 1997 constitution says some things that are different from the report we wrote, especially in respect to the composition of parliament and the executive. We recommended that the president should be an indigenous Fijian, nominated by the Great Council of Chiefs, elected by both houses of parliament. I think that is a good thing. That's something that I'd like to see in the constitution. We recommended that two-thirds of the seats be national seats and be contested from three-member constituencies, and that people be forced to make alliances at that level. They reversed that by saying two-thirds should be communal and one-third open. If there is some doubt in people's minds about the system of voting, let's look at it again. Although people are critical of the 1997 constitution, one thing it recommends is compulsory power-sharing. The constitution provides that any political party with more than 10 per cent of seats in parliament is constitutionally entitled to be invited to be part of cabinet, which I think is a good thing. That's why the Fijian Association went in. The *Soqosoqo ni Vakuvalewa ni Taukei* (SVT) is crying foul, unconvincingly, because they were invited. Instead they wanted a number of portfolios, which are the prime minister's prerogative. He invited them to participate—the question of portfolios is a matter of negotiation—instead, the SVT demanded terms and conditions. I do not know of any other constitution for a similarly situated ethnically divided society where indigenous concerns and rights are as well protected without breaching democratic principles.

VH: Fiji has ethnic groups other than the Fijians and the Indians. I think we've talked quite a bit about the Fijian and Indian communities particularly, but I wonder if you have any thoughts about the Rotuma situation, particularly at this time. It seems to me that over the years, Rotuma has been treated as a colony of Fiji. Given the present climate in Fiji, maybe Rotuma might consider exploring some other kind of relationship with Fiji, one perhaps that will give it more autonomy, something akin to a compact of free association with Fiji. Do you think this is something that Rotuma should consider?

BVL: This is an issue that came up before the commission in 1995, when we travelled to Rotuma and received a number of submissions. There were several concerns. One is that there was an independence movement led by Mr Gibson. There was a faction that wanted independence—not only them and other places like Rabi. So the independence action was certainly canvassed. But there are many Rotumans who didn't want it, because, they pointed out, 70 per cent of Rotumans live in Fiji. They are part of the Fiji economy. Let me put it this way: we recommended that the issue of independence is for the people of Rotuma to decide. I think we also favoured the idea of some kind of compact of free association that gives Rotuma greater autonomy while maintaining some kind of relationship with Fiji where you can come and work and so on. I think we were very sensitive about that; we did not dismiss the issue out of hand. We felt that it is something the people of Rotuma should work through. Fiji's interest in this is economic, the 200-mile economic zone, that's what it's all about. A lot of Fijians would say, 'Well, if Rotumans want independence, go to Rotuma', but they are Fiji citizens. I think that's not the issue; the issue is here's an island that is far away, in public consciousness as well as physically. If they want greater autonomy, the commission certainly favoured that, and we felt that they should explore some kind of compact with Fiji, perhaps the kind of relationship Tokelau has with New Zealand, for example. We were very sympathetic.

VH: What are your political plans now in relation to Fiji? Do you have intentions of going back and becoming actively involved in trying to figure out where Fiji should go or how it should resolve its problems?

BVL: I had my opportunity. I have said what I think is appropriate. Emotionally, Fiji will always be a part of me. That will always be there. I think that active politics is probably out now. The shadow lengthens and one is conscious of the small amount of time that's left. I really want to do other things. Eventually, after writing a biography of Jai Ram Reddy—a story of Fiji politics from 1970 to 1999, a period when I myself came of age and was involved in some capacity with Fiji's politics—I'll probably not go back to Fiji. I want to work on a multi-volume history of Australian relations with the Pacific from 1800 to 2000, because I live here now. I'd like to explain this part of the world to people in this country because Australia has been a dominant power in this region. That's one thing I want to do. Then I'd like to write some fiction. It's difficult but I'll try. I don't see myself being in academia for very long. I've had a good run. If something better comes up I'll certainly think about it. For the time being academic life seems to be the best alternative I have.

3

Curtain Call

Jack Corbett

This interview was conducted by Jack Corbett at The Australian National University (ANU) on 9 February 2015 for the purposes of the present volume. It offers a chance to reflect on the 15 years between Brij Lal's discussion with Vilsoni Hereniko in 2000, including political events in Fiji and the 2006 coup and 2014 elections in particular. Lal also reflects on the future of the discipline of Pacific History, particularly at ANU.

JC: The last time you did one of these interviews it was with Vilsoni Hereniko (see Chapter 2). You'd just been involved in the 1997 constitution process. And, aside from being a scholar, you were a participant in history. Over the last 15 years, your role seems to have changed, particularly in relation to Fiji. My first question is why, and what difference do you think that changing role has made?

BVL: Well the last 20 years have been years of—how should I put it—turbulence in Fiji's political history: the 1987 coups and then the coups of 2000 and 2006; and this period has seen enormous change in Fijian society. In terms of the demographic balance, the Indo-Fijian population has declined substantially, largely through emigration, to about a third of the total population while the indigenous Fijians have increased to about 60 per cent. This has enormous implications for the course of future developments in Fiji, including for the conduct of politics. Space has now opened up for debate on issues that were once simply impossible to imagine.

And then there is the whole question of a nascent coup culture in the country. There was a time when we believed that the proper process—the proper way—was through the democratic process, through elections and respecting the verdict of the ballot box. After 1987 people began to think that we could change our politics through the shortcut of military intervention. Having spent all my academic career studying the history of Fiji, the history of other developing countries, and the role that individuals played in trying to develop a political culture that respected democratic values—I am talking about people like A.D. Patel and Ratu Mara and Jai Ram Reddy later on—and to see democratic processes and values so blatantly subverted distresses me. I still feel that there is an obligation on me as a student of Fijian history to take a stance.

The second aspect of this was that given the state of repression, the denial of freedom of speech silenced a lot of people in Fiji. The country became an area of darkness as far as the freedom of expression was concerned. I was in a position to articulate a line of thought, whereas people living in Fiji were scared to voice their opinion because of fear of persecution for the temerity of speaking out. What distressed me considerably was that people I had expected, educated people, leaders of moral communities, to take a stand in defence of the rule of law and of democratic principles did very little. I could not do that, stand on the sidelines and do nothing. I felt that I had no choice but to take the stance I did and I don't regret that at all, despite being chucked out of Fiji and banned from returning. I would not call myself a public intellectual; that is too grandiose a claim. Rather, I see myself as someone who took a stand on matters of principle. And that is what I have done.

JC: Has it made a difference?

BVL: I think it has made a difference in the sense that I receive emails and messages from people who keep saying, 'Doc what you're doing is inspiring. We believe in what you are saying—but we can't say this ourselves'. Even people who publicly criticise me would say privately, 'Well what you are saying makes sense'. Mind you, I also get a quota of hate mail. And I think there is in a sense a disquiet among the powers that be in Fiji that I am weaving a separate narrative that a lot of people in Fiji silently find convincing. So I think there is that aspect to it. One should never underestimate the power of the pen—or the word processor.

3. CURTAIN CALL

It is very tempting to succumb to the attractions of power or proximity to power. It is far more difficult to stand your ground, to draw a line on the ground and say: this far and further.

But I write not because I want to make a difference or bring about change—I suppose I do—but because that is the only thing that I can do. I see myself as having no alternative, no choice in the matter. Something terrible was happening and I couldn't be a bystander. But I now want to write about the world that matters to me, that helps me better understand my past. I want to be a witness to the time and place in which I have lived. And I want to be able to leave my footprints—it sounds very egotistical—but I want people who come later on to know that some people did stand up and were prepared to be counted when it mattered.

JC: And you've paid a price.

BVL: I paid a price and it does hurt.[1] There is no denying it. It's hurting not to be able to return to one's place of birth. It's hurting because as the oldest living family member of my extended family, I have certain responsibilities and obligations which I can't fulfil. For example, attending funerals and marriages and being at the celebration after a birth. And I am very conscious of the passage of time. The shadow is lengthening. I do hope that one day I'll be able to go back just to be on the Fijian soil again. But if it doesn't happen then it doesn't happen.

I'm truly grateful to Australia. I can't say how grateful I am for the opportunities that this country has given me. And I am at home in Canberra. At least my immediate family members, my siblings and my children and others are now in Australia. So the sense of loss to some extent is mitigated by that fact, but it is still there.

I hope that one day I can say to the authorities in Fiji: 'Look, I've lost. You have won. The sanctions against Fijians travelling to Australia have been lifted, so why don't you reciprocate? And at least tell me why I can't go back. What wrong did I do? I stood up for certain principles and certain values. And you stood up for something that you believed in. The battle is over in a sense.' Unfortunately, I detect a sense of vindictiveness in

---

1 Lal is referring to 2009 when he was banned indefinitely from returning to Fiji (Lal 2011: 303–306).

all of this, this indefinite ban on my wife, who has never commented on political matters, and myself. And maybe fear as well, I don't know, the sense that the pen is mightier that the sword.

JC: Speaking of those principles and values. One of your biographical subjects and I suspect heroes, A.D. Patel, stood up for things like a non-racial franchise and so forth. These things have come to pass in Fiji. Why don't the ends justify the means in this context?

BVL: Many things that A.D. Patel stood for are now a reality: a common name, equal citizenship, non-racial designation of public institutions, particularly schools and the like. But in public life, means are just as important as ends. When you're talking about the project of nation-building, getting people behind the idea is vital, through consensus, dialogue and discussion: that is the way in which you will convince the people about the value and the importance of supporting something as big as this. What you have in this situation is that important institutions, particularly Indigenous Fijian institutions, have been unceremoniously dumped—for example, the Great Council of Chiefs. There is anger among many Fijians, there is frustration that is not articulated publicly but it's there, seething beneath the surface. The sense of humiliation is palpable. It won't go away.

I just hope that the government of the day will show more sensitivity and understanding. I welcome many of the developments that have taken place, such as the adoption of a common name for all citizens, equal citizenship, the end of racially discriminatory affirmative action programs. And I suspect that these changes are irreversible. But the way these changes have been brought about leaves much to be desired. The process is just not right. Violence as an instrument of public policy will always be counter-productive. And I also see a problem here. The problem is that you have an ethno-nationalist institution, the Fijian military, being the champion of multiracialism and the guardian of democracy. There's clearly a contradiction here. I also don't know to what extent Commodore Bainimarama's multiracial vision, as he has articulated it, is shared by people who are in his corner now because many of them were coup supporters. I'm talking about people like Inoke Kubuabola. Their support for Commodore Bainimarama is opportunistic. I am not sure that there has been a genuine change of heart.

This is partly because of the manner in which change has been brought about, without public consultation. There was a façade of consultation, nothing more. It is said that Fiji has returned to democratic rule, which is true but in a very limited way. The parliament is really a pliant institution. There is hardly any robust debate on important issues. There is no consultation with the opposition at all. The government has all the answers. 'This what I want and expect', and it gets done double-quick. But this is not how democracies work. Compromise and consultation are an integral part of the democratic process. Given that we live in a very complex world, stable government requires some give and take and preparedness on the part of all stakeholders to live with less than the optimal outcome.

JC: So what's the prospect for the future then?

BVL: Fiji is not out of the woods yet by any stretch of the imagination. The country is passing through a very, very critical period. I get the sense that one era in Fiji's colonial history—the twentieth century—with its assumptions and understandings about how politics ought to be organised, which interests should be given priority over others, has come to an end for a whole variety of reasons. One is the demographic transition I talked about. The fear of Indian dominance that so coloured Fijian political life and thinking in the twentieth century is gone. The second thing that has changed, in recent decades, has been the passing on of those paramount chiefs and those who believed in the racially organised political structure. Ratu Sir Kamisese Mara, who died in 2004, was the principal architect of that order, but even before his death his handiwork was being eroded by the forces of modernity.

One era has come to an end. But we don't yet know what the new one will look like. At the moment the rhetoric is about building a genuinely fair and equal multiracial society, levelling the playing field for all citizens, fostering a sense of national cohesiveness. All that is good and to be welcomed. What worries me, though, in this new dispensation is the role of the military. The kind of guardian role they have got in the constitution would give them the constitutional right 'to intervene in politics if they don't like it'. They have got the veto power, so to speak, over the political process. They can't be touched. Their budget can't be touched, so I think we just have to wait and see over the next maybe decade, to see how things progress. Those who supported the coup and all that followed may one day realise that they are riding a tiger they cannot dismount at will.

The second point I want to make is that the present order is dependent on the goodwill and whim of one or two individuals. We're not talking about representative democracy. We're talking about strongman democracy here. Today Commodore Bainimarama is around and so he will guard this structure. But what happens when he's gone? I don't see anybody on that side of politics who has the charisma, and the profile, to be able to see these things through and I don't know how seriously committed they are to his stated vision. Fiji First, the prime minister's political party, is a political party in the technical sense. Most people would agree it is in fact run by very few people. Stability will come to Fiji if there is a solid foundation based on the rule of law and genuine participatory democracy. While I can see the end of one era, I really cannot see the shape of the one that is going to come.

JC: Yeah, it's interesting. The question I have in regards to that is that for much of your life you've been associated with the National Federation Party (NFP). Are you still an NFP man? And do you see a role for those old parties in this new future?

BVL: I've never actually been a member of NFP. What attracted me to the party was the kind of inclusive, democratic, non-racial principles that it enunciated in the 1960s. I found that attractive. I strongly felt the political edifice constructed on the pillars of communalism and racial separation was bad for Fiji. There was a vision for the country which, as you've said, has been realised in part although not in the way its founders intended. I found that attractive. I found the vision of the leader of the Indo-Fijian community throughout the 1970s, 1980s and 1990s, Jai Ram Reddy, attractive. He realised that indigenous Fijians were not prepared to move to a common roll at all. They totally opposed it, and promulgated the 1990 constitution instead. So, he opted for the model of consociationalism—power sharing through group representation, but always respectful of democratic values, and always respectful of the sensitivities of the indigenous population. People, I hope, will see me as someone who has consistently believed in certain principles—of democratic values, the sanctity of the ballot box, the importance of dialogue and discussion in resolving difficulties. These are the kind of things that A.D. Patel and Jai Ram Reddy articulated. And in the process they lost. Both of them lost. But I think they were the right values and that the approach was right.

Now I am in a situation where a lot of indigenous Fijians write to me and say, 'Doc, you stood for principles and you never personalised issue'. That is endorsement that I have an attachment to certain values, and as it happened, in Fijian politics, it was the NFP which articulated those. I thought the Alliance party's approach of racially compartmentalised politics was inappropriate for Fiji. But the kind of party politics of the 1970s, 1980s and 1990s is gone. Old fears and phobias are gone. Now, every political party is required by law to have a multiracial membership. And that's a good thing. You already see, for example, in NFP the sort of things which I hadn't thought would happen. Credible Fijians, professional Fijians, are standing for what was once perceived to be an Indo-Fijian party. Once for Fijians to stand for an Indo-Fijian party like the NFP was tantamount to treachery and betrayal, but now, you don't have that sense at all. Now the president of the party is a young Fijian lawyer, and that's a good thing. That is the way of the future.

JC: That segues nicely to your scholarship and legacy as a scholar. For much of your career you've written about racial politics. Do those old ways of making sense of Fijian politics still hold?

BVL: I wrote about those issues, about the role of race in Fijian politics, because that is what situation was on the ground at the time as I found it. To be sure, there were cross-cutting issues that united communities across the communal divide but because of the institutional structure of politics, everything had to be put in racial terms: so many Indians in parliament, so many Fijians in parliament. Affirmative action was seen in purely racial terms. Race was not simply false consciousness. It permeated the very sinews of our important institutions. You were asked for your racial identity when you left and re-entered the country, when you opened a bank account, got your driver's licence, applied for scholarship, were considered for promotion. Its pervasive effect is difficult for the younger generation to imagine but it was palpable to those of us who lived through those times. I wrote about what I saw; it wasn't a figment of my imagination. What is happening now is a positive development. And it's partly because the architects of the old order are gone, the demographic situation has changed, old barriers and boundaries have collapsed from the impact of modern technology. Fiji is a much more open place now than it was two decades ago. As I have said before, Fiji is an island, but an island in the physical sense alone.

JC: Could you describe the experience of writing about issues of race in Fiji? If you were to start your career today as a young scholar of Fiji, what do you think you would write about?

BVL: Not all my work is about issues of race as you would know. I have written on a whole range of other subjects as well. If I were starting now, I would stay clear of politics and contemporary history. One thing I've learned writing about Fiji in the last 30 to 40 years is that it's been a really painful process, emotionally and intellectually draining, gut-wrenching. I keep revisiting those missed opportunities. I see with great clarity the mistakes we made and we haven't learned from those mistakes. Every time I revisit the past it's like opening a wound afresh. I sometimes wish I did not write about Fiji at all, that I worked on some other Pacific island or on some other topic in the remote past, rather than on something that is so close to the bone, as a writer, as a scholar, and as a participant. I enjoy writing about the past creatively and imaginatively. I think one can better capture the truth of the human experience through creative writing if it is properly done, and that is something I would have started doing much earlier in my career than as a part-time hobby. Stories have a way of connecting with people that dry social science scholarship cannot.

JC: Over the last 10 to 15 years there has been a notable shift in your focus. Not just on Indo-Fijians but on Indian diaspora more generally. What brought that about?

BVL: Two things. One is that I have continued to write about contemporary Fiji. I've done the historical part, I've written my books, I have lived at the interface between scholarship and practical action. Engagement and attachment are important to me, not detached and disinterested scholarship. The head and the heart have to meet. That's where I live. I use that scholarship to illuminate the present. So that's one strand in my work.

The other one came about quite unexpectedly. My first book was on the Indian indentured labourers to Fiji. And after that I wrote a series of articles on women and suicide and protest on the plantations. That work was finished by the late 1980s and around that time it began to be discovered by scholars working in different parts of the world—in the West Indies, in Mauritius, in South Africa. There was a revival in aspects of the work that I had done. It was my article on the experience of Indian indentured women on the plantations that aroused the initial interest, but my other work also began to get noticed by this broader constituency. A reinforcing factor was the emergence of the concept of an Indian diaspora. Before the 1990s there was no sense of such a thing but it suddenly came into vogue and became the focus of far-flung and loosely organised scholarly network. One result was invitations to conferences and to publish in this wider field, culminating in my editorship of the *Encyclopaedia of the Indian Diaspora* (2006), which was such a success. My interest in the Indian diaspora developed in a haphazard way, but it has now become an important part of scholarly work.

JC: I want to press you a little bit on the views of some of your critics. The first accusation would be that Lal is too Indian focused; his take on Fiji is very much an Indian view. How do you respond to that?

BVL: What is an Indian view? That is too simplistic a characterisation and very misleading. I would happily plead guilty to the charge of having a democratic point of view but not a racial point of view. When you talk about an Indian view of Fiji, essentially you are talking about views that are broadly concerning things like equal rights, equal citizenship, democratic space and equal opportunity for everybody. These have been associated with one community in Fiji. But in fact they are universal values. And that is what Indo-Fijians have been asking for all along from the 1920s onwards. Let's have a common roll, common citizenship, equal opportunity. And I happen to agree with that. So what is identified as an Indian view is in fact fairly broad concerns of people everywhere.

Let me give you a specific example—of the 1987 coup. I took a very prominent role as a commentator—and a book came out of that, *Power and Prejudice* (1988). A lot of people were saying at the time that I was taking the anti-coup stance because I was an Indian. The world saw events in Fiji through the lens of racial stereotypes: Indians were out to usurp the rights of the Fijians and the Fijians had no choice but to oppose that by force. It was seen as an indigenous versus immigrant issue. I argued that the coup was not about race only but about recovering power by a group that had lost it; race was used as a scapegoat for other interests and motivations. Issues of class and regional politics were involved. The quest not to give up power lay at the heart of the issue, especially by people who thought they had the right to rule by virtue of who they were, an entrenched elite. I am not sure I convinced many people at the time, but now most people agree with that analysis. It's become part of the mainstream thinking on the subject. I opposed the 2006 coup even though many Indo-Fijians supported it. A lot of people were perplexed. Some Indo-Fijians in Sydney wrote to my vice chancellor, Ian Chubb, to fire me because I was bringing disrepute to the university because of my opposition to the 2006 coup. My worst hate mail was from Indo-Fijians.

I acted the way I did because there was a commitment to certain principles. I wasn't doing it because Indians were the target in 1987. I felt then, as I do now, that the coup was wrong, that it was not about race but about other interests. I don't believe coups solve problems. As I have said so many times, coups compound problems. I believe passionately in the rule of law, in the values of democracy, in the sanctity of the ballot box, and in the processes and protocols of constitutionalism. I opposed coups not on ethnic but on moral and ideological grounds.

The second thing is, yes, if you look at my more creative writing, my faction, I write about my own community. And I do it because I am a part of it. I do it because I understand their background, I understand what makes them tick. I can feel the community's heartbeat. And I do it because I want to be a witness to my time and place. I am afraid I do not think I can write about other communities with the same degree of confidence and intimacy. I haven't written about the inner lived experience of the Fijian people because I don't have that intimate familiarity with Fijian culture. Their concerns and interests, I can see, I can understand, but I don't think I am in a position to articulate them with the same kind of confidence that I am of the world that formed and de-formed me. I would accept that I began my work looking at Indian indentured labourers but I branched out looking at the broader political history of the country. One of my great regrets really is that you don't have a substantial Fijian scholar from within, writing about changes taking place within Fijian society, profound changes. I mean Fijian society as it was in 1970 is not what it is now. There has been a fundamental transformation. What is going on? And I think this where I regret that after 30 to 40 years of university in Fiji we haven't produced many scholars that can tell us about the internal dynamics of the society. There is not another Rusiate Nayacakalou, Isireli Lasaqa or Simione Durutalo on the horizon.

JC: Postcolonialism is a frame for understanding some of these issues, why did you never take to it in your work?

BVL: Well, two things. One is that the time when I entered the academy way back in the early '70s, postcolonialism wasn't around. I read a lot of that literature in subsequent years and I am aware of the pertinence of some of their concerns and relevance to my work. But I have not been overtly postcolonial or postmodern in my work. This is partly because I want to create my own text. I don't want to be a footnote in somebody else's text. I had this rich field to explore, you know multiracialism, nation-building and so on, and I wanted to see it through my own eyes. I strongly believe that theory should emerge out of the data that you collect rather than the other way around. There is something of the literary scholar or artist in me, I suppose, who thrills to the particularities of the human experience in all its maddening diversity and complexity, and I am comfortable with that. History is a mansion with many rooms, and there should be room for all kinds of scholarship. Postcolonialism has a place in it, to be sure, but it should also know its place in the broader scheme of things. Among the scholars whose works I enjoy reading, and who were once my colleagues, all nontheoretical in the narrow sense, are fine writers of prose, such as Tessa Morris-Suzuki, Hank Nelson, Bill Gammage, Ken Inglis. Further afield a whole host of great American historians, from C. Vann Woodward to Arthur Schlesinger Jr, and in Britain, from E.P. Thompson to David Cannadine. But a short answer to your question is that I am egotistical enough to believe that my work should have my signature on it, not someone else's.

JC: So then you touched on this briefly. But the criticism would be that that text is still relatively atheoretical. Can you articulate why or what it is about your work that makes a theoretical contribution?

BVL: I am not sure that framing the question that way is very helpful. What matters in the end is not whether your work is theoretical or not, but the quality of the imagination and insight you bring to bear on it, whether your work opens a new window on the broader field. That, in the end, should be the true test of any piece of scholarship. Theory informs my work but I do not let it smother it. That is a choice I made a long time ago. I am not interested in the arcane debates about methodology and theory that take place in a discipline. I leave that sort of navel-gazing to others who have a taste for it. My main concern is to tell a story in a way that I connect to readers beyond the halls of the academy. I write to get read, not simply to get ahead. Look at historians whose works have altered our perceptions of the past, Henry Reynolds on Australian Aboriginal history, Eugene Genovese and Kenneth Stampp on American slavery, E.P. Thompson on the emergence of the English working class, and I think you will see what I mean.

JC: You mentioned before the absence of a sort of Fijian equivalent to yourself as a scholar. I wonder if you can reflect a bit on your generation of Pacific intellectuals. Both where you fit and what contribution that generation has made to our understanding of the region.

BVL: A lot of Pacific Islanders of my generation went to USP—the University of South Pacific—founded in 1968, to be trained to provide for the manpower needs of the newly independent countries or countries about to become independent. When they finished their studies they got absorbed into the bureaucracies of their countries. Some, very few, stayed on at the university to pursue academic careers, such as Rajesh Chandra, Vijay Naidu, Simione Durutalo [1956–1994], Vilsoni Hereniko. The older generation included Pio Manoa, Raymond Pillay, Satendra Nandan and Subramani.

But many USP graduates did not go into academia, though, of course, they made profound contributions in their own countries and regionally as well. The opportunity was there but other things intervened. One of my regrets is that more of us are not doing the kind of solid academic research that is needed. And I really would like to see more Pacific Islanders in Australia and New Zealand universities as well so that the Islander voice is represented. But now, the environment in the universities is very different. It's more outcome-driven, externally funded, project-oriented research. The bright ones go into consultancy or international civil service. And maybe that is the nature of the beast. I tried to train PhD students, to come up through the ranks, but other attractions intervened. So there is that regret. But I think that people of my generation have made a contribution, not in academia necessarily but more broadly to society.

JC: I guess the nature of things, particularly when reflecting on people who have come to the end of their careers, is to wonder where the next generation comes from, where the next Lal comes from. Does USP produce another Lal?

BVL: I certainly hope so, but I don't see any evidence of that for the moment. I think the pressures, the incentives and opportunities have changed. The idea of devoting an entire lifetime to scholarship on one country, let's take Fiji for example, that's not likely to be the case in the future because you don't have too many positions which encourage that kind of commitment, or support that kind of endeavour. You are forced to apply for research grants and research grants are determined by national priorities. You work on projects one after another. And who is there to say that these things are less relevant, to themselves and to the societies in which they work. I am not prepared to make that judgement that the kind of work that I have done is necessarily better than what other people are doing. We are all making our contributions in different ways, to the broader field and to the improvement to the lives of our people. But I do think that it would be good to have a few more people from the islands, breaking into the top echelons of Western academy and they're not doing it now.

JC: Part of that story is also that the nature of the academy, even at ANU, is changing. There are very few Pacific historians left at the ANU, for example. There's a question of whether your own position will be filled when you're gone. Are the opportunities that you were afforded going to be around?

BVL: The short answer is no. And now with the shrinking budget it means that you have got to reprioritise where you want to focus your energies. In this new order, Asia has become much more important than the Pacific Islands. So what you had in the '60s and '70s and '80s and '90s—a cluster of Pacific historians here working on the region, that's gone and I don't think I'll be replaced. Many Pacific historians are now well into their 60s. And I don't see new ones coming up. Yes, there are some in New Zealand, Damon Salesa, for example. But Judy Bennett and Jacqui Leckie at Otago or Clive Moore at Queensland are getting on in age. Many have retired: Ian Campbell, Peter Hempenstall, Hugh Laracy,[2] Doug Munro, Stewart Firth, Donald Denoon and Deryck Scarr come to mind, although some remain active researchers and writers. Hank Nelson and Alan Ward have died. So that cohort which came of age from the mid-1960s through to the late 1960s and early 1970s is gone, or is on its way out. And it's not for lack of trying but we have not been able to build or to get people in the discipline who will take the field further. Maybe it won't be history, but some other disciplines that will fill the void.

---

2   Sadly, Hugh Laracy died on 6 October 2015 (Salesa 2016).

But the discipline of history itself has changed. Now we have got to take a broader approach. Historians have to be more creative, to engage with cognate disciplines, to be prepared to retool to engage with other disciplines. But the old model of graduates coming out of ANU and then populating the provinces has gone.

JC: The question is to what extent this is in part a failure of your generation to cultivate successors or to what extent the humanities have suffered particularly in recent years. And whether we are going to see a vibrant historical scholarship on the Pacific—or just in general—in years to come?

BVL: Perhaps to some extent we are responsible. But I think that given that there are so few positions in Pacific history, for example, a lot of people didn't see any future in this. And many people trained at ANU in the 1970s and 1980s could not find academic employment. They went into high school teaching or into public service, people such as Andrew Thornley and Penny Lavaka. The necessities and the requirements have changed. I don't think Pacific history will die, only it will be done in a different way. But I think that the culture of the academy is such that it is not conducive to a lifelong kind of career in one field. That's the nature of the beast. We'll just have to wait and see.

JC: As you look back on your journey through Fijian history of the twentieth century, what would you say was the major challenge in writing it?

BVL: Fijian history is a deeply contested terrain. There is no unifying narrative about it. What one group viewed as good and desirable, another thought the opposite. One thought that on balance colonial rule was beneficial, the other thought it was baneful. One wanted primordiality as the foundation of Fiji's political culture, the other advocated ideology. One wanted common roll, the other communal. One was the landowning community, the other was primarily tenants. One deployed the metaphor of Fiji as a harmonious three-legged stool, the other rejected it. The list goes on. Unlike some other Pacific Island nations such as Tonga and Samoa with a homogenous cultural tradition, where history could be deployed in the project of nation-building, Fiji had no such advantage. Inevitably, what one writes is seen through a particular ethnic and ideological lens. That is why people shy away from examining too closely the contours of our history lest they discover a huge void.

So, we use warm and fuzzy catch phrases such as 'Fiji: The Way the World Should Be', and used to portray ourselves as the model of a functioning multiracial democracy, although we all probably knew in our hearts that things were not as rosy as we wanted the world to believe. Our task as scholars is to explore the corners and hidden crevices of our past, to force ourselves to look at the mirror. It is very easy to be accused of being biased. Inevitably, you are accused of taking one side or the other. The best thing to do in the circumstances is to declare your hand. As I have said on another occasion, value is a matter of judgement, and there can be no finality in matters of scholarly discourse. The most important thing is to be true to the evidence before you. I find it encouraging that there is more openness now, more willingness, to acknowledge the complexity and contradictions of Fijian history, but this wasn't the case when I began my journey.

JC: That brings us to your retirement, or pending retirement. Why now?

BVL: Well, many things. One is that I have been in this business for over 30 years, 25 of them at the ANU. I've seen the best. I've worked with the best. They're all gone. So there's a sense of isolation and a definite sense of loss. I'm talking about my colleagues in this corridor. I feel that the world which formed me is now gone. The sense of community, the sense of being together in the same business, of looking out for each other, is gone. We are a much more atomised group now, harassed and hassled, all furiously chasing the research dollar. I don't find the present culture of the academy satisfying any more. To justify your existence every year to academic bean counters is not what I joined the academy for in the first place. To tell the truth, I find the whole thing repugnant. We historians don't operate on an annual cycle, nor should we. The value of our work will be judged in the fullness of time, not tomorrow or the day after. I refuse to accept the bureaucrats are the best judges of the value of the work we do.

I have other things I want to do. I want to do volunteer work in the community, to give something back to this generous land which has been so hospitable to me and my family. I am actively exploring options in that regard in relation to remote and Aboriginal communities. I want to read and write more widely. As I mentioned before, I am really taken in with the idea of writing about the past creatively, imaginatively. I have been doing that on the side for some time, but I now want to make creative writing the centrepiece of my work. I have a novella in mind which I want to complete. It is about the autobiography of a tree, and how the tree has seen changes taking place around it over several generations. And I come back to the question of bearing witness to my time and place, to create a memory bank for future generations because the world I come from is unwritten, where memory is not neatly archived.

I have had a good innings. Now there is no retirement age, and I could go on for as long as I like. But when does fresh blood come into the system? We have a responsibility, I think, to prepare the ground for younger people to come up through the ranks. I'll still keep on writing. I'll still keep on doing the work in different ways maybe. But I don't have to be on full pay to do that. I will continue my association with the university or with the academy in some form but less constrained by the need to be on the treadmill all the time. And I really want to read more. A lot of my colleagues unfortunately don't see things that way. After 40 years they still want to write the book they never wrote that they know they will never write! But I am more than the sum total of words I have written. I have other obligations. I hope 'I have done the state some service', as the great Oscar Spate used to say. It's time to move on, to get off the treadmill.

JC: Well on that note, good luck! And thank you.

References

Lal, Brij V. 1986. *Power and Prejudice: The Making of the Fiji Crisis*. Wellington: New Zealand Institute for International Affairs.

———. 2011. *Intersections: History, Memory, Discipline*. Lautoka: Fiji Institute of Applied Studies, and Sydney: Asia Pacific Publications.

Lal, Brij V., Peter Reeves and Rajesh Rai (eds). 2006. *The Encyclopaedia of the Indian Diaspora*. Singapore: Editions Didier Millet in association National University of Singapore, and Delhi: Oxford University Press; Honolulu: University of Hawaii Press.

Salesa, Damon. 2016. 'Obituary: Hugh Laracy'. *Journal of Pacific History*, 51(1): 43–47. DOI: 10.1080/00223344.2016.1164284.

Indenture

4

Brij V. Lal: Rooting for History

Goolam Vahed

> I have come to the conclusion after a lifetime of reading and writing that accessible prose is valued by the lay reader. Stories draw people in. Storytelling, as Hannah Arendt once wrote, 'reveals meaning without committing the error of defining it'. The sharing of experience creates the possibilities for individual acts of imagination ... Imaginative works have that special power to connect (Lal 2011: 5; see also Arendt 1968: 105).

Having keenly followed Brij V. Lal's work on indenture since the 1980s, I was delighted when he invited me to contribute a chapter on South Africa for *The Encyclopaedia of the Indian Diaspora* (Lal 2006: 6). I teamed up with Surendra Bhana and we were two of the many scholars worldwide who contributed to the *Encyclopaedia*, which has received rave reviews. Thus began my relationship with a scholar whose life's work has inspired many individuals. We met for the first time in 2010 when he visited South Africa with his wonderful wife, Padma. We subsequently met at conferences in Mauritius in December 2011 and at Hyderabad in February 2013 where he presented carefully crafted lectures.

Although Lal is an internationally recognised scholar, his demeanour reflected his humble roots. He hails from Tabia, Labasa; the son of a petty cane farmer whose parents had no formal education. He was modest about his own academic contributions, but a cheerful soul. In Mauritius, we sat with scholars from Suriname, the Netherlands, and Trinidad deep into the night chatting about matters ranging from Bollywood to contemporary politics and the state of world cricket, while some took to singing Hindi film songs and *ghazals*. We in South Africa have largely adopted English as our home language and it was a revelation that Indian languages are alive in some of the former colonies where indentured Indians had emigrated.

Lal established a formidable reputation as a scholar on indentured labour in Fiji. His work evolved over the years and he has written prolifically and passionately on contemporary politics in the land of his birth. His books on Fiji include its twentieth-century political history, a biography of the Indo-Fijian leader A.D. Patel, an analysis of that country's coups in recent decades, and an account of constitutionalism in post-coup Fiji. Lal's scholarship and activism is widely acknowledged and he has received a string of academic and civic honours. He was elected a Fellow of the Australian Humanities Academy in 1996; appointed to the Fiji Constitution Review Commission in 1996; awarded the Officer of the Order of Fiji in 1998; promoted to full Professor in the Institute of Advanced Studies at The Australian National University (ANU) in the same year; awarded a 25th Anniversary of Fiji Independence Medal in recognition of his contribution to Fijian education; and was made a Member of the Order of Australia (AM) for his contribution to the promotion of Pacific scholarship through research and commentary. He was also banned from his homeland, a painful experience; he wrote, 'I now live forcibly exiled from the land of my birth' (Lal 2011: 6).

I first encountered Lal's works as a graduate student at Indiana University where, as a Fulbright student, I completed my Master's and Doctoral degrees. A class on bonded labour gave me the opportunity to research Indian indenture and I read up on current literature.[1] This began to broaden my understanding of the Indian diasporic experience. I also became acquainted with the influential works of E.P. Thompson, especially his monumental and pathbreaking study, *The Making of the English Working Class* (1963).[2] The work of this towering figure in labour history was liberating when juxtaposed with Louis Althusser and other

---

1   The earliest conference on Indian indenture was held in Mauritius in 1984. It was attended by Hugh Tinker and by scholars from the Caribbean and South Africa. This created a network of scholars working on indenture. Some of the papers were published in the collection edited by Uttama Bissoondoyal and S.B.C. Servansing (1986). Scholars like David Dabydeen, Brinsley Somaroo, Basdeo Mangru, Rhoda Reddock, Madhavi Kale and Marianne Ramesar pioneered the study of indenture in the Caribbean. Some of their early work was published in David Dabydeen and Brinsley Somaroo (1987). These studies focused on the economic contribution of indentured workers, control and resistance, the impact of the imbalanced gender ratio, folk songs, and family life.
2   The 50th anniversary of *The Making of the English Working Class* generated considerable discussion and commemoration. See e.g. Holland and Phillips 2014.

structuralist and functionalist interpretations that downplayed both workers' experiences and their ability to effect social change (see Elliott 2006). I also familiarised myself with the literature on slavery in the Americas, the work of James C. Scott on resistance (1985), and the emerging work of the Subaltern Studies Collective (Chaturvedi 2000), to get a better understanding of the history of bonded labour, industrial workers and the subalterns more generally. The lesson we took from these readings was that the working class, as Thompson tells us, 'made itself as much as it was made' (1963: 194). Many of these insights were applied in revisionist studies of Indian indenture.

Indentured migration to Natal was part of a new international circulation of labour that evolved after the British abolished slavery in 1833. To address the labour shortage on colonial plantations, around 1.3 million Indian contract labourers were exported to Mauritius, Jamaica, British Guiana, Trinidad, St Lucia, Granada and Natal between 1834 and 1916 (Y.S. Meer 1980; Northrup 1995: 156–57). Ironically, abolitionists were able to end the 'savagery' of slavery in part because of the availability of other forms of unfree labour that would come to be considered 'savage' in settler colonies (Singh 2014: 227). The 60,945 indentured migrants who went to Fiji between 1879 and 1916 constituted a tiny proportion of the overall number. The Pacific made up a small segment of the global trade in Indian indentured labourers.

Hugh Tinker's pioneering study, *A New System of Slavery*, provided a broad overview of indenture (1974). It was not the first such study. C. Kondapi (1951) preceded Tinker by two-and-a-half decades but Tinker (1921–2000) brought an activist bent to his subject (Munro 2009: 249–50). He had fought in the Indian army during World War II and worked in the Indian civil service before returning to England where he completed his doctoral degree at Cambridge University. He was a prolific author and academic who taught at Rangoon University and the School of Oriental and African Studies (SOAS). *A New System of Slavery* resonated with many left-leaning academics and activists during a time of global activism against the Vietnam War, civil rights in the USA, apartheid in South Africa, and more generally against underdevelopment in the so-called 'Third World'.

Tinker followed in the footsteps of other authors of studies of slavery in the United States where the period after the publication of Kenneth Stampp's *The Peculiar Institution* in 1956 saw an outpouring of scholarly works on slavery, the slave trade and resistance with a revisionist approach that gave the slaves voice and agency. Eugene Genovese's *Roll, Jordan, Roll* (1976), as well as the work of James C. Scott (1985), widened the definition of resistance to include those aspects of life that helped slaves to reclaim their humanity, such as culture, spirituality, materiality, desertion, music and work slowdowns.

Tinker viewed Indian indenture as simply an extension of slavery. This magisterial work stimulated studies of Indian indenture that sought to combine empathy for the indentured with solid empirical scholarship based on conventional archival sources such as correspondence between officials and commissions of inquiry (in the absence of memoirs, letters, diaries and other such sources). There was little by way of oral interviews with surviving indentured migrants. Tinker did not draw from studies that gave agency to the subaltern slave community, and by describing indenture as slavery he ignored the historically specific context in which indenture took place, namely colonialism (Singh 2014: 227).

Despite its shortcomings, *A New System of Slavery* was welcomed by many in the 'Third World' because of its focus on labour, race and class, and its clearly ideological and moral overtones. It stimulated works that expanded existing historiography in their ambition and scope. The prevailing work had focused on the workings of the system, including the legislation surrounding indenture and the horrible treatment meted out to many of the indentured (L.M. Thompson 1952; Weller 1968). In South Africa, early history writing was dominated by white scholars who showed little interest in the indentured experience. Some attention was given to Mohandas K. Ghandi's 21 years in South Africa but, overall, the emphasis was on the struggle against white minority rule. Regrettably, the opportunity to record oral histories of indentured immigrants was lost.

Lal differed from this scholarship in a very important respect. He established that knowledge of Indian origins was key to understanding the indentured experience. Decolonisation and concern with 'race relations' in the colonies in the 1950s and 1960s resulted in most studies on Indians focusing on the migrant population in the colonies rather than from whence they came. Much of this work was undertaken by anthropologists and sociologists. Historians who studied the indentured period tended to focus on the economic contribution of indentured labour, employer control on the plantations, the implications of the disparities in the gender ratio, and so on. There was little systematic profiling of the indentured populations or an exploration of their agency and lived experiences.

When Lal conducted his research for his PhD at ANU from 1977, there was little information available on Fiji, apart from his PhD supervisor's monograph, *Fiji's Indian Migrants* (Gillion 1962). Lal was curious to find out whom the indentured were, why they left India, and how they reconstructed their lives in Fiji, and he pioneered a study to find such information. He initially employed quantification to supplement conventional official archival sources such as the records of various government departments and commissioned reports. He analysed the Emigration Passes that contained information concerning the name, indentured number, next of kin, caste, age, gender and district of origin of migrants. This personal information was recorded by the colonial state to identify and track migrants' employment in the colonies and to monitor them in the event that they returned to India. Of the 60,000 migrants to Fiji, around 45,000 departed from Calcutta and it is on this group that Lal focused. The work was tedious. He spent 12 hours a day for five months viewing a microfiche machine in the dark room at the National Library of Australia. He analysed the passes, then coded them and analysed them via a computer that was, of course, a very basic machine in the 1970s (Munro 2009: 249).

While quantification has its critics, and like all historical sources is open to bias and misrepresentation, Lal pointed out in a subsequent study that his aim:

> unlike that of others who had worked on the records of overseas Indians, was to illuminate detailed aspects of the background of the indentured emigrants, and to identify every minute shift in trends, which had been of secondary importance to other researchers. To do this effectively required the examination of all the passes. It was, it must be admitted, an extremely tedious process, but the data that the analysis has yielded has not only opened up new areas for discussion but has also given me a solid base to pursue further research into the evolution of Fiji Indian society (Lal 1983b: 44).

The outcome of Lal's research was a two-volume doctoral dissertation (1980), a condensed version of which was published as *Girmityas* (1983a). These studies profiled the North Indian indentured population to Fiji. The picture that emerged, he wrote, 'goes against many assumptions and assertions that have been made about the emigrants' (Lal 1983b: 45). As he would note, the 'origins' challenged the prevailing idea that the *girmityas* were from the lowest strata of society. He found that the migrants represented a cross-section of rural Indian society. They were members of various castes, hailing from Bihar, the Indo-Gangetic plains, and surrounding areas.

While Lal may not have consciously been thinking about this, his findings served an important political purpose for segments of the Indian diaspora. During my visits to Australia from around 2004 and subsequent attendance at conferences of the Indian diaspora, I was struck by the differences in attitude towards India and Indian academics between Indian South Africans and many of those from other former colonies who believe that Indians from India look down upon them as having low-caste indentured origins and as people who have lost their 'authentic' culture, caste and religious practices (see Vahed 2007). The difference may be due to the fact that Mohandas K. Gandhi spent the years from 1893 to 1914 in South Africa, as a result of which India has always taken a special interest in the Indian diaspora in South Africa. This included the appointment of an Agent-General by the Indian government, who liaised between Indians and the government in South Africa between 1927 and 1946, and India's support for the anti-apartheid struggle, which began with India taking up this issue at the United Nations (Vahed 2015). My perception is that South Africans are generally much less critical of India and Indian academics. Lal's findings on the caste origins of indentured migrants would have helped to demolish many of the myths around origins.

Once he established the areas from whence the migrants came, Lal spent a year in India visiting them—places such as Balia, Baharaich, Ghazipur, Faizabaad, Gonda, Gorakhpur, Sultanpur and Azamgarh—to find out what motivated people to leave. He conducted extensive oral history interviews with the descendants of indentured emigrants and found that his informants frequently spoke of the recruiters' lies and deception. More important to Lal was that, as a result of his fieldwork, he acquired a deeper understanding of the migratory experience. He found that rural Indians had historically been on the move to places such as Assam and Calcutta or Mumbai for work. The idea of going out in the world in search of employment was therefore not a new one. Many thought that Fiji was somewhere near Calcutta and that they would return home after a short sojourn. In most cases, the journey into indenture became permanent emigration. Lal's 'history by numbers' was crucial for subsequent studies that explored other aspects of indentured life.

In Natal, for example, Surendra Bhana and Joy Brain, historians at the former University of Durban-Westville, embarked on a project in the early 1980s to computerise Natal's ships' lists. In 1986, when they had captured 95,382 names, they fed this information into a computer programme and undertook a statistical analysis. By this time, Bhana had read Lal's *Girmityas* and was in contact with him:

> Lal encouraged me to produce a book, even if it was statistical. I started writing up in 1987 under great pressure since I had [by then] decided to leave for the United States. On Brij Lal's advice, I proceeded with the book. I did additional research at Berkeley and had the book published by Promilla.[3]

Following Bhana's departure to the United States, Brain completed the outstanding names and published the list in digital format as a CD-ROM in 2003. The personal and social details of the 152,184 indentured passengers became easily accessible to anyone with internet access when the data was posted onto the University of KwaZulu-Natal, Gandhi-Luthuli Documentation Centre's website in 2005. When Cassim Badsha, a retired computer programmer with a passion for history, got his first glimpse of the lists, the PDF files presented themselves as an opportunity: 'It was a like a goldmine of easily accessible data for a programmer to develop a relational data base … The value of a relational database in this form is in its capacity to generate statistics—correlations, trends, and the like—with a few clicks of a mouse' (Waetjen and Vahed 2014: 67). This promises new ways of reading existing information.

> Statistics-wise we can now say so much more—like how many people died of suicides or drownings and hangings and snake bites and things like that—it's all recorded there … The data files ha[d] never been aggregated into one. Having done this, through this programme, and having stripped key areas and linked them to the total file, like doing searches by specific village or caste or ship etc. etc. has now given all the data greater meaning … Just those flat ships lists are pretty meaningless until you do this data mining … Now it is all available and it can be used as a subject content at high schools, at universities, by economists, by sociologists (Waetjen and Vahed 2014: 68).[4]

---

3   Surendra Bhana, email to author, 28 May 2013, cited in Waetjen and Vahed (2014: 60).
4   This section of the chapter is drawn from Waetjen and Vahed (2014: 65–69).

The data lists, as they currently stand, open up new and exciting possibilities for research. Badsha met with Goolam Vahed and Thirunagaren Moodley of the Documentation Centre at the University of KwaZulu-Natal on 6 August 2014 to discuss how to make the programme available to the general public via the Documentation Centre's website. Unfortunately, Badsha died before this project could materialise. There remains a possibility that his vision could be achieved. During October and November 2016, Julia Stephens, a Professor of History at Rutgers University in the USA, visited South Africa. She wrote to me in advance of the visit on 11 October 2016:

> I've been reading your article 'Passages of Ink' on the Ships Lists, which was very helpful, and was wondering whether there has been any work in the last couple of years with Cassim Badsha's database. I'm hoping eventually to do some interactive digital mapping and data analysis of Indian migrant families, and his work sounds of great interest. I would love to be in touch with him if that was possible, although I understand from the article that he may not be well.

When I informed Dr Stephens that Badsha had passed on, she wrote on 18 October 2016:

> Having recently started a new teaching position at Rutgers, which has a very large number of students form the US/South Asian diasporic community, I was really inspired by the collaborations that have been developing between family historians and scholars in Natal around these records ... When I didn't see anything online about the database, I feared that Cassim had never been able to complete the project. But I absolutely think that he was right that this is a gold mine for data analysis. I'd love to see the work he had started, and I think that I may be able to find help with continuing it. I'm just starting to learn how to do this sort of digital mapping and data analysis. I've been collaborating with people who know more, including the Center for History and Economics at Harvard. I know that a lot of people have put tons of work into generating this material, so I would want to use it in a way that does justice to their original vision.

At the time of completing this chapter I had not met Dr Stephens but I hope that with the permission and approval of Badsha's family, his project will come to fruition.

The ships' lists, as they currently stand, are used by individuals to trace their roots and by those applying for 'Overseas Citizen of India' (OCI) or 'Person of Indian Origin' (PIO) status. Like Lal, many academics of the

Indian diaspora are constantly faced with calls for assistance to trace their indentured forebears and these lists make it possible to access this information more easily.

Remarkably, Natal has taken the global lead amongst colonies receiving indentured migrants in creating this kind of relational database. Interested scholars and others in Suriname have recorded the names of indentured migrants while around half the names of migrants to Mauritius have been captured on computer. No such initiative has been undertaken to record the names of migrants in other colonies that received indentured migrants. However, at a conference on indenture held in Mauritius in 2012, initiatives were taken to systematically computerise the ships' lists and to place the data on a global relational database. Both Lal and I were nominated to that committee. Progress has been slow because of limited resources, work commitments and, importantly, the death of Badsha, whose programming skills were key.

The field of indentured studies has made great strides over the past three decades. Lal is a restless historian. He felt that although his study based on quantification was important, it made a limited contribution to historical explanation. He found that generalisations tended to be descriptive rather than explanatory and he began to search for other sources in his quest to explain cause and effect. Lal turned to biographies to provide a sense of how the indentured migrants negotiated a system barely one step removed from slavery. From numbers, he was now turning the indentured into people with ambitions, cultures and agency even while accepting that the structural nature of indentured industrial agriculture was essentially unfree. Yet it was also a system that some migrants used to escape restrictions in Indian society or to assume positions of power (such as *sirdars* or sub-overseers) within prevailing power mechanisms.

Lal brought most of his essays on indenture together in his collection *Chalo Jahagi* ('Let's go shipmates') (Lal 2000). This work inspired many. He explored new themes using innovative sources where possible. Written with a deep sense of the personal and eschewing methodologies that strangle rather than liberate history, probably without realising it, Lal stimulated many historians of the Indian diaspora. I was one of them. Writing inside of apartheid in which the chapters on my forebears were almost always headlined, 'The Indian Problem', whose history was erased and whose very futures were hemmed in by an aggressive racist system, to read Lal was not only to read shared histories and memories, but also to read hope.

Lal's *Chalo Jahaji* showed us that no matter how all-encompassing the system, people find innovative ways to challenge, work around and negotiate a life. *Chalo Jahaji* can be read as Lal taking his readers on a journey through indenture or taking the indentured on their journey to the colonies. The collection includes an emotive piece about Lal's journey to his ancestral village of Bahraich (Lal 2000: 25–39), as well as pathbreaking micro studies that focus on subject formation and agency. 'Kunti's Cry', for example, uses the attempted rape of an indentured woman by an overseer to examine issues of power, gender, violence and abuse on plantations. Lal also shows how this incident was used to mobilise anti-indenture activists (Lal 2000: 195–214). In addition, he translated Totaram Sanadhya's (written by his scribe, Benarsidas Chaturvedi) observations of plantation life, a rare and valuable document of the indentured period (Lal 2000: 261–72). As with good historical writing, Lal embraces C. Wright Mills' belief:

> the biographies of men and women, the kinds of individuals they variously become, cannot be understood without reference to the historical structures in which the milieux of their everyday life are organized … Whatever else he may be, man is a social and an historical actor who must be understood, if at all, in a close and intricate interplay with social and historical structures (2000: 62).

Ashwin Desai and I were similarly moved to conduct our own research on indentured labour (2010). Other excellent studies were emerging around this time, such as those by Rajend Mesthrie (1991), Marina Carter (Carter 1995, 1996; Carter and Torabully 2002) and Madhavi Kale (1998). Lomarsh Roopnaraine's study provided a more comprehensive story of bonded labour and of the continuity between slavery and indenture (2007). We were striving, like Lal in *Chalo Jahaji*, for a history from the bottom that did not provide the perspective of officials and the ruling classes. In the absence of oral histories, we relied on conventional archival sources such as correspondence between officials as well as commissions of inquiry. A valuable official source was the office of the Protector of Indian Immigrants, which had been set up in the 1870s following reports of the abuse of indentured workers. The Protector's files in the Natal Archives Repository contain a wealth of information on the lived experiences of the indentured, including many first-hand testimonies.

Ann Stoler correctly warns us that colonial archival documents are not neutral pieces of information but are imbricated in issues of power, control, fabrication and even memory (Stoler 2009). Instead of ignoring such archival evidence, however, like Lal in *Chalo Jahaji*, we sought the perspective of the indentured by reading these sources contrapuntally—'against the grain'. Texts, as deconstruction theory tells us, have a multiplicity of meanings and archival documents are no exception. While the research was tedious, the results were rewarding. Although the viewpoints of the ruling classes are undoubtedly overpowering in archival documents, we found the voices of the subalterns through their letters to and from family in India, remittances, their complaints to the Protector, their testimony in court cases, estates records, and even such actions as feigning illnesses, desertion and suicide. These actions are important for, as Gayatri Spivak tells us, the subaltern don't always speak with words. Her influential article speaks of a woman who questions the idea of belonging to one man and articulates this by taking her life. Her death is compounded by the absence of institutions where her resistance speech could be heard with the result that her reason for taking her life was not recognised. Hence, Spivak's provocative title, 'Can the Subaltern Speak?' (1988: 271–313). Many among the indentured also committed suicide, and Lal has written extensively on these individuals who were speaking through their actions (Lal 2000: 215–38).

In *Inside Indian Indenture*, Desai and I revisited the idea that there was a total breakdown of family and culture amongst the indentured, resulting in alienation (see, for example, Jayawardena 1968). Our study does not reduce the story of indenture to a simple one of victimhood. We show that the indentured and their descendants lived complex lives. While we focus on working-class formation, we show that race, ethnicity, language and regional origins were all important in the making of class. We also recognise the importance of culture by examining popular culture, sport, leisure-time activities, education, religion, music, sexuality and death amongst the indentured. This combination of social and cultural history sought to provide a nuanced perspective of the indentured experience.

One example is that of indentured women, described by Hugh Tinker as a 'sorry sisterhood'. Indentured women undoubtedly faced many challenges. They were paid lower wages and received fewer food rations than men. Women were sometimes forced to append themselves to men to gain access to food. Women's burdens stretched beyond issues of sustenance and labour. Many were subjected to sexual violence and an unforgiving, dismissive system. Yet some of the stories, such as Votti's, draw our attention to the ways in which some women confronted the multiple layers of oppression. To compile this story, we searched the archives, examining documents of the Protector of Indian Immigrants, court records, Immigration Department records and estate papers. The result is the story of a remarkable woman who confronted indenture, although it meant consecutive terms of imprisonment; and the perils of being a single woman who refused sexual 'favours' even when it meant beatings and ridicule and who adeptly used the legal system for protection. She emerges as a strong woman who used the full range of the 'weapons of the weak' (Desai and Vahed 2010: 6–10).

There are many Vottis in our narrative. Instead of portraying indentured migrants as passive objects of an oppressive system, we identified the multiple beginnings that made up the indentured experience; power relations on the plantations; the intricate ways that the indentured resisted and accommodated the system; and the culture and community that they created within the period of indenture but also beyond. The indentured were as much agents as they were victims and silent witnesses to unfolding history.

The scholarship on indenture, as with slavery and other working class histories, continues to mature and break new and exciting ground. *Coolie Woman* by Gaiutra Bahadur (2013), for example, is the fascinating story of a young woman who went to Guiana (now Guyana) in the early twentieth century as an indentured migrant. The story of this single migrant, who was pregnant, was 'recovered' by her great-granddaughter. Bahadur conducted research on three continents and examined masses of files in the colonial archives. The result is a rich and gendered study of the complex lives of indentured women, many of whom were fleeing into indenture to escape some form of mistreatment in India. They were subjected to further hardship during the voyage and in the colonies. This is a story of double diaspora as her descendants migrated to the United States.

Recent work on indenture examines culture, religion, family, leisure-time activities and resistance and accommodation. Another line of academic studies highlights the 'advantages' gained by indentured Indians in the colonies. They and later their descendants most likely enjoyed greater freedom and opportunities in the colonies than they would have had in India where caste, superstition, famine and religious strictures in particular severely circumscribed life chances. There is a caveat. We need to guard against romanticising the experiences of indentured Indians, and all subaltern history for that matter; a trap that is easy to fall prey to. We must, by all means, validate subaltern experience by retrieving their voices, but the stories that emerge do not necessarily make these individuals heroic or the system any less harsh. Future studies should aim to find a middle path between indicting the system and pointing to ways in which the indentured used it to make new lives.

Despite the advances in the historiography, several avenues of enquiry need further exploration. One area of great importance in Fiji and other colonies that received indentured labour, including Natal, is the relationship between Indians and the indigenous populations during the colonial period and into the present. This area has been probed to some extent by Caribbean scholars but much greater research is required in most former colonies because of the repercussions that persist to the present. Fatima Meer wrote that the presence of indentured Indians in Natal undermined the negotiating power of the Zulu vis-à-vis white settlers. Whatever the African 'perceptions of Indian indentured workers was in 1860', she wrote, 'included in it must have been the suspicion, if not the knowledge, that they had been brought in … to be used against them in ways perhaps not immediately understood' (F. Meer 1985: 48). In this regard, Desai and Vahed's (2016) revisionist study of Gandhi's South African years created a huge storm and much anger amongst Indian South Africans because it challenged the idea of Gandhi as a non-racial icon of the struggle against white minority rule in South Africa.

Walton Look Lai (1993) also addresses the poor relations between Africans and Indians, who were resented by Afro-Caribbeanists during and after indenture, while Bridget Brereton's (1979) study of Trinidad examines the colonial period. However, much work remains to be done. As Antoinette Burton reminds us:

> The will to a color-blind account of solidarities between Africans and Indians in the service of a transnational or global history of political resistance is in danger of disappearing important and often painful histories of racial dis-ease—histories that were the result of Gandhian legacies, British imperial policies, caste politics and local interactions between communities of color on the ground in various parts of Africa itself (Burton 2012: 14).

In Guyana, Fiji, South Africa, Trinidad and Tobago and elsewhere, the relations between formerly subaltern groups have not been resolved, as new global forces generate new kinds of tensions that often manifest as 'race' tensions. The focus on agency and resistance is important in the study of indenture, motivated as it is by the desire to show how the indentured labourers lived out of the gaze of their masters. But the indentured spent the major portion of their time working, not resisting or engaging in leisure activities. Since work was so important in their lives and occupied so much of their time, in order to focus on the 'lived' experience of the indentured we need, again, to focus in detail on their work, on what they did and how it evolved, and on labour routines and discipline on plantations. Work influenced so many other aspects of the lives of the workers—family, mortality, formation of community and leisure. They were not simply involved in a perennial struggle with their masters (resistance) and a labour history perspective on indenture will allow us to see how work influenced other aspects of workers' lives.

Research on Indian indenture would also benefit from examining the indentured experience in all of its manifestations, which should include the trades in and activities of African, Chinese, Comorian, Javanese, Japanese, Malagasy, Melanesian, Yemeni and others who participated in the indentured labour system. Focusing strictly on the Indian indentured experience creates an intellectual parochialism and distorts our understanding of the richly complex global indentured experience. If we do not study indentured labour as the global phenomenon that it was, the field of Indian indenture will be marginalised in global labour studies. Moreover, Indian indenture was part of bonded labour systems that included slavery and convict labour. During the eighteenth and nineteenth centuries, most of this labour was unfree and we can gain a deeper understanding of labour history through a comparative perspective.

While much research remains to be done, the flourishing historiography of Indian indenture will undoubtedly be a source of great joy to Lal. Michael Frisch writes in his book *A Shared Authority* that the main concern of public historians should be 'a fundamental commitment to the importance of that verb at the heart of memory, making it something alive and active as we confront our own world' (1990: 25). Lal, too, believes that a public historian's role should be to ensure that people do not forget the past, however painful that memory may be. He wrote in *Intersections*, 'I have done so [written his memoirs] principally in response to requests from complete strangers from around the world seeking information and reading material about their parents' and grandparents' place of birth' (Lal 2011: 6). At a public address on Fiji Remembrance Day in 2014, Lal said:

4. BRIJ V. LAL

> One of my life's ambition[s] has been to remember what others have forgotten or chosen to forget—to give our people a voice and a modicum of humanity, to give them a place at the table of history. We need to remind the new generation about our history: history doesn't only belong to the victors but to the vanquished as well. One thing I have done in life before I go is to give voiceless people a voice—a sense of place, a sense of purpose. People will remember this aspect by history. I do not celebrate struggles and sacrifices and sufferings of our people. What I marvel at is how ordinary people did extraordinary things in extraordinary circumstances. We, their descendants, have inherited those traits and legacy of our forebears. And that is that even in difficult circumstances, we never give up and we never compromise. There is a kind of dignity within us, where did it come from? It comes from people who travelled thousands of miles in difficult circumstances, but never gave up. This is the legacy of Girmit that I think we are celebrating, not those horrible things we read in books many years ago (Lal 2014).

There are many things to admire in Lal's scholarship—his deep love of documents and archives, his political commitment, his sober but occasionally partial style when he feels it is warranted, his erudite scholarship, his ability to be both irreverent and reverent, his ability to theorise but refusal to let it encumber his narrative, and his desire to place the subalterns at the centre of broader historical processes.

Lal has sometimes been seen as an empiricist and criticised for not writing highly theorised history, perhaps of the likes of Gayatri Spivak or Dipesh Chakrabarty. What is wrong with this? Too often, historical writing is judged on how abstract it is and how much theory it incorporates. History is about people and the strength of Lal's work is his ability to put human faces to our pasts, and to present characters with whom his readers can connect. This kind of history gives voice to the perspectives of ordinary men and women who in the past were neglected or suppressed for one reason or other—class, age, gender, race, ethnicity. Lal's project of telling the stories of ordinary and not so ordinary people in ways that are accessible to the wider public is important as we are living in a time when the academy valorises academic journals that are never read by those who feature in these stories. There is, unfortunately, little incentive in the academy to produce the kind of meaningful work produced by Lal.

Lal has contributed significantly to various historiographies through his books, edited collections, journal articles and conference presentations in what is an accomplished career in the academy and in public life.

His work blends autobiography and biography with social, political and historical analysis, and is both engaging and eminently readable. His books display impeccable scholarship on a range of subjects—indenture, his travels, academic life, the Indian diaspora and the discipline of History itself. His writing of history is not a passive response to the historical past. For him, the personal is historical. He actively engages with the past and present as a result of his experiences at the hands of the political elite in Fiji. He brings his own experiences to bear in his later writings as a result of his being a 'twice migrant'. He makes the point that the centre of gravity of many Fijian Indians is now the major cities of Australia and New Zealand. His *magnum opus* on Fiji Indians could well be subtitled 'from immigration to emigration'.

During March 2017, the Girmit Centre in Lautoka, Fiji, hosted an international conference on the abolition of Indian indenture, which I attended. This was my first trip to the country and I wrote to Lal in advance to ask whether he would also be attending. He replied on 4 November 2016:

> I don't think they will lift the ban. It is so silly. I lecture to students in Fiji via skype. They see my face, hear my voice, read my words and discuss my ideas and yet the government won't allow us in. It is petty vindictiveness, nothing more, especially as last week the government lifted travel bans on foreign journalists once banned from Fiji. I may not be present physically but my spirit will be there. They can banish me but they can't ignore my work.

Sadly, Lal was not given permission to attend the conference. I found this ironic, as the overriding theme at the conference was unity and reconciliation between Indo and indigenous Fijians.

The archives that Brij V. Lal minted, the oral histories that he recorded, the fields that his ancestors tilled and out of which he harvested the history of indenture, may no longer be his domain. But true to his indentured roots, he will remain a voice to be reckoned with in the land of his birth, Fiji; in Australia, his adopted home, and in many other parts of the world where he and his work are both appreciated and respected.

References

Arendt, Hannah. 1968. *Men in Dark Times*. San Diego, New York and London: Harcourt, Bruce and Co.

Bahadur, Gaiutra. 2013. *Coolie Woman: The Odyssey of Indenture*. London: C. Hurst.

Bhana, Surendra. 1991. *Indentured Indian Emigrants to Natal, 1860–1902*. New Delhi: Promilla.

Bissoondoyal, Uttama and S.B.C. Servansing (eds). 1986. *Indian Labour Immigration*. Moka, Mauritius: Mahatma Gandhi Institute.

Blackburn, Robin. 1997. *The Making of New World Slavery: From the Baroque to the Modern, 1492–1800*. London: Verso.

Brereton, Bridget. 1979. *Race Relations in Colonial Trinidad*. New York: Cambridge University Press.

Burton, Antoinette. 2012. *Black Over Brown: Race and the Politics of Postcolonial Citation*. Gurgaon, India: Three Essays Collective.

Carter, Marina. 1995. *Servants, Sirdars and Settlers: Indians in Mauritius, 1834–1874*. Delhi: Oxford University Press.

———. 1996. *Voices from Indenture: Experiences of Indian Migrants in the British Empire*. Leicester: Leicester University Press.

Carter, Marina and Khal Torabully. 2002. *Coolitude: An Anthology of the Indian Labour Diaspora*. Anthem South Asian Studies.

Chaturvedi, Vinayak (ed.). 2000. *Mapping Subaltern Studies and the Postcolonial*, 2nd ed. London and New York: Verso.

Cumpston, I.M. 1953. *Indians Overseas in British Territories, 1834–1854*. London: Oxford University Press.

Dabydeen, David and Brinsley Somaroo (eds). 1987. *India in the Caribbean*. London: Hansib/University of Warwick, Centre for Caribbean Studies Publication in cooperation with the London Strategic Policy Unit.

Desai, Ashwin and Goolam Vahed. 2010. *Inside Indian Indenture: A South African Story, 1860–1914.* Cape Town: HSRC (Human Sciences Research Council) Press.

———. 2016. *The South African Gandhi: Stretcher-Bearer of Empire.* Stanford: Stanford University Press.

Elliott, Gregory. 2006 [1987]. *Althusser: The Detour of Theory.* New York: Verso.

Frisch, Michael. 1990. *A Shared Authority: Essays on the Craft and Meaning of Oral and Public History.* New York: State University of New York Press.

Genovese, Eugene D. 1976. *Roll, Jordan, Roll: The World the Slaves Made.* New York: Vintage Books.

Gillion, K.L. (Kenneth Lowell Oliver). 1962. *Fiji's Indian Migrants: A History to the End of Indenture in 1920.* Melbourne: Oxford University Press.

Holland, Owen and Eoin Phillips. 2013. 'Fifty years of E.P. Thompson's *The Making of the English Working Class*'. *Social History,* 39(2): 172–81. DOI: 10.1080/03071022.2014.914784.

Jayawardena, Chandra. 1968. 'Migration and social change: A survey of Indian communities overseas'. *Geographical Review,* 58(3): 426–49. DOI: 10.2307/212565.

Kale, Madhavi. 1998. *Fragments of Empire: Capital, Slavery and Indian Indentured Labour in the British Caribbean.* Philadelphia: University of Pennsylvania Press.

Kondapi, C. 1951. *Indians Overseas, 1838–1949.* New Delhi: Oxford University Press.

Lal, Brij V. 1980. 'Leaves of the banyan tree: Origins and background of Fiji's North Indian indentured migrants, 1879–1916', 2 vols. PhD thesis, The Australian National University.

———. 1983a. *Girmityas: The Origins of the Fiji Indians.* Canberra: The Journal of Pacific History.

——. 1983b. 'Indian indenture historiography: A note on problems, sources and methods'. *Pacific Studies*, 6(2): 33–50.

——. 2000. *Chalo Jahaji: On a Journey through Indenture in Fiji*. Canberra: Division of Pacific and Asian History, The Australian National University; and Suva: Fiji Museum.

——. 2001. *Mr Tulsi's Store: A Fijian Journey*. Canberra: Pandanus Books.

——. 2011. 'When it is over'. In *Intersections: History, Memory, Discipline*, pp. 1–7. Lautoka: Fiji Institute of Applied Studies; and Sydney: Asia Pacific Publications.

——. 2014. 'Fiji girmitiyas: Ordinary people did extraordinary things in extraordinary circumstances'. Address on Girmit Remembrance Day, Auckland, 17 May 2014. Transcript and translation from Hindi by Thakur Ranjit Singh. In *Fiji Pundit*, 17 May 2014. Online: fijipundit.blogspot.com/2014/07/fiji-girmitiyas-ordinary-people-did.html (accessed 7 September 2014).

Lal, Brij V. (ed.). 2004. *Bittersweet: The Indo-Fijian Experience*. Canberra: Pandanus Books.

——. (ed.). 2006. *The Encyclopaedia of the Indian Diaspora*. Singapore: Editions Didier Millet in association National University of Singapore. Lautoka: Fiji Institute of Applied Studies; and Sydney: Asia Pacific Publications.

Look Lai, Walton. 1993. *Indentured Labor, Caribbean Sugar: Chinese and Indian Migrants to the British West Indies, 1838–1918*. Baltimore: The Johns Hopkins University Press.

Mangru, Basdeo. 1996. *A History of East Indian Resistance on the Guyana Sugar Estates, 1869–1948*. New York: Edwin Mellen Press.

Meer, Fatima. 1985. 'Indentured labour and group formation in apartheid society'. *Race & Class*, 26(4): 45–60.

Meer, Y.S. (ed.). 1980. *Documents of Indentured Labour in Natal, 1851–1917*. Durban: Institute for Black Research.

Mesthrie, Rajend. 1991. *Language in Indenture: A Sociolinguistic History of Bhojpuri-Hindi in South Africa*. Johannesburg: Witwatersrand University Press.

Mills, C. Wright. 2000. *The Sociological Imagination*. Oxford: Oxford University Press.

Munro, Doug. 2009. *The Ivory Tower and Beyond: Participant Historians of the Pacific*. Newcastle-upon-Tyne: Cambridge Scholars Publishing.

Nelson, Cary and Lawrence Grossberg (eds). 1988. *Marxism and the Interpretation of Culture*. Urbana: University of Illinois Press.

Northrup, David. 1995. *Indentured Labor in the Age of Imperialism, 1834–1922*. Cambridge: Cambridge University Press.

Ramesar, Marianne. 1994. *Survivors of Another Crossing: A History of East Indians in Trinidad, 1880–1946*. Mona, Jamaica: University of the West Indies, School of Continuing Studies.

Reddock, Rhoda. 1994. *Women, Labour and Politics in Trinidad and Tobago: A History*. London: Zed Books.

Roopnaraine, Lomarsh. 2007. *Indo-Caribbean Indenture: Resistance and Accommodation*. Kingston: University of West Indies Press.

Scott, James C. 1985. *Weapons of the Weak: Everyday Forms of Peasant Resistance*. New Haven: Yale University Press.

Singh, Hira. 2014. *Recasting Caste: From the Sacred to the Profane*. New Delhi: Sage Publications.

Spivak, Gayatri Chakravorty. 1988. 'Can the subaltern speak?'. In *Marxism and the Interpretation of Culture*, edited by Cary Nelson and Lawrence Grossberg, pp. 271–313. Urbana: University of Illinois Press.

Stampp, Kenneth. 1956. *The Peculiar Institution: Slavery in the Antebellum South*. New York: Alfred A. Knopf.

Stoler, Ann Laura. 2009. *Along the Archival Grain: Epistemic Anxieties and Colonial Common Sense*. Princeton: Princeton University Press.

Thompson, E.P. 1963. *The Making of the English Working Class*. London: Victor Gollancz.

Thompson, L.M. 1952. *Indian Immigration into Natal, 1860–1872*. Pretoria: Union Archives Printer.

Tinker, Hugh. 1974. *A New System of Slavery. The Export of Indian Labour Overseas, 1830–1920*. London: Oxford University Press.

Vahed, Goolam. 2007. 'Adaptation and integration of Indian migrants in Brisbane, Australia'. In *Indian Diaspora—The 21st Century—Migration, Change and Adaptation*, edited by Anand Singh. Special issue of *The Anthropologist*, 2: 37–51.

Vahed, Goolam. 2015. 'Nehru is "just another coolie": India and South Africa at the United Nations, 1946–1955'. In *Conceptualising the Roles of China and India in Africa: History, Contemporary Realities and Future Scenarios*. Special issue of *Alternation Journal*, 15: 54–85.

Vahed, Goolam and Surendra Bhana. 2006. 'Indians in South Africa.' In *The Encyclopedia of the Indian Diaspora*, edited by Peter Reeves, Brij V. Lal and Rajesh Rai, pp. 242–53. Singapore: Editions Didier Millet in association National University of Singapore; Lautoka: Fiji Institute of Applied Studies; and Sydney: Asia Pacific Publications.

Waetjen, Thembisa and Goolam Vahed. 2014. 'Passages of ink: Decoding the Natal indentured records into the digital age'. *Kronos*, 40(1): 45–73. Online: www.scielo.org.za/pdf/kronos/v40n1/03.pdf (accessed 6 March 2017).

Weller, Judith Ann. 1968. *The East Indian in Trinidad*. Rio Piedras: Institute of Caribbean Studies, University of Puerto Rico.

5

Girmitiyas and my Discovery of India[1]

Clem Seecharan

About 1880, in the ancient town of Ayodhya in the United Provinces of India, a young girl of the Parray clan gave birth to a son. She must have been deeply disgraced, because she was willing to go alone with her baby to a far-off island to which other people of the region were going. That was how the Parray woman came to Trinidad. She wanted her son to be a pundit.

V.S. Naipaul (on his paternal great-grandmother) (1984: 56)

I know very little about my ancestors in India … All that I shall ever know about my parents before they reached British Guiana [in 1901] is what is stated in the records of the now defunct Immigration Department [Ships' Registers]. They came from Basti in Uttar Pradesh, about sixty miles from Allahabad, Jawaharlal Nehru's birthplace.

Cheddi Jagan (1966: 13)

I grew up with many Indias, a tapestry of images—part fact, part fantasy—that have helped to shape me. I was born in British Guiana in 1950, on the edge of the plantation where several members of my family were taken, as 'bound coolies', from India, between 1875 and 1909. They were, like most of those who went to Fiji, *girmitiyas*: indentured labourers.

---

1 Originally published as the 'Foreword' to Brij V. Lal (2004), *Girmitiyas: The Origins of the Fiji Indians*, 2nd ed., Lautoka: Fiji Institute of Applied Studies.

I was given no idea of the India in which my people originated—no clue as to why they left. I imagined India as an undifferentiated place, vastly bigger than British Guiana, but not as big as England. It was axiomatic in popular lore that the *girmitiyas* were tricked by *arkatis*—the evil recruiters in India—into 'a new slavery': they took the place of African slaves in the colony. But we learnt nothing of our ancestral background; nothing beyond the embroidered tales of deception and kidnapping that were the unassailable explanation for their presence in British Guiana. We did not reflect on the emotions, the pain, probably still lingering in the rickety frames of the dwindling *girmitiyas* in our midst, in the late 1950s. We did not explore the terminal break with the 'motherland'—for most, a one-way journey. That recent India was an area of darkness; we did not try to comprehend it. Indeed, the India of the great Hindu classic, the *Ramayana*, the constructed India in Bombay movies, Gandhian India in revolt against British rule, and free Nehruvian India, had greater resonance for us than eastern Uttar Pradesh (the United Provinces (UP)) that, I would learn much later, was the home of my ancestors. If I had any notion at all of the Indian provenance of my ancestors it was that they were *not* Madrasis (Tamils): darker people whose rituals were alien to ours. We felt superior to them.

In 1966, I learnt from Cheddi Jagan's book, *The West on Trial*, that his people had come from Basti District, in eastern UP (Jagan 1966: 13–14, 24)[2]—that had prompted me to ask about the place where our family originated. I learnt nothing; the void remained, and no one seemed perturbed by it. My early years had been spent among several of my great-grandparents, former *girmitiyas*, yet the carnival of images in the boy's imagination must have considered them strange, companions of the framed Hindu gods and goddesses on our wall who looked over us: pictures that belonged to an India of magic. I must have seen them—these speakers of that funny language of our Hindu rituals—as somewhat mythical, evoking in me something surreal and timeless, as if, long ago, they had wandered too far away from home, got lost in the bush, and found themselves, purely by chance, on a sugar plantation in British Guiana: a long journey over land, among strange peoples. And even when

---

2   Cheddi was born on 22 March 1918 at Plantation Port Mourant, Corentyne, Berbice. His people were Kurmis. His birth certificate gives his name as 'Chedda'; just below that is recorded: 'Illegitimate'. His father was 'Jagan, Calcutta Immigrant, 88470, *Elbe*, 1901'. His mother was 'Bachaoni, Calcutta Immigrant, 88316, *Elbe*, 1901'. I am grateful to Professor David Dabydeen for a photocopy of this document.

5. *GIRMITIYAS* AND MY DISCOVERY OF INDIA

I was told, as late as 1955, that the last batch of former 'bound coolies' was returning to India, by a big boat that was pointed out to me in the newspaper, the boy of five still imagined them retracing those faint steps in the bush, walking for months, possibly years, through places with tigers and elephants and flying chariots.

Such were the labyrinthine fantasies the *girmitiyas* stirred in me! They persisted into my adolescence. They came not from a precocious imagination but out of 'historical darkness'. We really had no conception of this recent India that was the home of the *girmitiyas*. Inquiry, such as it was, fell for the tale—perpetuated by the *girmitiyas*—that they were all duped into going to British Guiana. Their curiosity ceased. The *arkati*, the infamous recruiter, still casts a long shadow. V.S. Naipaul (born 1932), whose people went to Trinidad as *girmitiyas* from eastern UP, recalls that he, too, was imperturbable about the 'historical darkness':

> I grew up with two ideas of history, almost two ideas of time. There was history with dates. That kind of history affected people and places abroad ... But Chaguanas, where I was born, in an Indian-style house my [maternal] grandfather [a Brahmin girmitiya] had built, had no dates. If I had read in a book that Gandhi had made his first call for civil disobedience in 1919, that date seemed recent. But 1919, in Chaguanas, in the life of the Indian community, was almost unimaginable. It was a time beyond recall, mythical. About our family, the migration of our ancestors, I knew only what I knew or what I was told. Beyond (and sometimes even within) people's memories was undated time, historical darkness. Out of that darkness (extending to place as well as to time) we had all come. The other where Gandhi and Nehru and the others operated was historical and real. The India from which we had come was impossibly remote, almost as imaginary as the land of the *Ramayana*, our Hindu epic. I lived easily with that darkness, that lack of knowledge. I never thought to inquire further (Naipaul 1984: 58–59).

The 'India from which we had come', was, in fact, more imaginary and remote than the land of the *Ramayana*. We, too, were comfortable with that darkness. But, as if to atone for this and the timelessness of the narratives we told ourselves, I became obsessed with time and dates— punctiliousness about time in my daily life: punctuality; and a passion for apprehending chronological time: the sequence of events and their contexts, the rudiments of an historical temper. I would lose patience with my own people for not being able to date things, even their own dates of birth or those of their children. I was also frustrated by the absence of a chronological sense. This, I suppose, was what gave me the yearning for a sense of history, and is the genesis of my efforts in recent years to teach and write aspects of Indo-Caribbean history.

It started with the historical darkness in my family: not until the mid-1980s was I able to establish the precise place of origin, in India, of most of my family. And it was not until Brij Lal's *Girmitiyas: The Origins of the Fiji Indians*[3] peeled back the shroud, casting unprecedented luminosity on our historical darkness, that this India, which had eluded me whenever I pursued my great-grandparents' antecedents, began to cohere.

My discovery of this book in early 1989, in the library of the Royal Commonwealth Society, five years after its publication by the *Journal of Pacific History*, gave me my first conceptions of nineteenth-century eastern UP. *Girmitiyas* also gave me the context for examining my great-grandparents' attitudes, including their motives for flight. Like an illumination, it unclogged my mind so that I could begin to see the efforts of the 'bound coolies' and their descendants in the Caribbean as an achievement worthy of celebration—though not of triumphalism. *Girmitiyas* is a foundation of my contribution to Indo-Guyanese history. It belongs with Nehru's *The Discovery of India* and C.L.R. James's *Beyond a Boundary*—these had cast a spell on me since the mid-1960s. *Girmitiyas* lit up my intellectual path away from the consuming historical darkness, which had delayed my creative spirit for a long time. I craved a history of our own—'a history with dates'.

Submerged ancestry: Kaila's world

It was my illiterate maternal great-grandmother, Kaila (1889–1956), who sparked something in me. She kindled my curiosity for the antecedents of the *girmitiyas*. When she died I was only six years old, but she still occupies a niche in my memory: a mythical persona almost, in my pantheon of Hindu goddesses, however dimmed by time and decades of unfaltering atheism. I think this idealised image of Kaila is a compound of the adulatory recollections of my extended family, and my own faded snapshots and later embellishments of her. But there were grounds for the construction of this somewhat ethereal persona: her abundant sacrifice for the family that betrayed no selfish motive; the absence

---

3   All quotes cited from *Girmitiyas* are taken from the original edition, published in 1983.

5. *GIRMITIYAS* AND MY DISCOVERY OF INDIA

of petty jealousy—that bedevilling feature of many Hindu joint families; the inexhaustible energy that fed her resolve to make life better for my maternal grandmother, her only child, and her five children. The fact that Kaila never flinched from what she saw as duty to family, until the day she literally dropped collecting firewood in the cemetery, enhanced the persona of unsullied magnanimity. It was a life of total devotion to the building of a new family, in a new place far away from home, for she had journeyed alone to British Guiana as an indentured labourer, in 1909, aged 20. She would never have contact again with anyone in India.

Much of what I remember of Kaila is a blur, but it is a haziness that is of a piece: there is much that is immanent and suggestive in the faded image. It still has the power to evoke in me eclectic visions, to draw me into its shifting meanings and inner complexities—its subtle narratives— while intimating ways of self-reflection that speak to a larger context: the dynamic of our Indian community in colonial Guyana.[4] I vaguely recall her visits to my grandmother, on Saturday afternoons, walking the six or seven miles from Plantation Rose Hall to Palmyra, and repeating the journey on Sunday afternoons. Palmyra, the village of my birth, was also the village of my maternal grandfather's family, the Sohans. Kaila and her husband, Jagarnath (1888–1958), had bought several plots of land there, as well as cattle, for my grandmother, Ramdularie (1916–1985), after she married my maternal grandfather in 1930, aged 14. But they continued to work and live at Plantation Rose Hall, in the rent-free 'logies' or barracks in the 'nigger yard', some of which were built during slavery—and looked so. Abstemious to the bone, every penny earned was guarded. That was why Kaila walked those miles to and from my grandmother's at weekends, whatever the weather. Yet she was unstinting when it came to her daughter, her grandchildren and me, her first great-grandchild, apparently the apple of her eye. She always brought fruits, sweetmeats, clothes, various things she made, for us.

A black, little woman, she was not quite of the Guyanese landscape: after nearly 50 years, she still looked and dressed as if she were from a foreign place. She belonged to that remote, incomprehensible India that possessed my boyhood. In my imagination she fused with those surreal Hindu images that looked out of the walls of our living room, the gods and goddesses that seemed to hover in midair. They awed me.

---

4   British Guiana became independent on 26 May 1966 as Guyana.

As I played at being a boss, a white overseer on the sugar plantation, ordering menial toilers about, my strange boyhood gift for wonder would magically transport Kaila to this India of which I knew nothing: the way Hanuman, the monkey god, fetched the mountain of curative herbs, in his hand, in the framed picture on our wall. But there were ordinary, day-to-day images, too. Kaila was as adept at the minutiae of wet-rice culture, as she was adroit in weeding and manuring sugar cane. Even now, nearly 50 years on, I can still place her on the *kharian* or threshing floor, driving our big-horned bullocks in endless cycles, tethered to a pole around which were packed tight bundles of freshly cut rice stalks (*padi*, unhusked rice). I can still see this busy little woman winnowing the *padi*, or helping to fill it into jute bags for the mill, sweeping up every grain with practised frugality. Nothing was wasted: the straw was fed to cows, the husk and broken rice to fowls and ducks, the cow cakes were dried for cooking or manuring the vegetable garden. The draconian thrift of village India had not been squandered in the comparative comfort of village Guyana. Fact and fantasy were inextricably interwoven in my apprehension of Kaila. One thing I did know for sure: she retained a deep affection for the *girmitiyas*, especially the few with whom she had made the crossing.

I remember her being in tears a few times—this stayed with me—and many years after she was gone I asked my grandmother, Ramdularie, the reason for her sadness. She said it had to do with the successive deaths of several of her friends from India, who were passing away month by month by the mid-1950s. They saw themselves as *jahajins*, ship-sisters, to the end. They were like blood relatives, their children forbidden to intermarry. On several occasions she had to upbraid Kaila for being so deeply pained that she would wail inconsolably at the funeral of one of her *jahajins*, imploring her to 'take' her soon: she could not wait to join them in the next life. Such was the bond of these *girmitiyas*! It grew stronger as they became fewer in the late 1950s. Brinsley Samaroo has reflected on the making of this bond:

> On board ship the castes and regions of India were mixed as in the depots, and the common tasks, assigned with little respect to persons, served as a great leveller. The only separation on board was by gender and marital status ... [r]eplacing the previous ties of caste and region was a new form of bonding which was started in the depots and strengthened on the ship. This bonding became greater on those ships which underwent difficult passages, for example in the churning, swirling waters of the *Pagal Samundar* (Mad Sea) so often encountered off the Cape of Good Hope.

5. *GIRMITIYAS* AND MY DISCOVERY OF INDIA

This brotherhood/sisterhood of the boat (*jahaji bhai/bahin*) was cemented when the immigrants joined together to resist ill-usage by European seamen. For this reason, the Indians resented being separated into different colony batches when they arrived in the Caribbean (Samaroo 1999–2000: 19).

It is not surprising, therefore, that the enigma of Kaila has accompanied me throughout my life, sustaining curiosity, as if there was something hidden in her life that belongs to me: a kernel of truth that was at the core of my being. I learnt to call this *identity*, an exercise of the imagination that spoke to one's essence, grounded in family as well as a wider context, community: belonging. But that was a mature consideration arrived at after much internal conflict and agony on the meaning of India—many imagined Indias that still find ways of drawing out a strange loyalty. Kaila and my other *girmitiya* great-grandparents are its source.

But Kaila's India remained elusive to my curiosity. From time to time my grandmother had tried to coax fragments of that past out of her, hoping to draw something from lapses in her taciturnity. She did not get beyond the exhausted tale that she was deceived into going to Demerara (British Guiana) to 'sift sugar'. Kaila was 20 when she went to the colony; she was 'single' and travelled alone. How credible was her fragment of a story? Was she married in India? Did she have any children? What was her mother like? Did she have a happy childhood? What did they do for a living? Did she miss those she would never see again? Did she dream of returning one day? Why did she leave home? Did she tell anybody that she was going away to work, possibly never to return? Why did she travel alone, unaccompanied by any relatives? How did she find the strength to break completely from her past and establish a foundation for people like myself to acquire ambition and self-belief? Some area of darkness! These questions, if asked at all over the years, were never answered. The gnawing secrets are interred with her. But, for me, the questions would not go away. They were sustained by my liberal education and the emerging historical temperament that was tormented by the historical darkness. That darkness that shrouded this woman, whose quiet consistency of purpose must have lodged in my imagination, fed my intellectual curiosity. It would later endow my pursuit of Indo-Caribbean history and historiography with the aura of a mission. This submerged history, which was Kaila's and mine, had to be written. The problem was how.

Joseph Ruhomon (1894), Peter Ruhomon (1947) and Dwarka Nath (1950), local Indian amateur historians, had made a bold start. However, the *girmitiyas*, as individuals, were silent in these pioneering studies. Even Bechu's fearlessly partisan writings on their behalf, in the late 1890s, had not sought to remedy this, although there were many thousands in British Guiana (Seecharan 1999). Agency was denied the 'bound coolies'. Amidst the supremacy of imperial institutions and definitions and the omnipotence of the colonial bureaucracy, individual lives, as well as the universe of the *girmitiyas*, were rendered voiceless. The intellectual means did not exist for the exploration of Kaila's world, including her inner promptings. After a while, curiosity just dried up. Everything would be subsumed under the resilient *arkati* thesis of deception and kidnapping, which brought closure on the imponderables. But, unlike Naipaul, I could not 'live easily with that darkness'. It grew worse the older I got. My intellectual *raison d'etre* was animated by this gaping void in self-knowledge, a strangled sensibility—a fault-line in my identity.

It would be a circuitous route to comprehension of Kaila's world. A few years ago, I reflected on this passion to know:

> My family grew rice but they had been cattle people for nearly a century in British Guiana. I took this for granted. It was many years later, in the 1980s, when I became deeply involved in my father's cattle business that I began to explore this family obsession with cattle. I turned to the National Archives in Georgetown [Guyana], to the Ships' Registers of indentured labourers (Seecharan 1997: 22).

This helped me to detect the vague contours of my *girmitiya* ancestors. I quickly ascertained that much of their caste instincts had accompanied them to the Caribbean; it was a major force in shaping their new world. The Ships' Registers had lightened the historical darkness; that elusive India was just peeping through its Himalayan clouds.[5]

---

5   These Registers are in the National Archives, Georgetown, Guyana. There are 188, 917 individual embarkation slips, bound in 358 volumes, with the name of the ship and the year of the voyage embossed on the spine. These slips have the names of the immigrant, their ship's number, any peculiar identification mark, their village of origin, as well as their *tahsil* (sub-district) or district. They also state their place of registration, and the nearest of kin, if any, accompanying them. The plantation to which they were sent is pencilled in.

5. *GIRMITIYAS* AND MY DISCOVERY OF INDIA

My first ancestor in the colony was Sohun (Sohan),[6] my mother's paternal grandfather, who went to British Guiana as a 'bound coolie' in the ship *Rohilla*, which left Calcutta on 11 February 1875. He was 22 years old and came from Doobaree Village, Azamgahr District, in eastern UP. He was indentured to Plantation Rose Hall, the same sugar estate to which Kaila and Jagarnath were taken later, in 1909 and 1908 respectively. When Sohan left the estate, sometime in the late 1880s, he bought some land at Palmyra Village, the place of my birth, on the edge of that sugar plantation. He started to graze cattle on the common pasturage, which abounded before the meteoric rise of rice cultivation during World War I. But Sohan continued to work as head cattle minder on neighbouring Plantation Prospect, an estate owned by a Mr Gill, one of the many Scotsmen in the district. I felt as if I had cracked an ancient code when I discovered in the Ship's Register that Sohan was of Ahir caste, the celebrated cattle rearers of UP and Bihar. I grew up with knowledge of our Ahir caste provenance, but that had engendered incredulity in me, from time to time. I needed official corroboration in order to accept our cattle pedigree as unimpeachable. The need for authentication was aggravated by the absence of any caste rituals that would have anchored the claim.

Many of Sohan's children, grandchildren and great-grandchildren were also cattle rearers. A few became infamous cattle rustlers. My maternal grandfather, Latchman Sohan (1908–1989), was not unimpeachable. The last of Sohan's 10 children, born when he was 55, Latchman was a spoilt child, pampered by his creole Indian mother, Surat, Sohan's second wife. He turned to heavy rum-drinking early and retained that passion all his life. He was also prone to violence in the home. Outside of the home, Latchman was a warm, magnanimous man, prodigal with his generosity, if a bit of a rogue, something of a folk hero. He was known as Skipper Ding, most called him Skipper, this was done out of affection. That he was a legendary cattle herder—masterful at the lasso—sustained a heroic image long after he had passed his best. The image in the home was less heroic. In the late 1930s, already a father of five, he would deftly escape pressing domestic chores, especially the demanding seasonal tasks of rice-planting and rice-harvesting. Skipper was not overly concerned with the maintenance of his young family, a task stoically assumed by his wife and her parents, Kaila and Jagarnath, over many years.

---

6   I have relied heavily on two people for information on Sohan, Jagarnath and Kaila: Ramdularie (1916–1985), Palmyra, East Canje, Berbice, interview, May 1982; and Latchman Sohan (1908–1989), Palmyra, interview, December 1985.

Skipper's life was one of perpetual flight. Escape through booze and excess of all sorts; escape to the hinterland of British Guiana, to the inhospitable grasslands of the Rupununi, on the Brazilian border, encountered in Evelyn Waugh's *Ninety-Two Days* (1934) and *A Handful of Dust*, his novel of the same year. For many years in the late 1930s to the early 1940s, Skipper drove cattle on the Rupununi Cattle Trail, the 180 miles from Dadanawa, through Surama and Kurupukari, to Takama, on the Berbice River. Often, after that drive through the rainforest—heat, mosquitoes, sandflies and a million things that bite, itches, sores and dog tiredness—he would abandon himself to a week's whoring in the brothels of Takama, until body and money were spent. He would hitch a ride back to Dadanawa for another drive. The cycle could be repeated several times before he returned home. Something of the Ahir had fused with the spontaneous anarchy of the Brazilian *vaqueiro* (drover) and images of the hard-drinking, brothel-hooked cowboy of the American west. To Skipper, money was a handful of dust. Eventually, he would drink his way home until he was broke. He was known to pull out his gun, threatening to shoot his whole family; wife and children would scatter into the darkness and the bush. The bravado spoke of futility: belated assertiveness in a home that had learnt to do without him. He never fired the gun, except once—when he killed a 'tiger' (possibly a leopard) and made it into the newspaper. He had become a legend.

I was groping towards the diverse forces reshaping us, removed from that India we could not apprehend. Yet, somehow, India still mattered. Throughout the 1960s I came under the spell of one of Sohan's other sons, Kaywal, popularly known as Kilpax (1901–1972), a self-educated man who gave me another kind of India. A reformist Hindu, an Arya Samajist, he devoured several daily newspapers, apart from the writings of Gandhi, Nehru and Swami Vivekananda. A chain smoker, possessed by the World Service of the BBC and All-India Radio, he was glued to his little light green 'Ferguson' radio as it crackled into the night. Next day he would seek me out early to survey world events: Nehru's speech to the Lok Sabha on Pakistan or China; President Johnson and Vietnam; trouble in the Congo; Castro, Sukarno, Nkrumah, Ben Bella, Nasser; and, inevitably, back to Nehru, Gandhi and names that I learnt to associate with India's freedom struggle: Motilal Nehru, Gopal Krishna Gokhale, Madan Mohan Malaviya, Abdul Kalam Azad, Sarojini Naidu and others. Jawaharlal Nehru, of course, was infallible. Kilpax had lots of time. When I thought we had exhausted the political deliberations of the day, he would deftly throw in a name to conjure with, and start firing

5. *GIRMITIYAS* AND MY DISCOVERY OF INDIA

again: 'Krishna Menon! Weak! Too much talk! And now the Chinese have walked into India! Ladakh stolen!'; or 'Jagjivan Ram, a Chamar, and Defence Minister!' I was drawn into his web. Another India, Nehru's, was taking shape in me. Kilpax was giving me his passion for argument and his enchantment with the spoken word, in English. And throughout my apprenticeship, he treated me like his equal, although I always called him *nana*: maternal grandfather.

Skipper's and Kilpax's father, Sohan, this patriarch who died in the mid-1920s, had left a very rich legacy indeed. His youngest daughter's grandson, Len Baichan (born 1946), was a Guyana and West Indies cricketer. He toured India and Pakistan in 1974–75 and Australia in 1975–76, and played in three Test matches. In his first, in Lahore in 1974, he made a century. He did not play a Test in India, but he travelled widely there and brought back lavish tales of the subcontinent, from the Khyber and Kashmir to Karnataka and Kerala, of legendary cricketers and film stars, of great palaces and maharajas, which he shared with me during many spacious hours, over rum, under that big samaan tree in the village. The cascading visions of India battling in me could not dry up. The curiosity, too, would not die. So my journey through the Ships' Registers, in 1985, had become an imperative. It would throw up light, feeding new questions, leaving many unanswered. But it was a journey that had to be made.

I discovered that my father's maternal grandfather, Sewnath (1881–1956),[7] like Sohan and Jagarnath, was an Ahir. He came from Kharaura Village, Ghazipur District, eastern UP, and embarked from Calcutta on 8 October 1892, aged 11. He went to British Guiana in the *Avon*, accompanied by his sister, Sonbersi, aged 22, and her husband, Raghu, aged 30. Raghu was also an Ahir. It is noteworthy that the Register has them as the parents of Sewnath. That was incorrect; nothing is known of his parents, but they did not go to the colony. The assumption of parenthood by his sister and brother-in-law was a ruse to evade scrutiny of his case: he was a minor and would have needed the approval of his parents to board the ship at Calcutta.

The trio was indentured to Plantation Albion, on the lower Corentyne Coast, about 12 miles from Rose Hall. Young Sewnath soon acquired a formidable reputation on the estate as a shovelman. Sometime during

---

7 I have relied heavily on Sarran Jagmohan (1920–2005) for information on Sewnath, Etwarie, Harpal, Ramsarran Maharaj and Jagmohan: Palmyra, interview, April 1986; personal communication from Toronto, Canada, dated 21 July 1994, 14 and 16 March 1995.

World War I, he had moved from Albion to Plantation Rose Hall where he continued as a shovelman. His earnings were better than most fieldworkers, and his astounding frugality and gift for spotting a bargain or a niche for profitable investment enabled him to buy several properties at Palmyra and neighbouring Sea Well, at the junction of the East Canje and Corentyne districts. Sewnath, like Sohan and Jagarnath, retained the Ahir's passion for cattle: he bought several head and soon established a subsidiary source of income.

A self-assured, orderly and meticulous man, Sewnath was scrupulous with his time. He often said things in parables, many centred on a theme: time is money. He had little time to spare, and was impatient with those who wasted his time. He managed that time dextrously, combining estate labour with cattle, sheep and poultry rearing, rice farming, the cultivation of fruits and vegetables, and money-lending. The idea of a holiday or a slack period did not sit easily with Sewnath and his wife, Etwarie. On Sundays, whatever the weather, they would work on their vegetable farm at Blendaal, on the west bank of the Canje River, several miles from Palmyra. Only the rapid descent of the solid darkness would stop them: the weary miles home were made in their donkey cart laden with plantains, eddoes, sweet potatoes, cassava, pumpkins, mangoes, sour-sop, sapodilla, and a range of other fruits and vegetables. As their first grandson, Sarran Jagmohan (1920–2005), narrated to me this tale of resilience, industry and utter devotion to the welfare of their eight children, he recalled: 'that donkey cart, with a small lamp dangling from the axle, had enough to fill a market. They grew most of what they ate; and they ate well, although they were very careful with money'. He added that they treated boys and girls with impartiality; some of the produce of their farm was always reserved for their married daughters.

Etwarie, my father's maternal grandmother, was a creole Indian, born in British Guiana around 1883. She was a Muslim; but when she married Sewnath in 1898, she took a Hindu name. She was hardworking, energetic and thrifty. I remember her, in her last years in the late 1950s to early 1960s: a wiry old woman, skeletal. I never saw her sitting still. For many years she was a weeder at Rose Hall, but her reputation as a rice planter was legendary, deemed the fastest and neatest in the area. Both Sewnath and Etwarie were impelled by a passion to uplift their children. They gave one of their properties to their eldest child, Sukhia (1899–1969), my paternal grandmother, and her husband, Jagmohan (1891–1938), whom she married in 1913, aged 14. Their second daughter was married to Jagmohan's younger brother, Mangal, who owned the best shop in the village in the 1930s. Etwarie died in August 1961, on polling day, having just voted for Cheddi Jagan. It was totally in character that she should have done her duty before moving on; her reliability, resilience and consistency of focus were as unfaltering as Kaila's. Unconsciously, I must have absorbed her habit of according girls the same respect she gave to boys. She could hold her own in any argument and never flinched from plain speaking or firm decisions.

The background of her first son-in-law, Jagmohan, is fascinating. It is enshrined in family lore. The tale is told of a man named Harpal (1846–1934), an Ahir *girmitiya* who had returned to India with his eldest son, Balgobin, in 1888. He had left his wife in British Guiana, having counselled her that if he did not return by a certain *jahaj* (ship), she should feel free to take another man. He did not return by that ship, and his wife, a Brahmin born in the colony, my father's paternal grandmother, soon invited a Brahmin man, another former *girmitiya*, Ramsarran Maharaj, to live with her. In early 1891, unannounced, Harpal (with his son) returned from India and went straight to his home at Warren (East Coast Berbice), as if nothing had happened. There he met the wife he had left behind pregnant by Ramsarran. Harpal had an amicable discussion with him and implored him to return to his home in a neighbouring village. Ramsarran pointed to the problem thrown up by the pregnancy, but Harpal assured him that he could handle that: he would bring the child up as if it were his own. Ramsarran left. This child, Jagmohan, my paternal grandfather, was born on 15 August 1891. He became a cattle herder, fathered 13 children and died prematurely, of pneumonia, on 17 September 1938, aged 47. He and his eldest son, Harold, who also died of pneumonia, were buried on the same day. Jagmohan grew up at No. 7 Village (East Coast Berbice), and worked for many years on Harpal's cattle farm. In his last years he was a cattle herder on an estate, Goldstone Hall, not far from Plantation Rose Hall. Ramsarran Maharaj returned to India for good, around 1898; there is no evidence that he had anything to do with his son Jagmohan's upbringing. The latter, a full Brahmin by birth, had taken to Harpal's Ahir calling, so that when he married my paternal grandmother, Sukhia, Sewnath's eldest daughter, Harpal probably saw that as keeping within the Ahir fold, his mother's Brahmin stock and the Muslim upbringing of Etwarie notwithstanding.

I had gone to the Ships' Registers looking for my *girmitiya* ancestors in chronological order, so Jagarnath and Kaila came last on my roster. My mother's maternal grandfather, Jagarnath (1888–1958), went to British Guiana in the ship *Ganges*, which arrived there from Calcutta in late 1908. He was indentured to Rose Hall. He was 20 years old and, like Sohan, also from Azamgahr District in eastern UP; his village was Azampur. He was Ahir, like Sohan, Harpal and Sewnath, my other great-grandfathers. I was not aware how far the Ahir pedigree permeated the family. From time to time people spoke of our Gwalbans Ahir background, but the Registers had established for me that our obsession with cattle was not fortuitous. It had its roots in ancient caste promptings; and our settling on a section of the British Guiana coast, with ample land for grazing, must have rendered the ancient calling irresistible. We would pursue it assiduously for some 120 years, until one by one our numbers dwindled as we fled hapless Guyana for the greener pastures of the Indo-Guyanese diaspora: New York and Toronto primarily.

Kaila's story, however, broke this Ahir monotony. I had not anticipated this. She went to British Guiana in the *Ganges* in September 1909. She came from Bhagwanpur Village, Gonda District, eastern UP, next door to Basti, on the border with Nepal. As noted before, she was 20 years old, and travelled alone—no relatives, man or woman, accompanied her. The Register gave her caste as Pasi. I had never heard of this, so it took me some time to discover that it was a low caste of palm tappers and catchers of wild birds and small game. It quickly dawned on me that her very dark complexion was, indeed, a badge of her low caste status. Pasis were an aboriginal caste, black people, so her name, Kaila, was probably a corruption of 'Kala': black. I learnt that the name Pasi comes from a word meaning 'noose', used in trapping small game. I reflected on this often, and concluded that by escaping her low caste ascription this remarkable woman had, indeed, escaped the noose.

My maternal grandmother had just died when I discovered Kaila's caste background—a very dark woman herself, I have no idea what her reaction would have been. My mother was not very pleased with this belated revelation. She did not belabour the point, but said that I should not make this public. Although I was aware of our Ahir roots, my caste instincts had never cohered; yet I recall a tinge of disappointment on learning of Kaila's low caste. This had surprised me. I must have felt vindicated, having discovered the strength of our Ahir antecedents, for I had become a passionate cattle rearer in my last years in Guyana, in the early 1980s.

5. GIRMITIYAS AND MY DISCOVERY OF INDIA

I like to think that the belated establishment of the diversity of my roots, Ahir, Brahmin, Muslim, Pasi, however submerged, has made me a broader person, equally proud now to claim a wider legacy. This, I suppose, has made me a better Guyanese and West Indian, more at ease with diversity and hybridity, better able to appreciate the achievements of the people of African descent in the region. It was a journey that had to be made; I had learnt much from it, but it left me with far more questions than when I started.

The curiosity grew thicker with my assembling of the fragments of my great-grandparents' Indian background. But the darkness over the real India that they had left, including their reasons for leaving, was not amenable to speedy dissipation. It was my discovery of Brij Lal's *Girmitiyas* that slowly opened for me sealed doors to the opaque world of the indentured labourers. It provided, at last, windows into Kaila's world that had eluded me since I was a child. This book would be the foundation of my belief that an Indo-Caribbean historiography was possible; and that it would debunk Naipaul's infamous dictum that the history of the 'West Indian futility' could not be written because 'history is built around achievement and creation; and nothing was created in the West Indies' (Naipaul 1962: 29).

I was fortified for the journey. This is what I wrote in 1997, reflecting on the place of *Girmitiyas* in the project:

> Towards the end of the 1980s I endeavoured to recover the real India of these north Indian 'bound coolies' in British Guiana. A fount of rare illumination presented itself with my encounter of Brij Lal's *Girmitiyas: The Origins of the Fiji Indians*. Here, in a refreshingly lucid and dispassionate way, the unexamined dogma of deception and kidnapping is scrutinised and largely debunked. Lal had unearthed compelling socio-economic reasons for their leaving ... [and] their role in shaping the temperament of the indentured labourers and their descendants in the sugar colonies. *Girmitiyas* also had a seminal influence on my way of seeing. The resilience of the Indians in Guyana, their thrift and ambition for their family—their achievements—are rendered more intelligible because we now have an authentic overview of real eastern UP and western Bihar, from the latter half of the nineteenth century (Seecharan 1997: xxxiii).

This is a magnificent legacy. How precisely did *Girmitiyas* help me to comprehend Kaila's world?

Discovering *Girmitiyas*: Out of historical darkness

At the beginning of the book, Brij Lal makes it clear that he challenges many of the standard assumptions about the *girmitiyas* and the world whence they came. It is, indeed, a fine scholarly achievement, revolutionary in its execution. He examines all the emigration passes (embarkation slips) of the 45,439 north Indian indentured labourers, who embarked at Calcutta for Fiji between 1879 and 1916. He gave me hope at the start of *Girmitiyas*: '[O]ur discussion has relevance for many other Indian labour importing colonies, particularly the West Indies, which drew their supplies from the north' (Lal 1983: 2). He repeats this at the end:

> [M]uch of what has been said ... also applies to those other Indian labour importing islands, in the West Indies especially, which drew their supplies from north India. All the British colonies operated under the same, or very similar, regulations and many of them shared the same facilities in Calcutta. Sometimes the same emigration agent officiated for several colonies simultaneously, and even the sub-depots and recruiters were shared (Lal 1983: 131).

No examination as thorough as this had been undertaken for British Guiana or Trinidad—this is still the case. The story he was telling was also the story of my people; this was the light I had yearned for most of my life. Buoyed by this, I turned to a groundbreaking article by the British social anthropologist Raymond Smith written in the late 1950s on the origins of the *girmitiyas* to British Guiana (Smith 1959). Smith's study was based on a sample of 9,393 emigration passes of north Indians, between 1865 and 1917, but the correspondence between his findings and Lal's is so compelling that any doubt that *Girmitiyas* does not constitute an accurate account of the origins of Indo-Caribbean *girmitiyas* as well is dispelled.

The only major difference between Fiji and British Guiana is the paucity of Madrasis (Tamils primarily) in the latter. Smith estimates that they comprised 4.4 per cent of the migrants to British Guiana. Lal states that they were 6.3 per cent. He is nearer the mark: Madrasis numbered 15,065 of the 238,909 *girmitiyas* taken to British Guiana between 1838 and 1917. In Fiji they were 23.8 per cent of all migrants. However, this disparity is not replicated for north Indian migrants. Smith estimates that 85.6 per cent of the indentured labourers to British Guiana originated in Uttar Pradesh and Bihar: 70.3 per cent in the former, 15.3 per cent in the latter. Lal states that 86 per cent of north Indian migrants to Fiji originated in this area: 75.5 per cent in UP, 10.5 per cent in Bihar. Both Smith and Lal observe that eastern UP and western Bihar primarily were the sources of these migrants, especially the former.

Nine districts in eastern UP, and a neighbouring district, Shahabad, in western Bihar, contributed 51 per cent of the Indian migrants to British Guiana. It is noteworthy that nine of the 10 principal districts that supplied labourers to the two colonies are identical. In British Guiana the five principal districts of recruitment were Basti, Azamgahr, Ghazipur, Gonda and Fyzabad. In Fiji, Basti, Gonda, Fyzabad and Azamgahr were among the five principal districts that contributed north Indian migrants; the other was Gorakhpur, neighbouring Basti, on the border with Nepal. Three of these districts had special resonance for me: Sohan and Jagarnath were from Azamgahr, Sewnath came from Ghazipur and Kaila originated in Gonda. They were becoming less remote, no longer imaginary. I could now locate them on the map—real places. My exploration of the *girmitiyas* was acquiring intellectual validity.

Brij Lal also establishes that, contrary to popular opinion, an overwhelming majority of the migrants were not from the lowest castes and outcastes. Raymond Smith corroborates this. Lal states that Brahmins and other high castes (Kshatriyas) comprised about 14 per cent in Fiji; middling agricultural and artisan castes were 39 per cent; low castes and outcastes contributed 28 per cent; Muslims were 15 per cent. Smith estimates that Brahmins and other high castes accounted for 13.6 per cent of the migrants to British Guiana; middling agricultural and artisan castes were 38.8 per cent; low castes and outcastes were 31.1 per cent; Muslims 16.3 per cent. Not only was there a remarkably high correspondence in the caste distribution of the two sugar colonies, but, as Lal observes, this also corresponded with the representation of the main castes in UP. The low caste Chamars, the largest single component among *girmitiyas*, contributed 12.9 per cent, 13.4 per cent and 12.4 per cent to British Guiana, Fiji and UP respectively, in 1901. Kshatriya castes constituted 9.2 per cent, 10 per cent and 7 per cent; Ahir 9.7 per cent, 9.2 per cent and 8 per cent; Kurmi 5.6 per cent, 5.1 per cent and 4.1 per cent; Pasi 2.2 per cent, 2.4 per cent and 2.6 per cent; and Muslims 16.3 per cent, 15.1 per cent and 13.5 per cent in British Guiana, Fiji and UP respectively, in 1901. Brahmins, however, were less inclined to go to the colonies as *girmitiyas*: they comprised 2.0 per cent and 3.7 per cent of migrants to British Guiana and Fiji respectively, but they accounted for 8 per cent of the population of UP in 1901. Lal summarises his findings:

> It is obvious that the evidence calls in question assertions about the predominantly low caste origins of the indentured migrants. Low castes, of course, contributed a large percentage of the total numbers migrating, but the proportion of high and middling castes is noteworthy ... It is clear that for most castes, with the exception of Brahmins, there is a broad correlation between their strength in the United Provinces and their contribution to the emigrating indentured population ... Muslims and Chamars, who constituted the largest component of UP society, also furnished the largest number of migrants. Kshattriyas and Ahirs, too, feature prominently (Lal 1983: 70–71).

Lal also establishes that, contrary to accepted dogmas, by the latter half of the nineteenth century, the impoverished districts of eastern UP and western Bihar were already immersed in a culture of migration: to Assam tea plantations, jute mills and myriad industrial destinations in Bengal, especially Calcutta, even Bombay textile mills. Many people were already on the move when they engaged for indentureship in the sugar colonies. The penetration of their agrarian economies by the British rendered many of the traditional caste skills superfluous; there was immense dislocation. Pressure on this old land in eastern UP was intense: the density of population in 1891 in Fyzabad, Azamgahr and Jaunpur districts, for instance, had reached 702, 790 and 816 per square mile respectively. The problem was exacerbated with the demise of many caste occupations, because virtually every non-agricultural caste was forced upon the land. This was a region of chronic land hunger and destitution for many people from the lowest and middling castes, but some high caste people were not immune from this plight.

In 1911, in UP, only 9.2 per cent of Ahirs were returned as earning a living principally from their traditional caste occupation: 'pastorals, cattle owners, breeders, dealers in milk produce'; 73.6 per cent were listed as cultivators. Among Brahmins, only 7.9 per cent gave 'priesthood' as their principal means of livelihood; 73.6 per cent as well were returned as cultivators. Among Kaila's people, Pasis, a mere 0.5 per cent still pursued their caste job; 63.3 per cent were cultivators; 23.4 per cent field labourers. The low caste Chamars had also virtually abandoned their ancient, despised trade of leather working: 39.1 per cent were returned as cultivators, while 35.9 per cent and 9.6 per cent were field labourers and general labourers respectively. It is significant that Kurmis and Koeris, the premier cultivators of the eastern districts of UP, indicated little occupational shift: 84.3 per cent and 87.9 per cent respectively were cultivators. But the influx of virtually every caste, seeking subsistence from the land, would have aggravated their land hunger as well as their vulnerability to the notoriously usurious moneylenders (Lal 1983: 72–73).

By the late nineteenth century, Kurmis, Koeris and Ahirs had earned a formidable reputation as cultivators, but the land was still monopolised by the high castes: Brahmins and Kshatriya (Rajputs and Kayasths). In the late 1880s these upper castes owned 79.8 per cent of the land in Basti, 83.2 per cent in Sultanpur and 67 per cent in Azamgahr. Yet Brahmins were not enamoured of agriculture and attributed ignobility to working on the land. In 1901, in Basti, the single largest source of migrants to British Guiana and Fiji, Brahmins comprised 12.6 per cent of the Hindu population and owned 19.3 per cent of the cultivated area. They owned more than any caste, despite being deemed 'inferior agriculturalists owing to their prejudice against handling a plough' (Nevill 1907: 76). The incompetence of Brahmins contrasted with the meticulous husbandry of Kurmis, Koeris and Ahirs, who were responsible for 24 per cent of the cultivated land; they were deemed of the 'greatest importance in the economic condition of the district' (Nevill 1907: 102–103). Ahirs held 8.2 per cent of the cultivated area, and were considered cultivators 'of a high order'. However, the crown for agricultural excellence was reserved for Kurmis. Dr Voelcker, an authority on agriculture in eastern UP at the end of the nineteenth century, had praised their 'minute methods'. He was deeply impressed with the husbandry of the agricultural castes as a whole:

> [N]owhere would one find better instances of keeping land scrupulously free of weeds, of ingenuity in device of water-raising appliances, of knowledge of soils and their capabilities, as well as the exact time to sow and to reap, as one would in Indian agriculture, and this not at its best alone, but at its ordinary level. It is wonderful, too, how much is known of rotation, the system of mixed crops, and of fallowing. I ... have never seen a more perfect picture of careful cultivation, worked with hard labour, perseverance and fertility of resource (Voelcker 1893: 11; also cited in Crooke 1972: 30–31).

Yet all these cultivating castes were at the mercy of landlords, hence the necessity for prudence in financial matters, if they were to elude the trapdoor to permanent debt bondage.

BEARING WITNESS

In Ghazipur District, the home of my paternal great-grandfather, Sewnath, his caste of Ahirs formed 'the backbone of the cultivating community', and were deemed 'hard-working and successful farmers' (Nevill 1909: 84). Yet they experienced acute land hunger, most being tenants of the Brahmins, Rajputs and Kayasths. In 1906 the upper castes in this district owned 82 per cent of the land; Ahirs owned a mere 2,283 acres although they were responsible for 14.3 per cent of the cultivated area. In the neighbouring district of Azamgahr, the home of my maternal great-grandfathers, Sohan and Jagarnath, Ahirs were also among the best cultivators, but they owned very little land: 7,601 acres or 0.6 per cent in 1879; 10,637 acres or 0.8 per cent in 1906. However, they believed that their ancestors were once the ruling race, holding the same high status as Rajputs and other Kshatriya castes. In view of the contemporary political ascendancy of Ahirs (Yadavs) in UP, it is not far-fetched to suggest that this belief in past supremacy must have been conducive to self-esteem and the sustaining of effort. The achievements of my *girmitiya* ancestors in British Guiana would seem to substantiate that. Their thrift and passion to own land certainly have their roots in the frustrated agricultural initiatives, the stifled skills of Ahirs in eastern UP as cattle rearers and farmers. I am unable to ascertain whether my Ahir great-grandparents' families, in Azamgahr and Ghazipur, had continued to pursue cattle rearing as their principal occupation despite the demise of their traditional calling; but the passion with which they pursued it in British Guiana suggests continuity, not merely the resuscitation of a folk practice. In any case, they would also have combined it with cultivation, as was the pattern with most Ahirs in UP. But their land hunger must have been acute, their indebtedness probably chronic.

As I read the *District Gazetteers* of eastern UP and other sources, animated by the emerging universe to which *Girmitiyas* had led me, I began to grasp the context in which my people's attitudes and skills had been shaped. For instance, the following by E.A.H. Blunt, an authority on eastern UP, on their capacity to pursue several activities simultaneously, in order to combat land hunger and the yawning trap of the moneylender, struck a chord. I readily set Sewnath and his wife, Etwarie, into this milieu. It is true that the latter was born in the colony and was of Muslim stock, but Muslims often manifested, even more than some of the other groups, a passion for thrift, entrepreneurship and ingenuity in performing several

5. *GIRMITIYAS* AND MY DISCOVERY OF INDIA

subsidiary occupations simultaneously. I could also appreciate the role of the joint family in the process. I was better able, too, to comprehend why land was at the heart of their endeavour. Blunt had written:

> A subsidiary occupation is a matter of great economic importance for it makes, especially amongst agriculturalists, all the difference between poverty and comparative ease …There are, in fact, many peasants who have other sources of income: dairy work, selling grass or fuel, basket weaving, the making of rope, gur (coarse sugar), and tobacco, the ginning, spinning and weaving of cotton, etc. … [T]he economic unit amongst the Hindus is not the individual but the joint-family … [O]ne or more of its members are often in separate employment and earning an income of their own, of which they usually remit a part to the common pool of the family (Blunt 1938: 30–31).

There must have been a consuming fear among small cultivators of the *mahajan* or moneylender: because of land hunger and the smallness of their plots, they were perpetually vulnerable to him. As Lal observes, debt burden in these eastern districts of UP was pervasive and deep-rooted, a perennial nullification of effort and enterprise. I could now better understand the reason for flight from this region to other parts of India and to the sugar colonies. I could see, also, why most of my *girmitiya* great-grandparents harboured such a passion for thrift, driven by that imperative for landownership:

> Debt was indeed one of the major problems for the small cultivator. The full extent to which the peasantry was indebted was revealed by an enquiry into the subject in 1868–9 … [I]n most districts indebtedness was pervasive … in Lucknow, between 66 and 90 per cent of the cultivators were estimated to be in debt; in Unao and Fyzabad 90 per cent; and in Sitapur between 60 and 80 per cent … *over three-quarters of the peasantry were shackled with debt* … Sometimes the debt had descended from father to son, while sometimes it was contracted for a marriage ceremony or to pursue a law suit. In addition … the peasants also had to borrow for agriculture or related purposes … *The cycle never ended; the cultivating tenant, one observer noted, 'is born in debt, increases his debt throughout his life and dies more hopelessly in debt than ever'* [emphasis added] (Lal 1983: 83–84).

Lal made me reflect further on the despair that must have claimed my people in late nineteenth century eastern UP, and the will of a few to escape. I could see that indentureship in British Guiana, though initially darkened by its bonded element, was not a static state: within a decade or so after their arrival, many became small farmers, owning a piece of land and a few head of cattle, in villages neighbouring the plantations. The break with the latter was not terminal: economic and social links were resilient. Released at last, their skills and ambition could grow, even flourish. This was my story, and I could no longer accept doublebilling on the historiography of oppression: to see indentureship as 'a new slavery', If I may borrow Pankaj Mishra's elegant phrase, I could not wallow in 'the tenacious pleasures of victimhood' (Mishra 2017: 27). It is absurd to equate Indian indentureship with African chattel slavery; to do so is to trivialise the unexampled savagery of the latter. Besides, the plantation experience of Indians, however oppressive, was certainly not a journey into despair. This bleak, somewhat political, interpretation—to assuage African fears of perceived Indian economic ascendancy—did not accord with the experience of my family in the colony. Lal had also made me think of my people in the context of the 200 famines in India between 1860 and 1908. I tried to locate Sohan, Harpal, Ramsarran Maharaj, Sewnath, Kaila and Jagarnath in that India where the 'constant and menacing spectre of famine ... stalked the land with increasing frequency and stubbornness' (Lal 1983: 120). This was a land of real slavery for landless people, whose traditional occupations had disappeared. This was probably the fate of the low caste Pasis, Kaila's people, landless labourers, many of whom would have been *sewaks* (bonded slaves). In fact, in 1905, as the *Gonda Gazetteer* recorded (Kaila's home district), many Kori agricultural labourers, possibly slightly higher in status to the aboriginal Pasis, were *sewaks*: 'practically the slaves of their employers' (Nevill 1905: 67). Brij Lal sketches the anatomy of this form of slavery in eastern UP:

> Many landless labourers led the lives of bonded slaves. This status began with the taking out of a loan by low caste men such as Chamars and Dusadhs. They then committed themselves and their descendants in perpetuity to the landlord until the loan was repaid. In return the landlord allowed the *sewaks* (bonded slaves) an agreed share of the produce of the field that they cultivated. In most cases, the share was barely sufficient to feed the *sewak* and his family. The landlord therefore provided further supplies, their value being added to the principal loan. The son of the *sewak*, once old enough, shared, and at his death succeeded to, his father's bond. In the meantime, the principal loan was perpetually being increased by the addition of the value of the food supplied by the landlord, and there was little prospect of the debt being repaid (Lal 1983: 87–88).

5. *GIRMITIYAS* AND MY DISCOVERY OF INDIA

The poverty of Kaila's people would have made them especially vulnerable to myriad diseases that were rampant, assuming epidemic proportions, in the latter half of the nineteenth century. In her home district, Gonda, cholera was endemic after 1875; violent epidemics were common. Between 1872 and 1881, this disease accounted for 11.5 per cent of the total mortality of her district. There were bad outbreaks in 1873, 1876, 1877, 1878, 1881, 1886 and 1888—10,000 died in the latter year. In 1893, 16,000 died from cholera. Smallpox visitations were also common in Gonda: there were epidemics 'of great intensity' in 1876 and 1880. Famine struck in 1874, 1877 and 1897.

This was the context, Lal argues, in which some people, men and women, in eastern UP and western Bihar, became enmeshed in a culture of migration. By 1900, for instance, migrants from these areas had monopolised the jobs in the jute mills and factories of Bengal. The five principal districts from which they came were Benares, Azamgahr, Ghazipur, Jaunpur and Allahabad. In 1911 a quarter of the UP migrants in Bengal were women; by 1921, at the end of indentureship, a third in Calcutta were women (Lal 1983: 64). Lal explores the phenomenon and concludes that it is incorrect to attribute blame on the *arkatis* for duping vulnerable people into migrating overseas. He contends that although an element of deception was necessarily imbedded in the recruitment process, there were potent economic forces that sustained the culture of migration, internally and externally. He confers 'agency' on the *girmitiyas*, autonomy as actors:

> [T]here was great upheaval in rural Indian society in the 19th and early 20th centuries, and this ultimately had its origins in the character of British rule in India. All strata of Indian society, the high castes and the low castes, the landlords and the landless labourers, were exposed to, and affected by, the widespread changes sweeping the Indian countryside. Many adjusted to their declining fortunes and stayed on in the village in the hope that things might improve. Others, from all groups and of differing social gradations, thought differently and left. *The recruiters may have painted rosy pictures of glorious prospects in the colonies, and may, thereby, have attracted many into their net. But there were forces at work in Indian society itself that were cutting the peasants off from the safe moorings of their traditional society. Not only men but women [as individuals] and families also migrated* [emphasis added] (Lal 1983: 89).

BEARING WITNESS

Girmtiyas is probably most revolutionary in its treatment of women indentured labourers. This enabled me to reach Kaila's elusive world. Over and over, I could see how these extraordinary women were suffused with the strength of character manifested by Kaila, as well as creole women like Etwarie and Ramdularie. Raymond Smith estimates that 43 women were recruited for every 100 men who went to British Guiana between 1865 and 1917: 82 per cent were between 10 and 30 years old; 52.6 per cent were between 20 and 30. Among men, 85.6 per cent were between 10 and 30. Lal's figures for Fiji corroborate Smith's with regard to the sex ratio as well as the age structure. It is clear that most of these people were very young; their whole lives were ahead of them. What is surprising, however, is the high incidence of women who migrated as individuals, unaccompanied by any relatives. Lal states that while 86.8 per cent of the adult males who went to Fiji were 'single', 63.9 per cent of the adult women were 'single'. Nearly two-thirds of the women were registered as single. I do not know what proportion of the *girmitiya* women to British Guiana were single, but in view of the remarkable correspondence of the statistical evidence from the two colonies, it is reasonable to assume that it was as high as Fiji. Kaila was in this 'single' category, although she was 20 years old when she landed in 1909. The incidence of single women is very surprising indeed. In 1891, in UP, 90 per cent of females were married between 10 and 14; between 15 and 19 only one in 15 was not married (Lal 1983: 103). In British Guiana, my creole-born paternal great-grandmother, Etwarie, was married at 14; my paternal and maternal grandmothers, Sukhia and Ramdularie, too, were married at 14. Lal's explanation of the high incidence of single *girmitiya* women is persuasive.

He rejects the notion that these women were primarily from the lowest castes, that they were mainly whores or women of loose morals. As with men, the women who went to Fiji were drawn from a broad cross-section of castes in UP: 4.1 per cent were Brahmins; 9 per cent Kshatriyas; 31.4 per cent from middling agricultural castes; 31.9 per cent from low and outcastes; 16.8 per cent were Muslims. He also observes that a high percentage of women migrants were registered outside of their home districts: 59 per cent from Basti, 66.5 per cent from Gonda and 'the overwhelming majority' from Azamgahr and Sultanpur (Lal 1983: 108). He contends that this was so not because they were tricked by *arkatis*, but because many had already left home or were driven out of their homes after the death of their husbands, during recurring epidemics. Indeed, many women were already on the move, going 'east', to Bengal and Assam, seeking a new life:

> Migration was not a new or unknown phenomenon for Indian women; thousands had left their homes before they met the recruiters and were shipped to Fiji and other colonies; had moved to other parts of India (Calcutta jute mills, Assam tea gardens, Bihar coalmines, Bombay textile mills) in search of employment, either on their own or in company of their male relatives. The journey to Fiji was part of a larger process of migration (Lal 1985: 57–58).

Although Lal acknowledges that an element of deception permeated the indentureship system, he does not see these women as 'helpless victims', merely 'pawns in the hands of unscrupulous recruiters'. He recognises them as 'actors in their own right'. He gives agency to these women. They were still very young, immersed in a hopeless environment, but with a broader vision of new possibilities spawned by the culture of migration of the late nineteenth century. Exposure to a wider world and anonymity, beyond their villages, expanded their horizons, and endowed the more enterprising with notions of escape from the ancient despair. Lal observes that some young women were in a desperate situation because their husbands had migrated and had obviously decided not to return; others were young widows or young wives marooned in a pitiable existence in the homes of their in-laws. He concludes:

> The fact that women were prepared to part with a life of drudgery and unhappiness for the largely unknown would seem to me to suggest that many of them must have been individuals of remarkable independence, enterprise and self-respect. These were certainly the values they nurtured and lived by in the colonies (Lal 1985: 147).

This could easily have been a commentary on Kaila's life in British Guiana, between 1909 and 1956. It led me to William Crooke's contemporary account of the role of women in agriculture in UP at the end of the nineteenth century. I had no doubts now of the pedigree of Kaila and Etwarie—the source of their meticulous cultivating practices, in rice or cane field, their continuity of focus, their balance and sense of proportion, which helped to guide their men-folk and rescue them from the excesses of plantation life. Crooke observed:

> Among a large section of the cultivating tribe the women freely assist the men in field labour; in fact, the effectiveness of husbandry may be to a large extent measured by the degree to which this is the case. You will constantly see the wife of the Kurmi or Jat sowing the seed grain as her husband ploughs, weeding or assisting in irrigation by distributing the water from one little patch to another, if she does not take a more active share in the work by helping to empty the well bucket or raising the water lift ... [S]he milks the cow, feeds the calves, picks pottage herbs in the fields, collects firewood or makes the cow-dung into cakes for fuel. She has to grind the wheat or barley, which is the chief food of the household, husk the rice or millet, and do all the cooking, besides taking her share in field work, and scaring the parrots and monkeys from the ripening crops. If she has any leisure she can devote it to ginning cotton or spinning thread ... If she misconducts herself she has to endure hard language and sometimes blows (Crooke 1972: 229–31).

This is also the source of their resilience and initiative, for although women were expected to endure and stoically perform their 'duty' to mothers-in-law, husbands and sons, they were not all compliant. A minority, pushed by the futility, became unlikely rebels. As noted above, because of the recurring epidemics in the late nineteenth century, many girls, married at 11 or 12, were widowed at 13 or 14. These girls became drudges, virtual slaves in the households of their late husbands. Remarriage was impossible; it was a disgrace to return to their parents' homes. They were washed up; there could be no worthy life ahead. They carried the stain of widowhood as if they were the authors of the premature demise of their husbands. Others were girls deserted by husbands, who had fled family debts or other communal exactions. Some were accused of sexual infidelity, which meant disgrace and ostracism in village society. The main difference between the latter half of the nineteenth century and previously was the possibility of escape for an intrepid, microscopic minority.

That explains why nearly two-thirds of the women who went to Guyana and Fiji travelled alone: 'single'. Many of the men, also, reportedly single, were probably in similar circumstances. Men and women had a lot to hide, much of it unimaginably painful. But it was easier for them to learn to forget when they were all in the same boat, to come to believe their constructed narratives that attributed all blame for migration to the *arkatis*, the ignoble recruiters. A collective amnesia was crucial to the building of a new persona and a new life. That was why the India of the *girmitiyas* was quickly claimed by historical darkness. That real India was too problematic for easy narration: it harboured too many secrets, it was reinvented as mythical, it had gone beyond scrutiny. The mythical India of the great Hindu classic, the *Ramayana*, with several of its named places located in contemporary UP, was constructed as an authentic representation of the motherland. The real eastern UP and western Bihar disappeared from the radar. The India of the *Ramayana* has endured, as I have written elsewhere, because it is a narrative that answered many of the monumental, urgent needs of the *girmitiyas*:

> The theme of Lord Rama in exile in the Dandak forest is resonant among Indians in the diaspora. His triumphal return to Ayodhya has a freshness; it offers a long reign of enlightened rule, when harvests were bounteous and 'mothers wailed not in their anguish for their babes'. It is an evocation of hope and renewal, even of their own triumphal return, however illusory. Essentially, it answered the yearning for a new beginning, reassurance that there was life after despair. It gave more—the Golden Age, a vision of a perfect India that eclipsed the dark, familiar one. That Hanuman, the monkey-faced loyal servant of Lord Rama, could scale and uproot mountains to get curative herbs to save a wounded Lakshman, Rama's devoted brother, made him the great shaper of possibilities; and his role in the rescue of Sita, the wife of Lord Rama, from the evil Rawan, made him the great defender not merely of chastity, but of *dharma* (Hindu duty) itself (Seecharan 1999–2000: 64–65).

I explain the special resonance of Sita with *girmitiya* women and their descendants thus:

> Indian women in the Caribbean empathised with a Sita of human proportions: the machinations of her husband's co-wife; exile; privations in the forest; kidnapping and imprisonment in Rawan's Lanka; and as related in the Valmiki version of the *Ramayana*, aspersions cast on her sexual purity, lingering suspicion and further banishment. The pathos is exhausting but the Sita persona spoke to women who were in virtual exile, had severed all links with their families in India, had to endure aspersions cast on their sexual life on the plantations (occasionally ending in murder by jealous partners), while toiling to reshape a life and recreate a family in a distant land. But even beyond the dark shadow of the plantation, this Sita endures among Indo-Caribbean women—a symbol of resilience—*not* merely a tendentious patriarchal construct of compliance (Seecharan 1999–2000: 65).

This Sita could absorb the guilt, the submerged pain of loss, the trauma of 'kidnapping' and 'exile'; the amnesia so essential to the reinvention of self. This Sita could fill the void of the recent past and allay the fears of the present. Sita has transcended the mythical state—an enduring redemptive force in the lives of most Hindu women.

It belongs to our family lore that among the few things Kaila took to British Guiana in 1909 was a copy of the slim *Hanuman Chalisa*, a celebration of the heroism of Hanuman. She could not have read it; she was illiterate. In my youth I recall seeing this tattered, incense-stained booklet among the family's religious paraphernalia. No one ever read it; that would have profaned it. It was enough that it spoke of the great shaper of possibilities and the defender of Hindu faith. It celebrated something precious or enduring to the world that my *girmitiya* ancestors had made in British Guiana. And the fact that Kaila supposedly brought the booklet from India also endowed it with sacred properties. Indias of the imagination were at the core of this new world.

I could not have arrived at the self-definition I have grown into, in the last three decades, without *Girmitiyas*. It has helped me to find the centre. But this book has also been at the heart of my work in Indo-Caribbean historiography; and I am proud to claim it as a groundbreaking text of this new chapter in Caribbean historiography.

References

Blunt, E.A.H. 1938. 'The environment and the distribution of the Indian people'. In *Social Service in India: An Introduction to some Social and Economic Problems of the Indian People*, edited by E.A.H. Blunt, pp. 1–41. London: His Majesty's Stationery Office.

Blunt, E.A.H. (ed.). 1938. *Social Service in India: An Introduction to some Social and Economic Problems of the Indian People*. London: His Majesty's Stationery Office.

Crooke, William. 1972 [1897]. *The North-Western Provinces of India: Their History, Ethnology, and Administration*. Karachi: Oxford University Press.

Jagan, Cheddi. 1966. *The West on Trial: My Fight for Guyana's Freedom*. London: Michael Joseph.

James, C.L.R. 1963. *Beyond a Boundary*. London: Hutchinson.

Lal, Brij V. 1983. *Girmitiyas: The Origins of the Fiji Indians*. Canberra: The Journal of Pacific History.

——. 1985. 'Kunti's cry: Indentured women on Fiji plantations'. *Indian Economic and Social History Review*, 22(1): 55–71.

Mishra, Pankaj. 2017. 'Welcome to the age of anger'. *Guardian Weekly*, 13 January, pp. 26–29.

Naipaul, V.S. 1962. *The Middle Passage*. London: Andre Deutsch.

——. 1984. *Finding the Centre: Two Narratives*. London: Andre Deutsch.

Nath, Dwarka. 1970 [1950]. *History of Indians in Guyana*. London: the author.

Nehru, Jawaharlal. 1946. *The Discovery of India*. London: Meridian Books.

Nevill, H.R. (comp. and ed.). 1905. *District Gazetteer of the United Provinces of Agra and Oudh, Vol. XLIV – Gonda*. Nainital: Government Press, United Provinces.

——. (comp. and ed.). 1907. *District Gazetteer of the United Provinces of Agra and Oudh, Vol. XXXII – Basti*. Allahabad: Government Press, United Provinces.

——. (comp. and ed.). 1909. *District Gazetteer of the United Provinces of Agra and Oudh, Vol. XXIX – Ghazipur*. Allahabad: Government Press, United Provinces.

Ruhomon, Joseph. 1894. *India: The Progress of Her People at Home and Abroad, and how those in British Guiana may Improve Themselves*. Georgetown: C.K. Jardine.

Ruhomon, Peter. 1988 [1947]. *Centenary History of the East Indians in British Guiana, 1838–1938*. Georgetown: The East Indians 150th Anniversary Committee.

Samaroo, Brinsley. 1999–2000. 'Chinese and Indian "coolie" voyages to the Caribbean'. *Journal of Caribbean Studies*, 14(1–2): 3–34.

Seecharan, Clem. 1997. *'Tiger in the Stars': The Anatomy of Indian Achievement in British Guiana, 1919–29*. London: Macmillan.

———. 1999. *Bechu: 'Bound Coolie' Radical in British Guiana, 1894–1901*. Kingston, Jamaica: University of the West Indies Press.

———. 1999–2000. 'The shaping of the Indo-Caribbean people: Guyana and Trinidad to the 1940s'. *Journal of Caribbean Studies*, 14(1–2): 61–92.

———. 2011. *Mother India's Shadow over El Dorado: Indo-Guyanese Politics and Identity, 1890s–1930s*. Kingston, Jamaica: Ian Randle Publishers.

Seecharan, Clem (ed.). 2001 [1894]. *Joseph Ruhomon's India: The Progress of her People at Home and Abroad and how those in British Guiana may Improve Themselves*. Kingston, Jamaica: University of the West Indies Press.

Smith, Raymond T. 1959. 'Some social characteristics of Indian Immigrants to British Guiana'. *Population Studies*, 13(1): 34–39. DOI: 10.2307/2172067.

Voelcker, John Augustus. c. 1893. *Report on the Improvement of Indian Agriculture*. London: Eyre and Spottiswoode.

Waugh, Evelyn. 1934. *Ninety-Two Days*. London: Duckworth.

———. 1934. *A Handful of Dust*. London: Chapman and Hall.

6
Reflections on Brij Lal's *Girmityas: The Origins of the Fiji Indians*

Ralph Shlomowitz and Lance Brennan

In Brij Lal's first monograph, *Girmityas: The Origins of the Fiji Indians* (1983), a number of central issues are addressed: the structure and operation of the recruitment system (Chapter 1), the regional origins of the migrants (Chapter 2), their social and economic background in India (Chapter 3), and the migration of women and children (Chapters 4 and 5). In the three decades since the publication of this monograph, our research group at Flinders University has addressed a set of related topics on the history of the health of Indians at home and abroad. Our first project focused on the health of indentured workers, including those going to Fiji, while in the second project, using John McDonald's econometric expertise, we attempted an anthropometric history of India (Shlomowitz 1996: chs 4, 6, 9, 11, 14; Brennan, McDonald and Shlomowitz 2013). This project owed its origins to Ralph noticing individual height data on the Emigrant Pass on the back cover of *Girmityas*. As a student of Robert Fogel, a pioneer of anthropometric history, he perceived the possibility of constructing a systematic analysis of changes in the welfare of rural Indians during the indentured labour period—if other emigrant passes and shipping lists included data on individual height as well as on age, caste and district of origin. They did. In this project, we followed Lal's lead in quantifying the data included in the Emigrant Passes of workers who departed from Calcutta, and then extended this to include those departing from Madras. These research projects have brought forth new evidence and new insights on many of the topics addressed by Lal. This chapter is not an evaluation of Lal's work. Rather, it offers a series of reflections on how Lal's pioneering scholarship can be fruitfully extended. These reflections are limited to Lal's first three chapters as we have little to add to the chapters on women and children.

In his first chapter, 'A Journey Begins', Lal argues that the success of recruitment depended on relative economic conditions: in 'a period of relative prosperity … Indians naturally expressed a reluctance to leave their homes', while in 'years of drought, scarcity and famine … distressed peasants sought any alternative to alleviate their grim conditions' (1983: 25, 26). Lal then shows that the number of recruits who were 'rejected as unfit' in sub-depots before despatch to Calcutta and between arrival in the Calcutta depot and departure for overseas were more marked in the years of famine and scarcity as recruiting authorities could then be more selective of who they permitted to go overseas (29, 31). The specific reasons why the recruiting authorities 'rejected as unfit', Lal suggests, 'are difficult to ascertain as our sources do not go beyond giving statistical aggregates' (30).

As one of our main sources used in investigating changes in the average height of Indians before World War I was the height of indentured workers that were recorded in the Emigrant Passes, we were concerned that the issues raised by Lal could bias our analysis in two ways. If average height varied by the ease or difficulty of recruitment, taller recruits being obtained in times of famine when recruiters could be more selective of who to accept, this bias would prevent us from adducing any possible secular change in height from our data. And if a minimum height restriction was in operation, possibly being a major reason for the rejection of some recruits as unfit, this would prevent generalisation from the height of indentured workers to that of the wider population.

Our response to the first of these concerns was to formally incorporate demand and supply variables in our multiple regression analysis: an increase in the demand for labour from the colonies being associated, other things remaining the same, with a decrease in average height as recruiters had to seek out additional recruits by tapping a worse-off stratum of Indian society. An increase in the supply of recruits brought about by famine conditions would have been associated, other things remaining the same, with an increase in average height as recruiters would have been able to procure recruits from a better-off stratum of Indian society.

6. REFLECTIONS ON BRIJ LAL'S *GIRMITYAS: THE ORIGINS OF THE FIJI INDIANS*

The resulting regression analysis showed strong support for this inclusion of supply and demand factors, and in this way we could formally evaluate if there had been a secular change in height (Brennan, McDonald and Shlomowitz 1997).

We had a number of responses to the concern that a minimum height restriction, common in recruiting for the army and police, was operative. One response was to inspect the left-hand tails of the height distribution for a possible shortfall.[1] Such shortfalls were not in evidence. A second response was to search for extant recruiting instructions in various archives. In the Natal Archives we discovered a number of such instructions, two of which are reproduced in the appendices to this chapter. These instructions placed importance on chest circumference, rather than on height or weight, as the main indicator of the required physical standard to perform the heavy physical labour required on overseas sugar cane plantations. For South Indian indentured workers going to Fiji, information on chest circumference was recorded on their Emigrant Passes (Brennan, McDonald and Shlomowitz 1994). And emigrants from both Calcutta and Madras had their chest measurements taken after arrival in Fiji—these measurements were summarised in unpublished minute papers in the Colonial Secretary's Office of Fiji and in the published Annual Reports on Indian Immigration, Fiji. We concluded that recruiting authorities used the information on chest measurement to indicate the physical standard of the recruit while the information on height was included for the purpose of identification.

Lal first traces broad trends in recruiting for overseas in Chapter 2, 'Places of Origin'. He shows how the initial enthusiasm for tribal labourers from Chota Nagpur shifted to the northern plains of Bihar and the United Provinces while tribal labour continued to provide the main source of labour to the Assam tea gardens (1983: 47). In our research, we have offered an epidemiological explanation for this pattern: tribals were more resistant to malaria in the tea gardens than other recruits but they were more susceptible than other groups to cholera *en route* to Calcutta, at the Calcutta depot, and on voyages overseas (Shlomowitz and Brennan 1990: 88, 89, 99).

---

1   'Tail' refers to the distribution of heights among the indentured workers, expressed as a linear graph. Usually this is seen as a bell-shaped figure. The left-hand 'tail' is the left side of this bell shape. A long left-hand 'tail' suggests that those selecting indentured workers in India had no regard for the shortness of the prospective worker, whereas a short 'tail' indicates a minimum acceptable height.

The main focus of this chapter, however, is Lal's use of the Emigrant Passes to document the districts of origin of Fiji's indentured workers. In our research on the height of Indian workers, we followed Lal in the quantification of the districts of origin of migrants to other destinations as well as Fiji and departing from Calcutta and extended the study to those departing from Madras. During the last half of the nineteenth century, the less populous western districts of United Provinces benefited from government expenditure and the development of irrigation and railways, therefore providing opportunities for the expansion of agriculture, and the employment of share croppers and agricultural labourers. It is not surprising, then, that the recruits leaving from Calcutta came mainly from the plains districts of Bihar and, especially, eastern United Provinces where—as in Basti—population growth and the landlord-dominated agrarian structures brought economic pressure on poor agriculturists even during good seasons, while in times of flood or drought the displacement of the poorer population from districts like Gonda made them receptive to the prospects of emigration (Brennan, McDonald and Shlomowitz 1998).

In a study we made of Muslim migration to Fiji from Madras—alongside climatic factors such as the recurring droughts in North Arcot—socioreligious factors were important in creating an atmosphere where people recognised the advantages of migration. The most numerous Muslim migrants were the Mapillas of Malabar district, a group oppressed by their Hindu landlords through rack renting and unwarranted evictions—some small Mapilla bands struck back with religiously accented violence, deliberately fighting to their deaths as martyrs. Although the British recognised the causes of the unrest, their response was ineffective: for the Mapillas, indentured labour in Fiji was a release from an environment at once economically, socially and politically hostile (Brennan, McDonald and Shlomowitz 1992: 403–405).

In Chapter 3, 'Social and Economic Origins', Lal uses the Emigrant Passes to quantify the number of migrants who identified themselves as coming from specific Hindu castes, or as Muslims, or as Tribals. By comparing the resulting statistics with the numerical strength of specific Hindu castes and of the Muslim community in United Provinces society between 1891 and 1911, he concluded that, other than the Brahmins, the indentured workers formed a fair cross-section of the rural population. Brahmin recruits were underrepresented: whereas Brahmins made up 3.7 per cent of workers, they comprised between 8.0 per cent and 8.4 per cent of the United Province population (Lal 1983: 70).

The under representation of Brahmins can be explained by both supply and demand forces. On the side of supply, Brahmins would, in general, be less likely than other groups to be so destitute as to need to emigrate as indentured labourers. And on the side of demand, recruiters may have been hesitant to accept those Brahmins who had little exposure to hard agricultural labour. That the two sets of instructions included in our appendices specifically exclude the recruiting of Brahmins for Natal may reflect this viewpoint. Similarly, in the 1870s, the British Guiana Emigration Agent stated: 'Brahmins are objected to in Demarara, and in future will be carefully excluded' (*Bengal Emigration Proceedings* 1874–75: 165).

That different colonies adopted at times different policies can be shown in the attitude of Natal's recruiting regime towards Muslim recruits, particularly in the period from 1886 to 1902. Whereas the Muslim proportions of the overall populations of United Province and the Madras Presidency in the Census of India of 1901 were 13.5 per cent and 6.4 per cent, the proportions of Muslims departing from Calcutta and Madras to Natal between 1886 and 1902 were only 1.8 per cent and 1.4 per cent (Bhana 1991: Tables 15–17, and pp. 72–74, 79–81 for social groupings). As there was no comparable underrepresentation of Muslims going to other colonial destinations, the underrepresentation of Muslims going to Natal was brought about by a directive for Natal, as indicated in the instructions in the appendix: 'Mahomedans'/'Muhammadans' were not wanted.

The exclusion of Brahmins and Muslims in these instructions brought forth this comment from the Emigration Agent for Natal in Calcutta to the Protector of Immigrants for Natal on 6 February 1899:

> I think it is a pity you should decline to receive Mahomedans, as they are far the strongest and efficient laborers, although perhaps more inclined to be turbulent than Hindus of the labouring castes. There is too a caste of Brahmins who are cultivators and not clerics, who are admirable workers in the field, usually farming their own small holdings. I do not think they should be refused, however I will guided by the form which I obtained from Madras (Indian Immigration Trust Board Papers, 1889, II/1/48, Reference No I 389/1889).

In our research, we too used the Emigrant Passes (and Shipping Lists) to quantify the social origins of the emigrants who departed from Calcutta and Madras. But where Lal employed classifications of caste that mix ritual and socioeconomic terminology, we preferred to follow the *Census of India, 1901*, which classified Hindus in terms of the ritual pollution involved in transactions of food and water between members of different castes (Brennan, McDonald and Shlomowitz 1998: 55–70). The classifications were based on information provided by local informants—usually high caste—to the Census ethnographers. We constructed four general caste categories to use in our statistical analyses: high caste, superior sudra, inferior sudra and scheduled caste.[2] We believed the advantage of this was that it did not pre-judge the socioeconomic position of the castes in our attempts to trace changes in wellbeing over time. In terms of migration to all the destinations, we replicated the underrepresentation of Brahmins in the emigrant population departing from Calcutta. Similarly, we found very few emigrants identifying themselves as Brahmin, Kshatriya or Vaishya departing from Madras. Even though these castes comprised 5.7 per cent of the Hindu population of the Madras Presidency in the Census of 1901, they formed only 0.15 per cent of the emigrant group (Brennan, McDonald and Shlomowitz 1994: 238).

Ralph first met Brij Lal in the late 1970s when Lal was a PhD student at ANU. Lal developed his doctoral thesis into the monograph under discussion. Ralph has followed Lal's outstanding career ever since with great interest and pleasure. When Lal convened a conference on Indian overseas migration and settlement he invited Lance to present a paper on behalf of the group, and later—after Lal became deeply involved in the writing of the Fijian constitution—Lance agreed to edit the papers given at the conference. This became a Special Issue of *South Asia*, entitled *Across the Kala Pani* (Brennan and Lal 1998). Ralph and Lance consider being Brij Lal's friend and colleague a great privilege.

---

2   That there was a measure of reality in the categories we employed is indicated by the demands in the 1990s for reserved educational and employment advantages similar to those enjoyed by the scheduled castes by a group calling itself the 'other backward castes'. This group comprised those castes that we denoted—somewhat inelegantly—as 'inferior sudra' (see Brennan, McDonald and Shlomowitz 2006: 117–62).

Appendix 1: Instructions to Local Agents and Recruiters working for the Government of Natal

Length of service required of Emigrant	1.	The Emigrant should be fit for 5 years' field labour.
Age of Emigrant	2.	The men should not be more than 40 or less than 18 years of age. The married women should not be more than 35 unless they form part of a family the members of which are able and willing to support them in Natal. Single women should not be more than 30 years of age and those with one or more children will be rejected unless they form part of a batch.
Hands	3.	The Emigrants' hands should show that they are agricultural labourers.
Caste of Emigrant	4.	Non labourers such as *Ex* Sepoys, Office or Salt Peons, *Ex* Constables, Fakeers, Brahmins, Bangle makers, Artisans and Beggars must not be recruited.
	5.	Malayalees, Muhammadans, Emigrants returned from Natal as invalids or undesirables, Indians from Lobito Bay, Educated Indians, Indians with weak intellect or known to be suffering from fits are not wanted.
Minors	6.	Minors who have quarrelled with their friends are frequently sent to Madras and are then claimed by their friends or they change their minds in a few days and express unwillingness to go to Natal. Minors, *i.e.*, under 18 must not be recruited and in the case of youths from 18 to 20, the Recruiter must take every possible care to satisfy himself that the Emigrant is not likely to change his mind in a day or two.

Willingness 7. The recruiters must take care that all emigrants are really willing subjects and are not being induced by small pecuniary gifts to emigrate as these men invariably cause dissatisfaction among the other coolies in Depot.

Source: G.A. Grierson, *Report on Colonial Emigration from the Bengal Presidency*, Calcutta, Government of Bengal, 1883, Appendix IV.

Appendix 2: Instructions for Surgeons

When examining and selecting Emigrants in the Mofussil before proceeding to this Agency

1. The Emigrant should be, first, free from contagious disease; second, in a fit state to undergo a sea voyage of two months; third, equal to ten years' field labour.
2. The men should not be more than 35 years old, and the women not more then 30, unless they form part of a family.
3. The chest should be round and well developed; flat chested men should be rejected.
4. The hands should have horns on the palmer base of the fingers showing that the emigrant is accustomed to hard work. Fakeers, Brahmins, Kyeths, Baniahs, Mahomedans, Shop keepers, Barbers, Toddy drawers, Bangle makers, Beggars and Weavers &c, should be rejected.
5. Cases of hernia, hydrocele and enlarged testicle should be discovered and rejected as these diseases usually develop in the colonies.
6. Bad cases of opthalmia or of diseased eyelids should be rejected. Slight opthalmia may be detained for treatment until cured. If the emigrant has lost an eye from this disease, or from any other cause on no account should he be accepted.
7. Emigrants with slight anaemia, or malarious fever, may be passed if it be considered that a few weeks' good feeding and careful treatment may put them right. Cases of enlarged spleen and chronic anaemia ought to be rejected.
8. Short Stature or slimness is not an objection if the emigrant be wiry and tough, and well able to handle agricultural implements.

The weight of males should be nearly proportional to height, that is, 8 stone 3lbs for 5 ft, and 5lbs additional for each inch over 5 ft.

9. Emigrants suffering from slight bowel complaints should be detained till cured. The abdomen should not be flat or puckered from chronic looseness, nor inflated from habitual indigestion. All cases of chronic bowel diseases should be carefully sought for and rejected. Opium eaters, sand smokers and ganga smokers must be rejected.

10. Of contagious diseases, measles and small pox have hitherto proved most troublesome, and every suspicious case should be carefully excluded.

11. The slightest signs of leprosy; varicose veins in any part of the body; Ulcers on legs or feet, and syphilis in any form, are regarded as sufficient to justify rejection. Cases of enlarge goitre are undesirable and liable to rejection.

12. Sickly children give much trouble. Not infrequently a large family has been kept back month after month at successive embarkations on account of a weakly child. All such children should be rejected.

13. Arrangements have been made for vaccinating the emigrants here.

14. Minors, whether male or female, under 16 years of age, are not allowed to emigrate unless accompanied by a responsible relative, and should not therefore be recruited.

Robert W.S. Mitchell
Government Agent for Natal Garden Reach, Calcutta, 1889

Source: Indian Immigration Papers, II/1/48, Reference No. 389/1889, Natal Archives, Petermaritzburg.

References

Bengal Emigration Proceedings, 1874–75, India Office Records, London, P/171.

Bhana, Surendra. 1991. *Indentured Indian Emigrants to Natal, 1860–1902: A Study Based on Ships Lists.* New Delhi: Promilla.

Brennan, Lance and Brij V. Lal (eds). 1998. *Across the Kala Pani: Indian Overseas Migration and Settlement.* Special issue of *South Asia,* 21(sup. 001): 1–237.

Brennan, Lance, John McDonald and Ralph Shlomowitz. 1992. 'The origins of South Indian Muslim indentured migration to Fiji'. *Journal of the Institute of Muslim Minority Affairs*, 18(2): 402–409. DOI: 10.1080/02666959208716261.

——. 1994. 'Trends in the economic well being of South Indians under British rule: The anthropometric evidence'. *Explorations in Economic History*, 31(2): 225–60. DOI: 10.1006/exeh.1994.1010.

——.1997. 'Toward an anthropometric history of Indians under British rule'. *Research in Economic History*, 17: 185–246 (reprinted in Brennan, McDonald and Shlomowitz 2013: 1–81).

——.1998. 'The geographic and social origins of Indian indentured labourers in Mauritius, Natal, Fiji, Guyana and Jamaica'. In *South Asia*, 21(sup. 001): 41–55. DOI: 10.1080/00856409808723350.

——. 2006. 'Caste, inequality and the nation state: The impact of reservation policies in India, c1950–2000'. *South Asia*, 29(1): 117–62. DOI: 10.1080/00856400600550831.

Brennan, Lance, John McDonald and Ralph Shlomowitz with Eva Aker. 2013. *Well Being in India: Studies in Anthropometric History*. New Delhi: Readworthy Publications.

Census of India 1901 (full text). Online: www.archive.org/stream/cu3192 4071145571/cu31924071145571_djvu.txt (accessed 7 March 2017).

Grierson, G.A. 1883. *Report on Colonial Emigration from the Bengal Presidency*. Calcutta: Government of Bengal.

Indian Immigration Trust Board Papers, 1889, Natal Archives, Pietermaritzburg.

Lal, Brij V. 1983. *Girmityas: The Origins of the Fiji Indians*. Canberra: The Journal of Pacific History.

Shlomowitz, Ralph and Lance Brennan. 1990. 'Mortality and migrant labour in Assam, 1865–1921'. *Indian Economic and Social History Review*, 27(1): 85–110.

Shlomowitz, Ralph with Lance Brennan and John McDonald. 1996. *Mortality and Migration in the Modern World. Varorium Collected Studies Series*. Aldershot: Ashgate Publishing.

Fiji Politics

7

A Political Paradox: The Common Franchise Question and Ethnic Conflict in Fiji's Decolonisation[1]

Robert Norton

> The moral vision that has shaped my interpretation is essentially modernist, democratic, and egalitarian. I will not contest that my approach is necessarily more justified or better than others with different points of departure. Value is a matter of judgment, and there can be no question of finality in scholarly discourse.
>
> Brij V. Lal (1992: xvii–xviii)

> Unless history displays conviction, interest, and involvement, it will not be understood or attended to. That is why subjective interpretation, while limiting knowledge, is also essential to its communication … History is persuasive because it is organized by and filtered through individual minds, not in spite of that fact. Subjective interpretation gives it life and meaning.
>
> David Lowenthal (1985: 218)

The engaging qualities we enjoy in Brij Lal's work were evident in one of his first publications—a lengthy paper on the indenture system in Vijay Mishra's edited volume marking the centenary of the first arrival of indentured Indians in Fiji (Lal 1979: 12–39). I vividly recall my first

---

1 Some statements in the present chapter are drawn from Norton (2015).

meeting with Lal that year at a lunch at Macquarie University with Chandra Jayawardena, my intellectual mentor and professor, who also had written a chapter on the indenture system for that volume. I found myself siding with Lal's redemptive concern in his paper as Jayawardena indulged in some light-hearted needling that I thought was a bit tough on this bright young scholar newly venturing on the academic stage. The hint of rivalry from the eminent senior scholar was further indication of Lal's calibre.

The involvement and conviction in Lal's writing express his deep personal commitment as grandson of an indentured worker and his interest, driven by postcolonial Fiji's traumatic political events, in counterfactual questions about what might have been. One of his major concerns has been with the decisions and events of the 1960s when British officials worked with political leaders to prepare Fiji for independence. Running through much of Lal's writing is the question: how might that process have been better conducted to lay foundations for a less troubled and more prosperous multiethnic Fiji?

I share Lal's interest in the decolonisation decade. I began my research in Fiji at that time and like him I have studied the official documents on the process of ending British rule. We have often exchanged ideas and sometimes disputed about the events and personalities of those years. In this chapter I want to take our discussions further, proceeding in the spirit of Lal's declared openness to alternative historical interpretations and his interest in counterfactual possibilities. I will first reexamine the course of political decisions and events, giving critical attention particularly to the principal Indian leaders' militant push for a common franchise. I will conclude by considering what decisions could plausibly have been taken by British colonial officials and Fiji's political leaders that might have averted the political difficulties and traumas that have beset Fiji since independence.

The question of how the electoral system should be reformed was the major issue of contention among Fiji's political leaders during decolonisation. Lal and some other writers on Fiji's modern history have maintained that the failure of the British rulers to introduce a common electoral franchise to replace the system of communal representation is substantially to blame for postcolonial Fiji's recurrent political violence and instability. The leading advocate for a common franchise in the 1960s was the India-born barrister A.D. Patel (1905–1969), founding president of the National Federation Party (NFP).[2] In a compelling biography, Lal details Patel's outstanding contributions to political leadership and debate in late colonial Fiji (Lal 1997). I share Lal's admiration for Patel, whom I knew and observed at election rallies. Powerful in intellect and personality, Patel was an eloquent exponent of his vision of an integrated, multiethnic nation. The most formidable lawyer and debater in the Fiji of his day, he was a tireless advocate for social and economic as well as political reforms. I cannot agree, however, that his campaign for a common franchise, in the militant way in which he and his NFP colleagues conducted it, was a positive factor for Fiji's political development in those critical years. Mistaken actions were taken, with harmful long-term consequences, by these leaders no less than by their political opponents and British colonial officials. I shall argue that the ethnic political polarisation in the 1960s was determined far less by the communal electoral system than by the militant campaign for its replacement by common electoral rolls and non-reserved parliament seats.

Studying the politics of a society so ethnically divided as Fiji at the time of its decolonisation, is likely to engender in a western scholar a tension between personal universalist social values and an understanding of deep-seated social and political realities that clash with those values. This has been my own experience in writing about Fiji. As a young researcher in the mid-1960s, imbued with the tenets of 'modernisation theory', I readily identified with the radical Indian leaders' ideology and attended more to their views and activities than to those of their opponents in the Alliance Party. That ideology made for the most compelling campaign rhetoric against the dull conservatism of the latter's discourse. But I also met frequently with Fijian leaders in the Alliance Party and attended some of their campaign gatherings in villages, gaining insight into the depth of Fijian opposition to the NFP's common franchise call. A standout feature of election campaigning at that time was a stark disjunction between the content and militant style of the NFP rhetoric and the indigenous Fijian perceptions and fears. I came to view the NFP's campaign for radical reform as an error of political judgement. Developing a balanced system of multiethnic political parties or coalitions and avoiding a strengthening of ethnic tension should have been the main objective in the decade

---

2 Originally named Federation Party, after the federation of sugar cane farmers' unions upon which it was initially built, the party was renamed National Federation Party (NFP) in 1968 when a small indigenous Fijian party joined it. For simplicity I will refer to the party as the NFP throughout the chapter.

of decolonisation. The push for a common franchise deepened the ethnic political divide and prevented the NFP from building a multiethnic alliance that might actually have proved more conducive to an agreement with its opponents for some reform in the direction it sought.

The politics of decolonisation

By the mid-1960s, Fiji's politics centred on rivalry between the NFP and the Alliance Party (Alley 1986: 28–51; Norton 1990: 75–106).[3] The interests and outlooks of the leaders had been shaped in very different social domains. The NFP's founders achieved popularity initially by their leadership of Indian sugar cane farmers in conflict with the Australian-owned Colonial Sugar Refining (CSR) Company. As the party extended its reach beyond the sugar districts, on the issue of Indian rights, its leaders and key supporters included lawyers, teachers, businessmen and trade unionists. It campaigned as a disciplined heroic body challenging colonial power. British officials, the NFP alleged, were resolved to end their rule with constitutional changes preserving the privileges and power of Europeans and their allies, the leading Fijian chiefs.[4] A.D. Patel, the NFP president, was inspired partly by the anticolonial history of India's Congress Party, which he had observed as a young man (Lal 1997: 107, 112–13). Three of the 12 NFP Indian candidates in the 1966 elections, including Patel, had grown up in India. Among the strongest supporters were many more who had come of age there, especially Patel's friends and associates in the Gujarati business community.

The Alliance Party was formed against the NFP as a coalition of indigenous Fijian, Indian, European and other groups. The leaders of its major body, the Fijian Association, were mainly several high-ranking Fijian chiefs who headed the colonial system of village administration that restricted most Fijians to only marginal engagement with the modern economy. These men had developed salaried and political careers in colonial bureaucracies. They clung defensively to their European political allies and were initially apprehensive about the ending of colonial rule.

---

3   Roderic Alley's excellent PhD thesis is the most detailed study (Alley 1976).
4   When speaking of 'the British', I refer to the UK government officials in Fiji or London. I use the term 'Europeans' as it is applied in the Fiji census to refer to white residents of Fiji, both citizens and temporary residents; predominantly of British ancestry, they or their forebears were mostly from Australia or New Zealand.

There was a paradoxical contrast in the contention about the electoral system. The NFP affirmed a universalist ideology and called for abolition of communal representation to affirm equality among the citizens and encourage national integration. Yet it remained essentially communal in its leadership and its following with frequent appeals to communal sentiments. The mainly Fijian-supported Alliance Party emphasised the strength of ethnic differences and the potential for destructive conflict. It insisted on the preservation of a communal electoral system to secure indigenous Fijians against the possibility of Indian dominance and thereby to ensure political stability. Yet the Alliance had significant success in building multiethnic leadership and support.

In the early 1960s, most Indian political leaders had adopted a moderate stance on constitutional issues, causing the colonial secretary to remark in a report to London late in 1963 that they were 'leaning over backwards to cooperate with both government and the Fijians'.[5] The common franchise question was not a major issue in the 1963 Legislative Council elections (Meller and Anthony 1968: 71). The change to a demand for radical electoral reform followed the launching of the NFP in mid-1964, a year after the first UN resolution pressuring Britain to end its rule over Fiji.[6] Four years earlier, the party's founders led a harvesting boycott by sugar cane farmers against the CSR Co.[7] Several Fijian, European and Indian political leaders had persuaded most Fijian growers to withdraw from the strike. Their conflict with the militant strike leaders contributed to the tension that grew as Britain moved Fiji toward self-government, for the two groups became the principal antagonists in the contention over constitutional reform.

Indian leaders had first called for a common franchise in the 1920s when only Europeans enjoyed elected representation in the colonial legislature.[8] The British officials refused to make the reform, arguing that it would lead to an Indian political strength that would imperil their

---

5   Macdonald to Marnham, National Archives (Kew), Records of the Colonial Office (hereinafter CO), 15 October 1963, CO1036/1263. See also Norton 2002: 145–46.
6   'Declaration on Independence for Colonial Countries and Peoples: The Situation With Regard To The Implementation Of The Declaration On Granting Independence To Colonial Countries And Peoples'. In *The Yearbook of the United Nations* 1963: 450, 456.
7   The strike was marked by some violence and arson attacks and army reserves were sent to protect farmers who wished to harvest their cane.
8   Indigenous Fijians were represented by nominees of the Council of Chiefs. Indian political leaders did not include Fijians in their argument for a common franchise until Fijians were enfranchised in 1963.

ability to safeguard the interests of the native Fijians (Lal 1992: 90–91). The Europeans insisted that political representation far out of proportion to their numbers was justified by their economic importance and their sharing with colonial officials the role of guardians of the Fijians. The Indians were given only three elected seats beside the Europeans' six. In protest their leaders boycotted the legislature for several years. The issue was soon eclipsed, however, by their concern with questions of education and lease access to Fijian land.

The call for common electoral rolls for Indians and Europeans was revived in the 1950s as Britain proceeded with decolonisation elsewhere. Britain's declaration a few years later of the plan to end its rule of Fiji, and United Nations pressure for this, encouraged a stronger push by Indian leaders for radical change, which brought them into acrimonious conflict with Fijian and European leaders of the Alliance Party. The latter agreed that a common franchise should be the long-term goal but insisted that social integration and a reduction of economic disparities must come first.

Several factors encouraged indigenous Fijian hostility to the common roll proposal. Especially since the 1940s, Fijians had feared a threat of Indian political domination and the decision to prepare Fiji for self-government alarmed them with the prospect of losing colonial protection. Their apprehension was deepened by the United Nations pressure on the UK to grant Fiji independence with a common franchise; they feared that the British might acquiesce and that Fijian interests, particularly their lands, would be in jeopardy. Until 1963, Fijians had not experienced electoral politics but were represented in the legislature by nominees of the Council of Chiefs. Most Fijians were subsistence villagers acutely conscious of Indian demographic, economic and educational superiority.[9] They had been encouraged by their leaders to view the hardline stand of the NFP leaders in the sugar dispute of 1960 as a threat to Fiji's stability and prosperity and a demonstration of those leaders' irresponsibility. Many Fijians believed allegations that the Indians aimed to drive out the CSR Co. and take control of the industry.

The extension of the franchise to Fijians compelled their political leaders to devise rhetoric for competition with new Fijian leaders emerging in the trade unions and the urban middle class. The established leaders stressed

---

9   Indians were nearly 51 per cent of the population, Fijians 43 per cent. Although the difference in population growth rate was lessening, the Indian rate was still substantially greater than the Fijian.

the need to promote Fijian unity to counter the risks that decolonisation would bring, particularly the threat of Indian dominance and their alleged objective of severing Fiji's link with the British Crown. The Fijian leaders were supported by European politicians, foremost of whom, John Falvey, sat with them as legal adviser on the Fijian Affairs Board.[10] This alliance was conspicuous at the first constitutional conference in London in 1965 where the Fijian delegates would not talk freely with the British officials until the officials agreed to meet them with the European delegates.[11]

The NFP's common franchise call had an inflammatory impact on the Fijian mood. Just as it helped to draw a large majority of Indians to the NFP, equally it helped mobilise most indigenous Fijians behind the Fijian Association and the Alliance Party. The Fijian Affairs Board chiefs making the transition from the security of their authority in the Fijian Administration and the Council of Chiefs to popular elections were advantaged by the NFP campaign they denounced. The Indian radicalism strengthened their popular relevance when social and economic change had been encouraging dissatisfaction with them.

The NFP campaign developed aggressive momentum as it extended beyond the sugar districts. With righteous fervour, the leaders promoted the party as a moral authority defending Indian rights and they condemned Indian opponents as traitors to their community. The demand for a 'common roll' ('one man, one vote, one value') was made the party's war cry and the symbol of its claim to legitimacy in Indian leadership. The primary objective, emphasised in campaign rhetoric, was to show the UK and the UN that the Indians were united behind the party. Electoral support grew from 64 per cent of Indian votes in 1966 to 77 per cent in 1968. But throughout the 1960s and beyond, it attracted only very weak and unstable indigenous Fijian support.

International and domestic political arenas

The militant push for a common franchise must be understood in relation to the universalist values central to the vision of social and political modernity that the United Nations was committed to uphold.

---

10   Since the 1920s, Europeans had nurtured their alliance with the leading Fijian chiefs to strengthen their own position against the Indian demand for political equality (Norton 1990: 37–40).
11   Trafford Smith to Jakeway, 17 August 1965, CO1036/1119.

NFP leaders hoped that the new Labour Party government in the UK (1964–1970), under UN pressure and recognising that the NFP was the major voice of 51 per cent of Fiji's population, would favour the demand for political equality. They especially valued the support of India, which, through most of the 1960s, was one of the severest critics at the UN against British colonial power.

The decision for a militant campaign was taken in the context of the importance of these external political agents. The NFP saw in them the prospect of persuading a reform that would ensure the Indians' security when self-government came.[12] This hope, together with the imperative to strengthen the NFP's dominance in Indian leadership, discouraged the party from compromising with its Alliance Party opponents. There appeared to be little incentive for moderation in the face of the Fijian and European resistance to radical change. Yet that resistance was the domestic political reality with which the NFP had eventually to come to terms near the end of the decade after an intimidating display of indigenous Fijian anger.

The NFP leaders' hope for international support was influenced also by the fact that they had fewer avenues for building a multiethnic following than did their Fijian counterparts, regardless of the political issues. Interests that sometimes encouraged some Fijians to unite with Indians in industrial disputes were submerged when ethnic concerns came to the fore. In the political arena there was, too, the old Fijian perception of Europeans as their protectors united with the chiefs in the face of the numerically and economically stronger Indians. The established pattern of political loyalties and alliances in Fiji helped induce the radical Indians to appeal to external agents on constitutional matters and to disregard pressures to compromise with Fijians and Europeans at home.

The constitutional talks of 1965

The NFP's reliance on perceived opportunities in the international political arena was reinforced by an impasse in discussions in Suva with their Fijian and European counterparts initiated by the colonial governor

---

12 British officials believed Patel was directly influencing the UN in the mid-1960s, although there was little firm evidence of this (Lal 2006: lxviii). British delegates to the UN found no evidence of attempts to influence UN delegates in the late 1960s. Shaw to Lambert, 7 March 1969, The National Archives (Kew), Records of the Foreign and Commonwealth Office (hereinafter FCO), FCO58/314.

early in 1965 in preparation for the first constitutional conference in London. The NFP leaders' withdrawal from the talks was provoked by leaks to the European-controlled media, which published articles allegedly deliberately misrepresenting the party's leaders and their common roll agenda 'with the object of creating animosity, misunderstanding and disharmony'.[13] The NFP leaders were convinced that the Fijians and Europeans were implacably set against compromise.[14] The Fijian leaders and the governor were angered by the Indians' action, particularly as they were hoping for some sympathy for 'the Fijian position over constitutional matters in return for the Fijians' declared willingness to meet the Indians wish for greater security of land tenure'.[15] Ratu Mara feared that 'without an indication of Indian willingness to compromise on such basic issues as common or communal rolls', he would find it very difficult to persuade the Council of Chiefs to agree to the new landlord and tenant proposals.[16] The tension arising from the failure of dialogue in Fiji was aggravated by the outcome of the London conference.

In planning Fiji's decolonisation, the British did initially favour replacing the communal electoral system with a common franchise, but soon concluded that this would risk political upheaval and ethnic violence that they might not be able to control, particularly as Fijians predominated in the army and police.[17] Concerned especially about the Fijian anxiety, the British delegates approached the constitutional conference resolved to make only very limited reforms of the electoral system. They offered a proposal, already discussed with officials in Fiji, which they argued would take a first step toward a common franchise by encouraging some voting across the ethnic divides but without removing ethnic reservation of seats. There would be three multiethnic ('cross-voting') electorates together covering the entire colony, each with a Fijian seat, an Indian seat, and a General Electors seat. Most electorates would continue to be

---

13 Annual general meeting of the Federation Party, Lautoka, 25 April 1965. Papers of A.D. Patel, Pacific Manuscripts Bureau microfilms, PMB 1152, reel 1. On the Suva talks see Lal 1992: 195–200; Alley 1976: 73–82; Scarr 2009: 130–134.
14 After withdrawing from the Suva talks, Patel sought private meetings with the principal Fijian and European leaders, Ratu Mara and John Falvey. Mara, fearing criticism from Fijian colleagues, asked Falvey to represent him. Patel declined to proceed in this circumstance. Robert Norton, taped interview with Patel, 31 October 1966. In Suva, before the London conference, the governor urged on the Fijian and European leaders the wisdom of taking a step toward a common franchise (Norton 2002: 148–49).
15 Jakeway to Trafford Smith, 8 April 1965, CO1036/1283.
16 Jakeway to Secretary of State, 17 March 1965, CO1036/1283.
17 Draft Colonial Office report on the conference for Foreign Office (undated), CO1036/1119.

ethnic (communal) in composition. The 'cross-voting' electorates were to comprise combinations of ethnic electorates. Every elector would belong to both an ethnic electorate and a multiethnic one and thus be entitled to four votes.

With difficulty, the British officials persuaded the six Fijian and six European conference delegates to agree to this innovation. But five of the six Indians held out for a full common franchise without reserved seats, refusing to offer a compromise until near the end of the conference when they suggested some common roll seats in addition to communal and cross-voting seats. The British officials were agreeable to this but the Fijians and Europeans could not be swayed. The Indians were aggrieved less by the rejection of their proposal than by the granting of 10 seats to the new category of General Electors (Europeans, Part-Europeans and Chinese) representing only 4.5 per cent of the population, and by the 14 seats given to Fijian electors (now including non-Fijian Pacific Islanders who with the indigenous Fijians formed 45 per cent of the population), while the Indians (51 per cent of the population) were allowed only 12 seats. The longstanding parity of representation had ended.[18]

The Indians returned to Fiji embittered and angry, disillusioned with the failure of the British to meet their expectation for sympathetic treatment: 'we are all bitterly disappointed and in a state of emotional tension', Patel told a BBC interviewer immediately after the conference.[19] The British delegates were deserving of criticism for not insisting on at least a more equitable outcome, as were the Fijians and Europeans for their refusal to agree at least to a trialling of some common roll seats.[20] The NFP Indians,

---

18   From 1937 until 1966, Fijians, Indians, and Europeans sat in equal numbers on the unofficial side of the Legislative Council. On the 1965 constitutional conference, see Alley 1976: 81–90; Lal 1992: 195–200; Lal 2006: lxiff; Scarr 2009: 136–40.
19   National Archives of Fiji (hereinafter NAF), CSO transfer file, 5/26/1. The Indian delegates had protested to the secretary of state for colonies urging that the proposals for the new constitution be amended as they would 'create grave racial disharmony' and 'irreparable harm ... to the country' (Letter to Greenwood, 12 August 1965, CO1036/1131). Greenwood responded that opposing the new constitution was 'likely to increase the suspicions of the other communities' and that cooperation in the introduction of the new constitution would help 'pave the way to further constitutional progress' (Greenwood to Patel 9 September 1965. In Papers of A.D.Patel, Pacific Manuscripts Bureau (PMB) 1152, Reel 1 'Letters ...'. Greenwood misidentified as 'Freeman' in contents list). After the conference, a senior London official and the Fiji governor tried, separately, to persuade the Fijians and Europeans to agree to the Indians being given an additional seat or two. Secretary of State to Jakeway, 9 August 1965, CO1036/1119; Jakeway to Trafford Smith, 16 November 1965, CO1036/1054.
20   The governor was later to say privately that the Fijians and Europeans had been 'too greedy'. Australian High Commissioner reporting discussions with Jakeway, Hamilton to External Affairs Canberra, 17 October 1966, National Archives of Australia (hereinafter NAA), A1838 316/1/6 part 6.

too, were at fault in maintaining a rigid stance for a full common franchise until close to the conference end after the Fijians and Europeans had very reluctantly agreed to the cross-voting proposal. The British delegates lamented that the NFP men had come to the conference only with a 'largely theoretical' argument for the common franchise but without a negotiating strategy for responding effectively to the Fijian and European opposition to such a reform; a failing that allegedly demonstrated their lack of understanding of Fiji's political realities.[21] Had the Indians made more realistic preparation for negotiation, the British said, they would probably have made some gains.

It was a poorly conducted and badly concluded conference that provoked a worsening of political and ethnic tension over the next three years, culminating in a dangerous crisis of ethnic conflict. The new constitution did, however, bring a major reform welcomed by all: a majority of non-official seats in the Legislative Council. The official side was reduced from a slight majority to just four out of 40 seats; 34 seats would be filled by popular election and two by Council of Chiefs' nominees. The next Legislative Council elections were the first in which political groups could compete for substantial influence in government.

The 1966 elections and the advent of Alliance Party Government

The highpoint of UN pressure on Britain over the Fiji question came in 1966. For the first time the colony was made a separate item on the General Assembly's agenda. The uncompromising UN resolutions were closely in tune with NFP election rhetoric. Town rallies with brilliant orators denouncing colonialism, especially its alleged injustices to Indians, mobilised an excited Indian public on an unprecedented scale. There were frequent declarations that the UN and 'world opinion' would compel Britain to introduce the common franchise and that this must be the 'last will and testament' of British rule. To speed reform, the NFP said, the UN

---

21   Trafford Smith to Jakeway, 20 August 1965, CO1036/1131. Fiji's governor had sent to London a lengthy report on the NFP that asserted 'there is little doubt that the long-term aim [of the NFP leaders] is to secure the political and economic domination of Fiji by the Indians'. It suggested that if the conference 'results in a ... constitution whereby ... Fijians and Europeans collectively outnumber the Indians in the Legislative Council, it will not be easy for the Party leaders ... to pursue their ambitions'. Jakeway to Secretary of State, 29 June 1965, CO1036/1125. It is not known if this advice influenced British government delegates to the conference.

was appointing a committee for an inspection visit to Fiji.[22] Britain must allow this, especially as the elections will prove the NFP is the voice of the Indians. And Britain must implement recommendations arising from the inspection that would undoubtedly back the NFP demand.

The Alliance Party's theme was that it alone had multiethnic support and leadership and aimed to build harmony and prosperity by preserving the communal electoral system to secure the interests of the different ethnic groups, particularly the indigenous Fijians. The Alliance would govern responsibly in the interests of all, whereas the NFP was a communal party whose radical electoral reform agenda was a threat to all. Moreover, its leaders had demonstrated their irresponsibility by their militancy in the sugar industry strike and by their withdrawal from the Suva talks. To its Fijian audiences, the party's Fijian candidates gave assurances that an Alliance victory would ensure that Fijians held political power when self-government came.

The Alliance Party dominated the new Legislative Council. It had won all 12 Fijian seats (attracting 66 per cent of the votes in the communal electorates), seven of the 10 General seats, and the three Indian seats in cross-voting electorates (but attracted only 15 per cent of the votes in the communal Indian electorates). In addition, the Alliance was supported in the Legislative Council by the two Council of Chiefs nominees and all three independent General members. The NFP secured only the nine communal Indian seats (with 64 per cent of the votes) and fielded only one non-Indian candidate (a Fijian cane farmer in a predominantly Indian electorate) (see Norton 1990: 75–106; Alley 1976: 176–264).

Given the strength of Indian support for the NFP, the governor, Sir Derek Jakeway, urged Ratu Mara, the Alliance president, to share with Patel the non-official seats in a new Executive Council. Mara, with his principal European ally John Falvey at his side, objected that this would upset his Indian colleagues and that in any case the parties were ideologically incompatible. Mara, Falvey and Patel had sat together in the Executive Council since 1964, and Jakeway was hoping to maintain an ethnic balance

---

22 This was true. See 'The situation with regard to the implementation of the Declaration on the granting of independence to Colonial Countries and Peoples: Fiji.' In *The Yearbook of the United Nations* 1966: 578–81. The UN request to inspect Fiji was refused by the British on the ground that such a visit was 'unnecessary'. The Fijian and European leaders firmly rejected the proposal.

among the non-official members.²³ But he had also resolved to nurture Mara to become Fiji's first prime minister and now readily accepted his argument, later stressing to London that it was Mara's decision 'to proceed with party political government'.²⁴ In his end-of-year report to London, Jakeway enthused about Mara's leadership, declaring that 'very soon we will have a situation of virtual self-government' and that now the governor 'can only exercise influence'.²⁵

Patel claimed at a party rally that he was invited to join the government but had refused in order to better serve the people as leader of the opposition. Privately he was aggrieved at the governor's decision and his resentment deepened as it became clear over the following months that Jakeway was content to allow Mara and his Alliance colleagues much rein in government. This situation was strengthened by Jakeway's introduction of the ministerial system in September 1967.²⁶ In his January 1968 report to London, Jakeway declared that 'the Alliance offers the best prospect of stable non-partisan government in Fiji and continues to deserve the support it has received from Her Majesty's Government'.²⁷

Political crisis and conciliation

Patel judged the governor's decisions and London's ready approval to signify official disinterest in considering further change as a matter of any urgency. Angered especially by the governor's failure to consult him about the ministerial appointments, he condemned the constitution as

---

23 Reporting to London on the eve of the elections, Jakeway had said 'a coalition government works best': 'A system of "Government" and "Opposition" is too likely to stratify on racial lines … It is our object to foster the seeds of union … They are there but need careful nurture … I only hope that they will still be there to tend after the elections'. Jakeway to Secretary of State, 12 July 1966, National Archives, Dominions Office (hereinafter DO), DO169/501.
24 Jakeway to Trafford Smith, 14 August 1967, FCO60/34. The governor retained 'full powers in respect of defence, external affairs, internal security, and the public service', and power to take control 'when necessary in the interest of public order, public faith, or good government'. Brief for UK mission at UN, 10 September 1969, FCO58/313.
25 Jakeway to Secretary of State for Colonies, 15 December 1966, CO1036/1667.
26 The new constitution required the governor to ensure 'appropriate representation of the various communities' in his Executive Council (Lal 2006: lxiv). He now appointed three Fijians, six Europeans (three of them officials) and only one Indian who had been elected to the Legislative Council by mostly Fijian votes.
27 11 January 1968, FCO 32/24. Jakeway's comments on the NFP were mainly negative.

'undemocratic, iniquitous, and unjust' and called for a new conference.[28] The NFP then commenced a long boycott of the Legislative Council, just as the UN again took Britain to task for allegedly mismanaging Fiji's decolonisation.[29] At public rallies and in the Hindi press supporting the party, there were renewed declarations that, despite opposition from Britain and the Alliance Party government, the UN would soon send an inspection team to Fiji.[30]

In by-elections for the vacant seats, in September 1968, the NFP waged a more aggressive campaign than before with the aid of two Fijians of high traditional rank. Their presence, speakers proclaimed, showed that not all the chiefs were with the Alliance Party. There were declarations that the constitution must be 'smashed' and denigration of the paramount Fijian chiefs (Mara and three of his Fijian colleagues in government) and European political leaders and business interests. The British rulers, Patel alleged, were resolved to perpetuate a European-dominated colonialist government. There was much anti-European rhetoric and stress on the need for Indian racial unity and denouncement again of Indian opponents for betraying their race (see Alley 1976: 235–59; Norton 1990: 98–102; Lal 1992: 203–06). Although indigenous Fijians were not to vote, there were attempts to win their favour by proposing that Fiji be made a republic with a Fijian head of state, and they were urged to unite with Indians against a shared oppression under the heel of the Europeans (Norton 1990: 97–100).

Winning back all seats with increased majorities was a pyrrhic victory for the NFP. Its attacks on the chiefs, together with the failure of Ratu Mara's strenuous personal campaigning, provoked an aggressive Fijian backlash that compelled the radicals to come to terms with dangers and constraints in the domestic political arena. There were marches and rallies in the towns, tacitly approved by Mara, directed against the Indian leaders and, for many marchers, against Indians in general. Before Mara and fellow chiefs subdued them, the protests came close to sparking widespread

---

28 *Legislative Council Debates*, 1 September 1967: 612. See also Alley 1976: 234–35; Lal 1992: 201. In the preceding months, the NFP had reportedly settled well into the role of 'opposition' and both parties had become 'increasingly anxious to present a public image of concern with national, not sectional or racial interests'. Acting governor Lloyd to Fairclough, 15 Sept. 1967, FCO32/21.
29 'The situation with regard to the implementation of the Declaration on the Granting of Independence to Colonial Countries and Peoples: Fiji.' *The Yearbook of the United Nations* 1967: 659–64.
30 Patel's speech at a rally at a Hindu temple. 1967. *Jagriti* (Nadi), 28 September; Editorial. 1967. *Jagriti* (Nadi), 30 September.

violence. As Brij Lal has observed, 'The 1968 by-elections changed the political dynamics of Fiji' (Lal 2006: lxix). The genie of aggressive indigenous nationalism had been released, weakening the Indians' political resolve, encouraging them to conciliation, and strengthening the Fijian conviction of entitlement to power. Though failing to win an Indian seat, Mara made political gains from the aftermath of the elections. But there was, too, a shocked recognition by him and his political colleagues that a catastrophe had been narrowly averted.

The changed NFP mood was also influenced by a shift of advantage to Ratu Mara in the international political arena. In personal meetings commencing late in 1967, he persuaded the government of India to recognise Fiji's difficulties and to sympathise with his cautious and gradualist approach to constitutional reform. India began late in 1968 to urge the UN to moderation on the Fiji question. Several months before the by-elections, two official emissaries from India, reciprocating Mara's visit to New Delhi, had met with NFP leaders. They had criticised the boycott and urged the NFP leaders to seek an extension of cross-voting and a reduction of seats for General Electors rather than continue to press for a common franchise.[31] They advised that some UN members were already moderating their position on Fiji and that the NFP leaders should work with their Fijian counterparts to achieve independence from Britain as soon as possible, and perhaps after that return to their common roll quest.[32]

Patel and Mara had begun private discussions soon after their separate meetings with India's emissaries. The talks were suspended as the by-elections drew near but were resumed soon after the Fijian protest crisis with the encouragement of another official emissary from India. The urgings of the Indian government men and the trend to moderation at the UN, encouraged by India, influenced the NFP leaders' efforts to reach agreement with the Alliance Party. In the mid-1960s, when UN pressure on the UK was strongest, Indian leaders had been sharply divided between a majority demanding radical change and a minority joining with Fijians and Europeans in a conservative approach to electoral reform. By the end of the decade, the militants themselves had become moderates favouring compromise.

---

31 Visit of Indian government officials 1967–1969, NAF, C163/16. See also Norton 2004: 166–67.
32 Karam Ramrakha, a party principal at that time. Personal communication, 19 July 2003.

Talks between the parties in Suva and at a conference with British officials in London led to the granting of independence to Fiji in October 1970 (see Alley 1976: 352ff, 380ff; Lal 2006: lxxii–lxxix; Norton 2004: 175–82; Scarr 2009: 165–88; Vasil 1972). The London conference of April–May 1970 presented a striking contrast to that of 1965, with political leaders now meeting in a mood of relaxed accord. The NFP leaders' willingness to temporarily shelve their common roll call and to accept a degree of Fijian political precedence was the most important factor in this, together with their suggestion that Fiji proceed to independence under Mara's government.[33] These concessions might have been more difficult to make but for a new NFP president, the younger and Fiji-born Siddiq Koya, appointed following Patel's death soon after the start of the Suva talks. Also important for the rapprochement was the shared concern that the party conflict had almost brought a catastrophe upon Fiji.[34] Mara's growing confidence in leading routine government, together with his strengthened success in the international arena, made him more open to conciliatory dialogue. In return for the NFP concessions, the Alliance leaders agreed to restoration of parity of elected representation of Indians and Fijians in a lower house of parliament, and a small reduction of seats for General Electors. Although all seats continued to be ethnically reserved, the proportion based in multiethnic electorates was increased. To Indian critics of the NFP's moderate turn, Koya replied that 'party interest [in a common roll] has been subordinated to the interest of the nation'. A common roll, he now insisted, can only be introduced 'if a significant number of Fijians accept it'.[35]

The dialogue in Suva had been conducted in camera by political elites who feared that to put their agreements to a popular test in elections before going to London would risk a renewal of ethnic polarisation that might break the accord. It was a major failing of the decolonisation process that it was not accompanied by a balanced development of multiethnic political organisation. This was at least partly because political competition

---

33 The Council of Chiefs was to control appointments to eight of the 22 seats in an upper house of parliament, with power to veto legislative proposals affecting specifically Fijian interests; the other senators would be nominees of the prime minister and the leader of the opposition.

34 Mara told the press after the London conference that the 'animosity' arising in the 1968 by-elections spurred greater efforts to find agreement 'between the races' because 'we realised we were right on the brink of disaster if we were not very careful'. 'Need to plug for all races says chief minister'. 1970. *Fiji Times*, 7 May: 3.

35 'Patience on common roll'. 1970. *Fiji Times*, 13 July: 3.

remained tied to the most ethnically divisive issue: the NFP's demand for radical electoral reform at a time of heightened indigenous Fijian feelings of insecurity and suspicion. In their confidential Suva talks, the leaders finally broke from that impasse. But by then ethnic opposition in political organisation had been set for many years to come; the major cause of the fragility of democratic government in Fiji.

During the 1960s, the NFP held only the nine Indian communal seats and it continued after independence to have only very weak indigenous Fijian support and less from General Electors. The Alliance Party maintained the allegiance of a large majority of Fijians and in the first postcolonial elections in 1972 attracted 24 per cent of Indian communal votes. But the party was soon challenged by an extremist Fijian group, which led it to lessen efforts to win Indian favour, and in subsequent elections the Alliance Party drew no more than 16 per cent of their votes.

Counterfactual questions

The NFP's common franchise campaign was so greatly at odds with the possibilities for political success that one must ask why it was pushed so strongly. There was, for several years, the hope that Britain's new Labour government, especially in the face of UN pressure and the strength of Indian support for the NFP, would override European and Fijian resistance to radical reform. More significant, however, was the NFP's impact on Indian political and social consciousness. The vibrant public rallies with combative oratory engendered feelings of strength and pride set against a colonial regime seen as supporting European power and privilege. These sentiments sustained the party's aggressive momentum despite its very weak prospects for success in both the domestic and international arenas.

The manner in which the NFP leaders pursued their radical reform goal was unwise given the strength of ethnic disparities, the very limited Fijian experience of electoral politics and their anxiety over the prospect of British rule ending. Patel, who dominated the NFP, maintained an intellectualist approach to reform, arguing the logical merits of a common franchise for building a new nation but paying little heed to the nature of the Fijian resistance. In this vision he was encouraged by doctrinaire principles of the UN declaration of December 1960, which demanded the ending of colonial rule 'without conditions or reservations'.[36]

While ostensibly aiming to promote political integration, the push for a common franchise contributed to ethnic tension by calling for the abolition of ethnic distinctions in political representation and by the NFP's emphasis on uniting Indians and attacking Europeans and leading Fijian chiefs whose alliance Fijians had long viewed as protective. An NFP principal, speaking on the outcome of the 1970 conference, acknowledged the danger in his party's failure to understand the Fijian fears. He stressed the importance of advice from the two Fijians who joined the party's leadership early in 1968:

> If they had not warned us about the deep undercurrents and the deep thinking of the Fijian people on many matters ... we might easily have taken the wrong path, and the two parties, locked ... in bitter confrontation, might have taken a path which may have been disastrous to the country.[37]

Brij Lal has pondered on how Fiji's decolonisation might have been better conducted, how different decisions might have been made and different paths taken. Pursuing such questions need not be the fruitless 'parlour game' famously derided by historian E.H. Carr (1987: 97) but can aid insight into the nature of constraints and potentialities at critical historical moments. A number of scholars, during the last 20 years, have argued persuasively for the value of counterfactual thinking, particularly about political events. They stress the importance of rigour in relating hypothetical alterations of past actions to known contextual constraints and realistic possibilities, and the need to avoid personal values or interests determining the conjectures (see especially Tetlock and Parker 2006: 14–44; for a critical review of the literature, see Evans 2014). These studies encourage me to consider afresh some 'might have beens' of Fiji's late colonial history, especially the possibility that existed for a stronger and more balanced development of interethnic cooperation in political parties.

---

36 'Declaration on granting independence to colonial countries and peoples'. In *The Yearbook of the United Nations* 1960: 44–50. The original UN statement on colonialism qualified its call for self-government by recognising the need to take account of 'the particular circumstances of each territory and its peoples and their varying stages of advancement'. United Nations Charter, June 1945, Chapter 11, Article 73, 'Declaration Regarding Non-Self-Governing Territories'.

37 Karam Ramrakha, *Fiji Legislative Council Debates,* 17 June 1970: 228.

Commentators on Fiji's political history, including Lal, have often attributed Fiji's difficulties substantially to an ethnically divided electoral system and have maintained that common electoral rolls and elimination of the ethnic reservation of parliament seats would have encouraged multiethnic collaboration on the basis of shared interests. While I certainly agree that this reform was desirable as a long-term objective, it is important to recognise that a common franchise is not a panacea for ethnic division in political life.[38] Shared material interests upon which interethnic unities might be built can also foster ethnic competition for scarce resources and a politics of ethnic patronage.

The prospect for the introduction of a common franchise in 1960s Fiji was minimal. It would be unrealistic to suggest that Ratu Mara and his Alliance Party colleagues could have been persuaded to make a major concession to the NFP call for this reform or that the British government might, in the prevailing political situation, have insisted on it. Given the strength of Fijian (and European) defensive hostility, and the British fears of instability and violence, these must be rejected as implausible counterfactuals.[39] Among the Fijian leaders, Mara was by far the most able and the most progressive in social and political vision. In the 1950s, he had advocated multiethnic schooling and a common franchise for town government.[40] But as the preeminent leader in the 1960s, he was constrained by the deep conservatism of colleagues in the Fijian Association and the Great Council of Chiefs and was himself averse to a common franchise at national level where Fijian interests were seen to be potentially at risk.

A more plausible counterfactual is an NFP willingness to moderate their common roll quest early in the decolonisation process.[41] This would have resulted in a less antagonistic and mistrustful opposition between the parties and might have opened the way for more interethnic cooperation on both sides. An attempt to continue dialogue in Suva in 1965 by discussing the electoral issue in a flexible way, signalling the possibility of compromise, might have encouraged at the first London conference

---

38   Trinidad and Guyana, societies with which Fiji is often compared, demonstrate this with their strong tendencies over many years to ethnic polarisation in electoral competition.
39   Fijians sympathetic to the call for a common franchise at that time were a tiny tertiary-educated minority.
40   A common franchise was introduced for town boards in 1967, and for Suva and Lautoka municipal councils in 1970.
41   The common franchise question was not an important issue in the 1963 Legislative Council elections.

a mood more conducive to an outcome acceptable to the party. This in turn might have favoured more interethnic collaboration in the 1966 elections instead of the aggravation of the ethnic political divide that did occur.

It is true that pressures and incentives for the NFP to remain firm in its call for the common franchise were strong. Aggrieved over the outcome of the 1965 constitutional conference, the NFP leaders remained hopeful of support in the international arena and they were determined to preserve their dominance of Indian leadership to persuade that support. The 'common roll' cry acquired powerful symbolic force, iconic of legitimate Indian leadership against alleged injustice and insecurity under colonial rule. To soften the demand in the Suva talks early in 1965 might have been seen to discredit the party's image as fearless champion of Indian rights.[42]

Yet there were moments of internal conflict that indicate the potential for the NFP to have modified its approach. There was, toward the end of 1967, strong support within the leadership for ending the boycott of the Legislative Council,[43] and after the meeting with India's emissaries early in 1968, there was again dissension about the boycott.[44] Moreover, popular Indian sentiment in support of the push for a common franchise was not comparable to the strength of indigenous Fijian sentiment against it. For most Indians, conditions for leasing Fijian-owned land and access to other economic opportunities were more important issues.

The NFP might have chosen to put greater emphasis on economic and social development issues, including those of special concern to indigenous Fijians and those cutting across the ethnic divide, matters that the leaders often did address at public rallies. Perhaps, had the NFP given more attention to those matters and softened its position on electoral reform, the colonial governor might, with Mara's assent, have established

---

42 In Alley's words, 'The stridency with which [the NFP] began propounding the need for a common roll was due, at least in part, to fears of Indian communal disunity at a time when it could be least afforded' (1976: 160).
43 This was overruled by Patel (Alley 1976: 327–28).
44 Fiji Political Intelligence Committee, report for February 1968. NAA, A1838/346 TS699/9/1 Part 2.

7. A POLITICAL PARADOX

the coalition government he had wanted following the 1966 elections.[45] This could have further strengthened efforts to build multiethnic cooperation for subsequent elections.

In this hypothetically different course of political events from an earlier moment in decolonisation, greater progress toward a true common franchise (multiethnic electorates with non-reserved seats) might have been made in preparation for independence. It is ironic that the traumatic experience of Fijian intimidation provoked by the aggressive push for radical reform contributed to the weakening of the Indian leaders' interest in the issue. When in 1975 Prime Minister Ratu Mara rejected the recommendation of an official inquiry for the introduction of some common roll electorates without ethnically reserved seats, the NFP leaders did not strongly protest.[46]

In 2013, long after Indian leaders had ceased to push for it, a regime backed by the almost exclusively indigenous Fijian army imposed a common franchise in the context of a greatly decreased Indian population,[47] a resolve to suppress Fijian ethnic nationalism, and the need for a self-validating nation-building mission. Once the major objective of radical Indian politicians and anathema to the Fijians, a common franchise now has central place in the ideology of a mainly indigenous Fijian government.

Archives consulted

National Archives of Australia (NAA)

National Archives of Fiji (NAF)

National Archives (Kew)
    Record of the Dominions Office (DO)
    Records of the Colonial Office (CO)
    Records of the Foreign and Commonwealth Office (FCO)

---

45 I don't discount the possibility that Jakeway might have overruled Mara's objection to power-sharing despite the hostility and mistrust on the part of Mara and Falvey against Patel at that time, although I think that was very unlikely. In old age, Mara told an interviewer that he regretted not having agreed to share power in government with Patel: 'Patel was an intelligent man. He would have worked along' (Hancock 2003: 34, cited in Lal 2011: 102).

46 The inquiry fulfilled a requirement in the 1970 constitution, inserted in compensation for the NFP agreeing to temporarily shelve their common franchise agenda (Lal 1992: 221–24). Not until a new constitution in 1997 were some multiethnic electorates without reserved seats introduced, although ethnic electorates remained in the majority.

47 The 2007 census reported that Indians were approximately 37 per cent and Fijians approximately 57 per cent of Fiji's population.

Pacific Manuscripts Bureau, College of Asia and the Pacific, The Australian National University
   Papers of A.D. Patel

References

Alley, Roderic. 1976. 'The development of political parties in Fiji', PhD thesis, Victoria University, Wellington.

——. 1986. 'The emergence of party politics'. In *Politics in Fiji*, edited by Brij V. Lal, pp. 28–51. Sydney: Allen & Unwin.

Carr, E.H. 1987 [1961]. *What is History?* 2nd edition, edited by R.W. Davies. Harmondsworth: London: Penguin Books.

'Declaration on granting independence to colonial countries and peoples'. In *The Yearbook of the United Nations*, 1960: 44–50. Online: cdn.un.org/unyearbook/yun/chapter_pdf/1960YUN/1960_P1_SEC1_CH5.pdf (accessed 7 March 2017).

'Declaration on independence for colonial countries and peoples: The situation with regard to the implementation of the Declaration on Granting Independence to Colonial Countries and Peoples'. In *The Yearbook of the United Nations*, 1963. Online: cdn.un.org/unyearbook/yun/chapter_pdf/1963YUN/1963_P1_SEC3_CH3.pdf (accessed 7 March 2017).

Editorial. 1967. *Jagriti* (Nadi), 30 September.

Evans, Richard J. 2014. *Altered Pasts: Counterfactuals in History.* Harmondsworth: Abacus.

Hancock, Kathleen. 2003. *Men of Mana:* Portraits of Three Pacific Leaders—Ratu Sir Kamisese Mara, Afioga Va'ai Kolone, Sir Robert Rex. Wellington: Steele Roberts.

Lal, Brij V. 1979. 'Fiji girmitiyas: The background to banishment'. In *Rama's Banishment: A Centenary Tribute to the Fiji Indians 1879–1979*, edited by Vijay Mishra, pp. 12–39. Auckland and London: Heinemann Educational Books.

———. 1992. *Broken Waves: A History of Fiji in the Twentieth Century*. Honolulu: University of Hawai'i Press.

———. 1997. *A Vision for Change: AD Patel and the Politics of Fiji*. Canberra: National Centre for Development Studies, The Australian National University.

———. (ed.). 2006. *British Documents on the End of Empire, Series B, Volume 10: Fiji*. London: The Stationery Office.

———. (ed.). 2011. *A Vision for Change: Speeches and Writings of AD Patel, 1905–1969*. Canberra: ANU E Press. Online: press.anu.edu.au?p=152161 (accessed 21 December 2016).

Lowenthal, David. 1985. *The Past is a Foreign Country*. Cambridge: Cambridge University Press.

Meller, Norman and James Anthony. 1968. *Fiji Goes to the Polls: The Crucial Legislative Council Elections of 1963*. Honolulu: East–West Center Press.

Mishra, Vijay (ed.). 1979. *Rama's Banishment: A Centenary Tribute to the Fiji Indians 1879–1979*. Auckland and London: Heinemann Educational Books.

'Need to plug for all races says chief minister'. 1970. *Fiji Times*, 7 May: 3.

Norton, Robert. 1990. *Race and Politics in Fiji*, 2nd ed. Brisbane: University of Queensland Press.

———. 2002. 'Accommodating indigenous privilege: Britain's dilemma in decolonising Fiji'. *Journal of Pacific History*, 37(2): 133–56. DOI: 10.1080/0022334022000006574.

———. 2004. 'Seldom a transition with such aplomb: From confrontation to conciliation on Fiji's path to independence'. *Journal of Pacific History*, 39(2): 163–84. DOI: 10.1080/0022334042000250715.

———. 2015. 'Brij Lal's biography of A.D. Patel—A Vision for Change: AD Patel and the Politics of Fiji'. *Fijian Studies: A Journal of Contemporary Fiji*, 13(1): 17–30.

Patel's speech at a rally at a Hindu temple. 1967. *Jagriti* (Nadi), 28 September.

'Patience on common roll'. 1970. *Fiji Times*, 13 July: 3.

Scarr, Deryck. 2009. *Tuimacilai: A Life of Ratu Sir Kamisese Mara*. Adelaide: Crawford House Publishing.

Tetlock, Philip E. and Geoffrey A. Parker. 2006. 'Counterfactual thought experiments: Why we can't live without them & how we must learn to live with them'. In *Unmaking the West: 'What-if?' Scenarios that Rewrite World History*, edited by Philip Tetlock, Ned Lebow and Geoffrey A. Parker, pp. 14–44. Ann Arbor: University of Michigan Press.

Tetlock, Philip, Ned Lebow and Geoffrey A. Parker (eds). 2006. *Unmaking the West: 'What-if?' Scenarios that Rewrite World History*. Ann Arbor: University of Michigan Press.

'The situation with regard to the implementation of the Declaration on the granting of independence to Colonial Countries and Peoples: Fiji.' In *The Yearbook of the United Nations*, 1966: 578–81. Online: cdn.un.org/unyearbook/yun/chapter_pdf/1966YUN/1966_P1_SEC3_CH2.pdf (accessed 7 March 2017).

'The situation with regard to the implementation of the Declaration on the granting of independence to Colonial Countries and Peoples: Fiji.' In *The Yearbook of the United Nations*, 1967: 659–64. Online: cdn.un.org/unyearbook/yun/chapter_pdf/1967YUN/1967_P1_SEC3_CH2.pdf (accessed 7 March 2017).

Vasil, Raj. 1972. 'Communalism and constitution-making in Fiji'. *Pacific Affairs*, 45(1): 21–41. DOI: 10.2307/2755259.

8

Constituting Common Futures: Reflecting from Singapore about Decolonisation in Fiji

Martha Kaplan and John D. Kelly

In 1996, Brij Lal was one of the authors, in important ways the principal author, of a report on Fiji's constitutional needs. The report, Parliamentary Paper #34 of 1996, was titled *The Fiji Islands: Towards a United Future*. This report is widely remembered for its inclusion, a spirit of inclusion stretching from detailed review of sometimes contradictory global standards for constitutional ordering of indigenous rights, minority rights and other protections, to the measured inclusion of a wide range of voices seeking ways to reconstitute Fiji, including ways to mend fences but also ways to remove them. The report is correctly remembered as an intervention into Fiji's politics reminding all of the necessity of a commons, the exigency of finding legal means to reconcile ethnic Fijian interests with Indo-Fijian presence and vice versa. However, it should not be neglected that this report also decisively turned the measure and focus of Fiji's politics towards the future. Both of these dimensions of the report—the insistence on building a commons for Fiji and the emphasis on the future as measure of the political good—are of interest here. Neither of these goals was novel, but we sense that this report, addressing its circumstances, was a significant moment in Fiji's fraught political dialogues. By making a common future the necessary good for Fiji's politics, Brij Lal, in a quiet way, helped to accomplish what generations of Indo-Fijian political leaders have sought to do: establish incontrovertible and equitable terms of belonging for the Indo-Fijians of Fiji.

Reflecting on the second half of the twentieth century, that twilight period now in the domain of 'history', we reflect as well on visions of a common future, and the circumstances that necessitate them. Fiji has a troubled place in the roll of nation-states. We want to reconsider that, by setting it in a much more salutary place in a grimmer political history—the decolonisation of places where the nation-state model did not easily fit. Here we relocate Fiji's decolonisation, and the political and intellectual interventions of Brij Lal, in a history that does not take 'countries', 'nations' and 'nation-states' for granted, but locates the last of the 'new nations' in the decolonisation era otherwise, not merely in a history of nation-states. Where Benedict Anderson depicted late decolonisation as a 'last wave', latecomers adopting an established form, we see creative variation, under extreme pressure, in a more complex history of situations. In short, we want to reconsider the decolonisation of Fiji within the history of partitions, to notice all that it was not. Yes, Fiji was fractious, troubled, ethnically torn asunder, falling repeatedly to military takeovers. It has been overswept many times by that all-too-frequent alternative to the nation-state normal, in which not democracy but the political army connects nation and state. But Fiji's ethnic fences were never remade into walls, and its streets, in fact, never ran with blood. It is not an accident that Fiji's decolonisation came late. Nor was this late date a feature only of local conditions. Many in Fiji were certainly ambivalent about decolonising, and no few, especially among chiefs and their supporters, were as hostile toward it as many, especially among Indo-Fijians, were avid for decolonisation. Not only for this reason, Fiji was amongst the hardest cases for independence seekers and the waning British Empire to constitute. Fiji's actual constitutional ordering followed, and we think was subtly but decisively shaped by, everyone's experiences of the reversal of efforts elsewhere.

Thus this chapter looks at the ordering of Fiji, its people(s) and their common future that was embodied in its constitution at independence in 1970. It brings together our interest in South Asian diasporas, dynamic Fijian political histories, and the specific post–World War II historical conjuncture that formed the world of nation-states—interests we share with Brij Lal. But the chapter also reframes consideration of Fiji through comparison with experiences elsewhere, and specifically with Singapore

8. CONSTITUTING COMMON FUTURES

(independent in 1963 as part of Malaysia, and in 1965 on its own as Singapore). And it raises questions about partition. In so doing, it seeks new insights into the situation that multiple agents believed they faced in planning Fiji's constitution.

Partition is not usually raised when we think about Fiji. But the 1950s and 1960s were an era of partitions. These followed double touchstones from the 1940s. One was the quintessential partition of allegedly irreconcilable cultural difference—the religiously justified national partition of India into India and Pakistan. The other was the quintessential Cold War partition of Germany into East and West. In varying admixtures, the 1950s and 1960s saw partitions invoking either or both principles, usually both. Kashmir was pushed into impossibility, Korea and Vietnam into standoffs, civil war further split Pakistan and endemically fractured Burma. Against this backdrop, planners, both imperial and local, had to reckon with religion, ethnicity and geopolitical filiations, local and global factions often redoubling the lines of potential conflict, especially in yet-to-be decolonised Fiji and Malaysia. Both Cold War politics and ethnic asymmetry were keys to the Malaysian civil war, which the Empire addressed as a communist insurgency and suppressed with a successful counterinsurgency campaign (including Fijian military participation). Suspicion of ethnic Chinese political aspirations in favour of Malay 'sons of the soil' bumiputera thereafter had two motivations, inspired both by proindigenous sentiments and Cold War anxieties. In Fiji, similar elements were in play, especially as the Empire's old guard reacted to 'the Nehru era'. What then do we learn about Fiji in 1970 if we read it in the wake of Singapore in 1965? Not a simple story. Even where ethnic and religious divisions overlapped with geopolitical anxieties, the Empire used more than one tactic, especially as failures taught their lessons. To bring the Fiji 1970 constitution into new focus, this chapter will relocate Fiji in the history of deployed partition strategies. We will consider geographical partition and electoral partition as two opposites to common futures in late decolonisation.

Fiji's late decolonisation is sometimes attributed to colonial assumptions about perceived primitivity and unreadiness. But we wonder whether it was actually complexity that held it off: ethnic complexity, the politics of decolonisation and rule, the politics of Cold War. And as well, the longstanding parochialism of the British in Fiji itself. Long after Indian independence, they misunderstood Gandhians as communists. Long after the Bandung conference, they did not see how the world was moving.

We think that they tried, in Fiji's 1970 constitution, in (ironically) their five-year plans, and in their newly ensconced, 'apolitical' and enshrined civil service, to sustain as much of the imperial civility and estrangement in governance as possible. We think that they left it to Fiji itself to find a path to commons and future.

To honour Brij Lal

Let us emphasise from the outset that this argument is our own; if it is flawed that is on us and not something to blame Brij for inspiring. The term 'common future' we borrow, of course, from Brij Lal's work. It is not the title of the 1996 parliamentary report, which perhaps avoided the set-piece politics of a 'common roll', and spoke of moving Fiji toward a 'united future'. But the issues intrinsic to the common-roll voting debate are perhaps the most durable theme of Lal's decolonisation history. Or perhaps, equally, the importance of the commons and the importance of the future: his deliberately modernist works generally inspire us to contribute to reflections on modern Fijian history. In the last 20 years, Brij Lal has published on an epic scale a textured and reliable history of Fiji's complicated political vicissitudes, accomplishing something remarkable in the world of history writing, giving his country a reliable history of its independence era, a history leading right to its present moment. Rare is the historian willing and capable to so commit to people who can answer back. Equally rare, obviously, is the academic who can work so effectively within and in fact against political crisis. Brij Lal has had a remarkable career. We contribute here a comparative chapter seeking to illuminate parts of the long history he has captured by way of a particular comparison. We hope that it embodies Brij Lal's scholarly commitment to writing untold history and acting to constitute and make real political possibilities.

We first came to Fiji in 1982. We first 'met' Brij through reading his scholarship on indentured Indian migration to Fiji. As John began his ethnographic research on Indo-Fijian business and devotional life, and archival research on Fiji Indians in world anticolonial history, and Martha her ethnography of Drauniivi past and present, and her historical ethnography of British suppression of Fijian anticolonial movements, Brij Lal's *Broken Waves* came to provide the essential framework, the first real history of Fiji as a nation, and the first truly synthetic and actually modernist vision of its past, present and future. Our works thereafter—

Brij's as a socially astute historian and John's and Martha's as historical anthropologists—have intersected productively over the years.[1] We must have 'met' in the mid-1980s via letters (pre-internet!), finally actually in person at a conference we invited him to in 2000. Initially, Martha's work on anticolonial Fijian political-religious movements (Kaplan 1989, 1990, 1995) and more recently on the export of Fijian Water (2005, 2007) may have seemed separate from John's Indo-Fijian historical anthropology (Kelly 1988, 1991, 1992), but over the years we (Martha and John) came to commit ourselves to writing in ways that challenge colonially constituted, ethnically separate histories of Fiji (Kaplan and Kelly 1994, 1999; Kelly and Kaplan 2001; Kelly 1995, 2005, 2011: 235–49). As our historical writings moved from events in the 1920s and 1930s into the decolonisation era (papers that eventually became our book *Represented Communities* (2001)), we began to pursue simultaneously, the historical origins of the Fiji coups and the lessons from Fiji's history for a political anthropology of decolonisation and the nation-state. In all this work, we recurrently take inspiration from Brij's histories of Fiji as a whole. Brij Lal's histories of modern Fiji lay the foundation for all future histories of independent Fiji. And his political engagements, his humane political commitments and positive political contributions will prove never to have compromised his insightful histories. He is an inspiration for all scholars who aspire to relevance.

No communities without representation

In this chapter, as in *Represented Communities*, we analyse literal constitutions and other constituting moments to argue for an anthropology of nation and nationalism that takes seriously the manufacture of social charters as well as colonial realities and legacies. At the beginning of the twentieth century, imperial polities organised most of the world.

---

1   For instance, Brij and John shared an important commitment to using historical knowledge to illuminate the potential for common and humane relationships in Fiji: each published a translation of Totaram Sanadhya's 'Story of the haunted line', an inspiring story of Totaram's salvation from despair through his devotion *and* through moral and humane exchanges of food and care between indentured worker and Fijian villagers in the late indenture era. Happily, Brij's version in the *Journal of Pacific History* reaches a global scholarly audience focused on Indian diaspora as well as Pacific scholars and university students (Lal and Shineberg 1991). John's version, included in a volume along with his translation of Totaram's *My Twenty-One Years in the Fiji Islands* (co-translator Uttra Singh) was published by the Fiji Museum (despite a delay caused by the 1987 coup), and makes available in English this important original text on Fiji–Indian history to Fiji citizens, as well as to tourists and visitors (Sanadhya 1991).

Within these predatory, hierarchical polities, peoples (often referred to as 'nations') were assorted 'racially' by colonisers. In European empires, races were ranked as more or less civilised. Following World War II, this world of empires was replaced by a UN world, reconstituted as a field of individual, bounded nation-states. Explaining this rapid change, Anderson identified nations as imagined communities of people aligned in horizontal symmetry, and found nationalism to be the culture of 'modernity' (Anderson 1983). Anderson argued as well that the nation-states began in the Euro–American world and spread in a last wave to the rest. We think twentieth-century history was less evolutionary and more complicated. While victorious Americans, impoverished British imperials and others planned a global order of formally symmetric nation-states in the new world order of United Nations, across the decolonising globe, asymmetrically situated agents, including cosmopolitans and 'sons of the soil', socialists, liberals, communists, and communalists, ethnic champions and utopian planners, faced dilemmas grounded in local asymmetries in the planning of new nations.

While agreeing that nation-states are not given by race or place, we have argued that the historical conditions of the current order of nation-states are specific and specifiable. We see the history of the nation-state to be very recent, coming into being after World War II when, for example, India and England turned from being colony and coloniser, to nation-states. The UN world was formed as anticolonial struggles, Marxist, anarchist, *swaraj* and others, found their possible end points within the form engineered by postwar American power. An American plan for a world of independent, limited liability political entities, a world in which very Protestant self-determination would orient political futures and organise and delimit political wills, was put in place post–World War II. Imperial trade preferences weakened as Americans deliberately destroyed currency and investment barriers, and decolonisation rushed forward, colonisers squeezed between their own exhaustion and bankruptcy and their well-earned rejection by the people in almost every colony. The Americans gave this movement its trading-zone vocabulary for mutual recognition, locating 'new men' seeking 'self-determination' everywhere. And this postwar order proved robust enough to sustain, across the late decades of the twentieth century, the postwar commitment, also, to peace. The UN charter banned war between nations and states. How much of this Pax Americana followed from respect for the new system and how much from fear of atomic weaponry is not easy to judge, but in some combination the system weathered the 'Cold War' that its own unresolved ideologies engendered, and even kept that Cold War cold while decolonisation proceeded to its hard cases.

Sutured together in the nation-state and the decolonisation era are the idea of the bounded, territorial and independent state, and the sharp demarcation of its citizenry. In the twentieth century's new version of self-evident human rights, people are endowed with rights by their states. In this new order, people gain economic and social freedoms, civil and political rights, first of all within the nation-state that is their own. These rights and freedoms were not legally imagined as the imposition of any outside force. They could only rise with the yeast of self-determination, the new state coming into its own. But history provided state-makers of the 1950s and 1960s, both imperial and local, with problematic real situations: diasporic realities, religious rivalries and international security entanglements added complexity to colonial race hierarchies, resulting in a range of situations of self and other awaiting the new schemes for rights determination. In India, partition was mandated as a last colonial act, truly mandated, the British argued, by the given differences of religion and community, an implacable divide unsurmountable in peace. From flattened and guilty Germany came the paradigm of the partition made necessary by global political alignment, military occupation reread as the form for, and therefore of, local political will. In Fiji, more than 20 years later, we see a constitution that tried to turn colonial race categories into communities of self-determination. We hope that the motives behind that 1970 Fiji constitution can be clarified by a review of events in Singapore in between. Singapore was affected by both kinds of motives for partition. Both in the imperial decisions to create a Malaysia including Singapore in 1963, and the Malaysian decision to separate them in 1965, we shall see the operation of the two partition logics, communal and transnationally political.

It is possible to narrate Fiji's history as a story of local struggle over rules for communal representation and communal privilege, a politics of movements to sustain or repeal colonial colour lines, to outline Fiji against colonial shadows. We know this because we have done it. Fiji's 1930s restrictions on democracy, even while self-determination was sought in many places globally in the 'Wilsonian Moment' following the Versailles negotiations (Manela 2007), make sense as an effort of official Fiji to insist on racial difference and hierarchy in order to swim against the tide of oncoming self-determination, long before the outset of actual decolonisation in the

British Empire (Kelly and Kaplan 2001). There is much to be said for this measure of Fiji's recent difficulties in the entrenchments of its late colonial past. We wish to add, now, some further reflections on motives behind Fiji's 1970 constitution, remembering the intense and recent genealogy of partitions communally and/or geopolitically motivated. Taking our analysis beyond the effects of British animus for Fiji's Indians, of late imperial contrariness and loathing for Gandhi and his successful Congress, we want to reflect on the more particular partition strategies, electoral as well as geographical, that put Fiji in 1970, into its first postcolonial shape.

Constitutions at independence: Fiji and Singapore

As we will see, at independence in 1970 the governance of Fiji depended upon an elaborate machinery of group representation. The 1970 constitution reproduced the unequal political relations formed in the colonial era in favour of ethnic Fijians and chiefly power, and through 'communal rolls' it reinforced and further reified 'race' as a category in Fijian social and political life. Surprisingly—from a Fiji perspective—Singapore's 1965 constitution had a 'common roll'. But this commons came only after partition.

Fiji's constitution at independence in 1970

In 1970, Fiji's national government (at independence the Commonwealth Dominion of Fiji) followed the so-called Westminster model, with a governor-general (a Fijian chief) representing the queen, and a bicameral legislature of appointed Senators and elected members of the House of Representatives. Electorally, the majority party's (or coalition's) leader became the prime minister. Most of the seats in the House of Representatives were 'communal' with three voters' rolls: Fijians, Indians and General Electors. To be a voter in Fiji, people were required to register themselves as members of one of those rolls, in accordance with their 'race' ('General Electors' were European, part-European, Chinese, and primarily, other Islanders, in the local terminology).

8. CONSTITUTING COMMON FUTURES

Under the 1970 constitution, the House of Representatives had 52 members. Twenty-two members were Fijians, 12 elected by Fijians, and 10 elected by all of the voters (on the national roll) in particular districts. Twenty-two members were Indians, 12 similarly elected by Indians, and 10 by all of the voters in their districts. Eight were General Electors, three elected by General Electors and five by all the voters in the districts. Note that at the time the numbers were not proportionate. In 1980, Fijians who were 44 per cent of the population elected 42 per cent of the elected representatives. Indians who made up 50 per cent of the population also elected 42 per cent of the representatives, while General Electors at 6 per cent of the population had 15 per cent of seats (Lal 1986: 76). The over-representation of General Electors worked largely to ethnic Fijian advantage, since General Electors tended to form coalitions with the predominantly ethnic Fijian party. The second house, the Senate, had appointed members, eight named by the Fijian Great Council of Chiefs, seven named by the prime minister (head of the party in power), six named by the opposition party, and one representing people from the island of Rotuma. Thus, change in the majority party in the lower house would make literally one vote difference in the upper house, and could not provide a majority there without Great Council support. As Brij Lal has summarised:

> The logic of the electoral system adopted at independence was that the voters of Fiji would continue to vote on racial lines. A racially based electoral system engendered racial voting, inevitably at the expense of the greater national good. Fiji after independence was not a 'nation' of diverse peoples with common hopes and aspirations but a coalition of competing ethnicities with their own communal agendas. Elections came to be seen not as contests between political parties with competing ideologies, but as zero-sum racial contests. An election lost was thus seen as a loss for a 'race' (Lal 2008: 78).

Singapore's constitution at independence in 1965

In 1965 Singapore's constitution also followed the Westminster model, with the prime minister coming from the party with the most members of parliament elected. It was unicameral. Read in light of Fiji's constitution, the most surprising feature of the Singapore constitution of 1965 is that Singapore's system employed a 'common roll'. Voters in each district were identified by residence in the district, but neither candidates nor voters were organised by communal categories. This is despite the fact that

Singapore, like Fiji, had been a multiethnic British colony. Singapore did and does require people to identify themselves for national identity cards according to 'race' categories. And these categories do figure in key aspects of citizenship such as eligibility for Housing Development Board flats, which are ethnically balanced. But in 1965 they did not shape electoral representation.[2]

What can we learn from the difference between these two electoral systems that reveals the electoral partition so consequential for Fiji? The creation of Singapore in 1965 was part of the disassembling of the Federation of Malaysia, that is, part of a geographical partition. In this fashion Singapore gained 'common-roll' democracy in 1965, something Fiji is still working on. But Singapore's commons came into being via dramatic, violent events, and while its freedom enabled its modernism to accelerate, it also turned Singapore inward. In contrast, as we shall see, Fiji's electoral system, for decades, made appeal to common future suspicious, and instilled partition into every electoral act.

Independent Fiji 1970

In Fiji's constitution at independence, visions of a common future were predicated on balancing colonial 'race' categories. Unity was literally envisioned as tripartite; 1970 Independence images of a 'three-legged stool' envisioned national leadership by ethnic Fijian chiefly elites and ethnic Fijian commoner landowners, with Indo-Fijians as the economic backbone and the British crown as guarantor of the parliamentary system.

---

2 See Kevin Tan (2014) for a comprehensive discussion of Singapore's constitution. There have been changes in Singapore's constitution and representative system since 1965. For example, in 1984 nonconstituency MPs were introduced. Since 1988, some districts are represented by Group Representation Constituency (GRC) slates, which also serve as town administrative councils and require an ethnically mixed slate. In 1990, nominated members of Parliament were introduced (K. Tan 2014: 54–55). And from 2016 on, election of the president (a largely ceremonial gravitas head of state position) was reserved for members of a particular 'race' (defined threefold in the law as Chinese, Malay and Indian or other) in the event that no member of that race had been elected in the previous five elections. Deputy Prime Minister Teo Chee Hean represented the change as one promoting general citizenship: 'Every community should aspire to producing leaders that may one day represent the nation in the highest office' (*Channel NewsAsia* 2016; but see also Jaipragas 2016). In independent Singapore, unlike independent Fiji, 'race' categories have not defined or restricted voting rolls.

8. CONSTITUTING COMMON FUTURES

Arguments for 'common-roll' voting were rejected in favour of 'communal rolls'. Thus colonial contradictions pervaded the postcolonial possibilities creating a political climate in which multiple Fijian coups took place.[3]

Whether Fiji was to have a common-roll or communal-roll system had been much debated in the move toward independence. Yet, ultimately, proponents of a common roll acceded to communal rolls, in order to ensure independence itself. In 1946, European, Fijian and Indo-Fijian representatives sat on Fiji's Legislative Council, a board advisory to the governor. The majority of representatives were European, and were appointed by the governor. The colony's European residents also had three elected representatives. The Indo-Fijians elected three representatives, and three Fijian representatives were appointed (Norton 1977: 8).

At the so-called Deed of Cession debate in the Legislative Council in 1946, European members argued that the original deed of cession 'giving' Fiji to Queen Victoria and her heirs in 1874 provided that the British would preserve and protect Fijian interests. These arguments were clearly directed at quelling Indo-Fijian initiatives for greater legislative representation. Fiji Indian Legislative Council Member A.D. Patel pointed out the irony of colonial claims to protect Fijians against foreigners, and made powerful humanistic and political economic arguments against the colonial position. He said:

> It should be well understood and well appreciated that we came here to play our part in turning this country into a paradise. Indians came here and worked here for those people who gobbled up half a million acres of free-hold land from the Fijian owners. We came and worked, under a semi-servile state, and thank God, saved the Fijian race from the infamy of coming under the same system. As a matter of fact, if anything

---

3   While Fiji's earlier coups were explicitly ethnic Fijian nationalist projects, in the military coup of 2006 the regime shifted the narrative of power seizure. It was not explicitly Fijian ethnonationalist (although the military forces and leadership are still overwhelmingly ethnic Fijian). Instead, it was a military coup similar to other military coups across the globe, in which the goals of military rule supplant other political stances. The regime propounded an 'anti-corruption' message and imposed military rule, claiming provocation, as colonial governments did, by disorder and disaffection. Colonial tactics, notably censorship of the press, were in full force. The implications for self-determination, and for advocacy of forms of belonging by Fiji citizens as a whole, or Indo-Fijians in particular, are sobering. The military leadership of the 2006 coup has succeeded in assembling around themselves a political party, Fiji First, that has won the 2014 elections, held on the basis of a single national voting constituency. Whether this victory will open postracial democratic possibilities for Fiji it is much too early to say. On the one hand, the single national constituency plan has ended multiple disproportions and ethnic unfairnesses in prior districting systems. On the other hand, any civil government led by coup makers is obviously compromised in its ability to secure democratic rights and civil freedoms.

the coming of my people to this country gave the Fijians their honor, their prestige, nay indeed their very soul. Otherwise I have no hesitation in saying that the Fijians of this Colony would have met with the same fate that some other indigenous races in parts of Africa met with (Patel 1946: 48).

A.D. Patel envisioned a Fiji in which sacrifice and service made Indo-Fijians part of the common future. But in the colonial era, it had been assumed that different populations or 'communities' had different natures and roles to play in the colonial polity, and would each be represented separately in the governing bodies of the colony. At this key moment in world history, with the impetus to world decolonisation taking shape, Fiji's colonial Europeans and Fijians sought to enhance the colonial Fijian 'polity within the polity' and to secure special Fijian paramountcy. Patel's arguments on behalf of the Indian contribution to Fiji failed to reshape the colonial Fijian chiefly position (see also Lal 1997). Even more crucially, as Fiji moved slowly towards independence, a model of representation based on 'communal' rather than 'common' electoral rolls dominated Fiji's politics, with fundamental implications for the future of Fiji as a nation.

The colonial British had ruled Fiji through a paternalist system of indirect rule based on their chiefly system, and preserved Fijian land ownership, such that ethnic Fijian kin groups currently own 83 per cent of the nation's land, inalienably. Indeed, the aristocratic British colonial rulers of Fiji formed a bureaucratic alliance with Fijian high chiefs. At independence in 1970, Fijian chiefs were Fiji's highest national leaders, and Fiji's first, and succeeding, constitutions have all been written to ensure various degrees of ethnic Fijian political paramountcy and landholding rights. Ethnic Fijians have predominated in civil service and in Fiji's military, but many still gain their livelihood partly from subsistence economic activities on communally owned land. In contrast, the Indo-Fijians came to colonial Fiji as indentured labourers, in the era of colonial capitalist plantations. Exploited in Fiji's sugar plantation system, they served as the economic backbone of the colony and nation. They also resisted European domination in Fiji, and joining with the nationalists in India, sought political and economic parity with colonial whites, and a path to self-determination. Farming on leased land, and entering diverse fields of professional and wage work, Indo-Fijians have predominated in many areas of business and wage labour, while ethnic Fijians predominated in government.

Throughout the twentieth century, many Indo-Fijians led Fiji toward independence. The majority of Indian indentured sugar plantation workers and their descendants shared—and contributed to—Gandhian initiatives to end British imperial dominance in India and to establish independence throughout Empire. Anticolonial political-religious initiatives by ethnic Fijians arose mainly in hill and hinterland areas, were of limited scope, and were suppressed by coalitions of British colonial officials and ethnic Fijian chiefs—many of whom held office in the system of indirect rule (Kaplan 1995; Macnaught 1982). World War II saw the end of the British imperial era, and the beginning of the UN era of nation-states. In Fiji, the war brought into sharp focus the differing colonial pasts and different visions of the future of ethnic Fijians and Indo-Fijians. Most ethnic Fijians envisioned a postwar world run along similar lines to the imperial politics of colonial Fiji. The majority of Indo-Fijians, like the Indian nationalists, were more attuned to impending decolonisation. Ethnic Fijians fought eagerly on behalf of the British during the war. Most Indo-Fijians followed Gandhi in refusing to fight for an imperial system that classed them as inferior. Colonial governors censored truthful news accounts about Congress's successes and India's inevitable independence. Faced with the Indo-Fijian challenge, British political rhetoric in Fiji forged an ever-stronger alliance with ethnic Fijians, drawing upon ethnic Fijian fears of Indo-Fijian population growth, and denigrated Indian and Indo-Fijian anticolonial resistance.

Cold War politics conflated colonial self–other relations with India and overseas Indians. Early twentieth-century colonial allegations of potential 'Bolshevism' embraced hinterland ethnic Fijians, especially their political-religious leaders and Jehovah's Witness converts as well as anticolonial Indo-Fijians and emerging unions of maritime workers (largely ethnic Fijian) and of cane growers (largely Indo-Fijians).

In 1970, Fiji had two major political parties that gave voice to the aspirations of Fiji's peoples for the nation-state. Because of constitutional requirements, each party had mixed 'racial' membership and fielded candidates of all three electoral categories ('Fijian', 'Indian', and 'General Elector'). Each, at times, espoused more or less pluralistic ideals. However, they swiftly became parties representing different ethnic groups. The largely Indo-Fijian National Federation Party (NFP) was founded in 1964 by leaders of cane growers' unions and other unions with a history of contestation against colonial policies. The largely ethnic Fijian Alliance

Party held power from 1970 to 1986, when the new, line-crossing Fiji Labour Party won the elections in alliance with the NFP, an electoral victory answered in 1987 by Fiji's first coups.

The legacy of these colonial divisions was played out in independent Fiji. Repeatedly in independent Fiji, ostensible pluralism in policy coexisted with colonial continuations of ethnic Fijian paramountcy. The ceremonies of independence in 1970 dramatised these ambivalences. On the one hand, for the first time in Fiji's history, Indo-Fijians and other peoples had a major role in public ceremonies. The celebrations were intended to represent Fiji as a 'three-legged stool'. Language policy gave equal status to English, Fijian and Fiji Hindi. But in fact, the independence ceremonies themselves, presided over by Prince Charles, gave special weight to royalty in political life, speaking to Fiji's 'chiefs and peoples', underlining the ongoing position of Fijian chiefs, a kind of authority, leadership and appeal to tradition not open to Indo-Fijians, who had no 'chiefs' (Kelly and Kaplan 2001: 131–32). The ambivalences toward pluralism seen in the independence ceremonies of 1970 were to harden into asymmetric and polarised political parties. Before the 1986 election, the chiefly led Alliance Party could represent itself as favoured by all communities or races except Indian (and even supported by many Muslim Indians, especially in the earlier elections). But after the new Labour Party and its coalition government proved there could be an alternative possible alliance to lead Fiji—one that did not include the chiefs—ethnic Fijian chauvinists in the military declared that the entire constitutional arrangement was flawed for not guaranteeing ethnic Fijian paramountcy.

Independence for Malaysia and Singapore 1963–65

Startling, from the perspective of Fiji's independence constitution, is Singapore's 1965 common-roll electoral system. But it is not startling at all when we look back to 1963. Singapore's initial independence was as part of the Federation of Malaysia. That Federation partitioned itself less than two years later, over visions of what should constitute a common, self-determining future. Viewing Fiji in the light of this history will demonstrate how several key elements of Fiji's first decades of independence may have been new to Fiji, but were not new in the history of decolonisation.

In 1963, an agreement for the establishment of the Federation of Malaysia was signed by Britain, Malaya, North Borneo and Singapore. What future, 'common' or not, was envisioned via the Federation? Planners attempted to align multiple imperatives: the first imperative seemed to be federation itself. In Singapore, most anticolonial proponents of independence had come to envision it as requiring linkage with Malaysia. In 1963, inclusion in the Federation was central to Lee Kuan Yew and the People's Action Party (PAP), and useful to the British and to Malayan leadership as well. Planners both local and international assumed that the size of the Federation was vital for economic development. Cold War concerns drove the formation of Malaysia, from local politics to the decisions of an increasingly weary Britain, and the increasingly involved US. But visions of the commons began with, and ended with, a contradiction. For Malaysian leaders, the political primacy of Malays was critical. For Lee Kuan Yew and majority Chinese Singapore, the goal was a 'Malaysian Malaysia' (see Lau 1998, especially 246ff). Ultimately, no common future was instituted and Singapore became independent in 1965 (Lau 1998; see also Hack, Margolin with Delaye 2010; Lee 2008; Shiraishi 2009; T. Tan 2008; Trocki 2006; Wang 2005).

In a late colonial history similar to Fiji's, the British had created special political ties with Malay leaders and peoples in colonial Malaya and viewed Chinese and Indian minorities on the mainland as anticolonial and potentially communist. There was particular concern that the overseas Chinese, on the mainland and in Singapore, might be linked to communist China. Suspicion of Chinese political aspirations predated the communist civil war in the 1950s. As early as 1946, Malay political leaders argued to the British that Singapore could not be included in an independent Malaysia because its large Chinese population would make Malays a minority in the country as a whole. After the counterinsurgency suppression, this acutely and widely felt suspicion led to the incorporation of the Borneo territories of Sarawak and Sabah into the Federation of Malaysia. Thus, by 1963 colonial Malay ties and history had developed into a vision for an independent, Malay-majority, Malay-centred Malaysia. Malaysian politics and policy coalesced in the party politics of the Alliance coalition (the United Malays National Organization (UMNO), Malayan Chinese Association (MCA), and the Malayan Indian Congress (MIC)). As Albert Lau has observed:

> The success of the Alliance formula … established the pattern of communally-based politics in Malaya for many years to come. Second, the years of fighting a determined communist-armed insurrection had given rise to an Alliance government that was staunchly anti-communist, autocratic and right wing (1998: 5–6).[4]

From the Fiji perspective, with an eye on the crafting of a common future, several aspects of the 1963 Federation stand out, especially representation in Parliament and the nature of citizenship within the new Federation. Lau went on to say:

> When the full terms for merger, with the exception of the financial arrangements, were made public on 15 November 1961, following the joint meetings of Malayan and Singapore officials, what was revealed was that, in return for autonomy in education and labour, Singapore agreed to a more limited number of seats than its population warranted, 15 instead of possibly 24 on a proportionate basis … The provision for special Singapore citizenship … also reflected Kuala Lumpur's desire to insulate the Federation politically from Singapore. In order that some 624,000 Singapore citizens, who were born outside of Singapore, would not be disenfranchised under the Federation's more stringent citizenship requirements for non-Malays, it was proposed that all Singapore citizens would continue to retain their Singapore citizenship while automatically becoming 'nationals' of the larger Federation. But Singapore citizens could run as candidates for a legislative seat and vote only in Singapore. Federal citizens, in turn, could run for a legislative seat or vote only in Malaya. In short these provisions were designed to reduce the danger of Singapore's Chinese threatening the political dominance of the Malay-dominated Alliance in Malaya. At the same time, the 'special position' of Singapore's Malay community was also safeguarded in the constitutional proposals, although Kuala Lumpur accepted that the 'special privileges' accorded to their kith and kin in Malaya would not apply in Singapore (Lau 1998: 14–15).

The federal government had authority over defence, external affairs and security (Lau 1998: 14). The Federation was to be a common market, and Singapore agreed to give 40 per cent of total revenue collected to the central government. Singapore provided a loan of SG$150 million

---

4   This Malaysian 'Alliance' coalition may have been an inspiration for naming Fiji's Alliance Party, headed by Ratu Mara, the party in power in Fiji from independence in 1970 until 1986. Similarly, Lee Kuan Yew spoke of the stability of a three-legged stool (and later of the power of a single-pronged seat, a 'shooting-stick') in 1965 speeches before and after separation (Kwa 2002: 108–32).

for development of the Borneo states (Lau 1998: 15–16). Like Fiji, this postcolonial new nation-state began with a tension over kinds of citizens, and the kinds were assorted along lines formed in colonial relations.

Initially, the Malaysian leadership and the Singapore leadership found common cause. But a series of differences built swiftly.[5] Of particular representational and electoral concern was whether Singapore's PAP and Malaysia's UMNO would contest elections throughout the Federation. In 1963, in a 'snap election' the PAP gained parliamentary strength. The PAP won over their leftist opposition (weakened in part by Operation Cold Store, in which leftist leaders were detained, jailed and deported) and also over UMNO-supported candidates (Lau 1998: 21–64; Lee 2008: 220–23; Trocki 2006: 24). The April 1964 elections were an important turning point. After the UMNO, the MCA and the MIC had established branches in Singapore, the PAP moved to participate 'as a Pan-Malaysian Party on a Pan Malaysian basis' (S. Rajaratnam quoted in Lau 1998: 99). This vision of the right of the PAP and of Singapore to participate electorally more broadly in Malaysia brought the party into conflict with the UMNO vision of Malay political preeminence. In the mainland election, the Alliance (UMNO, MCA and MIC) candidates won sweepingly. While there are intricate historical analyses of the electoral results (e.g. Lau 1998: 118–24; T. Tan 2008), the result was that the PAP abruptly had become an opposition party. The rapprochement between the two political parties (the PAP in Singapore and the Malaysian Alliance) was at an end, and soon after, so was the Federation.

By 1965, the Federation was at an end. Singapore's position within the Federation was increasingly couched as a conflict. The conflict was between a vision of a Malayan Malaysia, or a Malaysian Malaysia. Lee Kuan Yew and his PAP insisted, on behalf of Singapore, that it must be the latter. Political boundaries were hardened, charged speeches and newspaper accounts proliferated (Lau 1998, 2009). Some of the conflicts were federal versus regional, for example debates over national

---

5   The history of postcolonial Singapore's brief federation with and then separation from Malaysia has been largely chronicled with focus on Singapore and Malaysian party politics, regional relations and British, US and UN contexts (e.g. Hack, Margolin with Delaye 2010; Lau 1998; Shiraishi 2009; T. Tan 2008; Trocki 2006). The most powerful personifications of visions of Singapore's future are found in accounts focusing on Prime Minister Lee Kuan Yew, and on the PAP. It is beyond the scope of this paper to trace popular and subaltern future hopes. The partition itself was negotiated and announced to a stunned citizenry. This raises questions about the nature of self-determination that go beyond the space here.

development plans, and whether federal decision on the budget excluded Singapore representation while using Singapore revenue (Lau 1998: 214). But most powerful were the issues of rights of peoples, as communities, within the new polity. Lee Kuan Yew and the PAP were accused by UMNO leaders of discriminating against Malays in Singapore. The Singapore leaders challenged racially charged rhetoric and everything that precipitated violence (Lau 1998: 186ff; Turnbull 2009: 299–300). There were riots between Malays and Chinese in Singapore (Lau 1998: 161–210; Trocki 2006: 124–26). 'Before the riots, the PAP had assumed that it could work with UMNO. After the riots, the PAP knew it could not' (Lau 1998: 289). Singapore and Malaysia separated on 9 August 1965.

Conclusion: Fiji's common future

Brij Lal named his 2008 book on Fiji's decolonisation *A Time Bomb Lies Buried*, remembering the last memorandum written by Fiji's last British governor. The departing governor acknowledged that the British had failed to resolve the common roll–communal roll debates, and that 'One is therefore bound to regret that in effect a time bomb will lie buried in the new Constitution, and to pray that it may be defused before exploding' (Lal 2008: 79). No doubt the British had many touchstones for fears that an explosion could come. Malaysian history itself gave British colonials nightmares of communalist riots and a red menace lurking in diasporic politics. We think in Fiji they feared the latter much more. Strangely, Fiji's last governor, Robert Foster, was almost entirely ignorant of the Gandhian foundations of A.D. Patel's NFP non-violent non-cooperation; Foster attributed the peacefulness of Fiji's oppositional politics to Fiji's 'isolated position in the middle of the enormous Pacific … shielded to a very great extent from the influence of external ideologies and events' (quoted in Lal 2008: 99–100). Regardless of the British misapprehensions, when Fiji had its explosions, they were top-down and from the indigenous Right, and were conspicuously bloodless. And it was A.D. Patel who saw it coming. Debating, in Fiji's Legislative Council, the 1965 London conference that committed Fiji to communal roll on its path to independence, Patel protested (just four months after the separation of Malaysia and Singapore) that with communal-roll voting:

people get used to the idea of a racial separation, racial attitudes harden and people start thinking in racial terms and racial interests which leads not to one nation but, in the course of political development, it leads to claims for several nations (Patel 2011: 73; cited in Lal 1997: 183).

Patel responded to objections that India itself had had communal issues. 'I have been questioned about India and Pakistan. That division itself is a warning to us' (Patel 2011: 72). Patel feared partitions as much as Fiji's rulers feared Indian political assertion, and with misplaced anxiety the British sought to keep peace in Fiji by asymmetric electoral partition.

We do not write an historical anthropology of constitutions at independence in order to project the nation back into either place, quite the contrary (see Duara 1995).[6] We do not argue that either Fiji or Singapore was destined to have a common future, or that *not* having one is 'failure'. Neither do we argue that nation-states are morally inevitable or politically preferable forms. Instead, in this chapter we have focused on a moment in which global forces made nation-state forms inevitable, and actual nation-states came into being through powers and agencies local more than global. We hope it helps to reveal the many kinds of partition that have limited the development of political possibility.

The decolonisations of the 1950s and 1960s were thick with contradictory emotions, from anger and anxiety to vindication and hope. In large and small ways, actual agency of new and particular sorts developed in the new nation-states. Lee Kuan Yew called it 'the age of Nehru', praising his optimism and commitment to the future. But Lee also felt that

---

[6] A note on historiography, for Fiji and Singapore. We do not claim that the juxtaposition is novel, and apologise for not gathering a proper set of scholarship that takes up Fiji–Singapore comparison. Further, for both Fiji and Singapore there are histories of many periods and moments in which futures were envisioned differently and in which it could have been otherwise. Fiji's history is still too often told as an encounter of Europeans and indigenes, though Brij Lal's work has made it much better understood as a three-way encounter. Mobile histories of the islands remind us that Fiji and Tonga were not always distinct entities (Hau'ofa 1994). Labour historians remind us that the Indian labour diaspora followed on 'blackbirding' of Pacific peoples (Munro 1990: xxxix–li; Moynagh 1981). Mobile histories of the seas remind us that ships' crews, never entirely 'European' but gathered from ports across the globe, including India, intersected with Pacific peoples from the 1700s on (Clunie 1984). The self (and selves) of self-determination for Fiji could have been construed otherwise at many historical moments. But the colonial experience fixed prospects in Fiji, such that any understanding of Fiji's politics entailed both the rights of postcolonial indigenes, and the rights of labour-diasporic peoples. A range of histories of Singapore emphasise an emptied island made social by the British, or an entrepôt for commerce, or a Nanyang, i.e. Chinese diaspora, a site of colonial-era Indian diaspora (Rai 2014) or a regional centre of Malay power, or mobility and systemic connection whether ancient or current (Hack, Margolin with Delaye 2010). For discussion of Malaysian perspectives on Malaysia and its partition see Shamsul 1986; Shiraishi 2009; and T. Tan 2008.

Nehru's confidence in the future of cooperation between new nations was misguided. His own experience led him to insist on 'the unpleasant facts of life' (Rodringuez 2003: 68, 78). Singapore's successes followed from his single-minded commitment to its development.

Lee Kuan Yew in 1963 and the NFP (after A.D. Patel's death in 1969) were ready to accept serious limitations on the democratic position and powers of their people—Singaporean and Indo-Fijian respectively—in order to bring potentially workable democratic nation-states into being. In a different way each was nonetheless thwarted by sons-of-the-soil chauvinists who in Fiji refused to stick to rules that had been set, and in Malaysia simply recognised and rejected real difference. In both cases, the clear felicities and virtues of sensitivity to the special needs of indigenes became the licence for scepticism of democracy and civil and political rights, with tragic consequences.

Singapore was forced to go it alone. The Indo-Fijians have faced more painful and diffuse political dilemmas, in one strange situation after another. But now Fiji again has a chance to come together, to find a common future not just as a settler metropole but as a society of indigenes and diaspora. While Singapore has lost its larger federation, Fiji has repeatedly lost democracy, and paid a further price, in generations of out-migration of many of its most talented people from every group, especially the Indians. But it again moves toward a common future, a direction well set.

References

Anderson, Benedict. 1983. *Imagined Communities: Reflections on the Origin and Spread of Nationalism.* London: Verso (revised ed. 1991).

ChannelNewsAsia. 2016. 'Elected presidency: Amendments to constitution passed in parliament', 9 November. Online: channelnewsasia.com/news/singapore/elected-presidency-amendments-to-constitution-passed-in/3271856.html (accessed 23 November 2016).

Clunie, Fergus. 1984. 'Fiji's first Indian settlers'. *Domodomo,* 2(1): 2–10.

da Cunha, Derek (ed.). 2002. *Singapore in the New Millennium: Challenges Facing the City State.* Singapore: Institute of Southeast Asian Studies Publishing.

Duara, Prasenjit. 1995. *Rescuing History from the Nation: Questioning Narratives of Modern China*. Chicago: University of Chicago Press.

Hack, Karl and Jean-Louis Margolin with Karine Delaye (eds). 2010. *Singapore from Temasek to the 21st Century: Reinventing the Global City*. Singapore: National University of Singapore Press.

Hauʻofa, Epeli. 1994. 'Our sea of islands'. *Contemporary Pacific*, 6(1): 147–61.

Hermann, Elfriede (ed.). 2011. *Changing Contexts, Shifting Meanings: Transformations of Cultural Traditions in Oceania*. Honolulu: University of Hawaiʻi Press in association with the Honolulu Academy of Arts.

Jaipragas, Bhavan. 2016. 'What's behind Singapore's move to boost presidential chances of ethnic minorities?' *South China Morning Post*, 25 September. Online: scmp.com/week-asia/politics/article/2022077/whats-behind-singapores-move-boost-presidential-chances-ethnic (accessed 23 November 2016).

Kaplan, Martha. 1989. 'Luveniwai as the British saw it: Constructions of custom and disorder in colonial Fiji'. *Ethnohistory*, 36(4): 349–71.

——.1990. 'Meaning, agency and colonial history: Navosavakadua and the tuka movement in Fiji'. *American Ethnologist*, 17(1): 3–22.

——. 1995. *Neither Cargo nor Cult: Ritual Politics and the Colonial Imagination in Fiji*. Durham, NC: Duke University Press.

——. 2005. 'Outside gods and foreign powers: Making local history with global means in the Pacific'. In *Outside Gods: History Making in the Pacific*. Special issue of *Ethnohistory*, 52(1): 7–11. DOI: 10.1215/00141801-52-1-7.

——. 2007. 'Fijian water in Fiji and New York: Local politics and a global commodity'. *Cultural Anthropology*, 22(4): 685–706. DOI: 10.1525/can.2007.22.4.685.

Kaplan, Martha, and John D. Kelly. 1994. 'Rethinking resistance: Dialogics of "disaffection" in colonial Fiji'. *American Ethnologist*, 21(1): 123–51. DOI: 10.1525/ae.1994.21.1.02a00070.

——. 1999.'On discourse and power: 'Cults' and 'orientals' in Fiji'. *American Ethnologist*, 26(4): 843–63. DOI: 10.1525/ae.1999.26.4.843.

Kelly, John D. 1988. 'From Holi to Diwali in Fiji: An essay on ritual and history'. *Man* (n.s.), 23(1): 40–55. DOI: 10.2307/2803032.

———. 1991. *A Politics of Virtue: Hinduism, Sexuality, and Countercolonial Discourse in Fiji*. Chicago: University of Chicago Press.

———. 1992. 'Fiji Indians and "commoditization of labor"'. *American Ethnologist*, 19(1): 97–120. DOI: 10.1525/ae.1992.19.1.02a00060.

———. 1995. 'Threats to difference in colonial Fiji'. *Cultural Anthropology*, 10(1): 64–84. DOI: 10.1525/can.1995.10.1.02a00030.

———. 2005. 'Boycotts and coups, shanti and mana in Fiji'. *Ethnohistory*, 52(1): 13–28. DOI: 10.1215/00141801-52-1-13.

———. 2011. 'Shanti and mana: The loss and recovery of culture under postcolonial conditions in Fiji'. In *Changing Contexts, Shifting Meanings: Transformations of Cultural Traditions in Oceania*, edited by Elfriede Hermann, pp. 235–49. Honolulu: University of Hawai'i Press in association with the Honolulu Academy of Arts.

Kelly, John D. and Martha Kaplan. 2001. *Represented Communities: Fiji and World Decolonization*. Chicago: University of Chicago Press.

Kwa Chong Guan. 2002. 'Relating to the world: Images, metaphors, and analogies'. In *Singapore in the New Millennium: Challenges Facing the City State*, edited by Derek da Cunha, pp. 108–32. Singapore: Institute of Southeast Asian Studies Publishing.

Lal, Brij V. 1992. *Broken Waves: A History of the Fiji Islands in the Twentieth Century*. Honolulu: University of Hawai'i Press.

———. 1997. *A Vision for Change: AD Patel and the Politics of Fiji*. Canberra: National Centre for Development Studies, The Australian National University.

———. 2008. *A Time Bomb Lies Buried: Fiji's Road to Independence, 1960–1970*. Canberra: ANU E Press. Online: press.anu.edu.au?p=22441 (accessed 22 December 2016).

———. 2010. *In the Eye of the Storm: Jai Ram Reddy and the Politics of Postcolonial Fiji*. Canberra: ANU E Press. Online: press.anu.edu.au?p=25161 (accessed 22 December 2016).

———. 2011. *A Vision for Change: Speeches and Writings of AD Patel, 1929–1969*. Canberra: ANU E Press. Online: press.anu.edu.au?p=151821 (accessed 22 December 2016).

Lal, Brij V. (ed.). 1986. *Politics in Fiji: Studies in Contemporary History*. Sydney: Allen & Unwin.

Lal, Brij V. and Barry Shineberg. 1991. 'The story of the haunted line: Totaram Sanadhya's Fiji'. *Journal of Pacific History*, 26(1): 107–12. DOI: 10.1080/00223349108572653.

Lau, Albert. 1998. *A Moment of Anguish: Singapore in Malaysia and the Politics of Disengagement*. Singapore: Times Academic Press.

———. 2009. 'The politics of becoming "Malaysian" and "Singaporean"'. In *Across the Causeway: A Multi-dimensional Study of Malaysia-Singapore Relations*, edited by Takashi Shiraishi, pp. 92–124. Singapore: Institute of Southeast Asian Studies Publishing.

Lee, Edwin. 2008. *Singapore: The Unexpected Nation*. Singapore: Institute of Southeast Asian Studies Publishing.

Macnaught, Timothy J. 1982. *The Fijian Colonial Experience: A Study of the Neotraditional order under British Colonial Rule prior to World War II*. Canberra: The Australian National University.

Manela, Erez. 2007. *The Wilsonian Moment: Self-determination and the International Origins of Anticolonial Nationalism*. Oxford and New York: Oxford University Press.

Moore, Clive, Jacqueline Leckie and Doug Munro (eds).1990. *Labour in the South Pacific*. Townsville: James Cook University.

Moynagh, Michael. 1981. *Brown or White? A History of the Fiji Sugar Industry, 1873–1973*. Canberra: The Australian National University.

Munro, Doug. 1990. 'The origins of labourers in the South Pacific: Commentary and statistics'. In *Labour in the South Pacific*, edited by Clive Moore, Jacqueline Leckie and Doug Munro, pp. xxxix–li. Townsville: James Cook University.

Norton, Robert. 1977. *Race and Politics in Fiji*. New York: St Martin's Press.

Patel, A.D. 1946. *Speech in Legislative Council of Fiji, Extract from Debates of July Session 1946*. Suva: Government Press.

———. 2011. 'Debate on London constitutional conference, 15 December 1965'. In *A Vision for Change: Speeches and Writings of AD Patel, 1929–1969*, edited by Brij V. Lal, pp. 67–78. Canberra: ANU E Press.

Rai, Rajesh. 2014. *Indians in Singapore 1819–1945: Diaspora in the Colonial Port City*. New Dehli: Oxford University Press.

Reeves, Paul, Tomasi Vakatota and Brij V. Lal. 1996. T*he Fiji Islands: Towards a United Future: Report of the Fiji Constitution Review Commission*. Suva: Parliamentary Paper no. 36.

Rodringuez, S.J. 2003. *Lee Kuan Yew In His Own Words, vol. 1: 1959–1970*. Singapore: Hurricane Books.

Sanadhya, Totaram. 1991. *My Twenty-one Years in the Fiji Islands*, trans. from Hindi by John D. Kelly and Uttra Singh. Suva: Fiji Museum.

Shamsul, A.B. 1986. *From British To Bumiputera Rule: Local Politics and Rural Development in Peninsular Malaysia*. Singapore: Institute of Southeast Asian Studies Publishing.

Shiraishi, Takashi (ed.). 2009. *Across the Causeway: A Multi-dimensional Study of Malaysia-Singapore Relations*. Singapore: Institute of Southeast Asian Studies Publishing.

Tan, Kevin Y.L. 2014. *An Introduction to Singapore's Constitution*. Singapore: Talisman Publishing.

Tan Tai Yong. 2008. *Creating 'Greater Malaysia': Decolonization and the Politics of Merger*. Singapore: Institute of Southeast Asian Studies Publishing.

Trocki, Carl A. 2006. *Singapore: Wealth, Power and the Culture of Control*. London and New York: Routledge.

Turnbull, Constance M. 2009. *A History of Modern Singapore, 1819–2005*. Singapore: National University of Singapore Press.

Wang Gungwu (ed.). 2005. *Nation-Building: Five Southeast Asian Histories*. Singapore: Institute of Southeast Asian Studies Publishing.

9

Ethnicity, Politics and Constitutions in Fiji[1]

Yash Pal Ghai

It is clear that Fiji's constitutions hitherto have not enabled us to adequately deal with our problems. It is therefore necessary to adopt new approaches to constitution making, and imaginative and creative thinking on the design of our national institutions … We must think of new ways to regulate relations among our citizens and the state.

Brij V. Lal (1998: 117).

For an historian, Brij Lal has displayed a keen interest in contemporary constitutions and constitution-making, reflecting his concern with and involvement in politics. Constitutions and politics are inseparable in the

---

1   I have drawn on a number of my publications in the writing of this chapter, particularly Ghai 1988a, 1988b, 1988c, 1988d and 1989; Ghai and Cottrell 2007: 159–92; Ghai and Cottrell 2008; Cottrell and Ghai 2010.

I have also participated in discussions and negotiations on constitution-making in Fiji. In 1988, I was an adviser to the coalition government led by Dr Timoci Bavadra after its overthrow (having rejected a similar position in the caretaker government headed by Ratu Mara), especially on the Deuba Accord, and I was an adviser on its submission to the Constitution Inquiry and Advisory Committee; in 1996 I was principal adviser to the National Federation Party and the Fiji Labour Party in their submission to the Reeves Commission; in 2008 I was adviser to the UN Secretary General on the UN's engagement in the reconciliation process in Fiji; and in 2012 I chaired the Fiji Constitution Commission. Its draft constitution was banned and rejected by the prime minister and the attorney-general, without giving the public a chance to comment on it and a constituent assembly to debate it.

In most of my work and writings about Fiji, I have received much assistance from Jill Cottrell. I am grateful to her and Coel Kirkby for helpful and insightful comments on an earlier draft of this chapter.

South Pacific, particularly in Fiji. The constitution has seldom been far from Fiji's social, economic and political life. Constitutions in colonial and postcolonial states play roles different, in some respects, from those in more 'mature states'—certainly more ambitious, often simultaneously promoting and nurturing nationhood and the state. It is hard to understand the significance of constitutions in Fiji without immersing oneself in Lal's writings. I take the twin themes of this chapter from those in the quotation above: new approaches to constitution-making and new ways to regulate relations among citizens and the state. I also say something about relations between citizens and communities as well as the values and principles embedded in the constitution.

The several Fiji constitutions have been formulated through a variety of methods, in different contexts, with changing casts of individuals, community and the key decision-making bodies. There have been differences in contexts: pre-independence to post-coups, changing economy and notions of democracy, internal and external migration and variations in demography, literacy, education and skills, and so on. Decision makers on the constitution, and the degree of participation, has varied from a small, privileged group to the engagement of villagers in the remotest parts of the country. Processes have varied from the highly parochial to the global—with external influence and involvement and the incorporation of international norms. The method of adoption of the constitution has ranged from the relatively democratic to the most authoritarian, decreed and managed by the executive head of the government.

On relations between state and citizens, the experience of Fiji provides a number of valuable insights into the dynamics of politics and appropriate ways of structuring the state in multiethnic societies. Its multiethnic origins lie in colonialism, which not only has been globally the greatest creator of multiethnic political entities, but has also fashioned policies and institutions for the communities of such entities, yet is paid too little attention in contemporary studies of multiethnic states. The constitutional framework for the rights of citizenship and the organisation of state and power in Fiji since independence has been more critical than economic or social factors because of ethnic fragmentation and the dominance of the public sphere. There have been sharp divisions of opinion throughout its modern history between those advocating an integrated, non-racial state, based on individual rights (including equality), and those in favour of a political order based on ethnic communities. For a long time, citizenship in Fiji was subordinated to ethnicity.

Integration and consociation are perhaps not apt terms to categorise the division, but certainly there are echoes of this antithesis.[2] Many features associated with consociation have been present in the colonial and the postcolonial constitutions (such as separate communal representation, group rights, asymmetrical autonomy, power-sharing, separate educational systems, and entrenchment of rights to culture and land). Indigenous peoples' rights have been invoked, adding an extra twist to the integration–consociation polarity. But there have also been strong pulls towards political integration and broad-based, non-ethnic social justice policies. Fiji's experience shows that this polarity has limited intellectual or policy value. Consociation easily (and in Fiji's case seamlessly) slides into hegemony.

Independence constitution

Making of the constitution

Since independence, Fiji has had four constitutions, the first in 1970 and the latest in 2013. Constitutions terminating colonial rule are a sort of *rite de passage* to formal statehood for the territory and membership of the international community, becoming the focus of considerable attention and energy, determining the future form of state and politics. The colonial power becomes both the mediator between competing local communities and a partisan party—the latter especially if the colonial power has interests it wants to protect.

In Africa the impetus for independence came from local leaders, but in the South Pacific local leaders were generally not keen on independence, unsure perhaps of their ability to govern a new state and cope with the diversity of ethnic groups. Fiji was unusual in that the immigrant community of Indo-Fijians, by then outnumbering the indigenous Fijians, partly inspired by the struggle in India, supported independence, while the indigenous community opposed it, comfortable with British rule in which they enjoyed a superior status, with protection of their land rights and traditional institutions. But British appetite for further colonial

---

2   There is now considerable literature on consociation, by its supporters and opponents. A recent edited book that surveys the pros and cons of consociation is Choudhry (2008). The classical literature on the subject suggests that consociation is a modern western invention, but in reality consociation existed in empires in Asia and the Ottoman Empire for centuries.

rule had subsided, and the leaders of the indigenous community came under some pressure to accept independence. With the encouragement of Britain, discussions on independence began in the late 1960s between political parties, dominated by those of Indians and indigenous people. Perhaps because of the competing interests of the two communities, the discussions were held in great secrecy, in the expectation that agreement would be easier this way (a distinguished US political scientist favours closed negotiations for this reason).[3] This meant that people played little role in their future constitution.

Serious differences between the parties focused on the desirability of independence and the electoral system. A meeting of all the Legislative Council members was held in London, where some differences were resolved, through mediation, or more accurately, imposition by the British. The people of Fiji knew little about the issues discussed. The secret negotiations resumed on return to Fiji; only four active members from each party were involved; the papers and minutes were kept confidential.[4] There was little evidence of consultation by participants even with members of their own parties, despite complaints by their members and the Council of Chiefs. Lord Shepherd of the British government persuaded the negotiators to report on progress to the Legislative Council, shortly before the final constitutional conference in London in April 1970.

There was considerable confusion as to what the parties had agreed upon in the committee in Suva. British intervention was necessary to resolve several outstanding issues, and on elections agreement was possible only on the condition (put forward by Indo-Fijians) that the system would be reviewed after the first general elections. Reaching a settlement on the independence constitution in Fiji was harder than in any other South Pacific state, with the possible exception of New Hebrides/Vanuatu, but the debates in New Hebrides were fierce—and public. Looking at the 1970 constitution, one may get the impression—perhaps unfairly—that the leaders were more concerned with their own deals than the good of the country.

---

3   Jon Elster argues the virtues of constitution-making in secrecy because decision makers feel less threatened by pressure groups, can have free and frank discussions, and feel it is easier to change their minds when faced with a fairer alternative. The negative side is that there is lesser legitimacy of decisions, in part because of suspicions of motives of decision makers. See Conference on Democratic Transition and Constitution, 19–27 October 2001.
4   In 1986 when I began my study of the Fiji independence process, the records of the committee were still not publicly available. The late Ahmed Ali kindly loaned me the records—secretly—and I was not to make a photocopy!

Orientation of the constitution

The origins of the social, political and economic organisation of Fiji (largely adopted in the independence constitution) lie in British policies in the late nineteenth century (see France 1969). They were based on preservation of indigenous Fijian institutions (as understood, or even sometimes created, by the British),[5] particularly the chieftaincy, land and customary practices, which served both moral (protection of the vulnerable) and administrative convenience (indirect rule). Economic development was based on foreign, principally Australian, capital, largely invested in the sugar industry, and indentured labour recruited from India. The various communities of colonial Fiji—Fijians, 'Europeans', Indians, Chinese, 'part-Europeans', and 'others', who included Chinese and other Pacific Islanders, including Rotumans and sometimes part-Europeans—were segregated by race, which determined their entitlements, political rights and economic situation; there was no sense of a common political community or identity. Thus colonial policies both created and sustained these communities as distinct bodies.

The segregation of these communities and the isolation of indigenous people from the market meant that the relations among them were largely determined by administrative policies. This points to the importance of the political. Colonial history is interpreted largely in terms of administrative regulation, even the creation of racial claims and relations.[6] The effect of these policies, treating each community as a corporate entity, was to obscure the differences internal to each community.

The 1970 constitution hovered uneasily between integration and consociation. Other communities would generally provide political support to indigenous Fijians, as there were greater links between them and indigenous Fijians than with Indo-Fijians. It was on this assumption that the systems of elections and government were incorporated into the independence constitution.[7]

---

5 The Great Council of Chiefs, for example, as a formal institution was a colonial creation, as was, to a considerable extent, the 'customary' land tenure system. See Abrahamson 2009: 269 and esp. 271–72. As in Africa, perhaps even the 'traditional' identities that people adopt are the creation of the colonial powers.
6 See Lal 1992, an outstanding study of Fiji's history.
7 Indo-Fijians (close to 290,000) outnumbered Fijians (250,000) at independence, with minorities holding the balance (in favour of Fijians). After the 1990 coup, Fijians outnumbered the Indo-Fijians substantially, due to a higher birth rate, and the emigration of Indo-Fijians—so that Fijians did not have to rely on minority support (reflected in the separation of South Pacific voters from the roll of Fijians).

The constitution provided separate representation for the principal communities but, to meet the Indian insistence on a non-racial electoral system, some seats were racially allocated but voted for by electors of all races. Twenty-seven House of Representatives seats were ethnically elected (12 each for Fijians and Indians and three for 'Others'), 25 were voted on a common roll (10 each Fijians and Indians, and five 'Others') (1970 Constitution, Section 32). In the Senate, established principally to safeguard Fijian interests, eight members were nominees of the Great Council of Chiefs (GCC), seven were appointed by the prime minister, six by the leader of the opposition, and one by the Council of Rotuma (a small, remote island inhabited by Polynesians).

Various provisions protected the interests of indigenous Fijians, including their communal ownership of land (about 83 per cent of all land in the country, though not always the best land), preservation of their traditional social and political structures that were woven into the apparatus of the state. The Senate could veto certain legislation affecting indigenous Fijian privileges. A standard bill of rights protected all citizens,[8] but was qualified by the various collective rights for indigenous Fijians. The 1970 settlement was a mix of the democratic and the oligarchic, liberalism and ethnic separatism, equality and paramountcy of indigenous Fijians, market with restrictions on land and labour, a unitary state with significant autonomy for one community only, and freedom of religion with the close relationship of one religion (Christianity practised by indigenous Fijians) to the state. The system depended on maintaining the separation of races, or more accurately, keeping Indo-Fijians outside the alliance of others.

Notwithstanding the cross-voting national seats, the logic of the political system was dictated by the communal seats. Political parties were essentially racially organised to compete for the communal seats. The need to contest national seats was designed to compel each of the major parties to extend its appeal beyond the community they principally represented. For the most part this was not successful, each party being content to field a few candidates of other races. Native Fijian candidates sponsored

---

8   Based on the European Convention of Human Rights, found in most 1960s–1970s constitutions of former British colonies. In the Pacific, the Solomon Islands constitution is a prime example.

by the dominantly Indo-Fijian National Federation Party (NFP) were successful through Indo-Fijian votes, and so on.[9] In this way, cross-voting seats became an extension of communal seats.

This 'consociational' element in the voting was not reflected in the executive, designed on the Westminster parliamentary system of majoritarianism and the 'winner takes all'. The allocation of seats in the House of Representatives was such that, with a little support from their traditional allies, indigenous Fijians would dominate the executive. And any notion of what may be called 'sequential power sharing'—as in 'normal' situations, the major parties alternate in government—was, deliberately, excluded in the Fiji context.

Every government after independence was run by the Alliance Party, with Ratu Kamesese Mara as the prime minister, even in 1977 when his party lost to the dominant Indian party—a temporary hitch because, through a combination of Indian dithering and the natural inclination of the governor-general, Mara was asked to form government. A more serious challenge appeared in 1987 when an alliance of the NFP and the multiracial Fiji Labour Party (FLP) won, and its leader Timocy Bavadra became prime minister. Within the Fijian community, the new alignment reflected the distinction between the traditionalists and those who saw the communal lifestyle and politics as holding back the development of the Fijian community (the division to some extent reflected the differences between Fijians of the east and the west of the country). The constitution came under stress, as the fundamental assumptions of the protective policies about indigenous Fijians seemed to come apart, not only in terms of new emerging identities, but also because of the imperatives of the economy: incentives and efficiency could not be maintained in the face of the interaction of 'customary' rules and the market economy. Bavadra's government did not survive long: it was overthrown by an army officer, Sitiveni Rabuka, in May 1990. Though the coup was defended as the preserver of traditional chieftaincy, it marked the end of chiefly power and a swing to the commoners. But this was not evident from the constitution

---

9   A note on terminology: traditionally the indigenous inhabitants have been known as Fijians, and the second-largest community as Indians or more recently Indo-Fijians. The 1997 constitution called the country 'Fiji Islands' so the people 'Fiji Islanders'. The terminology did not 'take' well. The Bainimarama government wanted everyone to be 'Fijians' and the indigenous '*iTaukei*' (people of the land in Fijian language). Here for the sake of simplicity I retain 'Fijian' to mean the indigenous communities.

with which Rabuka brought the independence settlement to an end. Under him, the constitution-making process became the means to wage racial strife by another name.[10]

The 1990 constitution

Making of the constitution

As soon as a degree of public order was restored to Suva, and the government headed by Rabuka was installed, the governor-general set up a Constitution Review Committee in which the ousted coalition under Bavadra reluctantly agreed to take part though heavily outnumbered by Alliance and Great Council of Chiefs members. It was chaired by Sir John Falvey, a former attorney-general close to indigenous Fijians.[11] It was to review the constitution of Fiji and propose to the governor-general amendments to guarantee indigenous Fijian political interests 'with full regard to the interests of other groups'. The composition as well as terms of reference of the Committee favoured indigenous Fijians. Nevertheless, the process was more participatory than that for the 1970 constitution, though more manipulated (which often comes with participation). For the first time in Fiji, people had opportunity to give their views. The Committee held hearings in the four major towns and received over 860 written submissions and 120 oral submissions.[12] But the atmosphere in which these consultations took place was hardly conducive to any conciliatory recommendations. The Indo-Fijian community wanted a return to the 1970 constitution, while most Fijian individuals and groups wanted to enshrine Fijian dominance, differing only in the smallness of the role they would give to the Indo-Fijians.

The Committee recommended a unicameral legislature comprising 36 Fijians (28 elected and eight appointed by the Great Council of Chiefs), 22 Indo-Fijians, eight General Electors, one Rotuman, and up to four nominees of the prime minister. National constituencies, ethnically

---

10 Rabuka actually carried out two coups. The second (in September) forestalled the coalition caretaker government agreed upon in the wake of the first coup.
11 The Committee had available the services of a retired professor of law from the UK, Keith Patchett.
12 Lal (1992: 286–89) gives an account of the Commission, including of some of the submissions to it.

allocated by those elected by universal suffrage, were to be abolished, and all voting was to be communal. The prime minister's post was to be reserved for an indigenous Fijian.

Six members of the Committee, including all the Indian members dissented. As the process was leading nowhere and the economy was suffering from public disorder, the governor-general abolished Parliament and assumed executive powers—appointing Rabuka as the Commander of the armed forces. The governor-general convened a meeting on 24 September 1987 between political parties. On 27 September, the parties reached an agreement (the Deuba Accord) under which an interim government with members drawn equally from the two main parties would be established, and which would set up a new Constitution Review Committee (under a foreign expert) to propose a constitution acceptable to all, taking into account the aspirations of all communities.

Rabuka's response was rapid—on 28 September he carried out the second 1987 coup, declared Fiji a republic, and set up a government headed by himself and dominated by indigenous Fijians. He was soon replaced by Ratu Mara, thus returning the country to civilian, if not constitutional, rule.

Unlike the independence constitution, which was an elite-negotiated document, the 1990 constitution was more or less imposed on the people, in the face of unanimous opposition of one major community, Indo-Fijians, and considerable opposition from other communities. Having prepared its own draft (see Lal 1998: 10–11), heavily in favour of indigenous people, the Rabuka government set up the Constitution Inquiry and Advisory Committee chaired by a retired colonel, Paul Manueli, and weighted against Indo-Fijians. Its terms of reference were related strictly to the public reaction to the government draft, and to making proposals based on that reaction (Manueli 1989). Ratu Mara described the process: 'Citizens throughout the country were given the opportunity of making their views known, and eminent legal experts were called on for advice' (Mara 1997: 223). I had a different view: the committee was handpicked by the government and enjoyed neither popular support nor public credibility; the people had no effective participation and the constitution was to be brought in by force by the government (Ghai 1991). Brij Lal's evaluation of the process was less harsh, pointing to public meetings organised by the committee and oral and written submissions received (Lal 1998: 12).

Among the submissions received by the Committee was one from the military, which advocated 'absolute political dominance' by indigenous Fijians,[13] with controls on the press, judges appointed who would 'accept the situation', and the workers and the church cut off from what were viewed as subversive foreign influences, while the nation was subject to military discipline, and deprived of constitutional rule, for 15 years.[14]

Orientation of the constitution

The Manueli report, and the constitution based on it, were both racially based. Elections were to be entirely on an ethnic basis, with 37 seats for indigenous Fijians and 27 for Indo-Fijians out of 70 seats in the lower house. An appointed upper house was over two-thirds Fijian. Only an indigenous Fijian could be prime minister, and the president was appointed by the Great Council of Chiefs (GCC). There was a similar imbalance in the Senate. The over-representation of Fijians when they also had an absolute majority in the other house turned the justification of the second chamber on its head. Greater powers were granted to the executive than before, since the moderating role of the leader of the opposition (traditionally an Indo-Fijian) was removed and the prime minister had a direct and decisive say in appointments to various offices. The legislature and the executive were given unlimited powers to establish programmes and policies for 'promoting and safeguarding the economic, social, educational, cultural, traditional and other interests of the Fijian and Rotuman people' (s. 21(1) Constitution). Minerals were vested in the owners of the land underneath which they were found—a major shift of resources from the state to one community. The constitution enhanced the role of indigenous institutions, including the Native Land Commission, the Native Fisheries Commission, and the Native Lands Trust Board, removing review by the courts and the ombudsman of their decisions and acts.

What dominated Fijian elite views at this period were not just the question of the Indo-Fijian bogey, but also an outdated perception of Fijian society—rural, land-linked, chief-dominated and cohesive. The constitution of 1990 was biased towards rural Fijians (the 33 per cent of Fijians who lived in urban areas having only 13.5 per cent of the parliamentary seats). Many of the native institutions could not,

---

13 For the links between the military, religion and Fijian chiefly tradition, see Halapua 2003.
14 See Lal 1998: 14 for other measures proposed by it in favour of indigenous people.

as previously stated, be regarded as indigenous, but as instruments of those Fijians who controlled the state. Close control by native institutions by the state precluded other races from influence on state policies and undermined the capacity or willingness of the state to promote interethnic bargaining and accommodations. At the same time, these institutions were used to discipline Fijians as a racialised, dominant group separate from other citizens—thus amplifying their social, legal and economic segregation.[15] It gave a far more prominent role than in the past to the GCC, and thus greater control of the eastern chiefs over the western.

The coalition parties participated in elections held under this constitution in 1992, after a good deal of soul-searching (the differences over whether to participate actually broke the coalition). The election led to Rabuka becoming prime minister as an elected politician rather than as a coup-maker. (We cannot know how the history of Fiji might have been different if Bavadra, a statesman committed to the vision of a non-racial and just Fiji, had not died before the elections). Ironically, however, the constitution reinforced internal divisions among Fijians. Once Indians were sidelined, there was little to maintain the political unity of Fijians. The passing of power to commoners undermined the chiefly class, which had sedulously cultivated the ideology of traditionalism, and a sort of unity under eastern hegemony. No Fijian party, given the multiplicity of parties among Fijians, could form a government without the support of an Indian party. Needing Indian support to form a government, Rabuka agreed to a speedy review of the constitution.

The 1997 constitution

Making of the constitution

The failures of the 1970 and 1990 constitutions prompted the search for a new basis for the state and intercommunity relations, based on national harmony and equality. After considerable negotiations between the Rabuka government and the Indo-Fijian political parties, agreement was reached that an independent commission would undertake the review of the 1990 constitution and make recommendations for change. The Chair was the distinguished New Zealander Sir Paul Reeves (former governor-

---

15   I am grateful to Coel Kirkby for this insight.

general of his country), veteran politician Tomasi Rayalu Vakatora and The Australian National University Indo-Fijian scholar Brij Lal. The objectives of the review were the promotion of 'racial harmony and national unity and economic and social advancement of all communities, and bearing in mind internationally recognised principles and standards of individual and groups rights' (though there was a sort of proviso: the constitution 'shall guarantee full protection and promotion of the rights, interests and concerns of the indigenous Fijian and Rotuman people' (Reeves, Vakatora and Lal 1996: 2) The commission was to:

> facilitate the widest possible debate throughout Fiji on the terms of the Constitution of Fiji and to enquire into and ascertain the variety of views and opinions that may exist in order to formulate provisions of a Constitution that would meet the needs of a multi-ethnic and multi-cultural society (Reeves, Vakatora and Lal 1996: 2).

The Commission held many open meetings, covering much of the country, to receive the views of the public—and a few closed meetings (especially with senior officials of the government). It received 852 submissions altogether, including many presented to it at public meetings. It also received views of groups organised to participate in the process; they brought to the attention of the Commissioner views of overseas experts. The Commission considered that it obtained 'a picture of the hopes and concerns of the people of Fiji about their country's future'.[16] The media covered its meetings well. The Commission also sought information and ideas through papers from two sources: government departments and foreign experts, reflecting particularly on comparative research, and on issues it identified as critical to its recommendations. It supplemented this by visits to Malaysia, Mauritius and South Africa—all multiethnic states—to learn about their experiences, and meeting with a number of experts there, as well as in the US.

The Commission worked hard and in September 1996 produced a report, close to 800 pages long, providing the background to the review of the previous constitution and setting out the approach of the Commission, with clear explanatory notes—by far the most thorough and sophisticated analysis anywhere in the South Pacific of past practice, the rationale for change and the recommendations for a new constitution. What most

---

16 Reeves, Vakatora and Lal 1996: 59. Whenever possible, subsequent references to the 'Reeves Report', as it was called, will be presented in parenthesis within the body of my text, and referred to by paragraph, page or chapter number, as appropriate.

surprised the people was unanimity of analysis and recommendations in a highly contentious area, thanks in part to the skills of Reeves who let the two local members resolve differences between them (and the communities they represented) as well as the close and amicable relationship that developed between Vakatora and Lal.

Orientation of draft constitution (Reeves Commission)

A major objective of the Reeves Commission was the promotion of racial harmony and national unity—by encouraging and facilitating the formation of multiethnic governments (para 2.69). The key to this was the electoral system, but it would involve removal or adjustment of the four principal problems that the commission had identified: communal representation, the ethnic base of political parties, majority government and the indigenous 'paramountcy' principle. It dealt with the principle of paramountcy by highlighting its role in the protection of the rights and interests of indigenous Fijians, rather than in the domination of other communities, though it did recommend special powers for indigenous institutions.

On power-sharing, the Commission rejected proposals either for a requirement that the prime minister should appoint a specified number of ministers from the different communities or that the constitution should entitle every political party that had secured at least 20 per cent of parliamentary seats to a proportionate share in the cabinet (p. 18), as they would not fundamentally alter the nature of politics. Instead, electoral and other incentives were needed for parties to cooperate, merge and broaden their appeal for support (paras 2.76, 9.96).

It believed that the overriding goals of multiethnic government, racial harmony and national unity could not be achieved until the electoral system moved away from communal seats to non-racial open seats. It reversed the proportion between the two types of seats in the 1970 constitution, proposing a 70-member House of Representatives with 45 completely open seats, and 12 seats for indigenous Fijians and Pacific Islanders, 10 for Indo-Fijians, one for Rotumans and two for General Voters (the current term for 'others').

For the Senate, each province would return two members, without any racial restriction of candidates or voters (plus some limited representation of small communities who might not otherwise make it to the House), thus building on the 'distinctive identity' of provinces (para 9.177). To facilitate racial integration, the Commission opted for the Alternative Vote (AV) system for both the House of Representatives and the Senate (Chapter 10), rejecting both first past the post (as undemocratic) and proportional systems (as encouraging voting by ethnicity).

The Commission made several other recommendations to ease ethnic tensions, provide a strong protection of human rights, ensure social justice (especially through affirmative action for the genuinely disadvantaged, and rules about national institutions like the civil service and judiciary reflecting the national make-up), and to reinforce what they hoped would be a less confrontational style in parliament by providing for a committee system to carry out much of the work of scrutiny of government.

It was the Commission's hope that all its proposals would be regarded as part of a coherent and interdependent scheme and a fair balancing of the interests of ethnic groups. But the Joint Parliamentary Select Committee divided chapters of the proposed constitution among its subgroups that looked at each chapter in isolation.

Orientation of the 1997 constitution: Response to the Reeves Report

The recommendations of the Commission met with great hostility among the indigenous Fijian and a section of the Indo-Fijian Muslim community. But the report was sent to the Joint Parliamentary Select Committee (JPSC) to discuss the proposals and to agree on amendments if necessary.[17] Rabuka and the Indo-Fijian leader Jai Ram Reddy played a positive and constructive role. Many politicians were not happy at the emphasis on national identity at the expense of communal affiliations and institutions. A great number of them had become accustomed to and were comfortable with racially oriented electorates and politics. Others, who had not favoured the Commission's interest in comparative constitutions and experiences, emphasised the uniqueness of Fiji's circumstances; and that, as the president cautioned, national harmony would only come from the recognition of different races, cultures and customs (Parliament of Fiji, Annex II (2)).

---

17 For a detailed account of the deliberations and decision of the JPSC and the Parliamentary debate, see Lal 1998: 86–102.

Rabuka reminded the JPSC of the diversity of ethnic groups, cultures and faiths in Fiji, which give 'identity, solace and confidence to our citizens as individuals and distinct groups' (Parliament of Fiji, Annex IV(4)). In general, the JPSC accepted many of the values and principles of the Commission, but agreement on institutions was harder to negotiate, and in the end the provisions that would have given the two major communities equal rights in state institutions had to be watered down, maintaining the superiority of indigenous people. As with previous constitutions, Indo-Fijians had to yield to the indigenous-dominated military on political and constitutional matters.

The main amendments of the JPSC related to the system of government. It inverted the proportion between open and reserved seats. Out of a house of 71 members, only 25 seats would now be open; the balance would be divided among indigenous Fijians 23, Indo-Fijians 19, General Voters three and Rotumans one (representing slight over-representation of indigenous Fijians and the General Voters). This would reduce incentives to form multiethnic parties or mergers.

And the broadening of democracy was held back, by rejection of the proposal for an elected Senate. This eliminated further opportunities for electoral cooperation between parties of different ethnic communities. Its composition retained distinct ethnic elements: with 14 members nominated by the GCC, nine nominated by the prime minister, eight by the leader of the opposition and one by the Council of Rotuma. The requirement that at least nine of the 14 GCC-nominated members of the Senate approve certain legislation related to community rights especially on land, as well as the appointment of the president by the GCC rather than the more representative Parliament likewise retained the salience of the ethnic factor.

Perhaps realising that its decisions would reduce the prospect of power-sharing through the electoral process, The JPSC differed from the commission in opting for a mandatory coalitional government.[18]

---

18 One member of the JPSC, from the Fiji Labour Party, has explained why the Commission approach was rejected. His party, committed to non-racial distinctions, could not accept the notion of multiethnic government, but multiparty government, which the JPSC adopted, was more congenial (Krishna Datt, during a speech at the University of the South Pacific, 30 September 2003 (see Datt 2003)). The explanation is puzzling, since the vehicle for representation in the cabinet in the Commission proposal was parties, not ethnic groups as such.

It decided that any party that obtained at least 10 per cent of the seats in the House of Representatives would be entitled to a proportionate number of ministries.

After the 1997 constitution

Preferential voting is an appealing idea. But it is not surprising that AV has been sceptically received by many in the Fiji Islands. The system, being strongly majoritarian, makes it very difficult for a new party—or a party trying to recover from a serious decline—to get into Parliament at all. The system also worked quite differently from what the Commission had expected; it did not encourage cooperation between ethnic groups, but led to shady deals across ethnic lines, geared mainly to weaken those parties within ethnic groups committed to racial integration.

The formula for a power-sharing executive was more likely to help smaller parties. But it did not work at all well because of the lack of commitment of the leading parties to sharing power. In 1999, when the FLP won and invited Rabuka's Soqosoqo ni Vakavulewa ni Taukei (SVT) to participate, the latter responded with a number of conditions, which Prime Minister Chaudhry interpreted (with almost indecent haste) as a rejection. In 2001, after a coup and return to civilian rule, the SDL leader invited that FLP to participate while suggesting that there was 'insufficient basis for a workable partnership',[19] and went on to recommend a Cabinet with no FLP members.

Resolution of these disputes has involved repeated resort to the courts. In the first case, the Supreme Court held that Chaudhry was not bound to accept the conditions imposed by the SVT for joining government.[20] In the second case, the Supreme Court held the prime minister in breach of the constitution.[21] The matter went back to the court in 2004 over the precise interpretation of the constitution on allocation of seats.[22]

---

19   *Qarase v. Chaudhry*, [2003] F.J.S.C. 1, CBV0004.2002S (18 July 2003). The correspondence between the party leaders is appended to the decision.
20   *President of Fiji Islands v. Kubuabola* [1999] FJSC 8, Misc. Case No. 1 of 1999 (3 Sept. 1999).
21   *Qarase v. Chaudhry* [2003] FJSC 1 (the '2003 case').
22   *In re the President's Reference, Qarase v. Chaudhry—Decision of the Court* [2004] FJSC 1; MISC 001.2003 (9 July 2004). There was a dissenting judgment from Justice Gault on the issue of whether the prime minister could appoint senators or independent members of parliament as ministers without eating into his own quota in the Cabinet: *In re the President's Reference, Qarase v Chaudhry—Dissenting Judgment* [2004] FJSC 9; MISC 001.2003s.

The rules for appointments to the Senate were also litigated: was the FLP to get all the Senate seats for the opposition if it was the only opposition party entitled to sit in the Cabinet? The Supreme Court said 'Yes',[23] though one judge disagreed.[24]

These uncertainties in the constitution cannot be laid at the door of the Reeves Commission, but were consequences of the JPSC decisions. The Supreme Court emphasised:

> Conventions cannot be the subject of judicial prescription. They are matters for the elected representatives of the people to develop in working out the future governance of their nation. That, it is hardly necessary to say, mandates a degree of give and take and good faith on all sides (*Qarase v. Chaudhry* [2003] FJSC 1, para. 107).

One and a half more coups

Although eventually a power-sharing Cabinet did come into being, before the 'conventions' that the Supreme Court had advised could develop, another coup befell the country a few months later, in 2006, this time led by the head of the military, Commodore Bainimarama. The 1997 constitution was put into cold storage, though the government declared its resolve to return to constitutional rule, albeit after some fundamental reforms, particularly towards a non-racial Fiji. In 2009, the Supreme Court, reversing lower courts, declared that the 2006 coup was unconstitutional, and that the 1997 constitution was still valid and ordered the restoration of lawful government. Bainimarama, then self-appointed prime minister and his attorney-general, Alyaz Sayed-Khaiyum, ignored the decision and dismissed the Supreme Court—perpetrating yet another coup. The purported revival of the 1997 constitution did have the effect of rallying around it several groups who were opposed to the coup, even though they had previously been lukewarm about it. This gave the constitition new legitimacy.

---

23 *In re the Constitution, Reference by HE the President* [2002] FJSC 1; MISC 001.2001S (15 March 2002). See also the *Kubuabola* 1999 case above.
24 *In re the Constitution, Reference by HE the President (Dissenting Judgment)* [2002] FJSC 3; MISC 001.2001S (Justice Amet).

It must, however, be acknowledged that the first Bainimarama coup was popular with some sections of the people (mostly Indo-Fijian) and some civil society organisations. The 2007 project for a 'Peoples Charter for Change, Peace and Progress'[25] as a prelude to the making of the constitution, involving a significant number of organisations and well-respected individuals, was a sensible approach and produced some excellent proposals—though resisted by some, because of its connections with Bainimarama and his coup. But it lost its legitimacy, and many supporters, as the regime moved to the suppression of basic human rights and increasingly vindictive administration. Bainimarama and Sayed-Khaiyum seemed to change their mind about a return to democracy and continued their rule, backed by the armed forces, until September 2014.[26] Fiji was ruled primarily through a series of decrees, passed at the will of the prime minister (and legally unchallengeable), several of them quite draconian, targeting sources of independent thought such as the media and legal profession—and destroying the rule of law. The great harm that coups and the military rule do to democracy and the rule of law is seldom factored into discussions of the renewal of democracy. However democratic the new constitution, the system of government and the people's fear of the administration do not recover easily from the scars of the military regime.

Under some pressure from the international community, in early 2012, the government promised, yet again, to initiate a process for the writing of a new constitution, followed by elections. At this stage, I was approached by Sayed-Khaiyum to head the commission responsible for preparing the constitution, within broad guidelines.[27]

---

25 National Council for Building a Better Fiji, 2008. The Charter process had task forces on Good Governance (Legal, Political, Institutional and Constitutional Reforms); the Economy; and Social Cultural Identity and Nation Building.
26 I believe that Bainimarama and Sayed-Khaiyum (or at least the latter) did genuinely intend to move quickly to a new constitution. Sayed-Khaiyum asked me soon after the coup to go to Fiji to help write the constitution. I was unable to accept as I had just taken a senior UN post in Nepal to help in that country's constitution. In December 2008, I was asked by the Secretary-General of the UN to go to Fiji to explore the possibility of reconciliation between different political factions, leading eventually to a new constitution (Bainimarama had asked the Secretary-General for UN mediation). Based on our report, the Secretary-General agreed. I was to return to negotiate the terms and procedure for UN involvement, but the plan collapsed after it became clear that Bainimarama was not serious—perhaps just buying time?
27 The other members of the Commission were Taufa Vakatale, Penny Moore, Satendra Nandan and the South African Christina Murray.

Return to constitutional democracy?

The Ghai Commission

I agreed with most objectives the government had set out as the basis of the constitution except for immunity provisions. I was also impressed with the government's emphasis on a participatory process—and above all with its agreement to the independence of the commission and the making of the final decisions on the constitution by a representative constituent assembly.[28] I insisted, with success, on lifting of the restrictions on the right of assembly and public access to the Commission.

In order to ensure the government commitment to these assurances, I drafted a decree setting out the principles and objectives of the constitution, and the procedure (including the lifting of bans on meetings and security against victimisation in respect of submissions made to the Commission—and no immunities). The government, soon realising it had made a mistake with the process, divided the draft decree into one on the Commission and the other on the constituent assembly—and inserted in both the requirement that the new constitution must provide wide-ranging immunity for the military and other groups and individuals involved in the various past coups.

The new constitution was to *result from full, inclusive and fair participation of Fijians*. The Commission was to study the circumstances and needs of Fiji, and its constitutional history 'to avoid the mistakes of the past', carry out and commission research, use experts, keep the people informed, visit 'as many parts of the country as possible' (Fiji Constitutional Process (Constitution Commission) Decree 2012 (Decree No. 57 of 2012) s. 7(1)(b)), hold public meetings to receive oral and written submissions, which they were to analyse 'scientifically' and summarise in a report, prepare a draft constitution and any changes to existing laws that the constitution would require, and present it to the people along with an 'explanatory

---

28   When so invited by the Fiji government, I was confronted with the dilemma that I had faced a few years previously in my own country, Kenya, when the unpopular and dictatorial president Moi asked me to chair the Constitutional Review Commission. I consulted widely with civil society organisations, religious groups and friends on whether I should accept the offer. I did accept but on conditions that the president was not happy with but conceded—and the Commission did produce a good draft that was largely enacted into law. I made similar consultations in Fiji.

report'. It was then to seek and collect the views of the people on the draft, and submit the draft with those reactions for consideration by a constituent assembly. All in six months.

The draft constitution was to meet the needs of Fiji and the aspirations of its people, unite those people, be 'appropriately designed' to achieve 'true democracy, and respect for, and protection and promotion of human rights' (s. 3(d)). Another provision listed certain 'non-negotiable principles and values': (i) a common and equal citizenry; (ii) a secular state; (iii) the removal of systemic corruption; (iv) an independent judiciary; (v) elimination of discrimination; (vi) good and transparent governance; (vii) social justice; (viii) one person, one vote, one value; (ix) the elimination of ethnic voting; (x) proportional representation; and (xi) voting age of 18 years (s. 3(e)).

The commission prepared a small book to explain to the people both the objectives and process of the review, and held a number of meetings, on our own and through civil society groups to promote awareness of issues and options (Constitution Commission 2012). After that the process of consultation was very intense, with the Commission aiming to visit all areas of the country and holding hearings in 110 venues. We estimate that we heard from a very wide range of people and organisations—and at a late stage, the military. We also received many submissions by post and emails (locally as well as from the diaspora).

A remarkable consensus within the Commission enabled us to meet our deadline of the end of December 2012. By this time, we had lost the confidence of the prime minister and the attorney-general, who curtailed our activities (the former threatened to deport me if I did not stop meeting with trade unions, civil society, and political parties—I did not and he did not). Copies of our draft constitution were confiscated from the printers, and a small number was burnt. However, in accordance with the Decree we were able to present the draft constitution to the president, who, having praised our report at a farewell reception by the Commission, was subsequently compelled by the prime minister to strongly criticise it. We were stopped by the government from the next and final task—that of engaging the public on our recommendations and preparing a dossier of their reactions for the constituent assembly. In fact, the government ensured that there would be no constituent assembly, and took over the task of writing and promulgating the constitution—taking considerably longer than it promised, concentrating on developing an electoral system that would ensure it victory.

Orientation of the 2012 draft

I do not intend to examine the provisions of the Commission's draft constitution in detail—partly because it never became a constitution! My focus is on our analysis of the problems facing the country, and how these could be resolved, and how to give effect to the fundamental principles that the constitution must incorporate. The Ghai Commission agreed with many of the objectives of the Reeves Commission, and indeed the fundamental principles as set out by the government. As far the Reeves Commission was concerned, there were differences of approach, it being more cautious and conservative than us. As far as the government was concerned, despite promises to make submissions to us, neither the prime minister nor the attorney-general made submissions, though we were given to understand that the government position was no different from that of the military.

The issues

Ethnicity

There is wide acceptance among scholars and the public that the most fundamental causes of Fiji's contemporary problems lie in history and in its various constitutions shaped by that history. At the root is the organisation of politics, state and economy on the basis of ethnic communalism—the colonial legacy. This much is evident from the narratives of Fiji's two major communities: both victims of forces beyond them, deprived of free choice and will and victims of the colonial system. Instead of dealing with the forces that subordinated and in many respects exploited them, they regarded the other community as the obstacle to the advancement of its members—and made little effort to understand the suffering of the other.

Culture

We also noticed a crisis of culture. Fiji is caught up in a culture that is based on the organisation of an outdated economy. The demands of people embedded in this culture (for free and better education, health, housing and transport) cannot be met without a radical change in that culture and the values and institutions that sustain it. 'Culture' as applied to indigenous Fijians has become very encompassing, and deeply attached to religion, politics and economy, which cause particular problems in organising the state and planning the economy. Privileging one culture or religion above others in a multiracial society is no recipe for peace, unity or development. This problem is compounded by generational change, which makes culture a source of conflict not as between different cultural traditions but also within each culture.

Lack of trust in public institutions

People have little trust in political leadership and public institutions, a result of ethnic conflict and increasing levels of corruption compounding the sense of crisis that is widespread. The rule of law (for long a positive and important feature of state and society in Fiji) has been undermined. The frequency of coups has produced a feeling of hopelessness all too evident to the Commission in public hearings.

Democratic deficit and weakness

Fiji's democracy is without deep roots, without a real understanding of its importance or procedures. Racial politics have dominated at the expense of the values of democracy; operating within previous frameworks well past their usefulness. The succession of coups and military or military-influenced governments have also undermined democratic values and prevented the accumulation of democratic experience.

Approach of the Commission

The Commission developed an approach to the issues founded in the belief that the fundamental need was to shift the identity, politics and institutions of the people of Fiji from their bases in community to those based on equal citizenship. It suggested that the challenge was to create out of its diverse communities an identity as a nation founded on common values and aspirations, without dispensing with its rich cultural diversity. Once the foundations of that national identity have been agreed upon ('nation-building'), the values, institutions and procedures of the state must be reformed to reflect the Fiji nation and its aspirations ('state-building' or 'restructuring').

The Commission looked for approaches and solutions through which every community would be better off than otherwise. It proposed greater separation between state and society. The shift to non-racial state values and structures would be easier if the values, culture and practices of ethnic communities became their own responsibility. In this way, institutions like chieftaincy or religious practices would not be threatened or undermined but become matters for the community. The separation of state and society would actually protect culture and make it possible for members of ethnic communities to cooperate and work constructively in the public sphere, in the affairs of the state as well as the economy. For these reasons, the Commission recommended that the GCC (which the government had abolished) should be separated from the state, becoming purely a voluntary institution for communal affairs of Fijians.

The Commission had become conscious of how relatively unorganised the people were, except for the guidance and structure provided by faith organisations or through traditions and culture (especially for indigenous Fijians), and thus of their lack of knowledge of the purpose and nature of the state, or their own rights as individuals and organisations. It decided that civil society, even with its weaknesses, must be encouraged, including because, as the Reeves Report put it, civil society has a vital role to play in providing opportunities for members of different communities to come together (para 3.52).

Land

The Commission was aware that the customary land system had protected the indigenous communities, and it received advice that the system, with administrative reforms, could form a good basis for the developmental use of land. So it proposed a mechanism for a national dialogue on land involving state bodies, land owners (most of these Fijians) and tenants (mostly Indo-Fijians). The draft proposed some underlying principles to guide negotiations including security of land rights, better administration of land, responsible use of land, and participation and consultation. However, to increase the sense of security, all existing rights in land were recognised, as was the prohibition on permanent alienation of customary land except to the state, as well as freehold land and rights to it recognised in existing law.

Under the 1997 constitution, 'social justice' meant affirmative action, especially—as applied—for Fijians. Yet people from both main communities were poor and victims of discrimination. So the Commission relied upon the broad permission for affirmative action in the human rights chapter, and the recognition of economic social and cultural rights, such as education, health, food and water as enforceable, drawing on constitutions such as those of South Africa and Kenya. An addition was a right of access to markets—reflecting submissions the Commission received about the difficulties of access in the light of inadequate roads and boat services.

Conclusion

Process

Fiji has had, in 45 years, four constitutions, five coups and a period of eight years without a constitution. The fact that the last military regime felt it necessary to establish a constitution and then hold elections under it may suggest the importance, or even the necessity, of a constitution. A country with Fiji's fragmented communities, deep social divisions, diverse languages, religions and cultures, and lack of nationalism needs some sort of consensus on key institutions and procedures to run the country prescribed in a constitution. Fiji's history shows that broad consent is necessary to maintain the semblance of a state, a functioning economy, and a measure of law and order—and the evasion of sanctions from abroad. Constitutions and the making of them have therefore been a central aspect of Fiji's history.

The alternative is military rule, of which Fiji has ample experience (but surprisingly missing otherwise in the South Pacific). These days a constitution serves another purpose: warding off the disapproval of, even sanctions by, other states or interstate organisations (an important factor for Fiji's military that flourishes on its peacekeeping role—in other countries). Fiji's retreats from military regimes were perhaps dictated more by this consideration than legitimacy at home—for legitimacy at home was often secured by the military regimes through substantial support from important sections of indigenous, European and South Pacific communities.

The processes of law-making were marked by the circumstances surrounding its period. The 1970 constitution was to grant independence and establish the system of government. Like most decolonising constitutions the process was negotiated, not open and participatory, with Britain playing a major role.[29] The constitution itself was designed

---

29   Some other Pacific constitutional processes were far more open, especially Papua New Guinea and Vanuatu. For a comparative study of constitution making in the South Pacific, see Ghai 1988a.

to protect indigenous Fijian interests, which it did at great cost to ethnic trust. The process was highly secretive, on the initiative of local negotiating parties, not Britain. Certainly compared to constitution-making in other parts of the South Pacific, Fiji was the least democratic.

The 1990 process was more open and participatory. But it was still heavily influenced by political parties, and the military. As an exercise in genuine participation, or consensus-building, the process was a failure. The Manueli Committee was seeking comments on a draft prepared by Rabuka and his advisers. The military kept a firm control over the process, so that the resulting constitution was not negotiated, but imposed.

In substantive terms, the constitution represented an intensification of the racial factor and removed the few features not based on race as such. But it contained the seeds of its own destruction by being so blatantly racist, and undermining Fijian unity, that it was hard for the international community to do other than oppose it.

The 1995–97 process was excellent in many ways, but had two weaknesses. The Commission spent a fair bit of time educating itself, but did little to educate the people on the issues, which probably affected the quality of public participation (dominated as it was by political parties). One result of this might have been that though a large number of individuals and organisations made their submissions to the Commission, they were mostly cast in the old moulds of racial politics (delivered duly by the followers of old, established parties, on party instructions). Second, and perhaps more seriously, the report and recommendations of the Commission were presented to parliamentarians, rather than to the people, thus giving politicians the ultimate decisions, with the intrusion of racial politics as well as the convenience of politicians, with the focus shifting away from the national (as recommended by the commission) to the racial.

The process under the 2012 Commission was different from any previous process, to some extent building on the Reeves model. The process was highly participatory (despite many restrictions by, and fear of, the military). It would have been the most participatory in the South Pacific if the military had not truncated it, cutting out public debates on the Commission's draft, and then the convening of the constituent assembly, which would have made the final decisions on the constitution. It would have made a difference also if public debate on anything to do with the constitution had not been curtailed by the government until nearly the start of the process, making civil education almost impossible. This degree of democracy was too much even for the regime that claimed to have its basis in public support. Political parties had little impact on the process, and, in the early stages, were not keen on participation (but did warmly endorse the draft in a joint statement of all parties—a rare occurrence in Fiji). The government and the military (insofar as it is possible to separate the two) had slightly more impact, but did not really like the process as it was eventually inscribed in the decrees. And if the recommendations of the Reeves Commission were mutilated by politicians, the recommendations of the 2012 Commission were far more extensively affected by the military-based government. While the 2013 constitution has some echoes of the 2012 draft, the government introduced the provisions it had wanted all along, without fulfilling its commitment to a constituent assembly.

Orientation

Each of the constitutions had a clear orientation. The independence constitution was built on the colonial model (of divide and rule); in this respect Fiji was unusual, for in most former colonies, the independence constitutions represented a major departure from the colonial mode of representation and governance. The 1970 constitution seemed a curious mixture of consociation and integration, but really it was designed for the dominance of indigenous Fijians. In the background was the military, which would be run by the indigenous aristocracy, which transcended civilian and military rulers. Then again, Indo-Fijians regarded the constitution as transitional, leading to a fully non-racial and democratic dispensation (and insisted, successfully, on the review of the electoral system to promote integration, before the following election; Mara resisted it but a commission was set up. Its recommendations for proportional voting were disregarded).

All subsequent constitutions had the stamp of the military. Whether Ratu Mara used him or not, Rabuka demonstrated the teeth of the army as well as the collaboration between the army and aristocracy. The 1990 constitution demonstrated the superiority of the army (over the aristocracy) and its conception of 'indigenous' rule, founded on the clear dominance of the indigenous communities, of the eastern origin. It vested indigenous leaders and institutions with impunities, and dealt a severe blow to the principle of the separation of powers, which had until then commanded considerable respect. But by the very virtue of undisputed indigenous rule, Rabuka created major divisions within the indigenous community—of which he became a victim as the outlines of the 1997 constitution unfolded.

The 1997 constitution was not the Reeves constitution. The Reeves Commission had the vision of racial harmony and national unity, moving away from ethnic political parties and the racially based electoral system. It emphasised human rights and the equality of all the people of Fiji, without encroaching on the traditional rights of indigenous communities to their land as well as culture, manifested in the Great Council of Chiefs. Its caution in that respect may be seen as a kind of a transitional constitution, whose full realisation would have been the 2012 constitution by the Ghai Commission. The 1997 constitution was really the constitution of politicians brought up in the traditions of the 1990 constitution, but with greater attempts at a multiracial governance system. Their error was to disregard the expert advice of the Reeves Commission—a not unusual vice of politicians everywhere.

In one sense the 2012 Commission aimed at the full realisation of the objectives of the Reeves agenda, but with a fundamental restructuring of institutions. In many ways, it was faithful to the professed objectives of the Bainimarama and Sayed-Khaiyum regime, perhaps too faithful, so that it had to be destroyed—burnt. Together Bainimarama and Sayed-Khaiyum devalued the notion of a constitution driven by the people, or indeed of a constitution. The decree, a magical trick by which they had ruled Fiji for nearly seven years, continues to reign—in spirit. Fijians all (*iTaukei* (indigenous Fijians), Indo-Fijians, Euro-Fijians, Sino-Fijians and the South Pacific Islanders) will have to wait for a people-driven constitution, which is the foundation of their polity and which respects their identity as Fijians above all.

References

Abrahamson, Allen. 2009. 'The lie of the land: Suturing the jural and the ritual in Fiji, Western Pacific.' In *Law and Anthropology: Current Legal Issues Volume 12*, edited by Michael Freeman and David Napier, pp. 269–91. Oxford: Oxford University Press. DOI: dx.doi.org/10.1093/acprof:oso/9780199580910.003.0011.

Arjomand, Saïd Amir (ed.). 2007. *Constitutionalism and Political Reconstruction*. Leiden and Boston: Brill.

Choudhry, Sujit (ed.). 2008. Constitutional Design in Divided Societies: Integration or Accommodation? Oxford: Oxford University Press.

Conference on Democratic Transition and Constitution. 2001. FRIDE/ Gorbachev Foundation of North America, Madrid, 19–27 October.

Constitution Commission. 2012. *Building the People's Constitution: Your Responsibility A Guide to Constitution Making for the People of Fiji*. Suva: The Constitution Commission.

Cottrell, Jill and Yash Ghai, 2010. 'Between coups: Constitution making in Fiji.' In *Framing the State in Times of Transition: Case Studies in Constitution Making*, edited by Laurel E. Miller with Louis Aucoin, pp. 275–308. Washington, DC: United States Institute of Peace.

Datt, Krishna. 2003. Speech at the University of the South Pacific Conference on Democracy and Good Governance, 30 September (on file with author).

Elster, Jon. 2001. 'Ideal and reality in constitution-making'. Paper prepared for Conference on Democratic Transition and Consolidation organised by the Fundación para las Relaciones Internacionales y el Dialogo Exterior and the Gorbachev Foundation of North America, Madrid, October 2001. Online: www.constitutionnet.org/files/Elster%20Fride.doc (accessed 25 January 2017).

France, Peter. 1969. *The Charter of the Land: Custom and Colonisation in Fiji*. Melbourne: Oxford University. Press.

Freeman, Michael and David Napier (ed.). 2009. *Law and Anthropology: Current Legal Issues Volume 12*. Oxford: Oxford University Press.

Ghai, Yash. 1988a. 'Constitution making and decolonisation'. In *Law, Politics and Government in the Pacific Island States*, edited by Yash Ghai, pp. 1–53. Suva: Institute of Pacific Studies of the University of the South Pacific.

———. 1988b. 'Systems of government I'. In *Law, Politics and Government in the Pacific Island States*, edited by Yash Ghai, pp. 54–75. Suva: Institute of Pacific Studies of the University of the South Pacific.

―――. 1988c. 'Systems of government II'. IN *Law, Politics and Government in the Pacific Island States*, edited by Yash Ghai, pp. 76–105. Suva: Institute of Pacific Studies of the University of the South Pacific.

―――. 1988d. 'Political consequences of constitutions'. In *Law, Politics and Government in the Pacific Island States*, edited by Yash Ghai, pp. 350–73. Suva: Institute of Pacific Studies of the University of the South Pacific.

―――. 1990. 'A coup by another name? The politics of legality.' *Contemporary Pacific*, 2(1): 11–35.

Ghai, Yash (ed.). 1988. *Law, Politics and Government in the Pacific Island States*. Suva: Institute of Pacific Studies of the University of the South Pacific.

[Ghai, Yash]. 1991. *The Fiji Constitution of 1990: A Fraud on the Nation (A Report by the Fiji Labour Party and the National Federation Party)*. Nadi: Sunrise Press. (I wrote this report. My name does not appear on the title page, but see the preface).

Ghai, Yash and Jill Cottrell. 2007. 'Constitutional engineering and impact: The case of Fiji.' In *Constitutionalism and Political Reconstruction*, edited by Saïd Amir Arjomand, pp. 159–91. Leiden and Boston: Brill.

―――. 2008. 'A tale of three constitutions: Ethnicity and politics in Fiji.' In *Constitutional Design for Divided Societies: Integration or Accommodation?*, edited by Sujit Choudhury, pp. 287–315. Oxford: Oxford University Press.

Halapua, Winston. 2003. *Tradition, Lotu and Militarism in Fiji*. Lautoka: Fiji Institute of Applied Studies.

Lal, Brij V. 1992. *Broken Waves: A History of the Fiji Islands in the Twentieth Century*. Honolulu: University of Hawai'i Press.

―――. 1998. *Another Way: The Politics of Constitutional Reform in Post-Coup Fiji*. Canberra: Asia Pacific Press.

Manueli, Paul. 1989. *Report of the Fiji Constitution Inquiry and Advisory Committee,* Suva: Fiji Constitution Inquiry and Advisory Committee, August.

Mara, Kamisese. 1997. *The Pacific Way: A Memoir*. Honolulu: University of Hawai'i Press.

Miller, Laurel E. with Louis Aucoin (eds). 2010. *Framing the State in Times of Transition: Case Studies in Constitution Making*. Washington, DC: United States Institute of Peace.

National Council for Building a Better Fiji (NCBBF). 2008. Online: www.pidp.org/pireport/special/draftcharter.pdf (accessed 24 January 2017).

Pacific Islands Development Program website. Online: www.pidp.org/pireport/special/draftcharter.pdf (accessed 24 January 2017).

Parliament of Fiji. 1997. Report of the Joint Parliamentary Select Committee on the Report of the Fiji Constitution Review Commission. Parl. Paper No. 17.

Reeves, Paul, Tomasi Vakatora and Brij V. Lal. 1996. *Towards A United Future: Report of the Fiji Constitution Review Commission*. Suva: Government Printer (Parliamentary Paper No. 34 of 1996, Parliament of Fiji).

Cases

In re the Constitution, Reference by HE the President (Dissenting Judgment) [2002] FJSC 3; MISC 001.2001S (Justice Amet).

In re the Constitution, Reference by HE the President [2002] FJSC 1; MISC 001.2001S (15 March 2002).

In re the President's Reference, Qarase v. Chaudhry—Decision of the Court [2004] FJSC 1; MISC 001.2003 (9 July 2004).

In re the President's Reference, Qarase v. Chaudhry—Dissenting Judgment [2004] FJSC 9; MISC 001.2003s.

President of Fiji Islands v. Kubuabola [1999] FJSC 8, Misc. Case No. 1 of 1999 (3 Sept. 1999).

Qarase v. Chaudhry [2003] FJSC 1.

10

The Fiji Election of 2014: Rights, Representation and Legitimacy in Fiji Politics[1]

Stewart Firth

In his message to the nation on Fiji Day, 10 October 2014, President Ratu Epeli Nailatikau saw recent events as holding great hope for the future. He talked of 1987 as the 'beginning of a cycle of instability, division and hatred—four disruptions to parliamentary rule, a rebellion in the military and in 2000, the detention of our elected representatives for 56 days'. History had now come full circle, he said, as the new members of parliament 'gathered in precisely the same place where the first coup happened 28 years ago', and as the nation finally put this era behind it (Fiji Day Message 2014). This chapter explores three recurring themes in the history of Fiji's politics and in the light of the recent election: rights, representation and legitimacy, all of which have recurred in Brij Lal's writings. They have all been contested and the contest over them has been at the heart of that country's political misfortunes.

Rights are moral claims, and the circumstances of Fiji's colonial situation, where an indigenous population kept its land and culture and an immigrant population sought a recognised place in society, made rights

---

1 Republished with permission from *The Round Table: The Commonwealth Journal of International Affairs*, 104(2) (2015): 101–12. DOI:10.1080/00358533.2015.1017254.

a central political issue. The moral claim of the Fijians was based on their prior occupation of the Fiji Islands, stretching back thousands of years, and the moral claim of the Indians was based on their presence, as individuals, in a polity with roots in British liberalism and its philosophy of equal citizenship. Where the Fijians claimed group rights, the Indians claimed individual rights, while the British—seeking to maintain their own predominant position—steered a pragmatic course that mostly ended up on the Fijian side of the argument. The debate did not end with independence in 1970. On the contrary, independence opened the way for a continuing contest over rights in Fiji, one that took the country from democracy to a series of coups—two in 1987 and another in 2000—that were justified by an appeal to the primacy of the group rights of the original inhabitants of the country.

The debate over rights in colonial Fiji quickly became one about representation, which in the 1920s and 1930s meant representation in the colony's only parliamentary body, the Legislative Council, and which was later to mean representation in the parliament of an independent Fiji. The Fijians, their Europeans and Indians of Muslim faith favoured group representation that would be achieved by means of communal voting rolls, in which the qualification for candidates and voters would be based on ethnic or religious identity; most Indians of the Hindu faith (and they were the overwhelming majority) favoured instead the kind of representation that existed in liberal democracies, where ethnic and religious identity was irrelevant in qualifying candidates to stand and electors to vote, and where all that mattered was status as a British subject. Legitimacy is the third theme in Fiji's political history. Legitimacy, it has been argued, 'is the quality that transforms naked power into rightful authority; it confers upon an order or command an authoritative or binding character, ensuring that it is obeyed out of duty rather than because of fear' (Heywood 1999: 141). Nothing matters more to a government than the acceptance of citizens that it has a right to govern them. That right has different origins, however, in different cultural circumstances. In the precolonial chiefly societies of Polynesia and Fiji, leaders established their legitimacy by birthright and by demonstrating their descent from high-ranking ancestors. They were societies in which genealogies mattered a great deal because they were the keys to power, authority and resources. In the western liberal tradition to which Fiji was also heir, the legitimacy of a leader is said to derive from successful performance of the legal requirements to achieve leadership, that is, from winning an election conducted under law and according to the constitution. The issue is not one of majorities or voting systems. What matters is adherence to the legal rules whatever they may be. In Fiji's political history, both kinds of legitimacy, traditional and modern, have been at stake in the fate of governments, and there has been a constant tension between them.

On 19 May 2000, the day when armed men took control in Suva and overthrew the government, they erected a sign outside the parliament at Veiuto. It read: 'Be Warned Chaudhry: Fiji Indigenous Rights are Paramount in Fiji. We Will Fight to Uphold Them'. The phrase 'indigenous rights' became a constant drumbeat in Fiji over the next few months, especially from the coup leader George Speight himself. After parleying with Speight, the army arrested him and hundreds of his followers in the raid on Kalabu Fijian School.

Yet even with Speight out of the way, the mobilising power of 'indigenous rights' remained, as became evident when rebel soldiers mutinied at the Queen Elizabeth Barracks in November 2000 with the aim of doing what Speight had failed to do: establish a Matanitu Vanua (indigenous Fijian government) dominated by Bauan chiefs, with Ratu Jope Seniloli as president and (probably) Adi Samanunu Cakobau as prime minister. The rebellion was put down, Army Commander Commodore Frank Bainimarama avoided assassination, and within a year Fiji had returned to democracy following an election in August 2001. The election, however, returned a government that stood for advancing 'indigenous rights', and that operated in coalition with members of the Conservative Alliance-Matanitu Vanua (CAMV), who were even more committed to that cause than the government. The government of Fiji should be in the hands of Fijians and their chiefs, CAMV declared, and land that Fijians had lost should be returned to them (Tuitoga 2007: 209).

The outsider who did not know Fiji might have been forgiven for imagining that this was another case of colonial dispossession that had left an indigenous people on the margins of society. The appeal to 'indigenous rights' suggested this was the case, because the discourse of such rights had its origins in the situation of indigenous people in settler societies such as the United States, Canada, Australia and New Zealand, where recompense for past wrongs committed by the settler population has been incorporated into law and become part of a common understanding of national history. The idea of special rights that belong only to the descendants of Fiji's original occupiers is one that continues to exercise a strong hold over the imaginations of a minority who see the United Nations Declaration on the Rights of Indigenous Peoples of 2007 as guaranteeing them a form of self-determination entrenching indigenous dominance. Some Fijians like to think of themselves as members of a small and unique indigenous group whose very survival is at stake in the governing arrangements of their country.

Reality

The reality is very different. The British did not dispossess them of their land during the colonial period, 1874–1970, in fact quite the opposite. The aim of Fiji's land ordinance of 1880, in the words of the governor Sir Arthur Gordon, was 'to make the alienation of native land as difficult as possible' (Newbury 2010: 103); and the ordinance and its successors had that effect over the long-term, ensuring that indigenous Fijians would enter the twenty-first century with as much land (more than 83 per cent) as they had owned 100 years before. As for participation in government, indigenous Fijians held a dominant position in the governing affairs of their country after independence in 1970, with only a short interregnum between the election of an Indo-Fijian, Mahendra Chaudhry, as prime minister in May 1999 and his forcible removal by Speight's nationalists a year later. Thereafter the pattern resumed, with first an elected indigenous prime minister, and then, after the coup of 2006, an unelected one.

In the whole history of independent Fiji, the head of government has been indigenous 97 per cent of the time, and the military forces, which have played a central role in politics, have remained overwhelmingly indigenous in composition. As the Ghai Constitution Commission (see Ghai this volume) put it in 2012:

> The origins of indigenous peoples' rights lie in their status as a minority, subjected to discrimination, politically vulnerable, with their culture under threat. It is not obvious that indigenous people would be entitled to special rights if they were a majority, in control of the state, and owners of 90 per cent of the land (Constitution Commission 2012: 16).

The political context of the appeal to 'indigenous rights' in Fiji, then, is different from the expected one. Group rights, it has been pointed out, 'are often articulated as demands for group freedom, but they are also feared as vehicles for group oppression' (Jones 1999: 354). As indigenous Fijian youths rampaged through parts of Tailevu in August 2000, throwing petrol bombs into the homes of Indian farmers and threatening them with knives and garden forks, it seemed that such 'rights' in the Fijian setting were little more than excuses for thuggery against people of another race and a means by which unemployed, alienated young men from the villages could revel in a sense of power.

Rights have been contentious in Fiji's modern history. Against the group rights claimed by Fijians, the newcomers could counterpose another set. In acquiring Fiji through a Deed of Cession, the British recognised that the original occupiers of the land held rights over it by virtue of prior possession. Cakobau and the other chiefs who agreed to cede the possession, dominion and sovereignty of Fiji to Queen Victoria could not have done so, after all, if they were not deemed to have held dominion and sovereignty in the first place. Assuming control of the new British colony, Governor Sir Arthur Gordon told disappointed white settlers that the circumstances of Fiji's cession prevented it from becoming a white man's colony, and for the next 96 years of colonial administration, the British would see in the cession a promise of protection owed to the indigenous people of Fiji. The British did not use the term 'indigenous rights' but they acted as if such rights existed, and believed that the Deed of Cession had imposed upon them responsibilities of trusteeship towards the indigenous people of Fiji. In the negotiations over independence in the 1960s, their preferred outcome, as Brij Lal wrote, was 'Fijian leaders, in control, taking Fiji into independence' (Lal 2006a: lxxiv).

The Deed of Cession came to assume symbolic significance for indigenous Fijians, too. Many saw it as a charter guaranteeing Fijian paramountcy. When Sitiveni Rabuka seized power in 1987 he revived the old claim, cherished by Fijian nationalists, that independence should have been a literal reversal of the Deed of Cession, returning the country not to all the people of Fiji but to the Fijians alone:

> The Fijians felt that their land should have been handed back to the chiefs who, in good faith, ceded the islands to Queen Victoria for her to protect. So far as the Fijian people are concerned, this is the missing link—the handing back of their beloved country to them, and not to the strangers who, in the course of time, would decide the Fijians' fate in their own country (Tagupa 1991: 142).

This interpretation of the Deed of Cession sustained the hopes of the nationalists for decades, and appeared again in the rhetoric of 2000, but had no historical substance. As Ratu William Toganivalu said in 1970, 'there was nothing in the Deed of Cession to say that when England was to hand over Fiji that it was to hand it over holus-bolus to the Fijian people alone' (Tagupa 1991: 142, 145).

What about the people who had migrated in large numbers from the Indian subcontinent to work on the plantations of Fiji? What rights did they have as settlers and the descendants of settlers born in a new land? This was the question that exercised the leaders of the Indian community from the 1920s onwards, and their answer was to appeal to the rights of British subjects. The Indian leaders of that period were influenced not only by the movement for independence in India itself, but also by the fate of Indians in other parts of the British Empire, which was seen as responsible for their personal humiliation and that of a great civilisation.

Representation

Indian leaders such as Vishnu Deo and S.B. Patel took their lead from the Indian National Congress, and saw local events as part of a wider struggle taking place in countries as far away as Kenya, where, as in Fiji, Europeans were resisting Indian claims to equal treatment. The question of the rights of Indians in British colonies, moreover, immediately raised the issue of their political representation; hence the attachment of the Indian leaders to the principle of the common voting roll, drawn up irrespective of race, in elections to the Legislative Council. In their view, British subjects in Fiji should all be on the same voting roll, not divided into separate rolls according to racial identity. That is why, when election of Indians to the Legislative Council was introduced in 1929, the three who were elected decided upon a plan of action even before its first meeting. They would move a motion proclaiming that political rights along racial lines were unacceptable, demand that Indians be given a common franchise with other British subjects in Fiji, enumerate Indian grievances in detail, and then resign.

When they did so, they were heroes in India—Gandhi himself congratulated them for their patriotism—but suspect in Fiji. Governor Sir Murchison Fletcher saw Fiji Indian politicians of this kind as 'the uninformed tool of an extraneous organization which is dangerously seeking opportunity to use the Colony for the purposes of its world-wide attack upon the British Raj' (Gillion 1977: 140–41), and their dramatic resignation merely confirmed the Fiji government's view that communal voting should remain. Fletcher explained his reasoning to the Legislative Council in 1933:

> There is an essential difference between this Colony and a country such as England or Australia that Fiji lacks the homogeneity of race and racial sentiment which is ordinarily found elsewhere [sic]. In Fiji there are three principal groups, European, Fijian and Indian, each having an independence of outlook which it will not willingly surrender or merge, and the Europeans and Fijians have emphatically refused to subordinate their separate interests to that Indian preponderance which would in their belief eventuate, if the Indian request for a common roll for the Legislative Council were granted (Fletcher 1933).

In the 1936 constitutional reform, which remained in essence until 1963, the three elected Indian members of the Legislative Council continued to be chosen by voters in communal constituencies. Resignation and boycotts, meantime, became characteristic of the way Fiji Indians interacted with the emerging representative institutions of Fiji in the years before independence. In a deeply divided society, political styles diverged. Where Fiji Indian leaders were blunt and outspoken in their demands the indigenous Fijian leaders were deft and polite, concealing as much as they revealed, yet quietly determined to maintain their position.

In some ways, Fijian society remained static until well after the mid-twentieth century, with commoners subjected to a chiefly order that had the full backing of the British colonial administration, though we should remember that Fijians were already beginning to live away from their villages. The chiefs were the principal beneficiaries of the British presence. They stood at the apex of an indigenous hierarchy, and their powers over commoners were enshrined in law. Commoner Fijians engaged in repeated acts of resistance against the government in the early decades of the colonial period, and were never as satisfied with their subordinate position in an aristocratic society as the British and the chiefs liked to think. As Robert Nicole has pointed out, the accepted version of Fiji's history—the one found in landmarks, celebrations and school texts—elevates Ratu Sir Lala Sukuna to the status of a national hero, while little is ever heard of Apolosi Nawai, who captured the imagination of thousands of commoner Fijians in the early decades of the twentieth century with his vision of a Viti Company that would bypass the stranglehold held by Europeans on the copra trade (Nicole 2011: 97). Commoners never completely reconciled themselves to chiefly dominance. Writing of Deuba village in the mid-1940s, anthropologist William Geddes said people resented having to leave their own gardens to undertake communal work for the *roko*, the women complained about the work involved in preparing mats and food for chiefly ceremonies, and the preference shown to chiefs in being given government and army jobs was a source of widespread grievance (Geddes 1945: 88). At the same time, commoners invariably showed deference towards chiefs in their presence. 'Ambivalence' is the word that best captures this characteristically Fijian attitude, which was a mixture of resentment and respect. To be 'Fijian' was to assert a strong and distinctive identity that justified claims to paramountcy in a divided society and gave access to resources, above all, land. But to be 'Fijian', despite the unifying effect of this identity on the entire indigenous population, was not to be part of an undifferentiated group of people who all thought the same way. As many have pointed out, the idea of a single *iTaukei* identity papered over deep divisions in the Fijian community, and delivered power to the chiefly class who spoke in the name of all their compatriots. The assumption behind the representation of communities that inspired the idea of communal constituencies was that cultural identity came first and individual interests second, and that chiefs were in the best position to represent all Fijians.

The communalism of village life was supposed to be reflected in the communalism of Fijian political representation, and until 1963 Fijians did not vote at all. Instead, they were represented in the Legislative Council by five nominees of the governor acting on the advice of the Great Council of Chiefs. For Fiji's greatest chief, Ratu Sir Lala Sukuna, representation of this kind was the only kind compatible with Fijian tradition. He considered democracy un-Fijian and thought Fijians would never understand a system based on the counting of heads. Sukuna died in 1958, and by then the forces of modernity and individualism were rendering outmoded his vision of a people bound by obedience to chiefs and unquestioning attachment to the vanua.

Representation was the key to power, and was therefore a central issue in the negotiations over independence that gathered pace from 1965. In his final dispatch before independence, the last governor, Sir Robert Foster, concluded that a 'calm search for a just solution to the problem of representation proved virtually impossible: feelings ran too deep' (Lal 2006a: 517). On the Indian side, A.D. Patel stuck to his advocacy of a common roll as a matter of principle. At the Marlborough House conference in 1965, the Indian group led by Patel submitted that a communal role stood for divided loyalties, would magnify communal differences and would stand in the way of parliamentary democracy; in short, it should be abolished. The only solution for Fiji was a common roll, as he told voters in the Sigatoka Valley during the 1966 election campaign:

> We have to bring everyone together and the only way to do that is by means of common roll. We can no longer think along the lines that we are Fijians, we are Indians, we are Europeans or Chinese. We must think of ourselves as citizens of Fiji, that we are nationals of Fiji (Patel 25 September 1966, cited in Lal 2011: 94).

The Fijians led by Ratu Mara held precisely the opposite view, for 'the great Fijian fear was that a Common Roll Legislature would change the law on land and deprive them of their security of ownership', as he told Trafford Smith of the Commonwealth Office. The Fijians were not convinced 'that written safeguards against such action would be adequate' (Lal 2006a: 207). Fijian fears on this score were heightened by the demographic facts. By the mid-1960s, the Indian population was 51 per cent of the country's population and the Fijian 41 per cent, suggesting that any voting system based on numbers alone would deliver a permanent majority to the Indians. A supporting assumption—that most people would vote for candidates of their own race—seemed to be borne out by the victories of the Federation Party in the by-elections of 1968, and likely anyway in the social circumstances of Fiji. Whatever the democratic merits of A.D. Patel's argument, and they were considerable, the Fijians saw the common roll as a road to disaster and would not countenance it as the basis for entering independence. In this insistence they had the support of the British government, whose policy after the 1965 conference was to recognise 'that election on a straight common roll basis was not practicable for Fiji until a greater degree of integration of the Co [colony's] communities had been achieved', the position that remained when the British cabinet accepted independence for Fiji in 1970 (Stewart 1970).

The death of A.D. Patel in 1969 removed Fiji's most able proponent of a common roll from the Indian political leadership. According to Governor Foster, Patel's successor Siddiq Koya was 'a plump little lawyer, full of intrigue and calculation, who wears the mask of amiable geniality which occasionally slips to reveal the hatchet man beneath'. A 'wheeler-dealer if ever there was one', wrote Foster, 'he probably has no basic principles' (Foster 1970). The consequence was a change in the political atmosphere, with Koya more willing to compromise with Mara in the interest of achieving independence, and making the key concession that deferred consideration of a common roll for five years, when it was to be the subject of a Royal Commission. Once that time came and the Street Commission recommended 25 open seats to operate alongside communal seats, Mara was able to dismiss its proposals as a threat to the peace of the country.

Institutionalisation of race

Race was institutionalised in the post-independence politics of Fiji, which entered independence in 1970 with a constitution that preserved communal representation and indigenous rights. In the lower house all 52 seats were reserved for one racial group or another, Fijian, Indian and 'General'. Twenty-five were filled by a system of election called 'cross-voting', which specified the race of the candidate while allowing everyone to vote; and 27 were filled by communal voting, which specified the race of both candidates and voters.

Democracy lasted for as long as the Alliance Party won elections, but in 1987 the elections were won by a coalition consisting of the National Federation Party (NFP) and the new Fiji Labour Party, with a Fijian prime minister, Timoci Bavadra, and a cabinet consisting of both indigenous Fijians and Indo-Fijians. That was too much for Rabuka, who staged Fiji's first coup in order to overthrow what he called an 'Indian-dominated' government, plunging his country into the first of its periods of military government. Later that year, he issued a decree requiring 'that a new Constitution replace the Constitution under which [the people of Fiji] attained independence on 10th October 1970' (Declaration—Republic of Fiji Decree 1987, No. 8, 1(a), reproduced in Lal 1988: opposite page 118). Fiji's second constitution, promulgated in 1990, abolished cross-voting and strengthened communal voting. The paramountcy of the indigenous Fijians was to be maintained in the crudest of ways, by giving 37 of parliament's 70 seats to Fijians, with 48 per cent of the population, and only 27 to Indo-Fijians, whose numbers had dropped but still amounted to 46 per cent. By various other stratagems, the votes of urban Fijians counted for much less than those from rural areas. Justifying a constitution extraordinarily skewed to the advantage of Fijians, President Ratu Sir Penaia Ganilau called it 'a continuation, and enlargement, of an idea which has become an established part of our power-sharing arrangements' (cited in Lal 1992: 327), an argument that failed to convince the Indo-Fijian community, for whom it was both an insult and an imposition. Internationally, too, Fiji's 1990 constitution was widely condemned.

The 1990 constitution provided for its own review within seven years. Well before then, Rabuka, now the elected prime minister, appointed a Constitution Reform Commission. He was driven by considerations of political survival. Fiji had not done well since the 1987 coup. Almost 66,000 people left Fiji permanently between 1987 and 1994, most of them Indo-Fijian, and in the process they deprived the country of some of its best and most skilled citizens, leaving behind an economy in decline. By the mid-1990s, politicians on all sides recognised that Fiji needed a constitution that would restore its place in the international community and revive the country's economic fortunes. In the commission, the Fiji-born academic Brij Lal sat alongside the former New Zealand Governor-General Sir Paul Reeves and former minister and speaker of the Fiji House of Representatives Tomasi Vakatora. They confronted in the most tangible way the urgency of finding a constitutional solution that would take account of 'the rights, interests and concerns of all ethnic groups' (Lal 2006b: 129).

The outcome of their deliberations was the 1997 constitution. The Fiji parliament accepted much of what the commissioners proposed but, on the key issue of representation, reversed their recommendation. The Commissioners suggested that, in a parliament of 71 seats, there should be 46 open seats and 25 communal; the government decided on 46 communal seats and 25 open. The difference was significant. It meant that communal representation remained the central and defining characteristic of Fiji's electoral system with an experiment in a common roll now added, rather than the opposite. The 1997 constitution also provided for something else the commission had not recommended—power-sharing—but it was only in 2006, and then only for a few months, that a Fiji government included opposition members in its cabinet as the power-sharing provision required.

In any case, the military commander Frank Bainimarama soon led his troops to a coup that replaced representation with intervention. The attempts of the representative leaders of Fiji to rein in the military proved futile, and the government of Laisenia Qarase, elected in 2001 and again in 2006, became ineffectual. Talk of the government disciplining the military commander for his open opposition never led to action, and an emboldened commander finally acted on the logic of his situation. He despised the elected government; he had the guns, so he overthrew it. Bainimarama depicted his 2006 coup as a courageous act of constitutionalism aimed at saving the people of Fiji from destruction at the hands of the elected government. Extraordinarily, he claimed to have done nothing illegal or unconstitutional:

> The Republic of Fiji Military Force could have carried out unconstitutional and illegal activities, but had not done so and will not do so. It believes in the rule of law and shall adhere to the Constitution. It not only adheres to the rule of law and Constitution, but more importantly believes in adherence to the spirit of the law and the Constitution (*Fijilive*, 5 December 2006).

Bainimarama abandoned this pretence of legality within three years. In April 2009, acting through a senile president who was unaware of what was happening, he abrogated the constitution, declared a state of emergency, deported foreign journalists, censored the media, brought the legal profession under direct government control and sacked, among others, the Ombudsman, Supervisor of Elections, Auditor-General, Director of Public Prosecutions, the Governor of the Reserve Bank and the Commissioner of Police. In the process, Bainimarama created a new and unprecedented political atmosphere, in which criticism of the government became treasonous. Together with Attorney-General Aiyaz Sayed-Khaiyum, Bainimarama governed Fiji under a state of emergency for the next three years, as they issued a succession of decrees that were the antithesis of legislation in a system of parliamentary representation.

Yet the problem of representation in a future Fiji remained. Like all military rulers, Bainimarama discovered he could not rule by decree forever. He began a cautious liberalisation in early 2012, and appointed a Constitution Reform Commission, led by constitutional expert Yash Ghai. The commission was instructed to break with Fiji's long history of race-based, single-member constituency electoral systems. Any new constitution would have to include provisions for: one person, one vote, one value; the elimination of ethnic voting; and proportional representation. As it happened, the Bainimarama government spurned Ghai's draft constitution and came up with one of its own, the 2013 constitution that is now the law of Fiji. The new constitution—Fiji's fourth since independence—stipulates that the 50 members of parliament will be elected by proportional representation with the proviso that 'a political party or an independent candidate shall not qualify for any seat in Parliament' unless they receive at least at least 5 per cent of the votes (Constitution of the Republic of Fiji, 2013, section 53(3)). In the 2014 elections, this system delivered a clear victory for Bainimarama and his Fiji First Party, which gained 59.2 per cent of the vote, with SODELPA (Social Democratic Liberal Party) winning 28.2 per cent and the NFP 5.5 per cent. The independents and other parties, including the once-mighty Fiji Labour Party, failed to clear the 5 per cent hurdle and are not in the new parliament.

Legitimacy

As much as it is a story of rights and representation, the journey taken by Fiji since independence is one in which legitimacy plays a key part. High chiefly rank remained a qualification for important government or military office in Fiji throughout the British colonial period and is only now beginning to lose its significance. The brilliantly talented Fijian commoner Rusiate Nayacakalou was thought to be almost a genius by his headmaster at Suva Methodist Boys' School in the 1940s, but the Great Council of Chiefs would not award him a scholarship to study in New Zealand because he was not of chiefly rank. Other commoners suffered similar fates.

A bright boy of chiefly rank, on the other hand, found all doors were open. Such was the case for Ratu Mara, who inherited the title of Tui Nayau from his father and married one of Fiji's highest-ranking chiefs, Adi Lala Mara. As the paramount chiefly head of the Burebasaga Confederacy, she held the title of Roko Tui Dreketi, and as Mara's wife was Radi Ni Nayau. Identified early as a promising future leader, Mara was educated at Otago University, Oxford, and the London School of Economics, and groomed for leadership by both his chiefly peers and British colonial officials. Sir Robert Foster, the last governor, found Mara a dignified aristocrat who inspired 'awe rather than confidence' and was given to 'a dictatorial arrogance which does not make him easy to work with', a man who 'believes (without being anti-Indian) that Fijian paramountcy is proper and natural' (Foster 1970). These characteristics were not always seen as negatives by the British, though, who thought he was the best person to take Fiji into independence. Of high rank by birth,

Ratu Mara also possessed a modern kind of legitimacy, as the country's chief minister under self-government in the 1960s and its first prime minister, elected according to law under the constitution of 1970.

The key point in his favour, as far as the British were concerned, was that Mara embodied both forms of legitimacy, and both would assist in conferring upon his commands, and those of his government, 'an authoritative or binding character' (Heywood 1999: 141). He would, they hoped, bring stability to the country. And for a while he did. Mara lasted longest as a political leader, both as prime minister and president, because he combined traditional and modern forms of legitimacy, but his successors encountered endless difficulties. Ideas of indigenous rights and Fijian paramountcy, after all, suggested the existence of claims to authority that were prior to any that might arise from being elected. From the point of view of group rights, the result of an election was only one consideration in determining who the government should be; another might override it in the service of a greater interest, as both Rabuka and Speight claimed when they took over parliament by force and declared themselves to be in charge. In effect, they declared the elected governments of Bavadra and Chaudhry illegitimate because, in their view, they failed to meet the test of protecting indigenous rights.

Bainimarama's 2006 coup was different. By his actions he was declaring an elected government illegitimate, but on different grounds, namely that it was corrupt and that a thorough clean-up was needed for the sake of the country. This approach extended the justification for armed takeovers beyond the issue of rights into the terrain of government performance: if a government was not performing well, it deserved to be overthrown by force. And, as happened in 2009, if the courts were thought to be wrong in reaching a judgement, they should be ignored and the constitution abrogated.

Conclusion

For the moment stability has come to Fiji. Has Bainimarama cut through the Gordian knot of rights, representation and legitimacy and finally set Fiji on a genuinely democratic path? The appeal of indigenous rights, revived by SODELPA in the election, seems weaker than ever, especially to younger Fijians. The common roll has triumphed at last, but more than 40 years after independence and in a political atmosphere that, at least in the person of Bainimarama, lacks the respect for representative institutions that once characterised Fiji's leaders and their debate over the country's electoral arrangements. The final release of the auditor-general's reports has revealed overspending by the Fiji military forces in the years following the 2006 coup. These shortfalls are unlikely to be made good by the new government, which is not disposed to admitting mistakes (*Pacific Beat*, 22 October 2014). As for legitimacy, Bainimarama is inclined to see parliament as the instrument of his continued domination of Fiji's affairs, useful but in the end dispensable.

When Ratu Mara died in 2004, a state funeral service was held in Albert Park before a gun carriage bore his body through the streets of Suva on its way to the wharf, where it travelled by sea to his birthplace in the Lau Islands. As the gun carriage passed, heads were bowed and a hush fell over the entire crowd, children as much as adults, in mute testimony to the respect he inspired. Looking back, that day seems to have been a turning point in the history of Fiji, more so than we realised at the time. Within less than three years, the government would be in the hands of a military leader who had little time for the old Fiji of aristocratic privilege, the Great Council of Chiefs and the Methodist Church, and who would deal telling blows to each of them during his years as self-appointed prime minister.

In a formal sense, the Fiji of Mara and the chiefly order has gone forever. Yet a new kind of chief has arisen in the person of Frank Bainimarama, whose election campaign made much of his personal achievements as Fiji's leader. His legitimacy is modern and charismatic rather than traditional, and his personal vote of 202,459 votes—far more than that for any other candidate—shows his cult of the leader has widespread support. Bainimarama is the foundation stone of the current political order and has rendered himself indispensable to Fiji's current stability. The corollary is that Fiji's stability may not endure after he leaves the scene.

Acknowledgement

The author thanks Dr Colin Newbury, Linacre College, Oxford University, for his perceptive comments on a draft of this chapter.

References

Constitution Commission (The). 2012. Draft Constitution: the Explanatory Report. Suva. Online: resources.news.com.au/files/2013/01/07/1226549/110668-aus-world-file-fiji-draft-constitution-explanatory-note.pdf (accessed 16 November 2016).

Constitution of the Republic of Fiji. 2013. Online: www.paclii.org/fj/Fiji-Constitution-English-2013.pdf (accessed 16 November 2016).

Declaration—Republic of Fiji Decree 1987, No. 8, 1(a). Reproduced in Brij V. Lal. 1988. *Power and Prejudice: The Making of the Fiji Crisis*. Wellington: New Zealand Institute of International Affairs.

Fiji Day Message by H.E. The President, 2014: 10 October. Online: fiji.gov.fj/Media-Center/Speeches/2014-FIJI-DAY-MESSAGE-BY-H-E-THE-PRESIDENT.aspx (accessed 10 October 2014).

Fijilive. 2006. 'Army chief defends take over'. *Fijilive*. 5 December.

Fletcher, Murchison. 1933. 'Address by His Excellency the Governor, 13 October'. *Journal of the Legislative Council (Fiji)*. Suva: Command Paper no. 30.

Foster, Sir Robert. 1970. 'Fiji: final despatch before independence': despatch from Sir R Foster to Sir A Douglas-Home, 8 October. In *British Documents on the End of Empire, Series B, Volume 10: Fiji*, edited by Brij V. Lal, p. 514. London: The Stationery Office.

Geddes, W.R. 1945. *Deuba: A Study of a Fijian Village*. Wellington: The Polynesian Society.

Gillion, K.L. 1977. *The Fiji Indians: Challenge to European Dominance, 1920–1946*. Canberra: The Australian National University Press.

Heywood, Andrew. 1999. *Political Theory: An Introduction*, 2nd ed. New York: St Martin's Press.

Jones, Peter. 1999. 'Group rights and group oppression'. *Journal of Political Philosophy*, 7(4): 353–77. DOI: 10.1111/1467-9760.00081

Lal, Brij V. 1992. *Broken Waves: A History of the Fiji Islands in the Twentieth Century*. Honolulu: University of Hawai'i Press.

———. 2006a. 'Introduction.' In *British Documents on the End of Empire, Series B, Volume 10: Fiji*, pp. xxxv–lxxvii. London: The Stationery Office.

———. 2006b. *Islands of Turmoil: Elections and Politics in Fiji*. Canberra: Asia Pacific Press.

Lal, Brij V. (ed.). 2006. *British Documents on the End of Empire, Series B, Volume 10: Fiji*. London: The Stationery Office.

———. (ed.). 2011. *A Vision for Change: Speeches and Writings of AD Patel, 1929–1969*. Canberra: ANU E Press.

Newbury, Colin. 2010. *Patronage and Politics in the Victorian Empire: The Personal Governance of Sir Arthur Hamilton Gordon (Lord Stanmore)*. Amherst, MA: Cambria Press.

Nicole, Robert. 2011. *Disturbing History: Resistance in Early Colonial Fiji*. Honolulu: University of Hawai'i Press.

Pacific Beat. 2014. '2007 audit shows military overspend'. *Pacific Beat*. Radio Australia, Fiji, 22 October.

Stewart, M.M. 1970. 'Fiji independence': memorandum by Mr Stewart for Cabinet Defence and Oversea Policy Committee, 8 January. In *British Documents on the End of Empire, Series B, Volume 10: Fiji*, edited by Brij V. Lal, p. 435. London: The Stationery Office.

Tagupa, W.E.H. 1991. 'The unanticipated Republic of Fiji: The Deed of Cession as the constitutional basis of legitimacy'. In *Sovereignty and Indigenous Rights: The Treaty of Waitangi in International Contexts*, edited by William Renwick, 135–46. Wellington: Victoria University Press.

Tuitoga, Anare. 2007. 'Tailevu North: Five years down the line'. In *From Election to Coup in Fiji: The 2006 Campaign and its Aftermath*, edited by Jon Fraenkel and Stewart Firth, pp. 204–212. Canberra: ANU E Press. Online: press-files.anu.edu.au/downloads/press/p54581/pdf/ch152.pdf (accessed 11 January 2017).

Family Album

Figure 2. Brij and Padma with granddaughter Maya Lal-Parks
Source: Photographed by Yogi Lal-Parks, 15 May 2016, and reproduced with her permission and the permission of the subjects.

Figure 3. Three generations. From left to right: Brij Lal, Yogi Lal-Parks, Jayan Kenneth Lal-Parks (in front), Christopher Lal-Parks, Maya June Lal-Parks (in pram), Padma Lal, Niraj Lal, Sally Cunningham and Ash Arjun Lal Cunningham (in the baby wrap)

Source: Taken at the foot of the Sydney Opera House by a passing individual, January 2016, and reproduced with the subjects' permissions.

FAMILY ALBUM

Figure 4. Family group: Yogi, Jayan (in front), Brij, Padma, Niraj
Source: Taken in Canberra after Brij's investiture by a passing individual,
18 September 2015, and reproduced with the subjects' permissions.

Figure 5. Brij and Padma after the investiture
Source: Taken at the shores of Lake Burley Griffith, Canberra by Yogi Lal-Parks, 18 September 2015, and reproduced with her and the subjects' permissions.

Literature

11

Unfettering the Mind: Imagination, Creative Writing and the Art of the Historian

Tessa Morris-Suzuki

A cry in the night

> It was perhaps an hour later, or perhaps the following night, that I was once more wakened by the stammer of a tugboat's engine, and now I seemed to hear beneath it a troubled, human cry. This time it was futile to hold the bedclothes against my ears; I could not escape a sense of responsibility (Hutchinson 1969: 9).

Those are the opening words of a novel that has lurked in the depths of my consciousness ever since I first read it as an undergraduate around the start of the 1970s. In some quiet way, it has shaped my understanding of history, and now as I approach the end of my university career, still struggling with questions of historical justice and responsibility, I have found myself returning to it and rereading it, each time discovering something new in its pages. It provides, I think, a good starting point for some reflections about works that bring together the art of creative writing and the craft of the historian.

The novel, *Johanna at Daybreak*, was written by British author Ray Coryton Hutchinson (1907–1975) and published in 1969. Today it is little known and rarely read. Hutchinson's early work earned much praise, and his posthumously published novel *Rising* was listed for the Booker Prize, but his books somehow fell out of fashion and into an obscurity that is only occasionally lifted as, here and there, a contemporary reader rediscovers his writings (Green 1985). In a recent blog, the novelist Peter Hobbs writes:

> I've always found it strange how the reputations of so many writers have very little to do with the quality of their work. It can take many decades before there's a levelling out or reappraisal. In the short and medium terms weak writers may be lauded, and great writers forgotten. R.C. Hutchinson seems to have been in the latter category—he's almost unknown amongst writers of my generation or younger … Great writing is often far from where the publishing noise is, and where the headlines are, and sometimes it can get lost for a while. But it tends to find its way, at least to people who care for it.[1]

The obscurity is understandable. The 1950s and 1960s were decades of social realism in British literature, when the literary prize lists were dominated by the Kingsley Amises, Angus Wilsons and Margaret Drabbles of the world. But through these decades, R.C. Hutchinson went on doing as he had always done: writing novels on vast, sprawling Dostoyevskian themes of life and death, evil and remorse, faith, redemption and revolution. Many of his works are set in places far from the English Home Counties where he lived. His stories unfold in the foggy backstreets of wartime Germany, the steppes of revolutionary Russia and the guerrilla hideouts of Latin America. Hutchinson reaches boldly for the great metaphysical questions of life, and sometimes falls short—slipping into passages of prose that are overheated, overlong or overburdened with religious imagery. But when his work succeeds, it succeeds magnificently. At its best, his writing has that power peculiar to the creative arts. It can change the way you see the world.

In the opening pages of *Johanna at Daybreak*, Hutchinson drags his readers out of their comfortable chairs and transports them, without explanation or apology, into a bleak and dreamlike place that proves to be a refuge for displaced persons set in the chaos of the Netherlands just after the end

---

1 'Peter Hobbs hails R.C. Hutchinson and his "brave, compassionate, moral" novel "A Child Possessed"'. *Faber and Faber*, 22 April 2013. Online: faberfindsblog.co.uk/peter-hobbs-hails-r-c-hutchinson-and-his-brave-compassionate-moral-novel-a-child-possessed/ (accessed 17 November 2016).

of World War II. More disconcertingly still, his first-person narrative takes the reader inside the mind of Johanna Schechter, a German woman who has lost her memory.

Over the past two decades or so, questions of memory, commemoration, trauma and historical responsibility have become staples of historical research and the subjects of countless books, articles and conferences. Whole research institutes are devoted to these themes. But when *Johanna at Daybreak* was published, few historians had yet ventured into the labyrinthine realms of memory. Hutchinson is adventurous in his choice of topics; and his novels, like much good creative writing, reach into dimensions of history that often escape the more sober and constricted prose of the academic historian.

For Johanna, memory loss is a refuge, but an insecure one. The past keeps threatening to seep through cracks in her amnesia, just as in Michael Hanneke's haunting film *Caché* (Hidden) (2005) it seeps up through the cracks in the complacent middle-class world of contemporary Paris. For Johanna, a certain name or encounter has the troubling power to light a spark in her mind:

> as if I had once seen it on some signpost or in a newspaper headline, but there was … no reason to pursue it on my own account. I had learnt the folly of such researches … The past, for me, was such a region as precocious children invent to scare each other, a cavernous darkness peopled with menacing shadows, and I did not need to distress and alarm myself by turning in that direction: the present was enough for me to cope with (Hutchinson 1969: 19).

So Hutchinson invites his readers to see the world through the eyes, not of the victims of evil, but of someone who, at an obscure subconscious level, is aware that she is a wrongdoer, but has found psychological defenses to seal herself off from confronting that knowledge. The daily routines and dramas of the displaced persons' hostel absorb all her energy and all her waking consciousness. Only in her dreams does she seem to hear the 'troubled human cry', and know for a fleeting moment that she cannot 'escape a sense of responsibility'.

BEARING WITNESS

Escaping the despotism of the past

The theme of historical responsibility is a universal one, of which Johanna's story is just an extreme illustration. For most readers too, 'the present is enough for us to cope with', a place whose absorbing routines allow us to create a comforting amnesia, even if in a less drastic form than Johanna Schechter's loss of memory. But the novel resists simple universalisms and generalisations, and allows room to evoke the multiplicities of memory and forgetting. In *Johanna at Daybreak*, the counterpoint to the main character's amnesia is the mental confusion of the tragic but somehow majestic Debora Stahl, a Jewish woman whose refuge lies, not in forgetting the past, but in forgetting the present: Madame Stahl, despite all the evidence of her shabby and chaotic surroundings, believes herself to be living still in the glittering social world of her 1920s youth. It is the arrival of Debora Stahl and her husband Walther in the displaced persons' hostel that makes the first decisive breach in the walls of Johanna's amnesia, starting a process that will ultimately force her to confront the 'cavernous darkness' of history.

Johanna's final nemesis, though, lies in encounters with her own family, among them her brother-in-law Albrecht, a fellow German whose life has been torn apart by the consequences of Nazism, and who is unrelenting in his determination to remember:

> 'Yes,' [Albrecht] continued, 'I tried to forget all that. But now I don't want to forget it. In a way I was responsible myself for what happened, because we all were—we stood and watched them making a world where things like that could happen. And we can't say, "Well, it's time to put all that behind us"—that would just be a cowardly evasion.' His voice had remained cool and colourless, but now, as a dry bay leaf under a magnifying glass will suddenly burst into flame, it yielded to the passion that he had been suppressing: with a fury that pierced my ears and brain like a heated wire he said, 'Those things are not to be forgotten! *I tell you, I will not let anyone forget them*' (Hutchinson 1969: 166, emphasis in original).

'I will not let anyone forget': that, surely, might be a motto for the historian. But the reader, confronting Albrecht's remorseless righteousness, can also see that work of memory is at times a kind of violence. The novel invites us to consider the nature of and need for that violence. It poses questions, not only to those who escape into amnesia, but also to those who insist on remembering. The novel, unlike the academic text, is not expected to offer tightly argued conclusions; the questions do not have simple answers.

Most centrally of all, *Johanna at Daybreak* takes up a question with which scholarly history still struggles: the issue of forgiveness, or, more precisely the problem of the withholding of forgiveness. Recent debates about historical responsibility, apology and reconciliation have encouraged new waves of writing on the ethics and politics of forgiveness. Jacques Derrida, in the late 1990s, published a series of challenging philosophical essays on the subject, in which he argued that forgiveness in the true sense of the word can only be absolute, unconditional and independent of the remorse of the offender. Forgiveness, in Derrida's terms, is an ultimate act of self-determination by the wronged victim, but at the same time an act that becomes virtually impossible: 'forgiveness forgives only the unforgivable' (Derrida 2001: 32; see also McGonegal 2009: 41–42).

But R.C. Hutchinson in the 1960s was more concerned with the question of unforgiveness. What happens when our apologies or sense of responsibility for the past are insufficient to melt the hearts of those we have wronged? What happens if the past is simply unforgivable?

In my research on issues of historical conflict and reconciliation in Northeast Asia, I have become increasingly aware of the power and perils of the longing for forgiveness. The wrongs of the past create injustices that persist into the present. This places burdens of responsibility even on those who were not personally responsible for the original sin, but who have failed to right enduring injustices that flow from this sin. Which of us can endure the terrible moral absolute which R.C. Hutchinson lays out before us: a world in which there are only 'two sorts of people—one lot who goes through hell, and the other lot that makes them, or else just stands back and does nothing' (Hutchinson 1969: 305)? In people who inherit a responsibility-laden past or present, the hunger for absolution can become intense and laden with emotion. To be forgiven by those who 'go through hell' is to have a burden lifted from our shoulders, our self-esteem restored, our hearts liberated. Receiving heartfelt forgiveness is calming and deeply comforting.

But the longing to be forgiven can be a dangerous emotion. It may impel those with uneasy consciences to force their awkward words of apology onto others who lack the time or energy to take on the demanding task of forgiving. Worse still, people who apologise for the past may, all too easily, assume that their apology is one side of a simple reciprocal exchange: that the automatic result of any apology, however thin or light, will be an instant offer of forgiveness. This vision of the apology–forgiveness exchange as a reciprocal—almost a commercial—barter encourages the apologiser to feel cheated when instant forgiveness fails to materialise: 'I said sorry. Why are they still complaining?' The sense of guilt, or at least responsibility, is then radically but all too easily inverted into that strange phenomenon: the perpetrator's sense of victimhood.

The unfulfilled longing for forgiveness can lead to a renewed rejection of memory and of the past. When Johanna Schechter is confronted by the walls of unforgiveness, her overwhelming temptation is to retreat again into amnesia:

> Detachment: that was an operation which the mind could manage with its own resources. The past, I thought, need not command us. The burdens which arrived each day—the stress of fending for oneself, the pain of watching in the glass a creature who will presently grow old and useless—these should suffice to fill one's mental horizon: only perversity would make one look backward to revive old causes of distress. Yes, I needed to be vigilant; but now it occurred to me that I was expert in such vigilance already—I had only to re-employ the faculty of suppression which I had wantonly discarded (Hutchinson 1969: 306).

But the cost of amnesia is isolation, a retreat from human society, for fear that any encounter with others may once again stir the agonising pangs of memory. In the final pages of *Johanna at Daybreak*, R.C. Hutchinson evokes the story of the seventeenth-century Italian convict Jacopo Frugoni, who escaped from prison and fled eastward across the Mediterranean in a stolen boat, only to find that escape brought a more frightening form of captivity. In every port where he stopped, he was seized by the terrifying certainty that he had seen familiar faces in the crowd, and was about to be recognised. The terror only subsided when he set sail alone again on his boat; but then he would be assailed by a new fear—the fear of unending solitude, to which he now seemed condemned. Those who deny the past, Hutchinson suggests, are condemning themselves precisely to that endless solitude. True apology acknowledges the right of the victim to withhold forgiveness. The only escape from solitude is to face the past and the present in a world where one remains unforgiven.

But this is a novel, not a philosophical text. Academic writing abstracts. It draws the fine threads of specific themes out of the tangled fabric of everyday life, and holds them up to the light. The novel, on the contrary, finds its life in the midst of the tangle. Derrida's reflections on the ethics of forgiveness are searching and profound, but utterly abstracted from the actual world, where people never confront problems of memory, responsibility and remorse as pure philosophical issues. They confront them while at the same time struggling to cope with the everyday: buying the bread for tomorrow's breakfast, listening to the distracting bass notes of music from a neighbour's party, worrying about the quarrel they have just had with their parents or their children. The power of creative writing is its ability to put the philosopher's big questions back into the midst of the tangle of everyday life.

And it is in that tangle itself that *Johanna at Daybreak* finds some kind of resolution. Memory is painful; forgiveness does not come cheaply, and may not come at all. The only path to accepting responsibility is the step-by-step path through the infinitely complex everyday world of human existence:

> Side by side—our hands still touching—we went into the house, to be greeted by the fumes from a pan of milk which someone had let boil over and by the pervasive bickering of children. Enveloped in that orchestra of inveterate sounds and smells, I realised that I was back on the painful course I could never finally escape from—itself my one escape from the despotism of the past (Hutchinson 1969: 314).

Retrieving lost lives

It seems light years from the dark postwar Europe of R.C. Hutchinson's *Johanna at Daybreak* to the languid evenings of Brij Lal's *Mr Tulsi's Store*: a work of history and imagination, prose and poetry set in Fiji, which was sometimes referred to by Indian migrants and those left behind as 'the Ramnik Dvip, the colorful islands or the islands of paradise' (Lal 2001: 27). As he traces the lives of the Indian indentured labourers of Fiji, their descendants, and their distant relatives in India and its diaspora, Lal always keeps a light touch. Recalling a favourite phrase of the late geographer Oskar Spate—'one does not have to be solemn to be serious' (Lal 2001: x)—he conjures up the characters of his own Fijian childhood and early adulthood with an observant eye and a wry sense of humour: the grasping storekeeper Mr Tulsi, 'his ample stomach parked comfortably on his knees'; Mr Tom the overseer, barking out orders in 'broken CSR Hindustani' (Lal 2001: 49, 54). The Indo-Fijian landscape evoked his words is a changing, vanishing world laden with longing:

> I miss them, as I miss the touch of smell and sound,
> The pungency of cane fires, embers reddening the ground,
> The feel of warm rain on grass fresh mown,
> Swimming in swollen rivers, menacing, brown (Lal 2001: 208).

Hutchinson was a novelist using his craft to probe deep questions of history and philosophy. Lal is an historian adopting the skills of the creative writer to break out of the straightjacket of academic prose. If Hutchinson is adventurous in his choice of themes, Lal is adventurous in his use of the written form. *Mr Tulsi's Store* and his other 'factional' writings (as he calls them) freely combine personal reminiscences, short stories and poetry into a web of language that brings a vanished past back to life in all its complexity and sensuality. Brij Lal's journey through time is a circuitous one, building up layers of history one on another. It takes us through the dusty village streets and cane fields of Tabia, his Fijian childhood home, back to the Indian villages that were the starting point of the *girmitiya* (indentured labourer) diaspora, and forward to the diaspora's multiple stopping places, in Trinidad, Guyana and Surinam, even Honolulu and Canberra. There are, it seems, no permanent end points, only way stations on an endless voyage.

There are also no simple morals or conclusions, though the journey is full of suggestions about the meanings of the past. Education, books and the power of words figure prominently in the itinerary. For the children and grandchildren of the *girmitiyas*, education was a means to liberation from the weight of the history of indenture, and books were the windows through which their minds escaped into new and bigger worlds: 'The same texts which taught us to obey the laws also taught us read books, to cherish the pleasures of the imagination. Nothing is more dangerous to the established order than an unfettered mind' (Lal 2001: 20). That faith in the power of words and imagination to change the world is sustained and grows through Lal's account of English literature classes at school, and of that great social experiment, the University of the South Pacific, where he studied in the early 1970s. The same theme reappears, too, in his account of his travels around the Fijian Islands in 1995, collecting submissions for a new Fijian constitution, of which he was to be one of the authors. With the enthusiasm of a connoisseur, Lal records, not just the multitude of political suggestions presented to the constitutional commission by people from all walks of life, but also the language and the metaphors in which people expressed their dreams for the future of their country. In the multitude of submissions, Fiji appears as a house, a mother, a human body, a flower garden, a loaf of bread that just needs a little yeast.

This is a deeply nostalgic journey, but not a sentimental one. *Mr Tulsi's Store* charts the vast changes that have overwhelmed Indo-Fijian society. It brings back to life, through words and imagination, the vanished *girmitiya* village with its mango trees and thatched-roof houses, its endless cycle of religious rituals, its huddles of old men seated on the verandah of the village store, playing games of riddles and telling stories about the motherland. But this is no idyllic past. The world that Brij Lal evokes is a harsh and sometimes an unforgiving one. Its people struggle with poverty, insecurity and the loneliness of separation—separation from the India they have left behind, and from the mobile younger generation, who move on and away in search of better lives. The power of tradition and of old beliefs can be sustaining, but it can also feed superstition and exploitation, or constrain and ultimately destroy lives. It cages the dreams and imaginations of women and divides Hindus from Muslims, and Indians from Fijians. The pain beneath the humour and nostalgia is nowhere more evident than in the chapter of *Mr Tulsi's Store* just titled 'Ben', where Lal recalls the life and death of his eldest brother, who stayed at home and worked, in part so that his younger siblings could have the education and possibilities that he would never enjoy.

All the writings in *Mr Tulsi's Store* are infused with the feeling that the author experiences in his own encounters with India: 'a vague sense of loss' (Lal 2001: 34). The loss of which they speak is not only the vanishing of an Indo-Fijian village world; it is also the loss of the dreams of a multiracial Fijian democracy: 'the Fijian turmoil has traumatised the spirit that informed our idealism and our unbounded youthful optimism about the possibilities of unlimited progressive change. So much potential, so little of it realised' (Lal 2001: 103). Expelled from Fiji by the Bainimarama government in 2010, Brij Lal remains an exile from the land of his birth, and the last chapter of *Mr Tulsi's Store* is a poem of farewell.

'I will not let anyone forget': the words spoken by R.C. Hutchinson's Albrecht came to my mind when I read *Mr Tulsi's Store*. In the mouth of Albrecht, they are the angry cry of the righteous. But Brij Lal's writings fight a war against forgetting in a quieter and more peaceable way.

He insists that we remember, not just the grand tales of the tides of history and the rise and fall of empires, but also the irreplaceable small pasts of the individuals caught up in history's flows and vortices. He makes each of those small lives, and the landscape in which they were lived, matter to his readers. And that, in a way, is what history is all about: the reality of those millions of human lives that have gone before ours. The infinite complexity of each of those lives, with its pains and hopes and loves and visions of possibility. History can only rescue small fragments of a tiny fraction of those lives from the abyss of oblivion; but every fragment rescued adds to our understanding of what it is to be human.

Brij Lal's work is also, as he puts it, a 'small act of rebellion' against the academic enthusiasm for 'word games and jargon-laden, obscurantist prose, the converted talking to the converted, pandering to the educational establishment's demand for narrowly defined, peer-reviewed research, publishing to get ahead, or get funded, not necessarily read' (Lal 2001: xi).

It is, indeed, rather revolutionary in the challenges it poses to our assumptions about 'writing history'. History, as Brij Lal shows, may be written as poetry (as of course it was for many centuries in the past). It can be written as short stories in which the remembered and the recorded past is mixed in complex ways with imaginative re-creation. What matters is that its creative power should make the past come to life for readers in a very different time and place. Like the very different fictional writings of R.C. Hutchinson, Brij Lal's 'factional' writings place the big philosophical questions of history back into the endlessly complex tangle of life in which they are always played out: the world, not just of the mind, but also of the emotions and of all the physical senses.

Returning to the magic mountain

We live in a time when education and media are changing with dizzying speed. Twenty years from now, I am sure, universities will have changed beyond recognition, for better or worse. But as academics we seem oddly trapped in routine patterns of communication: the 80,000-word academic book, complete with copious footnotes; the peer-reviewed journal article; the 20-minute conference presentation in panels that never leave enough time for questions and answers. Are we unable to communicate in other ways, or only afraid of trying?

11. UNFETTERING THE MIND

Brij Lal's evocations of the past through essay, 'faction' and poetry point a way out of timorous straightjackets of scholarly communication; and his experiments in creative writing are interestingly paralleled by the work of another scholar who (like Brij Lal) has deeply influenced my work and life. Kang Sang-jung is a *Zainichi* Korean scholar of political science: *Zainichi* (literally, 'living in Japan') being the word commonly used to describe colonial-era migrants to Japan and their descendants. Of the same generation as Brij Lal, Kang is, like Lal, a child of the diaspora. In the 1990s he became well-known for his writings and public commentary on postcolonial themes, including his critique of orientalism in Japan's cultural images of his Asian neighbours (Kang 1996). But more recently, Kang Sang-jung, like Brij Lal, has turned increasingly to creative writing—novels or combinations of essay and fiction—to convey his ideas to an audience that extends beyond the walls of academia.

In *Omoni* (Mother), published in 2010, Kang moves almost imperceptibly from one form of storytelling to another. The book begins with Kang's reminiscences of his mother, U Sun-nam, and his account of her early life in the far south of Korea and journey to Japan as a 16-year-old bride. But as we follow her journey through the firestorms of the wartime bombing of Nagoya and the death of her first infant son, Haruo, we gradually start to see the world through U Sun-nam's own eyes. The book transforms itself from biography into novel:

> In late autumn the days retreated swiftly, and a chill air drifted through the neighbourhood. As the sun set behind Bannichi Mountain, the 'dong, dong' of a bell sounded from somewhere in the distance. Every time that sound reached her ears, the memory of her lost son Haruo returned, and Mother gently rubbed her swollen stomach, the sign of impending birth. 'It's like Haruo is being born again. Bet this one'll be a boy. Sure to be' (Kang 2010: 101).

Omoni, like Brij Lal's *Mr Tulsi's Store*, evokes the harsh realities of a migrant community whose world seems utterly remote from those of the book's contemporary readers; the creative language of the novel takes over from conventional academic prose because it has the capacity to bring that world to life on the page. Just as *Mr Tulsi's Store* rescues the ordinary but extraordinary lives of Tabia and its inhabitants from oblivion, *Omoni* rescues lives of a group of first-generation Korean migrants to Japan.

In the books that have followed, Kang has experimented with novel writing, not only as a way of reaching back into his own past, but also to convey ideas about society and history to readers who would be unlikely ever to pick up an academic work of postcolonial thought or political theory. These books reflect Kang's growing fascination with the work of Japan's most famous modern novellist, Natsume Soseki. Soseki is often seen as a quintessentially Japanese novelist whose work (in the words of one scholar) was shaped not just by western literary aesthetics but also by 'that ancient Eastern philosophy of resignation which some have described as the heart of traditional Japanese spirituality' (Odin 2001: 215). But Kang suggests that Soseki's novels can be re-read as deeply ironical and critical commentaries on society: commentaries full of relevance to the twenty-first-century world.

Kang's 2013 novel *Kokoro* borrows its title and elements of its structure from Natsume Soseki's most famous book. The Japanese word *kokoro* is not easy to translate into English because (as the nineteenth-century Japanophile Lafcadio Hearn observed) it elides into a single word the notions of heart and also of 'mind, in the emotional sense; spirit; courage; resolve; sentiment; affection; and inner meaning, just as we say in English, "the heart of things"' (Hearn 1896: front matter). Soseki's *Kokoro* (first published in 1914) is an exploration of the human psyche in the form of two first-person narratives written from the perspective of each of the novel's unnamed main characters. The first narrative is told from the perspective of a drifting, lonely young student, who becomes for a while the disciple of an older man he meets by chance on a visit to the seaside. The second narrative takes the form of a letter written by the older man—known only as 'Teacher' (*Sensei*). Here the relationship is inverted, as the older man confesses to the younger the fatal error that will consume his own life: for *Sensei*'s letter to his student is also an extended suicide note.

Kang Sang-jung's *Kokoro* gives the dual first-person narrative a contemporary and slightly irreverent twist by turning it into an email correspondance between a student and the author, in his role as *Sensei*. A core theme of Natsume Soseki's novels is the anomie and isolation of ordinary people caught up in a world that was changing with bewildering speed. Kang takes Soseki's ideas as a starting point for exploring the equally profound confusion and loneliness that many people in Japan today experience, above all in the wake of the triple disaster:

the earthquake, tsunami and nuclear meltdown of 11 March 2011. In its final pages, the novel also becomes a moving reflection on its author's own loss: the death of his son.

In *Kokoro no Chikara* (The Power of Kokoro), published in 2014, Kang returns to the theme of human anxiety in a turbulently changing world. Like *Mr Tulsi's Store*, *Kokoro no Chikara* is an adventurous mixture of literary forms. It consists of a series of essays, interleaved with chapters of a short novel. Both the essays and the novel take us back again to Natsume Soseki's classic. They also evoke another great modern novel that was being written as Soseki wrote *Kokoro*, though it would be published 10 years later: Thomas Mann's *The Magic Mountain* (Der Zauberberg). Set in a tuberculosis sanatorium in the Swiss mountains above Davos, Mann's novel, like Soseki's, follows the meandering fate of an individual adrift on the currents of modernity. Mann's main character Hans Castorp, during his seven years in the sanatorium, encounters and struggles with most of the philosophies and ideologies of modern Europe. But *The Magic Mountain* ends with its moral dilemmas unresolved and its main character still drifting and uncommitted. Castorp leaves the sanatorium only to confront the horrors of World War I on the battlefields of the Western Front.

The unconventional novel contained in Kang Sang-jung's *Kokoro no Chikara* brings Soseki and Mann together across time and continents. As General MacArthur's occupation forces take control of a defeated and war-devastated Japan in 1945, a multinational collection of people—diplomats from Japan's wartime allies, Germany and Italy, politicians from the vanished state of Manchukuo and others—gather in the limbo of an old hotel in the Japanese mountain resort of Hakone, waiting for their fates to be decided. Among them are two men: Hans Castorp, who has survived World War I to become the representative of his family's trading company in Japan; and Kawade Ikurō, the 'student' from Soseki's novel *Kokoro*, who has lived in Germany and become a translator working for the Japanese Foreign Service. In the rarified world of the post-defeat Hakone hotel—a world not unlike that of Mann's sanatorium—the two characters strike up a friendship, and the narratives of *The Magic Mountain* and *Kokoro* flow into one.

Through the characters of Castorp and Kawade, and their conversations in the mountains of Japan, Kang explores the themes of the passage of time and the search for meaning in a world ruled by the remorseless laws of the competitive economy. He contrasts the dreamlike Davos of Thomas Mann's magic mountain with the Davos that we know today: that gaudy stage where the World Economic Forum performs its annual rituals. Universities, he argues, have become too much like the second Davos, and not enough like the first. We need more magic mountains—more spaces where time slows down and there is scope for reflection and conversation, unpressured by the demands of global economic competition (Kang 2014: 106–14).

For Kang, the appeal of the characters of Castorp and Kawade lies in the fact that their discussions and self-doubts do not lead to any grand conclusions. They are outsiders, never quite in tune with the age in which they live. But their unease and their restless search for something better does not end with the drum-rolls and clashing cymbals of ideological certainties or revolutionary deeds. *Kokoro no Chikara* ends in the 1960s, with Japan and Germany rapidly recovering from the scars of war, and equally rapidly forgetting the lessons of defeat. Kawade, the 'student' of Natsume Soseki's novel *Kokoro*, is now on the brink of old age, and finds himself at odds with a society in which the pursuit of wealth and power threatens to sweep away the memories of the past. His teacher's suicide, he realises, was itself precisely an act of rebellion against 'an age in which everything was reduced to money, an age when friendship was betrayed and even blood bonds were sundered, an age when people fell into utter loneliness, an age filled with desire and ostentation' (Kang 2014: 185).

The real strength of the heart, though, lies not in acts of rebellion like *Sensei's* suicide, but rather in the act of survival: going on living, while remaining at odds with the spirit of the age you live in. Like Johanna Schechter, Kawade finds himself back on the 'painful course he could never finally escape from', the path of day-to-day survival in an unforgiving world.

Stories without end

Creative writing shakes up our senses and questions our certainties. R.C. Hutchinson makes his readers share the experience of Johanna Schechter's amnesia, and so become more conscious of the amnesia in their own lives. Kang Sang-jung prompts us to imagine what happens to literary characters after the last page of the novel, intertwining their lives with ours. Brij Lal enriches our visions of the forms in which history can be passed on from one generation to another, challenging us to tell and write our histories in new ways. These works—blurring the boundary between fact and fiction, history and literature—are deeply disconcerting to the conventional academic view of the world. They bring direct and sometimes raw emotions into a space usually ruled by the abstract intellect. They make history and social thought personal, breaking down the barriers that shield the life of the mind from simple, total life.

Because they are unfamiliar and unsettling, it is easy to marginalise them. Hutchinson's novels have remained 'great forgotten works' partly because they failed to fit comfortably into the accepted literary conventions of his day. Brij Lal's and Kang Sang-jung's excursions into the realms of fiction and 'faction' are almost certainly seen by some academics as peripheral, distractions from the real work of the scholar. But the challenge of these writings goes to the core of scholarship. Why, and for whom, do we read, research and write? How do we communicate ideas, and to what audience? How can we share, not only ideas, but also the passion and imagination to expand and live those ideas? How can we make our words alive and dangerous, so that they go on creating small new worlds in many minds, long after our readers have reached the last full stop (or the last question mark) on the final page?

References

Caché. 2005. Dir. Michael Hanneke, prod. Margaret Ménégoz and Veit Heiduschka, starring Daniel Auteuil, Juliette Binoche and Maurice Bénichou.

Derrida, Jacques. 2001. *On Cosmopolitanism and Forgiveness*, trans. Mark Dooley and Michael Hughes. London: Routledge.

Green, Robert. 1985. *R.C. Hutchinson: The Man and his Books*. Metuchen, NJ and London: Scarecrow Press.

Hutchinson, R.C. 1969. *Johanna at Daybreak*. New York and Evanston: Harper and Row, 1969.

Kang Sang-jung. 1996. *Orientarizumu no Kanata e: Kindai Bunka Hihan*. Tokyo: Iwanami Shoten.

———. 2010. *Omoni*. Tokyo: Shueisha.

———. 2013. *Kokoro*. Tokyo: Shueisha.

———. 2014. *Kokoro no Chikara*. Tokyo: Shueisha.

Lal, Brij V. 2001. *Mr Tulsi's Store: A Fijian Journey*. Canberra: Pandanus Books.

McGonegal, Julie. 2009. *Imagining Justice: The Politics of Postcolonial Forgiveness and Reconciliation*. Montreal and Kingston: McGill-Queen's University Press.

Odin, Steve. 2001. *Artistic Detachment in Japan and the West: Psychic Distance in Comparative Aesthetics*. Honolulu: University of Hawai'i Press.

'Peter Hobbs hails R.C. Hutchinson and his "brave, compassionate, moral" novel "A Child Possessed"'. Faber and Faber, 22 April 2013. Online: faberfindsblog.co.uk/peter-hobbs-hails-r-c-hutchinson-and-his-brave-compassionate-moral-novel-a-child-possessed/ (accessed 17 November 2016).

12

Autobiography and Faction

Doug Munro

Brij Lal started his professional career as an historian, but from the mid-1990s he has become increasingly involved in autobiography and creative writing. He called the latter 'faction', which as the name suggests is a quasi-fictional genre that mixes fact with fiction. The impulse to writing in a less-academic mode stemmed indirectly from his love of good literature and good writing generally. The direct impulse was much earlier and dates from his postgraduate fieldwork in India in 1978, when he was aged 26. For almost six months he lived in the impoverished rural areas of northeast India that provided the bulk of the *girmitiyas* (Indian indentured labourers) to Fiji. On visiting his grandfather's village, while keeping a diary, he went through a gamut of emotions that brought to the surface questions of identity and heritage, and he thought there and then that writing in a more creative vein might be the way to make better sense of such experiences (Lal 2003; Raicola 2007). But he did not know how to write in such a manner and neither did he have the time to learn. He explained to me, 'I was climbing the academic ladder and had to pay my dues'.[1] Had he known about it, Brij would have been heartened by the autobiography of Alan Bullock, an historian for whom he has high regard. It contains the encouraging statement that Bullock's father 'did not share

---

[1] Unattributed quotations are taken from interviews I conducted with Brij in 2000 and 2007. Some of the statements in the present chapter are drawn from Munro 2009: 243–309.

the view of many critics of his time that novels had an ephemeral character and did not deserve to be included in the discussion of serious literature' (Bullock 2000: 244).

Brij felt awkward about his literary aspirations; the closet novelist was seemingly on his way to becoming a novelist *manqué*. Although he hankered to write in a non-academic vein, he felt inhibited. Always a lover of good literature, Brij would have agreed with fellow historian Hugh Trevor-Roper, who told a friend, 'I have read no books … only dry and dusty sixteenth-century leases and records of debt and bills and docquets of inconceivable philistinism. What a price one pays to write history! But I hope to get back to literature soon' (quoted in Worden 2015: 4). But academics are only supposed to read fiction, not to actually write it. What would people think if he did so? Then several things happened. The deaths of his mother (in 1981), his brother Ben (1992), which was a devastating person blow (Lal 2001: 139–52), and then his father (1996) made him realise that much was at risk of being lost if he did not recapture on paper some of their shared moments. There was a need to 'shore up fragments before they slipped away' and to preserve things for the future generation, including his own urbanised children, Yogi and Niraj, who were disconnected from their Indo-Fijian roots. Brij was also approaching middle age, when the shadow begins to lengthen: 'you become aware of the limited time you have, and you want to make sense of things' is how he described it to me. His first forays into non-academic writing were in the mid to late 1990s, and were written in longhand, as were his lectures and sometimes even conference papers (although nowadays his creative writing is typed onto a computer screen). His first effort at non-academic writing concerned his 1978 visit to Bahraich, his grandfather's village, when he was a PhD student. Then came 'Sunrise on the Ganga', which recounted his reactions to India 20 years later. He also wrote about his older brother, the result of which was 'Ben's Funeral'.[2] These were followed by 'Mr Tulsi's Store', about that perennial evil of Indo-Fiji rural life, the moneylender—perhaps the rough equivalent of ticket touts in England in terms of avariciousness.[3]

---

2   The latter two were initially published in Ganguly and Nandan 1998: 91–108; and National Federation Party 1997: 69–76, respectively.
3   Moneylenders and other wicked middlemen were an institutionalised part of agrarian life in India. They followed Indian indentured workers to their places of employment. See generally Catanach 1970 (the late Ian Catanach was one of Brij's PhD examiners).

Brij's training as an historian prompted the realisation that a pivotal period in Indo-Fijian rural life, the 1930s through to the 1960s, needed chronicling before it receded from memory and was overtaken by the forces of change:

> It is an enormously important period in Indo-Fijian history. Indenture has ended, new cultural and social institutions were being set up, schools and newspapers were being established. This was a time when education was becoming important … How did this community so near to the shadows of indenture create that type of world—village life, the ways in which they celebrated life, and mourned its passing, the ways in which they created voluntary associations of self help, the way they saw themselves as a people and their place in the larger scheme of things? I was part of that world of post-war village life: prehistoric, no running water, electricity or tar sealed roads, no telephones. I was part of that world for which there was no documentation. It was a very important part of our life and of Fijian history overall. But how do you write about that past when you don't have records and people's memories are fading and many of them are dead? (from Munro 2009: 286).

Writing about village life during his childhood presented unexpected difficulties because he had only his early memories upon which to draw, and yet he had to be truthful to lived experience. At the same time, he had to move beyond his familiar academic parameters. He was trying to write about the experience of a generation from memory—to capture the spirit of the age. Although he had to write *as* an historian, he could not write *like* an historian. As mentioned, his children's reactions impressed upon him the urgency of recreating on paper the lost world of his own childhood: they simply could not comprehend a universe so alien to them. Yogi had only lived in Fiji as a young child, almost entirely in Suva. Niraj, who was born in Hawai'i, had only spent brief periods in the country. In short, Brij aspired in his autobiographical and faction writing to 'connect today's disconnected and dispersed generation of Indo-Fijians with their historical and cultural roots' (Lal 2003: 46. See also Chand 2013; Sharma 2007). For comparisons, see historian James Walvin's autobiography of growing up in the Greater Manchester area in the 1940s and 1950s, which stresses how the present is different from even the recent past (Walvin 2014). In similar fashion, one of the reasons that Walvin wrote his autobiography stemmed from talking to his sons and grandson: 'they listen to my tales as if I were talking about a lost Amazonian tribe. It was utterly beyond their ken.'[4]

---

4   James Walvin, email to author, 26 November 2014.

'Mr Tulsi's Store', 'Return to Bahraich', 'Ben's Funeral' and 'Sunrise on the Ganga' were smuggled into *Chalo Jahaji* (2000), his collected essays on Indo-Fijian indenture. He was not laughed out of court on account of their inclusion, and it did announce his intention to go beyond strictly academic writing. It helped to discover that he had a collective of colleagues in the Coombs Building at The Australian National University (ANU) who enjoyed writing creatively and provided reassurance and encouragement (Lal 2011: 15): Tessa Morris-Suzuki had written children's stories and poems; Mark Elvin had written both poetry and fiction, including a trilogy under the pseudonym John Mark Dutton (Lal 2011: 132); William C. (Bill) Clarke was also writing poetry and facilitating the publication of poetry by Pacific Islanders; Donald Denoon was trying his hand at novels, freely admitting that his first efforts read like 'an interminable seminar' (Borrie 2004; Fuller 2001; Clark 2000; Denoon 1996); and Hank Nelson was also beginning to write creatively. Lal would have been further reassured had he realised that others associated with ANU had also published fiction—for example, the historian Manning Clark (1969, 1986).

Another boost was the formation, within the (then) Research School of Pacific & Asian Studies (RSPAS), of a publishing arm named Pandanus Books. Its managing editor, Ian Templeman, was himself a poet who wished to encourage creative writing. In 2000, Brij founded the journal *Conversations*, under the imprint of Pandanus Books, as an outlet for the creative endeavour of colleagues in RSPAS. Out of this confluence emerged his first faction book, *Mr Tulsi's Store* (2001). Published by Pandanus Press, and containing several chapters that were originally published in *Chalo Jahagi* and in *Conversations*, *Mr Tulsi's Store* made something of an impression; it was highly commended at the ACT Arts Council 'Notable Book of 2002' award, and in San Francisco was judged one of 10 'Notable Books of the Asia Pacific' in that year's Kiriyama Prize.

Brij thought he was on to something new. He thought he had coined the word 'faction' (fact + fiction = faction) and had no idea that faction was an established literary style, although the term was late in finding its way into the major reference books (e.g. Drabble 1995: 341; see also Stead 2008: 306n). He was very surprised to learn, for example, that many writers during the 1930s were writing in an 'ambiguous, first-person descriptive vein, a then fashionable genre which blurred any clear line between fiction and autobiography—truthful to experience but not necessarily to fact (Crick 1971: 96n). Another example of faction that approximates the matter and substance of Brij's faction is Eric Braithwaite's *The Night we Stole the Mountie's Car* (1971), whose discrete stories are set on the Canadian prairies during the 1930s.

There is also a seemingly identical genre that rejoices under the name *roman à clef* (literally, novel with a key), the invention of which was attributed to Madeleine de Scudery (1607–1701), 'who created it to disguise from the general reader the public figures whose political actions and ideas formed the basis of her fictional narratives' (Boyde 1999: 155). In that sense, faction has been around for a long time.

The actual word 'faction' is of much more recent origin. The *Oxford English Dictionary* traces the term back to 1967 and even now it is hardly a household word. And neither is it 'a particularly helpful term. Most novels, if one were so inclined, could be described as factions: only works of fantasy would seem to be excluded' (Riemer 1996: 65). It stands to reason that the routine disclaimer in so many novels that resemblance to any person, living or dead, is transparently disingenuous. Nonetheless, in Brij's case, his use of the term is a remarkable example of someone replicating an existing genre, down to the very name, without realising its existence.

To complicate matters, it was not clear what Brij actually meant by faction. In a rare moment of ambiguity he wrote:

> In recording my experiences, I have privileged truth over accuracy, attempting to catch the thoughts and emotions rather than dry facts about village life. For obvious reason, some names have had to be changed and some conversations imagined. I have tried to recall the past creatively, imaginatively, rendering factual, lived experience through the prism of semi-fiction. I call this kind of exercise 'faction' writing. It is the most satisfactory way I know of remembering a past unrecorded by written events (Lal 2001: x).

It is the phrase 'to recall the past creatively, imaginatively, rendering factual, lived experience through the prism of semi-fiction' that confuses in the context of *Mr Tulsi's Store*. Most of the chapters in the book are not faction at all. They are autobiography. Brij at that time was conflating faction and autobiography and lumping the two under the rubric creative writing. Only two of the book's 12 chapters are outright faction, namely 'Mr Tulsi's Store' (where an avaricious moneylender gets his comeuppance) and 'Kismet' (where a newly appointed secondary school teacher falls for one of his students). Degrees of licence are exercised in these two chapters: names are changed, conversations are invented or reconstructed, events and episodes extraneous to 'what actually happened' may be pressed into service. But the inner kernel of such recounting is written as he observed or was told. Whatever the extent of literary licence, they are about, or based upon, real people, actual events and lived experience. The autobiographical chapters, by contrast, are as accurate to fact as he can make them.

Autobiography

Brij has no desire to publish a full-scale autobiography. Instead, there is a dispersed and extensive corpus of autobiographical writings whose content is both professional and personal, with the proviso that his nuclear family is largely off limits, the major exception being the account of his family accompanying him to the ancestral village (Lal 2001: 127–38). This, in fact, was the experience that inspired him to actually start writing faction.[5] Take the autobiographical chapters in *Mr Tulsi's Store* (2001). The contents cover a broad spectrum and involve episodes as varied as village life during his childhood, his secondary schooling, his undergraduate years at the University of the South Pacific (USP), the fieldtrip to northeast India, his employment at the University of Hawai'i, and his involvement in Fiji politics, whether as constitutional adviser, a chronicler of elections, or as a commentator on political proceedings.

The opening chapter in *Mr Tulsi's Store* is 'Tabia', his home village close by Labasa (Lal 2001: 1–23). It provides necessary context for what follows by explaining the institutions and dynamics and a village life based around sugar cane production and community inaction. It also foreshadows a dominant theme in the chapters that follow—namely, the value placed on formal education and his immersion in it. He had illiterate grandparents and parents; his mother learned enough of the alphabet to scribble her name in Hindi, but that was the extent of her literacy. Brij was the second boy from Tabia to go to university and he is under no illusions about how it boiled down to sheer chance of having the benefit of inspired and accomplished teachers. In the words of historian

---

5   The contradiction remains that many academics attach great importance to family yet largely exclude it from their memoirs and concentrate instead on their professional life. See, for example, Mansfield 2012.

Patrick Collinson, 'I know of no autobiography or memoir by a historian which does not attribute his or her commitment to the subject to some gifted teacher' (Collinson 2011: 47), and so it was with Brij. As he relates in 'Labasa Secondary' (Lal 2001: 59–80), they introduced him to good literature, which he soaked up like a sponge. Elsewhere Brij has remarked:

> I belong to a tradition and a generation which does not regard a few lines of mangled English as poetry. Grammatically incorrect 'English' that passes for modish prose is, for me, an exercise in language abuse. William Shakespeare, Matthew Arnold and John Steinbeck are not, for me, Dead White Males whose works have no relevance. I read them with the same devotion and interest as I read Albert Wendt and MG Vassanji, Chinua Achebe and Prem Chand. And great poetry often provides deeper insights into the human condition than post-modern theory: TS Eliot and Stanley Merwyn are good examples (Lal 2007a: 199).

His teachers were nothing if not adventurous. One of them was Vijay Mishra, now a professor of English literature at Murdoch University in Western Australia. He introduced his brighter students to *Lady Chatterley's Lover*, for which he 'would have been lynched at Mahatma Gandhi High!' (Lal 2001: 71).[6] Another teacher was Krishna Datt, later a Labour parliamentarian, who taught history with an 'infectious enthusiasm':

> He opened up his own personal library to us, lending us books by Geoffrey Barraclough, Denis Mack Smith, Percival Spear, L.C.B. Seaman, A.J.P. Taylor. I am not sure we understood the complex arguments and themes these historians espoused, but that was not the point. The books opened up a window to a past—even if that past was remote to all of us—that connected us to a wider world, other human experiences in history. The process of learning, I suppose, was more important than the content. Krishna also had a marvellous sense of theatre. I vividly recall him turning up to class one morning with a large placard around his neck with the opening words of the *Communist Manifesto*, 'Workers of the world unite. You have nothing to lose but your chains.' And he created a minor furore in the school by suggesting that Hitler's birthday should be remembered because he was an important—evil but important—figure in 20th century history (Lal 2001: 75).

---

6   A little over a decade later, Brij wrote a chapter for a collection edited by Mishra (Lal 1979: 12–39), who by then was a university lecturer. Walvin (2014: 58–59) discusses the court case in England over allowing the sale of the unexpurgated version of *Lady Chatterley's Lover*, commenting that when he read the book as a 19-year-old he could not see what the fuss had been about.

A third outstanding teacher was Subramani, who took over from Mishra and who became Fiji's finest writer of fiction and professor of English at the University of the South Pacific. *Dauka Puran*, set in central Vanua Levu during the mid-twentieth century, is the longest novel written in Fiji Hindi (Subramani 2001).

A criticism of educational practice in the colonial Pacific has focused on the overtly Anglocentric outlook of the curriculum. School children sang 'Bobby Shafto' and 'Sussex by the Sea' rather than songs in their own language. School textbooks, whether history, geography or English, were equally bereft of local content (see Lal 2004: 239–49). There is some validity to such criticisms. Or to put it another way, there is nothing wrong with gaining, through books, 'a little of that wisdom which Ulysses gained through knowing many cities and many men's manners and customs' (Spate 2006: 33), but not to the exclusion of one's own country or locality.[7] Brij is remarkably unconcerned about such qualms (Lal 2011: 191–92), feeling instead that the set reading, and especially the English and European classics, 'opened up new horizons beyond our joyless villages and fed our imagination, inculcating a love for the written word' (Lal 2001: 71): Elsewhere he has written:

> Reading stories from the Caribbean or Africa in our remote rural school, we felt connected to other parts of the world. The stories and pictures opened up new horizons for us, helped us momentarily escape the mindless routine of village life. That in its own way was also an empowering, enlarging experience. We understood that bad as things were around us and for us, we were not alone in our miseries and predicaments. The need to know, to connect with the world around us has remained with me. The passion to know more has only intensified with time (Lal 2011: 3).

Brij has few regrets about his time at Labasa Secondary School. It was there that the enjoyment of reading was inculcated, but it:

> had to be cultivated, which was never easy for people coming from non-literate, oral cultures. Now reading is an integral part of my being, indispensable to sanity. For me, most knowledge still comes through the written text, not the latest technology (Lal 2011: 212).

---

7   The *New Zealand School Journal* for primary school students achieved a nice balance between overseas and local topics, but with the aid of human and financial resources unavailable in Fiji. See O'Brien 2007. For a discussion of criticisms of the Eurocentric curricula, see Partington 2015: 255–57.

It appals him that Fiji has no reading culture to speak of. His secondary school education also showed that there were alternatives to the 'intellectual and cultural isolation' that was part and parcel of the 'mentally deadening routine of village life' (Lal 2001: 79–80). It also provided the escape route from the thatched-roof huts, the cane fields and the narrow mindset of Tabai. With the aid of the Canadian Third World Scholarship, he secured a place at the recently established University of the South Pacific and fled the dead hand of village life.

Brij's increasing detachment from his roots is by no means an isolated case. From at least the late 1950s, British working-class boys (and sometimes girls) were able to embark on university studies as recipients of state scholarships. Victor Bailey, who is now a history professor at the University of Kansas, was the first person in his extended family to go to university, in the mid-1960s, and he too would probably have never aspired to a university admission without the blessing and encouragement of good school teachers. In terms that largely replicate Brij's's experience, Bailey notes:

> the tendency for the entire University experience to take you away from your home background. The demand to think critically and widely can only lead to some element of alienation. You return to your old stamping ground with a different outlook. The old terrain feels horribly claustrophobic, terribly conformist. You can't imagine ever living and working in those environs again. In my case, there is also the accent issue. After a few years in different settings, the Yorkshire accent tends to soften and you begin to sound 'posh' to the ears of family and friends, as if you are sedulously trying to distance yourself from the old ways. And of course you return with a different set of political positions, which sound daft and idealistic to your erstwhile friends.[8]

In a somewhat similar fashion, Peter Corris (an historian of the Pacific Islands labour trade) used his education at the University of Melbourne as the vehicle by which he could 'get well clear of the a caring but stultifying, secular but puritanical, working-class upbringing', as well as to acquire a wider outlook on the world (Corris 2007: 62).

---

8   Victor Bailey, email to author, 28 March 2015; see also Walvin 2014: 195–202; LaMahieu 2014. With Brij, it was not a matter of accent but, rather, his facility in Hindi becoming somewhat rusty through lack of practice (Lal 2011: 197–98). Again by contrast, Brij notes how few people of Indian heritage in Trinidad can now speak in Hindi at all (Lal 2011: 152).

Brij's time at USP is recounted in 'From Labasa to Laucala Bay' (Lal 2001: 81–103). Again, he had marvellous teachers but more than hints at the tribal nature of the student body in a regional university that was supposed to transcend matters of race and nationality. At one point, in a passage that bespeaks the later Lal, he expresses regrets over this very point:

> to our great shame, we derided Indo-Fijian students such as Robin Singh who wore the sulu, spoke Fijian and preferred Fijian over Indian food, as social misfits not worthy of our affection and company. In retrospect, not getting to know Fijian students better, understanding their fears and hopes, I count as a sad missed opportunity (Lal 2001: 90).

Brij's intention was to qualify as a high school English teacher, but the prospect of a mandatory course in transformational grammar deterred him from pursuing his romantic interest in the novels of the Brontë sisters. So he switched to history. A major influence was the activist historian Walter Johnson from the University of Hawai'i, who was teaching at USP for a semester. He knew the people he lectured about—Franklin Delano Roosevelt, Adlai Stevenson, Martin Luther King—and he taught things in which he had participated, such as the Civil Rights Movement. As well as being a productive scholar, he had been the co-chair of the Draft Adlai Stevenson campaign, and had Stevenson won, Johnson would have been in the White House, as Arthur M. Schlesinger Jr was during John F. Kennedy's tenure. Johnson's example reinforced the notion that USP had a practical mission to provide a trained workforce for the decolonising Pacific (Lal 2001: 96). The intellectual climate at USP at that point was critical to Lal's evolution as an historian engaged in practical issues of the day.

Brij's marks were good enough to enable him to pursue postgraduate study at metropolitan universities but he has little to say about getting his MA and PhD from the University of British Columbia and The Australian National University, respectively. He returned to USP as a teaching staff member in 1981, and then he moved to the University of Hawai'i in 1983 (Lal 2001: 111–26). Given the politicised atmosphere, he is convinced that he would have been 'a part-time academic dabbling full-time in politics' had he remained in Fiji (Lal 2001: 102). He has a point but I think he is being too hard on himself here; his productivity would have declined but he would still have published a respectable academic corpus. He made his mark at the University of Hawai'i as both a teacher and a scholar and he freely admits that he was driven, in part, by a fear of failure. He is the first to admit that he had opportunities in Hawai'i that would never have been available at USP, but these had to be grasped. In the sterner—yet paradoxically more encouraging—environment of Hawai'i, he was able to achieve goals that would have been out of reach in USP's environment of complacency and underachievement. Brij was rather amused when I grimly described USP as a halfway house between a protection racket and a sheltered workshop. He later penned the lament that his *alma mater* had reneged on its obligation 'to produce [the] enduring, fundamental scholarship which [it] was so centrally located to produce ... So much potential, so little of it realized' (Lal 2001: 102–03). As he said more diplomatically on a subsequent occasion, despite the implied criticism of USP's insularity,

> We must continue to publish research that adds a vital sentence to the larger global conversation of scholarship ... We must engage and sensitively with the outside world, breaking the mould of self-referential, 'ghettoising,' inward looking academia (Lal 2011: 126).

Hawai'i, however, had its own dissatisfactions, one of them being the visa problems that prevented Brij's wife, Dr Padma Narsey Lal, gaining permanent employment in her field of resource and environmental biology. What he doesn't say is that local attitudes toward the situation in post-coup Fiji, especially from the Hawaiian sovereignty movement but not confined to it, disturbed him. There was widespread sympathy for Fijians as *iTaukei* (people of the land); the perception was that the 1987 coups were legitimate and justified given that indigenous Fijians had been hard done by. Events in Fiji were seen through the prism of the Hawaiian experience of dispossession. There was a reluctance on the part of many Hawaiians to believe what he was saying—that the coups were about power—and some students in his Honours courses wished they had a Rabuka in Hawai'i (Munro 2009: 261). There was also the feeling on Brij's part that this outpost within the United States was too much a foreign country. When a job offer came from the ANU, he accepted with alacrity.

Brij's autobiographical writings provide insights into his educational experiences and his professional career at the level of influences, satisfactions and motivations. There is the enquiring mind, the driven scholar, the need for engagement with his subject and the world at large, the love of good literature. The latter, in turn, has resulted in Brij writing both his histories and his factions with an eye to a broader lay audience rather than 'for a like-minded, narrowly-focused fraternity of specialists' (Lal 2011: 4). On a personal note, it is entirely in character that my 2009 Christmas present from Brij and Padma was a book subtitled *Adventures in the World of Books* (Carr 2008).

Presented as piecemeal contributions, his self-accounts are discontinuous and partial. They taper off when he returns to the ANU in 1990 and some important episodes are omitted. They are not evasions, it's just how it happened; and he has written more autobiography than any other historian of the Pacific Islands, barring Robert Langdon (1995). Even when trying to avoid imposing one's own expectations, there is still regret, for example, that he does not mention the extent to which the research and writing of *Broken Waves* (1992), which several contributors to this volume mention appreciatively, exhausted him and disrupted other schedules. There is also a silence about the protracted business of disengaging from the University of Hawai'i, and the occasion when he (temporarily) lost one half of his job at the ANU, until the intervention of a concerned administrator (see Munro 2009: 262, 281). The same selectivity applies to his work as one of the three Constitution Reform Commissioners in 1996–97 (Lal 2001: 153–68). He reveals some of the public face of the Commission and especially the dynamics of receiving submissions around the country, but little of its private workings. The reason is that he was sworn to secrecy.

What he does make clear is the depth of his affection and regard for another of the three-man Commission, the late Tomasi Vakatora, who was not one to be trifled with. As Brij recalls, the first meeting of the Commission 'was a pleasant enough encounter. "See, there is no blood on the flour, Tom," I said, pleased at the way things had gone. Back came the immediate reply: "Not yet". "What had I let myself into," I say to myself' (Lal 2001: 167; 1998: 174). Vakatora had a reputation as a hard-line ethnonationalist. Coming from opposite ends of the political spectrum, he and Brij seemed the antithesis of one other. Yet they confounded the sceptics in striking up a strong working relationship (and an enduring friendship) because each shared a vision for a more inclusive and less racially motivated Fiji. It might have helped, too, that each came from a humble background, in Vakatora's case from the mangrove swamps of the Rewa Delta (Vakatora 1988). It was a remarkable relationship that recalls the meeting of minds between the German Stresemann and the Frenchman Briand, who put aside national differences in the greater cause of lasting peace in Europe during the 1920s (Wiskeman 1966: 60–62).

But, as in Europe, it was not to be. The work of the Commission was undone, first by key recommendations being watered down by the Joint Parliamentary Select Committee, and second by the 2000 coup.

In describing his outlook as an historian, Brij makes clear that he needs a sense of engagement with his subject—the heart and the head must come together, which helps explain why the grandson of the *girmitiya* would write about the indenture experience in Fiji. A similar engagement, along with a sense of moral responsibility, accounts for his forays into the contemporary historiography of Fiji. He was initially disturbed that a democratically elected government was overthrown, in 1987, by those unable to surrender their power and perquisites at the behest of the ballot box; in more recent years he is disturbed by human rights violations by a government determined to quell dissident voices. As he has written:

> I live at the interface of scholarship and practical engagement with society. I am what the French might call *spectateur engage*, a politically engaged but independent intellectual (although intellectual is not a label I am comfortable with). I take my rights, roles and responsibilities as a citizen seriously. I live in society, not above or outside it. I am part of the history about which I write. I write to communicate, not obfuscate, to be read rather than simply to get ahead. I would like to have my voice heard on matters of consequence, to make a difference, if I can. Writing as accessibly as I can is my private act of resistance and revenge against some of the dominant intellectual fashions of our time (Lal 2011: 4).

There is the widespread feeling that writing about the very recent past is perilous. The familiar canards are lack of perspective, intrusion of personal feelings, loss of objectivity and the unavailability of sources. Brij has no truck with these criticisms and he has put up a reasoned defence of his position (Lal 2011: 39–57), arguing that the genre need not be one whit inferior to histories of the more distant past (see Munro, 'Indenture and Contemporary Fiji', this volume).

It is also the case that Brij's intellectual upbringing—for example, the influence of Walter Johnson (Munro 2009: 246–47)—made him receptive to writing contemporary history and to commenting upon current affairs. There is a tradition of 'participant history' among Pacific historians that commenced in the late 1940s with J.W. Davidson's involvement in the moves towards self-government in Western Samoan (Munro 2001: 91–116; Hempenstall 2007). Does Brij write 'better' history as a result of his engagement and participation? Ultimately, in my view, it boils down to personal preference, and Brij is happier when patrolling the borders of scholarship and practical action, as opposed to the likes of the historian of Tudor and Stuart England J.H. Hexter, who live their affective lives in another time and another place (Hexter 1961: 6–9), arguing that historians should be immersed in the archival material of their period and stay well away from the passions of their day and age. Brij begs to differ with such a hands-off approach: 'There is an unmatchable excitement about doing contemporary history' (Lal 2011: 57). In other words, it is a matter of temperament, and I tend to agree with historian Michael Kammen that there is 'not the slightest correlation between involvement and detachment on the one hand and the quality of a historian's work on the other' (Kammen 1982: 15). It's not a matter of the intrinsic superiority of one over the other. Rather, it boils down to what one wants to do and can do best. Brij is not in the least worried that the various instant histories of the 1987 coups vary one from the other. There is no single definitive text, he says, no master narrative:

> The idea that one day when all the facts are available, when the first primitive drafts of contemporary, or eye witness history, will be transformed by a master historian into a standard, universally uncontested account, about the full significance of what happened in the past, is mere fantasy (Lal 2011: 44–45).

As a public intellectual, Brij feels that silence is not an option. Rather he is duty-bound to speak truth to power, and Brij is fond of quoting Schlesinger that: 'A society in which citizens cannot criticize the policy of the state is a society without the means of correcting its course' (Lal 2011: 5, 138, 305). For his pains he (and Padma) have been banned from re-entering Fiji (Lal 2011: 303–306). In November 2009, after giving a radio interview, he was taken to the military barracks, aggressively 'interviewed', roughed up, and told he had 24 hours to leave the country. In January 2010, Padma, who had never publicly expressed a political opinion, was detained at the Nadi International Airport, incarcerated in a guarded hotel room and put on the first plane to Australia the next day. At the time, she was a senior research adviser to IUCN (International Union for the Conservation of Nature). Padma was then barred from re-entering Fiji, simply for the 'sin' of being Brij's spouse. In an act of sheer vindictiveness, the Fiji authorities won't even allow her to transit through Fiji, which has impacted on her career as an environmental consultant in the Pacific Islands.

Brij is not the only eminent academic to have been deported from one or other part of the world. In 1963 the young Terence Ranger, a lecturer at the University College of Rhodesia and Nyasaland, had his movements restricted and was then given his marching orders from Southern Rhodesia (now Zimbabwe) for his advocacy of racial equality and support for African nationalism (Ranger 2013: 127–48). And Benedict Anderson was banned from Indonesia in 1972 for his criticisms of the Suharto regime and only allowed to return in 1998 (Anderson 2016: 89). In neither case did the prohibitions have serious repercussions; Ranger and Anderson simply shifted their research interests to other parts of East Africa and Southeast Asia, respectively. Anderson considers himself lucky to have been kicked out of Indonesia because it forced him to do fieldwork elsewhere, to get away from a 'one-country perspective', and he had the linguistic skills to engage in fieldwork in both Thailand and the Philippines. There was an unintended bonus: 'Had I not been expelled, it is unlikely that I would have written *Imagined Communities*', the book for which he is most famous (Anderson 2016: 55). In Brij's case, exclusion from Fiji would have been serious had it come at an earlier juncture in his career, given that he never wanted to specialise in a different island group. It is fortunate that the ban was only a few years away from formal retirement.

Brij also got more excitement than he bargained for when writing a biography of Jai Ram Reddy, whose three-decade political career in Fiji was on the opposition benches. In an intriguing essay (Lal 2015: 59–72), Brij relates the 'making' of the biography and the extent to which Reddy was involved; the latter was cooperative in providing documentation and freely discussed most issues but otherwise maintained an arm's-length stance.[9] Brij also reveals his difficulties with the project, some of them due to a rare case of writer's block in initially putting pen to paper. Another problem was Reddy himself, who demurred when he read a completed draft, on the grounds that, 'There are too many things here that will unnecessarily upset too many people. I have finished my career and I want to be left alone in peace' (Lal 2015: 68). Compromises were reached, but not without heartache and tension, and publication eventually went ahead. In the final paragraphs of his essay, Brij reveals himself in searing terms, with his own three decades of anguish tumbling into the open:

---

9   See also Morgan (2015: 131–52) for the more positive reflections of a biographer who has also dealt with living subjects, in his case the British politicians James Callaghan (1912–2005) and Michael Foot (1913–2010).

> I relived the tumultuous events of the post-independence years that I had witnessed as a bystander: the pettiness of political leaders, corrupt and self-serving; the rampant racism; the arrogance of power; the coups and chaos; the fractured hopes and betrayal of promises; and the struggle of one man, not perfect by any means, hobbled by bitter divisions among his own people and facing the wrath of men convinced of their God-given right to rule irrespective of the verdict of the ballot box; the struggle by one man to find an honourable middle course for his people and for his country. All that sacrifice, all that anguish and heartache, came to nought in the end. To relive all this was a deeply painful experience for Reddy, as it was for me. I know in my heart that I would not be able to write this book now; the grief is simply overwhelming at how we ended up where we are: in a cul-de-sac where the prospects of genuine democracy look exceedingly bleak, where guns, not good arguments, rule the day (Lal 2015: 73–74).

Brij's feelings could be summed up in the words that his friend Vincent O'Sullivan used in another context: '[There is] a difference between the silence after the music, and the silence when there is no more music' (O'Sullivan 2003: 165).

His more recent autobiographical writings have become ever more reflective and sombre, revealing more of the so-called 'inner man'. It came as a complete surprise to read about his sadness that he cannot share with his Australian friends, unless they happen to be Hindu, his religious and cultural heritage: 'My inner world remains a mystery to them. I regret very much not being able to share my cultural life more fully, more meaningfully, with people whose friendship I genuinely value' (Lal 2008: 213). Longstanding friends had no idea that he felt this way. Conversely, when he was still allowed to enter Fiji, Brij found it difficult to connect with younger Indo-Fijians and to village life generally. Escaping his poor rural background carries unexpected penalties, which others seldom realise.

Also, in what might serve as a 'signing off' essay ('Coombs 4240: a room of my own'), Brij speaks of his 25 years in his office at the ANU, his home away from home with which he has deep communion. It recalls Kipling's poem *Sussex*:

> God gave all men all earth to love
>   But, since our hearts are small,
> Ordained to each one spot should prove
>   Beloved over all.

This fabled space had character all of its own—festooned with posters and photographs, crowded out by bookshelves, a littered desk where Brij could still find anything (except people's addresses). It was where he did most of his writing. 'Coombs 4240' also contains reflections on the changes to university life since he started out. He does not like what he has seen and experienced and he registers a firm and heartfelt protest at the consequences of the corporate/management model of university governance (Lal 2011: 127–38). He is dismayed by the supine response from the academy: 'The troubling thing is how meekly academics have capitulated to such pressure. By our acquiescence we have been complicit in the making of the mess that confronts us today' (Lal 2011: 136). Neither is Brij at ease with the new regime governing PhD supervision, which he feels involves too much bureaucracy and handholding. He likes even less the bean counting when it comes to assessing academic writing and how this prioritises productivity over creativity.

Another 'signing off' essay is 'When it is over' (Lal 2011: 1–7), which also serves as an *apologia pro mea sua*. Here, he expresses his discomfort that 'the narcissism of the younger generation [of Pacific historians] sometimes erases the historical subject itself … It is for me too late to change. Nor, if truth be told, would I want to' (Lal 2011: 5, 134–35). Like myself, he is happy being the type of historian he is. We have no desire to being other than what we are.

It's a good time to be going into retirement, especially when Brij's own part of the ANU, the School of Culture, History and Language, has been comprehensively gutted in yet another restructuring. But the real significance of 'When it is over' is to reveal what lies behind his work ethic, his commitment to his craft and, indeed, what impels him to further exertions when he has already done enough. He once said to me, 'I'd be enormously dissatisfied if I didn't accomplish what I set out to do'. It explains why he is so taken by Mary Oliver's poem 'When death comes', which reads in part, 'When it's over, I don't want to wonder whether I have made of my life something particular, and real … / I don't want to end up simply by having visited this earth' (Oliver 1992: 10–11, quoted in Lal 2011: 1)

Faction

Brij's faction stories are concerned one way or another with the Indo-Fijian, whether at home or abroad. These texts get beneath the surface appearances to the internal dynamics—the egos, the stresses and strains of relationships, patterns of conflict and power, defining the rules of the game. There is no nostalgia when it comes to village life: the irony is that Brij sets out to recapture a world he is glad to have escaped. That world is portrayed as containing little joy and much sadness as people cope with the hardships of daily life, the pervasive turmoil of personal relationships and the frequent enough injustices of social interactions. Some may find it strange that Brij finds creative writing far more difficult than writing scholarly history. The New Zealand historian and novelist Ann Beaglehole finds creative writing easier because there are no footnotes, and neither is there the endless checking and verification of text and footnotes alike.[10] Brij, by contrast, finds having to conjure up his own storyline far more taxing and burdensome.

The best-known of his faction stories is 'Mr Tulsi's Store' (Lal 2001: 45–57). More precisely, Mr Tulsi was the moneylender at Brij's home village of Tabia and the story revolves around Brij's own family. The two brothers at loggerheads are his father and uncle, and the father never forgave being betrayed by his sibling. In 'Kismet' (Lal 2001: 185–205), Brij rather regrets deploying the first person because people jump to the conclusion that the story is about himself, when in fact it is about one of his school teachers. But events similar to those described did happen; there *was* the romantic entanglement between teacher and schoolgirl, and the two *were* of different faiths. 'Mr Tulsi's Store' and 'Kismet' stray from strict factuality. But they are as true to experience and lived emotions as Brij can make them, and they recall J.B. Priestley's comment on the television series *Hancock's Half Hour*—that every episode 'told us more about the human condition, more about the failure of 1950s society, than 100 student demonstrations' (quoted in Goodwin 1999: 222). Or as historian Max Beloff has said:

> Sometimes I think the novelist may be a better guide to what we need to know and understand. Trollope's political novels are worth innumerable academic theses about nineteenth-century politics; Paul Scott's *Raj Quartet*

---

10 Ann Beaglehole, telephone discussion with author, 27 November 2016. See also 'Beaglehole, Ann'. n.d. *New Zealand Book Council Te Kaunihera Pukapuka o Aotearoa*.

is more illuminating than anything else that has been written about the 'transfer of power' in India. Historians do a more mundane job and are perhaps rightly less well regarded and less well rewarded (Beloff 1992: 24).

All the same, there is a credibility gap with 'Kismet', which occurred within a watching and a gossiping society. It is most unlikely that such an affair could have gone on for so long before being discovered. Or at least that is my perception, whereas Brij, not at all defensively, assures me that I would be surprised at how many secrets *do* remain hidden in small communities.

Brij's latest faction book is entitled *Turnings* (2008) and one of those 'turnings' refers to the crossroads in his career when he was combining writing conventional history and faction. Being freed from the shackles of the eternal footnote has an appeal, yet Lal constantly reminds that he writes faction as a historian:

> I revisit the village but with a historian's mindset, disciplined imagination: you say 'I am on trial, I am on oath to tell the truth'. So in what I describe I try to capture the inner truth of that experience' (quoted in Athique 2006: 213, 330–31).

Thus, 'Marriage' (Lal 2008: 35–51) graphically relates the frictions that can occur when the bride moves in with her husband's family. Again, the family involved was Brij's. In 'Across the Fence' (Lal 2008: 71–94), Gita gets a sweet taste of what life is like on the outside but has to return to the drudgery of looking after a small shop and an unappreciative invalid husband. In 'The Dux of Naisinu' (Lal 2008: 13–33), the impossibly idealistic school teacher gets unjustly caught up in the local rumour mill and is professionally ruined. In 'In Mr Tom's Country' there is an overtly political message. Mr Tom, a former Colonial Sugar Refinery inspector, is outraged at the treatment of Indo-Fijians, who are the economic backbone of the country: 'You take them out and the whole place will fall apart. Just like that. What wrong have they done? How have they wronged the Fijian people? Their only vices are thrift and industry' (Lal 2008: 147). This is Brij's one faction story where the main character is not in Indo-Fijian.

Brij's faction broadly follows the trajectory of his writings on Indo-Fijian indenture, and indeed the broad contours of his own life. His stories have increasingly moved away from the village setting, a function of Brij increasingly feeling out of place when visiting Tabia. Moreover, the actual themes in his indenture writings—of qualified survival and enforced adaptation (not necessarily for the better)—recur in his faction writing. And just as Brij has written scholarly articles about Indian indenture in sugar colonies besides Fiji (e.g. Lal 1998, 2000: 41–66), as well as second wave of migrations (Lal 2011: 139–55), his faction has chased the later diaspora (or second migration) of expatriate Indo-Fijians adjusting to their new places of abode.

The transmigrations following the 1987 and 2000 coups and the compromises of relocation are the stuff of his later faction stories. A notable example is 'An Australian Fusion' (Lal 2008: 173–95), which explores the recurring tensions between the older generation trying to hold onto the values of their homeland and a younger generation embracing the norms of the host society. Ramesh is set in his ways and secure in his cultural values, and has enormous difficulty in reconciling to the fact that his daughter is becoming Australianised and spurning her Indian heritage, which she thinks is a sham in any case. He eventually recognises that he has to make adjustments or else he will ruin his marriage and tear his family apart. That particular story is too close to the bone for some Indo-Australian youngsters—and their parents—let it be said. Perhaps, then, faction writing and conventional history have more similarities than differences in that their central concern is to get to the heart of the human experience.[11] Brij feels that his faction stories will stand or fall by the quality of the writing, how far they plausibly evoke a past time and the extent to which they plausibly express moments of action and passion.

Denouement

There is a synergy between Brij's faction writing and his writing of conventional history; he writes his faction with the mindset of an historian but one freed from the fetters of the eternal footnote. There is another way of looking at it in the sense that his faction represents a return to his roots in English literature. He had initially intended to major in English language and literature at USP but was repelled by a course in transformational grammar and turned to history instead (Lal 1992: 245). This was the first of his several 'turnings'. His computer-based PhD thesis on the origins of the Fiji Indians represents another bend in the road, and such work

---

11 Another tale of compromise and adjustment is recounted in 'Kumkum: Maya's story' (Lal 2007b: 309–27).

was certainly out of character with his inclinations: 'It was a PhD. It had to be done' is how he matter-of-factually described the situation to me. It comes as no surprise that he was only too glad to escape the world of quantification at the first opportunity and return to the documentary and humanistic history with which he was more comfortable. In the same way, he familiarised himself with comparative electoral systems, not for its own sake or as a matter of abiding interest but because it was necessary to his constitutional advising (Lal 1997: 39–72). Again, he opted out of this line of country when the need passed. Another bend in the road was, from the early 1980s, branching out into contemporary history—and this before the 1987 coups that were instrumental in the 'contemporary turn' in Pacific Islands historiography. When he turned to faction in the late '90s, it was not a digression but, rather, closing the circle and returning to what he started off doing.

James Walvin's autobiography of childhood and adolescence has already been referred to. Like Brij, Walvin grew up in straightened circumstances—a working-class background in the Great Manchester area—and he too received a university education only by virtue of a competitive scholarship. Walvin's maternal grandfather said to him in his inimitably blunt style, 'You're a lucky bugger' (Walvin 2014: 202). And so is Brij fortunate to have coincided with a window of opportunity that enabled kids from poor families to go to university on scholarships. But they still had to work for it.

References

Anderson, Benedict. 2016. *Life Beyond Boundaries: A Memoir*. London: Verso.

Athique, Tamara Mabbott. 2006. 'Textual migrations: South Asian-Australia fiction'. PhD thesis, University of Wollongong.

'Beaglehole, Ann.' n.d. *New Zealand Book Council Te Kaunihera Pukapuka o Aotearoa*. Online: www.bookcouncil.org.nz/writer/beaglehole-ann/ (accessed 6 March 2017).

Beloff, Max. 1992. *An Historian in the Twentieth Century: Chapters in Intellectual Autobiography*. New Haven/London: Yale University Press.

Borrie, Jan. 2004. 'Creative endeavours'. *Quarterly Bulletin* (ANU), 5(1): 9–11.

Boyde, Melissa. 2009. 'The modernist *roman à clef* and cultural secrets, or I know that you know that I know that you know'. *Australian Literary Studies*, 24(3–4): 155–66. DOI: 10.20314/als.dfae519805.

Braithwaite, Errol. 1971. *The Night We Stole The Mountie's Car*. Toronto: McCelland & Stewart.

Bullock, Alan. 2000. *Building Jerusalem: A Portrait of My Father*. London: Allen Lane.

Carr, Bob. 2008. *My Reading Life: Adventures in the World of Books*. Melbourne: Viking.

Catanach, Ian. 1970. *Rural Credit in Western India: Rural Credit and the Co-operative Movement in the Bombay Presidency, 1875–1930*. Berkeley: University of California Press.

Chand, Pratap. 2013. *A Fijian Memoir: Footprints of a Girmitiya's Grandson*. Lautoka: Vicas Press.

Clark, Manning. 1969. *Disquiet and Other Stories*. Sydney: Angus & Robertson.

——. 1986. *Collected Short Stories*. Ringwood: Penguin Books.

Clark, Margaret with Jim Collinge and Martin Lodge (eds). 1999. *John Mansfield Thompson: Notes Towards a Biography*. Wellington: Steele Roberts.

Clark, William C. 2000. *Pacific Voices, Pacific Views: Poets as Commentators on the Contemporary Pacific*. Canberra: Centre for the Contemporary Pacific, The Australian National University.

Collinson, Patrick. 2011. *The History of a History Man—or, the Twentieth Century Viewed from a Safe Distance*. Woodbridge, UK: Boydell Press.

Corris, Peter. 2007. 'Doing history'. *Overland* (Melbourne), 187: 61–63.

Crick, Bernard. 1981. *George Orwell: A Life*, 2nd ed. London: Secker & Warburg.

Denoon, Donald. 1996. 'An accidental historian'. *Journal of Pacific Studies*, 20: 209–12.

Drabble, Margaret (ed.). 1995. *Oxford Companion to English Literature*, 5th ed. Oxford: Oxford University Press.

Fuller, Peter. 2001. 'Profile: Donald Denoon'. *Quarterly Bulletin* (ANU), 2(2): 10–12.

Ganguly, Debjani and Kavita Nandan (eds). 1998. *Unfinished Journeys: India File from Canberra*. Adelaide: Centre for Research in the New Literatures in English, Flinders University.

Goodwin, Cliff. 1999. *When the Wind Changed: The Life and Death of Tony Hancock*. London: Century.

Hempenstall, Peter. 2007. 'Overcoming separate histories: Historians as "ideas traders" in the trans-Tasman world'. *History Australia*, 4(1): 04.1–04.16. DOI: 10.2104/ha070004.

Hexter, J.H. 1961. *Reappraisals in History*. Evanston, IL: Harper Torchbooks.

Kammen, Michael. 1982. 'Vanitas and the historian's vocation'. *Reviews in American History*, 10(4): 1–27. DOI: 10.2307/2701816.

Lal, Brij. V. 1979. 'Fiji girmitiyas: Background to banishment'. In *Rama's Banishment: A Centenary Tribute to the Fiji Indians*, edited by Vijay Mishra, pp. 12–39. Auckland and London: Heinemann Educational Books.

——. 1992. *Broken Waves: A History of Fiji in the Twentieth Century*. Honolulu: University of Hawai'i Press.

——. 1997. 'A new electoral system for Fiji: Recommendations of the Fiji Constitution Review Commission'. In *Electoral Systems in Divided Societies: The Fiji Constitution Review*, edited by Brij V. Lal and Peter Larmour, pp. 39–72. Canberra: National Centre for Development Studies and Stockholm: Institute for Democracy and Electoral Assistance.

——. 1998. 'Understanding the Indian indenture experience'. *South Asia*, 21: 215–37. DOI: 10.1080/00856409808723356.

——. 2000. *Chalo Jahaji: On a Journey through Indenture in Fiji*. Canberra: Division of Pacific and Southeast Asian History, The Australian National University.

——. 2001. *Mr Tulsi's Store: A Fijian Journey*. Canberra: Pandanus Books.

——. 2003. 'The road to Mr Tulsi's store'. *Meanjin*, 62(4): 42–48.

——. 2004. *Bittersweet: The Indo-Fijian Experience*. Canberra: Pandanus Books.

——. 2005. *On the Other Side of Midnight: A Fijian Journey*. New Delhi: National Book Trust.

——. 2007a. 'Pacific history matters'. *Journal de la Societe des Oceanistes*, 125: 193–200. DOI: 10.4000/jso.894.

——. 2007b. 'Kumkum: Maya's story'. *Cultural Dynamics*, 19(3–4): 309–27. DOI: 10.1177/0921374007080297.

——. 2008. *Turnings: Fiji Factions*. Lautoka: Fiji Institute of Applied Studies.

——. 2011. *Intersections: History, Memory, Discipline*. Lautoka: Fiji Institute of Applied Studies and Sydney: Asia Pacific Publications.

——. 2015. '"End of a phase of history": Writing the life of a reluctant Fiji politician'. In *Political Life Writing in the Pacific: Reflections on Practice*, edited by Jack Corbett and Brij V. Lal, pp. 59–74. Canberra: ANU Press. Online: press.anu.edu.au?p=319171 (accessed 16 January 2017).

Lal, Brij V. (ed.). 1992. *Pacific Islands History: Journeys and Transformations*. Canberra: The Journal of Pacific History.

Lal, Brij V. and Peter Hempenstall (eds). 2001. *Pacific Lives, Pacific Places: Bursting Boundaries in Pacific History*. Canberra: The Journal of Pacific History.

Lal, Brij V. and Peter Larmour (eds). 1997. *Electoral Systems in Divided Societies: The Fiji Constitution Review*. Canberra: National Centre for Development Studies and Stockholm: Institute for Democracy and Electoral Assistance.

Lal, Brij V. and Allison Ley (eds). 2006. *The Coombs: A House of Memories*. Canberra: Research School of Pacific and Asian Studies, The Australian National University.

Langdon, Robert. 1995. *Every Goose a Swan: An Australian Autobiography*. Sydney: Farm Cove Press.

LeMahieu, D.L. 2014. '"Scholarship boys" in twilight: The memoirs of six humanists in post-industrial Britain'. *Journal of British Studies*, 53(4): 1011–31. DOI: 10.1017/jbr.2014.110.

Mansfield, Bruce. 2012. *Summer Is Almost Over: A Memoir*. Canberra: Barton Books.

Mishra, Vijay (ed.). 1979. *Rama's Banishment: A Centenary Tribute to the Fiji Indians*. Auckland and London: Heinemann Educational Books.

Morgan, Kenneth O. 2015. *My Histories*. Cardiff: University of Wales Press.

Munro, Doug. 2001. 'J.W. Davidson—the making of a participant historian'. In *Pacific Lives, Pacific Places: Bursting Boundaries in Pacific History*, edited by Brij V. Lal and Peter Hempenstall, pp. 98–116. Canberra: The Journal of Pacific History.

——. 2009. *The Ivory Tower and Beyond: Participant Historians of the Pacific*. Newcastle-upon-Tyne: Cambridge Scholars Publishing.

National Federation Party. 1997. 'Ben's funeral'. In *Fiji: The Road Ahead*, pp. 69–76. Suva: National Federation Party.

O'Brien, Gregory. 2007. *A Nest of Singing Birds: 100 Years of the* New Zealand School Journal. Wellington: Learning Media Limited.

O'Sullivan, Vincent. 2003. Untitled eulogy. In *John Mansfield Thomson: Notes towards a Biography*, edited by Margaret Clark with Jim Collinge and Martin Lodge, pp. 163–65. Wellington: Steele Roberts.

Oliver, Mary. 1992. 'When death comes'. In *New and Selected Poems Volume 1*, pp. 10–11. Boston, MA: Beacon Press.

Partington, Geoffrey. 2015. *Party Days*. Sydney: Xlibris.

Raicola, Verenaisi. 2007. 'Fiji, a home like no other'. *Fiji Times*, 13 December, p. 7.

Ranger, Terence. 2013. *Writing Revolt: An Engagement with African nationalism, 1957–67*. Woodbridge: James Currey and Harare: Weaver Press.

Riemer, Andrew. 1996. *The Demidenko Debate*. Sydney: Allen & Unwin.

Sharma, Kamlesh. 2007. *Rahul's Road: Memories of a Fijiindian Childhood*. Canberra: KPS Publications.

Spate, Oskar. 2006. 'The salad days'. In *The Coombs: A House of Memories*, edited by Brij V. Lal and Allison Ley, pp. 23–33. Canberra: Research School of Pacific and Asian Studies, The Australian National University.

Stead, C.K. 2008. *Book Shelf: The Reader as Writer and the Writer as Critic*. Auckland: Auckland University Press.

Subramani. 2001. *Dauka Puran*. New Delhi: Star Publications.

Vakatora, Tomasi. 1988. *From the Mangrove Swamps*. Suva: Institute of Pacific Studies of the University of the South Pacific.

Walvin, James. 2014. *Different Times: Growing up in Post-War England*. York: Algie Books.

Wiskemann, Elizabeth. 1966. *Europe of the Dictators, 1919–1945*. London and Glasgow: Fontana Library.

Worden, Blair. 2015. 'Introduction'. In *Hugh Trevor-Roper: The Historian*, edited by Blair Worden, pp. 1–41. London and New York: I.B. Tauris.

Worden, Blair (ed.). 2015. *Hugh Trevor-Roper: The Historian*. London and New York: I.B. Tauris.

Tributes

13

Aloha e Brij

David Hanlon

Other contributors to this volume will no doubt comment on the undeniable quality and absolutely stunning volume of Brij Lal's scholarship. In this short essay dealing with Brij's time in Hawai'i, however, I would like to focus on other attributes that help explain his rise as one of the most prominent and certainly the most prolific Pacific historian of his generation. I have always been struck by Brij's persistence, courage, graciousness and upbeat ways. Those attributes certainly showed themselves in Hawai'i, but first there is the story of our simultaneous hire by the Department of History back in 1983. The position in Pacific history had been deemed an important one given the University of Hawai'i's geographical location. Gavan Daws had served with distinction as the department's Pacific historian. Tim Macnaught ably replaced him but decided, after securing promotion and tenure, to return to Australia. The search for Tim's successor proved difficult and frustrating. Invitations to apply were sent to established historians in the field but most declined. Ian Campbell taught for a term in 1981 but he declined the offer of a tenured position. There was a hopeful breakthrough when Stewart Firth agreed to accept the departmental search committee's offer of a regular, tenure track position. Stewart arrived in August of 1982 but by October of that year, had decided that the cost of living in Honolulu was just too prohibitive (Lal 1987: 3–4).

Division along generational, ethnic and political lines characterised the Department of History in the early 1980s. Political differences, coupled with professional rivalries that became personal, added to the tense environment. When it came time to choose Stewart's successor, those divisions showed themselves quite clearly. Brij and I were the finalists for the position; department members split their votes evenly between us. The tie vote was recorded on a blackboard in the department's library and was left up for several days for any and all to see. The stalemate was broken when someone observed that the department actually had a second position in Pacific history that had gone unfilled for a number of years. The decision, then, was to hire the both of us. At the risk of deluding myself, I'd like to think that things ultimately worked out well for all parties concerned, here and in the broader region.

I wanted to establish a strong personal as well as professional relationship with my new colleague, and decided to introduce Brij and his family to the island of Oʻahu. Shortly after they arrived in late July 1983, I took Brij, Padma and young Yogi on a ride around the island; Niraj would arrive on the scene later. When we got to the cane fields above Haleiwa on the North Shore, an auspicious place to stop given Brij's family history, I spied a pickup truck selling sweet Kahuku watermelons by the side of the road. I thought at the time that watermelon would be an appropriate welcoming gift. I pulled over, got out of the car, and began to purchase a whole melon when I realised I didn't have enough money with me. Brij graciously stepped forward, paid for the watermelon himself, and gave it to me as a gift! I still cringe every time I recall that trip around the island with Brij and his family.

The size, formality and hierarchy of the department surprised Brij. It took some getting used to. Life in Hawaiʻi also took some adjustment and was never easy for Brij and his family, as attested to by the chapter 'A Sojourn in Hawaiʻi' in his autobiographical collection of stories entitled *Mr Tulsi's Store* (Lal 2001: 111–26) The cost of living was the highest in the United States. This was particularly true for housing where the lack of quality added insult to the high rents being charged. Brij and his family started out in faculty housing, and later moved to a small cottage behind a large house on Kealaʻolu Street in the Kahala area of East Honolulu before purchasing a townhouse in Hawaiʻi Kai, one of the island's newest suburban developments at the time. A little more than a year after his arrival, the US Immigration and Naturalization Service ruled that Brij could only be granted a temporary visa because he was occupying a position for which there existed qualified American scholars. Reports of the ruling reached the newspapers. Already overburdened by the demands of teaching, research and advising students, Brij found his days crowded with meetings to attend, forms to fill out and telephone calls to return, all of this related to his visa status. Had that determination not been reversed by his persistence and the efforts of colleagues, university administrators, and Hawai'i's congressional delegation, Brij's sojourn in Hawai'i would have been short.

The 1980s was a tumultuous time on campus and in the broader state. Native Hawaiians were demanding sovereignty, and the redress of injustices and wrongs that followed the overthrow of the monarchy in 1893. There was a natural affinity and alliance between Hawaiian and Pacific studies in this period, and Brij was very much a facilitator and supporter of that alliance. He got along well with Haunani-Kay Trask, the head of the Center for Hawaiian Studies and the campus's most outspoken advocate on behalf of Native Hawaiian rights. Brij encouraged those Native Hawaiian students who sought to do a doctorate in Pacific history because there existed no real equivalent degree option in Hawaiian history. Being supportive of Native Hawaiian causes did not mean for Brij the abandonment of scholarly standards, however; he let it be known that politics could not substitute for a rigorous engagement with the archives.

Brij and I worked well together on behalf of Pacific history, while effectively bridging the divide that separated our respective supporters. We sometimes gave private, not-very-flattering nicknames to one or two of our more pompous senior colleagues, and had a good laugh when using those names. Things turned around quickly for Pacific history. We revised the curriculum, and added new courses. Under Brij's leadership, enrolment in our undergraduate Pacific history courses doubled, and there were soon more than a dozen students doing advanced degree programs in the field. Students from other fields of study found their way to our courses and seminars as well. Brij offered a graduate seminar on the Southwest Pacific during the fall 1985 semester that enrolled more than 20 students, an unheard of number for a seminar then and now. Brij's presence also helped attract a number of leading scholars in Pacific history to Mānoa: Ahmed Ali, Greg Dening, Francis X. Hezel, S.J., Kerry Howe, Barrie Macdonald, and Caroline Ralston all addressed formal gatherings sponsored by the Department of History or other units on campus.

BEARING WITNESS

During his time in Hawai'i, Brij kept a keen eye on political developments in his native Fiji. The coups of 1987 brought great pain and sorrow that were exacerbated by the distance that separated him from his extended family and homeland. At the same time, he was energised to speak out, and in ways that required great courage. There were those in Hawai'i who also hailed from Fiji but who held decidedly different views on the causes and cures of political unrest there. Brij was threatened on more than one occasion with bodily harm, but these efforts at intimidation did not deter him from speaking out or privately confronting his harassers. Later, his ceaseless advocacy for true democracy in Fiji would earn him official banishment and exile from his homeland. The courage to advocate, protest, criticise and speak out was honed in part in Hawai'i, I think.

Among our assignments as young assistant professors was the teaching of History 151 and 152, or World Civilization as it was known then. It was an impossible two-course sequence taught in a lecture format to audiences of between 300 and 400 students in large auditoriums. The avowed purpose of the course was to provide students with a sense of the sweep of the human past. Undaunted, Brij came to relish the assignment and carried it out with energy, enthusiasm and considerable success. He has written and spoken about the skills that he developed teaching that course, skills that served him well in his later academic and public career. Less well known are the binders of meticulously researched, handwritten lectures that he developed for the course and that he keeps in his office to this day. I remember an occasion a number of years ago when Brij was on campus during one of his frequent visits to Hawai'i. He stopped by the Department of History to say hello to former colleagues. While in the department offices speaking to the staff, Brij was introduced to a young assistant professor and recent hire who knew Brij by reputation. In the course of casual conversation, the young academic mentioned that he was giving a lecture that day on indentured labour. Without hesitation, notes or time to prepare, Brij offered to deliver the lecture himself, and proceeded to do so. To this day, that young academic, now a tenured associate professor with an impressive list of scholarly publications, speaks with an awe and amazement about Brij's feat.

It is not necessary to list here all of Brij's many books. Bob Kiste, the former director of the Center for Pacific Islands Studies at Mānoa, and I used to have a running joke when Brij's name came up in conversation in the years after his departure from Hawai'i. 'Another year, another book by Lal,' we'd say, 'how does he do it?' Like everyone else, we were stunned by his prodigious output. Brij was not just an incredibly productive scholar, he was a generous one as well who sought to give voice and make space for others. He brought many of us along on his own intellectual journeys, as evidenced in the numerous volumes he edited by himself or with colleagues, and that followed conferences in Canberra or elsewhere in the region that were characterised by their substance, hospitality and intellectual camaraderie.

I have always been impressed by the diversity of mediums through which Brij communicates. He is committed to the peoples about whom he writes and through histories that don't always use footnotes. He is a public intellectual who believes in accessible prose and good stories. Since leaving Hawai'i, Brij has become an advocate of what he calls 'faction', or the use of creative writing to impart the human stories that are often left out of academic histories. I and other contributors to this volume may risk embarrassing Brij with our words of praise on the occasion of his retirement from The Australian National University, but the truth is that he has embarrassed us with his incredible productivity, unflappable collegiality and his deep caring for the peoples of the Pacific about whom he writes with true commitment.

Hawai'i did not make Brij, but it certainly nourished and encouraged him. The energy, talent and drive that would make Brij such a force in Pacific history from the 1990s on was already on display in this corner of the region. His arrival here coincided with the publication of his first book, *Girmitiyas: The Origins of the Fiji Indians* (1983). There soon followed an edited collection of essays on Fiji politics published by Allen & Unwin, and a series of articles appearing in scholarly journals including the *Journal of Pacific History*, the *Indian Economic and Social Review*, and *Pacific Studies*. Brij later co-edited with Bob Kiste and Kerry Howe a much-needed volume on twentieth-century Pacific history put out by the University of Hawai'i Press.

At the same time, Brij proved a model citizen within and beyond the confines of the Mānoa campus. He gave numerous talks at the East-West Center, on other campuses in the University of Hawai'i system, and to teachers' workshops and local public schools. Along with the late Professor Leonard Mason of the University of Hawai'i Anthropology Department, Brij served as a consultant for Hawai'i Public Television's series on contemporary Pacific Islands cultures. He did not shirk his service obligations to the History Department: he sat on a variety of committees that dealt with the administrative, procedural and programmatic concerns of academic life. He was always there and with that cheerful, energetic, can-do-anything attitude of his. He was supportive of colleagues of all ranks and did not forget those who had helped him to this point in his career. Brij joined with other members of the History Department in establishing a fitting memorial tribute for the late Professor Walter Johnson, an early mentor and supporter whom Brij had encountered during his student days at the University of the South Pacific when Johnson was there as a visiting professor. Within two years of his arrival in Hawai'i, Brij successfully applied for promotion to the rank of associate professor with tenure, something that usually requires five or more years of research, teaching and service from the recently hired. The only vice I saw Brij exhibit during his time here was an obsession with cricket, a bad habit to be sure but one that was difficult to indulge in the Hawai'i of the 1980s.

Brij developed a special bond with the Center for Pacific Islands Studies at Mānoa, and its director, Bob Kiste. The Center was funded largely through a grant from the United States Department of Education, and was designated as a National Resource Center for the Pacific Islands, the only one of its kind in the United States. Based on the postwar area studies approach, the Center offered an MA degree in Pacific Islands studies and had an active community outreach program. Brij soon became one of the Center's core affiliate faculty members, and was instrumental in helping it to develop an active publishing program that soon became the envy of the entire region.

It was an exciting time for Pacific Islands studies at Mānoa. I remember vividly the numerous planning meetings leading to a well-crafted proposal that secured a funding grant from the university administration to start *The Contemporary Pacific: A Journal of Island Affairs*. We made a strong effort to recruit distinguished contributors to our inaugural issue and managed to secure submissions from scholars such as Harold Brookfield, Greg Dening, Stewart Firth, Johan Galtung, Stephen Henningham, Fran Hezel and Roger Keesing. Brij served as the journal's first editor. The meetings he chaired were models of their kind. He would come in with a set agenda that dealt primarily with decisions on whether or not to accept a manuscript for publication. Brij would describe the submissions' contents, summarise the readers' reports, and offer his recommendations. The thoroughness of his preparation was such that there was little need for comment or extended discussion. Those of us who later followed

Brij as editor of the journal had to confront the reality that we were not Brij Lal, and that our recommendations required supporting documentation and more extensive discussion from the members of the editorial board. Brij and I also served as founding members of the editorial board for the Pacific Islands Monograph Series (PIMS), a publication outlet for quality manuscripts on the Pacific Islands that might otherwise go unpublished because of sales and marketing considerations. Bob Kiste often expressed amazement that so many of the series' first volumes had to do with history; he thought it serendipitous but Brij and I knew better. Brij's concerns for the promotion of scholarship extended to students. With the support of Bob and the Center, Brij edited a collection of student writings entitled *Wansalawara* (Lal 1987) that helped establish a tradition of support and encouragement for student scholarship that is still very much alive and active today at the Center. Brij's debt to the Center led him to edit a Festschrift in honour of Bob Kiste on the occasion of his retirement. Brij also made it a point to return to Hawai'i for the launch of that book, *Pacific Places, Pacific Histories: Essays in Honor of Robert C. Kiste*. The introduction that he wrote for that volume is an eloquent testament to his deep gratitude to Bob and the Center (Lal 2004: 1–27).

As successful as he'd been at Hawai'i, Brij felt the pull to be nearer to events in his still-troubled homeland of Fiji. An appointment at The Australian National University offered him the opportunity he sought. Brij left the University of Hawai'i in 1991, though he returned on numerous occasions to give talks, participate in conferences or simply drop in to say hello while in transit to or from other destinations. In 2005, Brij served as an external examiner for the Center for Pacific Islands Studies. The review was required under the terms of the National Resource Center grant that funded the Center's programs. Brij's past history with the Center did not mean a pass. He chaired the review committee and authored, shortly after his return to Canberra, a lengthy report that combined praise and appreciation with a healthy dose of constructive criticism. That was the thing about Brij; his personal warmth and congeniality never compromised his insistence on excellence.

Let me close this all-too-brief remembrance and reflection by addressing Brij directly. It has been an honour and a privilege to count you as a friend and a colleague for more than 30 years, Brij. Thank you for all of the many ways that you supported and assisted me, and so many others here in Hawai'i. Please know that the aloha that you have shown so many of us here over the years is not forgotten and is more than reciprocated.

References

Lal, Brij V. 1983. *Girmitiyas: The Origins of the Fiji Indians*. Canberra: The Journal of Pacific History.

——. 1987. 'Introduction.' In *Wansalawara: Soundings in Melanesian History*, edited by Brij Lal, pp. 1–11. Honolulu: Center for Pacific Islands Studies, Occasional Paper. University of Hawai'i at Mānoa.

——. 2001. *Mr Tulsi's Store: A Fijian Journey*. Canberra: Pandanus Books.

——. 2004. 'Place and person: An introduction'. In *Pacific Places, Pacific Histories: Essays in Honor of Robert C. Kiste*, edited by Brij V. Lal, pp. 1–27. Honolulu: University of Hawai'i Press.

Lal, Brij V. (ed.). 1987. *Wansalawara: Soundings in Melanesian History*. Honolulu: Center for Pacific Islands Studies, Occasional Paper. University of Hawai'i at Mānoa.

——. (ed.). 2004. *Pacific Places, Pacific Histories: Essays in Honor of Robert C. Kiste*. Honolulu: University of Hawai'i Press.

14

In the Shadow of the Master Carver

Kate Fortune

Working with Brij Lal as assistant editor on the huge project that became *The Pacific Islands: An Encyclopedia*, published by University of Hawai'i Press in 2000, was in every way a wonderful, exhilarating, stimulating experience. My involvement began in 1996, when I was living in Canberra. I had been working in the Publications Branch of the National Library of Australia, when I saw an advertisement in the *Canberra Times* that caught my attention. In mid-June I went to be interviewed in the Coombs building at The Australian National University. Supplied with very specific directions by a helpful receptionist, I crossed the interior courtyard, climbed a series of stairwells and followed seemingly endless quaintly angled corridors. I am accustomed to navigational challenges—orienteering is my chosen sport—but the honeycomb layout of Coombs building would test the resourcefulness of any explorer. Eventually, of course, it became familiar territory for me, but (even as a seasoned staff member) I never lost my original sense of delight that the best way to go down was sometimes to go up a few steps first (and probably to turn left initially if you needed to end up in a right-hand wing).

My employment at ANU commenced at the start of September 1996, with the title of Research Assistant: Pacific Islands Historical Encyclopedia at the Research School of Pacific and Asian Studies, and with an office right next to Brij Lal. From that very first morning, I arrived at work with a smile on my face, reading the names on each door and feeling as if I were skimming the shelves of the 'Pacific section' of the library. Donald Denoon, Hank Nelson, Deryck Scarr, Robert Langdon, Niel Gunson, Gerry Ward, Dorothy Shineberg, Darrell Tryon, Tom Dutton, Ron May; and also, in close proximity, Atholl Anderson, Bill Gammage, Matthew Spriggs, Peter Bellwood, Michael Bourke, Peter Dauvergne, Sinclair Dinnen, Bronwen Douglas, Geoffrey Hope, Kurt Lambeck, Ewan Maidment, Alan Rumsey, Peter Sack, Nicholas Thomas, Michael Young … what a treasure trove of Pacific scholarship!

Brij's door was always open. We would have quick informal chats every few days, but the formal project development was achieved through our regular monthly sessions when the two of us made and confirmed plans, discussed progress, agreed on new directions and dealt with problems. The role of the full editorial board, chaired by Professor Donald Denoon, was also significant. At least three years before I joined the team, they had developed the concept of a Pacific encyclopedia and set the original parameters, devising a thematic approach—and they continued to have the final say on possible topics and contributors, as well as reviewing submissions. Board meetings were held quite frequently in the early days, but Brij himself always seemed to me to be the heart and soul of the project.

For the long duration of this project, Brij's clear focus and intelligent vision never wavered, and his enthusiasm remained steady. I cannot imagine a better colleague, quick to understand and unravel any confusing query I brought to him, constantly alert to a drifting current and aware of whatever correction was required to get us back on course. His vast knowledge of Pacific history is matched by a thorough understanding of cultural, political and economic issues, closely linked with a gifted teacher's ability to explain a broad context and define useful connections.

All these attributes were essential to the encyclopedia project, but in a way, none of them would have been sufficient without one further special talent. Brij is the most highly skilled and efficient networker I have ever encountered, and I am sure that is the key 'secret ingredient' in our final achievement. His contacts across the Pacific are apparently infinite, and he is tireless in maintaining them. As far as I can see, he remembers everyone who has ever crossed his path, every speaker at Pacific conferences, every university colleague from his whole career. I'm sure he still spends hours every day on the phone and on emails; he always did in my time, and could

14. IN THE SHADOW OF THE MASTER CARVER

produce email addresses for anyone I needed to contact. If I reported to him that some potential contributor was unable to deliver the material we wanted, he would think about it briefly, then cheerfully come up with a fresh suggestion. If he couldn't identify a name instantly, he would supply it within 24 hours, occasionally perhaps after also consulting with someone else (like Max Quanchi) who had been involved in the project from the beginning.

Over time, I realised that Brij also maintains significant personal and social contacts in his own time. He and Padma work as an amazingly effective team, on a number of occasions hosting informal gatherings at their home. I was introduced to many visiting Pacific historians in this way, enjoying both the Lals' warm hospitality and the stimulating discussion of academic issues and political ideas on which Brij thrives. I especially recall an evening in honour of Kerry Howe, visiting from Auckland, when we relaxed in the garden under one of Canberra's glorious summer night skies.

On such memorable occasions, part of the enjoyment of the conversation arose from my awareness of Brij's keen intelligence and wide range of interests. I could see the respect in which he is held by his peers, and the way his articulate and thoughtful opinions are sought by those around him. I observed the way he provides useful feedback to other people on their research and writing, and I noted the appreciative response that such generous professional support invariably elicits.

Brij is astute in his judgements and wonderfully decisive. I very much appreciated this promptness and thoroughness in dealing with anything to do with the encyclopedia. When I provided him with copies of entries as they came in to the office, he was always quick either to advise on who else should read them, or to assess them himself and to comment on any that needed a supplementary article or just a little further information. Here, too, he was able to offer a range of possible names for me to contact, and his recommendations were always well chosen and wise.

Brij seems to have endless composure, superhuman patience and extraordinary diligence. University concerns, faculty budgets and academic business matters obviously impose considerable burdens (both time and energy) on senior staff members, added to normal teaching responsibilities on top of travel to conferences, etc. From my office next door, I observed his huge workload and came to have enormous respect for the effortless way he appeared to handle everything—while maintaining his own research and writing. I can't even imagine how he finds time to keep up his own formidable research output, because he is in constant demand as a speaker and a commentator, and those books and articles keep on appearing in print.

When it was time to take our vast project to a publisher, it was Brij's experience and his personal link to the University of Hawai'i Press that streamlined the process and facilitated the production of a very handsome book. Our publishing editor, Pamela Kelley, clearly trusted Brij. He has earned a considerable—and well-deserved—reputation of delivering a quality product.

An encyclopedia of the Pacific Islands on this scale had never been attempted before (and in this new digital age may never be repeated). It seems to me it might be compared to the building of a large sea-going Māori *waka* (canoe) in the way it requires teamwork—with a variety of skills—but also leadership, with everyone working under the guidance of the master carver. The vision behind the selection of the tree, the coordination to get the huge log conveyed to the right spot, the astute imagination behind the design, the strong emphasis on and respect for traditional techniques, the patience and the personal charisma to lead a team constructing a useful vehicle from the various components, and finally the sheer energy required over a long period of time to achieve something of this size and weight. I found Brij to be an inspirational motivator, and it was a privilege to work with him. Thanks to him, I consider my involvement in this project to have been an immensely satisfying job.

15

Meetings with the Three Lals: That's Brij Lal, Professor Lal and Brij V. Lal

Jack Corbett

I first met Brij Lal, the persona, in a book: his 1997 life of A.D. Patel. At the time I was in the first year of my PhD studies at The Australian National University (ANU), struggling with all manner of questions. Some of these were bound up in the mechanics of thesis writing—design, method, significance—but little questions beget bigger ones and so I was also searching for answers to life's great puzzles. I'm not sure I found many, but a PhD does force you to resolve to tackle such challenges in a certain way and thus to tacitly accept some well-worn intellectual values and beliefs. This is a pragmatic step as much as anything—a PhD cannot cover everything, not much at all really—and so, I was coming to learn, that to embark on telling a microstory requires borrowing some of the scaffolding from elsewhere, even if you intend to interrogate this at a later date.

For the PhD I was interested in political leadership, and, so, in addition to reading biographies and autobiographies of Pacific leaders, I was attempting to digest the literature on leadership, politics and democracy in the Pacific Islands. I was conflicted. I am a sceptic of donor efforts to promulgate 'good governance' around the world, and yet, despite my persistent reservations, I remain a democrat. At least, I was coming to realise this when I first met Brij Lal.

The Patel biography has many interesting and important themes but, in that moment, the one that resonated most was the uncompromising prosecution of a case that A.D. Patel, and through him Brij Lal, made for 'one vote, one value'. The phrase, so often repeated as to appear a meaningless trope, captures a powerful imagining of how the world could and should be, the radicalism of which is born out in the Gandhi-inspired vision that A.D. had for Fiji. Inevitably, practice falls short of the ideal, and the public lives of both Brij and A.D. are testament to the messy and unpredictable way human affairs, under any regime, are governed. The irony of this vision being achieved in Fiji by non-democratic means would be painfully apparent to both men. Nevertheless, the sentiment retains romantic value for me and influenced how my PhD took shape. Put simply, I began to put aside perennial questions about whether democracy was appropriate in a Pacific context, and started to think about the *people*, like A.D., who practised it. The link, for me, was the realisation that if I believed in democracy, with all its imperfections, then the PhD didn't have to (re)resolve questions about its appropriateness. I had decided where I stood and as a result was free to roam on the assumption that this form of government represents a good in its own right. Indeed, at times, to echo Bernard Crick (2000 [1962]), democracy might even require us to take up our pen in its defence.

Later in 2010, I met Brij Lal in person after attending a guest lecture he gave in a course on Pacific history. I was trying to track down the autobiographies and biographies of Pacific leaders and cornered him to seek his assistance. I don't recall much of the conversation—no doubt he was helpful—but I do remember his clothes. He wore a bula shirt—not a luridly colourful one but it carried the unmistakable pattern—dress pants and an Australian-style bush hat. At first glance, it struck me as an odd combination. On reflection, it still is, but perhaps it is also an apt ensemble that reflects both his personal history, his inherent pragmatism—it was a warm day—and his capacity to stand out in a crowd. Certainly, it told me something about his jovial character that I had not picked up from the book.

I next met Brij Lal later that year, this time via email. I had just finished reading his 2010 biography of Jai Ram Reddy and had decided to review it (it later became the first piece of writing I published in an academic journal). I sent the review to my then supervisor—Peter Larmour—for his comment and advice about where to publish it. He suggested that, once accepted, I ought to send it on to Brij. In the fullness of time, when the review was in press, I emailed him a copy. In return, he offered me a cup of tea in the Coombs Tea Room, and so, I met Brij Lal again for what was to become the first of many discussions. I would like to be able to say I remember every word of wisdom he offered me over that cup of tea, but what stands out—perhaps because he regularly repeats it—is his advice that 'great work gets in the way of good work', or, to put it another way, there are only two types of PhD: complete and incomplete. It is a mantra I now repeat to my students.

At the end of that first year Peter left the ANU for a chair at the University of the South Pacific and so I was in need of a new supervisor. I have since learnt that searching for a supervisor is a funny business, at any stage of candidature, but it seemed a particularly strange thing to be doing at a time when I already had a topic, had given my proposal talk and made a start on my empirical work. Essentially, the broad intellectual parameters of what I was doing were established—or at least I was fairly dogmatic that I wasn't going to alter my direction—and so I was seeking a supervisor who wouldn't want to tinker too much. Peter's preference was Brij and, I was told, he was happy to take me and my project on. Despite this advice, I was somewhat apprehensive—Brij is a polarising figure, both politically and intellectually, and Pacific Studies at the ANU is rife with factions, rivalries and intrigue (not to mention I had just reviewed his book).[1] What I admired about Peter was that he seemed able to work between the lines whilst, as Brij's student, I would become firmly ensconced in one camp. However, these doubts dissipated at the first panel meeting that Brij attended. He laid my proposal on the table, declared that I had achieved good progress, but said that he felt the value of the project was that it was about political people—the human dimension—and his only fear was that I would get side-tracked by the types of rigid theoretical arguments common in my discipline of political studies. It was music to my ears. And so, I began to regularly meet Professor Lal in his office.

Much of Professor Lal's writings, both academic and creative, revolve around questions and notions of home and belonging. I have never been to Labasa or the India of his ancestors. I have, however, been to Suva, Honolulu, Port Moresby, the leafy Canberra suburb of Aranda and, more

---

1   I submitted the review to Vicki Luker, the executive editor of the *Journal of Pacific History*, who passed it on to the then review editor, Doug Munro. That is how Doug and I first came into contact. Doug had already commissioned a reviewer (Ghai 2011) so we agreed that he send my review to the *Journal of Imperial and Commonwealth History*, where it was accepted (Corbett 2011).

recently, Jervis Bay, all places that Brij has, for a time, called home. But, despite this, for me, Professor Lal's true home is his office in the Coombs building, among his books, a cup of tea by his side, and a pen and paper close at hand. Professor Lal's office has its own biography (see Lal 2011: 127–38, so I will not describe it in detail). It is busy, not encumbered by administrative documents or student papers, but writing and reading, and what invariably strikes me every time I enter are the overflowing shelves that line every wall, the contents spilling onto piles on the floor. I have often stared enviously at the titles, knowing that many can no longer be purchased, but must be borrowed or bequeathed. Most are about the Pacific, particularly Fiji, and he has an opinion on the quality of all of them. ANU history professors loom the largest in his opinion of what scholarship ought to be: Oskar Spate, Ken Inglis, Bill Gammage and Hank Nelson to name but a few whose titles are regularly taken down from the shelf for approving inspection.

I have fond memories of that office. In the beginning, our conversations were about my PhD, its content and status, but as time passed they more often concerned cricket, departmental gossip, career and general life advice. As I start to supervise PhD students myself, I am developing an appreciation of the uniqueness and complexity of each relationship. Invariably some do not work out—and not all of those supervised by Professor Lal will share my warm recollections—but looking back I am humbled by how generous he was to me with both time and counsel. Indeed, at the beginning I worried about how frequently he wanted to meet—was I so far off track that I required constant oversight?—but I came to recognise that was not his purpose; he just cared. One reason for my initial concern was that he was never particularly effusive in his praise; he always focused on what could be improved, on how a piece could be made better. Indeed, amidst what I can only assume is a typically anxious process full of fear and self-doubt, it seemed to me that he spent much of his time extolling the virtues of his other students in my presence. It was only later, once I got to know these others, did I learn that he had nice things to say about my work behind my back as well.

Peter had many arguments for why Professor Lal would be a good supervisor but his most perceptive was that he would help kickstart my career. This has been true in several ways, not the least of which is his willingness to read and comment on applications and resumes, often at short notice. He is always quick to point out failings, but quicker still to recommend remedial action. So far, he has not led me astray. In many ways, this should not come as a surprise. Professor Lal has studied the profession at length, sought to measure himself by its standards, and ultimately judges others by what he sees as markers of good scholarship: frequent production discernible by quality of style and substance. As academic practices are increasingly scrutinised by governments and their publics searching for value, this lesson is increasingly poignant. But perhaps it is easy to miss because he has achieved so much more than a continual stream of books, articles and chapters. His work as a 'participant historian' is well known, but what I find most endearing is his desire to inculcate a passion for writing, in a variety of styles and for different audiences, in his students. In many ways, this is the inversion of the bean-counting ethos that seems to have gained ascendency in the academy. Instead, he draws on an alternate scholarly tradition that values a vibrant intelligentsia that contributes to the cultural life of a nation and its people. These traditions only remain alive while those who care about them seek to instil them in each new generation of the profession.

I am told that it is not uncommon for the relationship between supervisor and student to persist long after the PhD begins to gather dust. It also changes. Once, with Professor Lal's help, I gained a postdoctoral fellowship at the ANU, he and I became colleagues and friends, although he remains a mentor. More importantly, Brij V. Lal and I began to talk about collaborating on a topic of shared interest: life writing (Corbett and Lal 2015). As an early career researcher, our collaboration brought home to me what it means to be a senior academic, and what it takes to get there.

To some extent, I only met Brij V. Lal, author of countless books and edited volumes, founder of journals and book series, convenor of workshops and keynote speaker at international conferences, after my PhD was submitted. Of course, I knew he was a big cheese—you don't become a professor at the ANU without attaining some distinction in your chosen field—but I am still growing my appreciation of his standing in the field. As a PhD student I had a singular focus and the time to pursue it. Once employed, things inevitably changed and it is only once I started to balance these other priorities—teaching, administration and so forth— with the type of work that Brij V. Lal has spent a lifetime pursuing that I began to realise just how prolific he has been.

Meeting Brij V. Lal taught me what it means to be an academic, as opposed to a scholar. Academics have to publish and to do so they need journals and book presses. As an impressionistic young student I just assumed these things had a perennial existence and that if my work was good enough, it would get published. Brij V. Lal taught me that there is more to the story—that books, journals and academic standards are not a given, they have to be created and maintained—and, as a result, he impressed upon me the essence of what it means to be part of a profession. In particular, he emphasised the difference between submitting and being asked to submit, and the difference between getting published and being read. He showed me how pivotal editors are and stressed the importance of keeping them happy. Above all, by example and direction, he taught me that being an academic was a craft. It required skill and patience in equal measure, and, while it was easy to scorn the profession while praising its purpose, one does not usually exist without the other. In a sense, it resembles democratic politics; you can't have the game without its players, and Brij V. Lal is a well-practised player of the academic game.

And so, to use a term for a cricketing feat that I am yet to achieve, we have met a hat-trick of Lals. Brij Lal, whom I first encountered in a book about a long-dead politician; Professor Lal, whose office, for me, will always be synonymous with the very best traditions of the ANU; and Brij V. Lal, a collaborator, friend and mentor of merit and distinction. No doubt there are other Lals that his other friends and family know better than I. But I feel fortunate to have met and learnt from the three I know, for each of these Lals has marked my work for the better, influenced how I think about academia, and helped me to understand what being a scholar can and should be.

Acknowledgements

Thanks to Doug Munro and Ceridwen Spark for their careful edits and suggestion. The usual disclaimers apply.

References

Corbett, Jack. 2011. 'Review of *In the Eye of the Storm: Jai Ram Reddy and the Politics of Postcolonial Fiji*'. *Journal of Imperial and Commonwealth History*, 39(2): 344–46. DOI: 10.1080/03086534.2011.568745.

Corbett, Jack and Brij V. Lal (eds). 2015. *Political Life Writing in the Pacific Islands: Reflections on Practice*. Canberra: ANU Press. Online: press.anu.edu.au?p=319171 (accessed 17 January 2017).

Crick, Bernard, 2000 [1962]. *In Defence of Politics*. London: Continuum.

Ghai, Yash, 2011. 'Review of *In the Eye of the Storm: Jai Ram Reddy and the Politics of Postcolonial Fiji*. By Brij V. Lal.' *Journal of Pacific History*, 46(3): 399–400. DOI: 10.1080/00223344.2011.632947.

Lal, Brij V. 1997. *A Vision for Change: AD Patel and the Politics of Fiji*. Canberra: National Centre for Development Studies.

——. 2010. *In the Eye of the Storm: Jai Ram Reddy and the Politics of Postcolonial Fiji*. Canberra: ANU E Press. Online: press.anu.edu.au?p=25161 (accessed 17 January 2017).

——. 2011. *Intersections: History, Memory, Discipline*. Lautoka: Fiji Institute of Applied Studies and Sydney: Asia Pacific Publications.

16

The Boy from Labasa

Nicholas Halter

Brij Lal and I began our journey across inland Victoria in October 2014, almost four years since he had first agreed to supervise my PhD. My peers at The Australian National University (ANU) were surprised, to say the least, that I would embark on such an expedition with Brij. The prospect of sitting in a car alone with your supervisor for an entire weekend was daunting, and there was little in the flat, dry and barren landscapes of country Victoria to distract him from inquiring into the progress of my thesis. Our destination was Boort, a tiny town of wheat farmers in the northwest of the state, and birthplace of one of Brij's closest friends at ANU, Hank Nelson. Brij had recently co-edited a Festschrift for Hank titled *The Boy From Boort* (Gammage, Lal and Daws 2014), and we agreed to visit the town simply because neither of us knew anything about it. Origins are important to Brij and me, and for this reason I gladly accompanied him to Boort. He had written and reflected much on his own upbringing in Labasa, Fiji, and this visit to country Victoria was an opportunity to see the land that had shaped his dear friend, and witness the modest beginnings that he and Hank both shared.

On our journey, Brij reminisced on his early days in the Coombs building at ANU with Hank and other colleagues. Hank's down-to-earth and unassuming demeanour spoke to Brij's ideals. Brij was a man who treasured Australia's egalitarian principles—principles that assisted an ambitious young Indo-Fijian to rise to the top of his academic field, and principles that later comforted a man exiled from his homeland for defending democracy. Brij admired his unpretentious, straight-talking colleagues. He detested bullshit and obfuscation, constantly reminding me that good scholarship was the ability to express complex ideas in clear and simple language. Whilst he expected hard work and diligence from his students, Brij was also a larrikin at heart. He was quick to make a witty pun, and his smile and laugh were infectious in the Coombs corridors.

I have often wondered if it was my direct and honest first encounter with Brij that won him over. He never ceased to embarrass me by regaling to others the story of our initial meeting, which I had asked for on the reasoning that I wanted to 'check him out'. I was 23 years old, naïve and underqualified, and I had no idea how famous (or infamous) Professor Lal was when I walked into the Coombs Tea Room to meet him. My proposed research topic was on Micronesia rather than Fiji, and only after lengthy discussions did we decide that a study of Australian travel writing was more appropriate. Later, I was surprised to learn that Brij's own journey to ANU began with an introduction as blunt and uninformed as my own. He had written a letter to the demography department at the time asking to begin a PhD, and his letter was passed around the building until it landed on the desk of Ken Gillion who agreed to take him on (Munro 2009: 248). I am grateful to Brij for repeating this act of generosity and trust towards me.

My close relationship with Brij was unusual compared to my peers. He would visit me at least once a week in my office, take me on walks around the Canberra bushlands, and invite me to his family home for special occasions. Brij shared much of his life with me, far and beyond other students whose supervisors were aloof or, more commonly, overloaded with teaching, grant-writing and research responsibilities. Never overbearing, Brij was adept at carefully balancing the role of friend and mentor simultaneously. I felt reassured knowing many students had sat in his office before, and Brij had seen them through to the end. Brij told me that his own time as a student at ANU was far different. Not only was he sent to Menzies Library to study alone for a year at the command of his supervisor, but he also submitted his thesis (in two volumes) for examination within three years, unchecked by any of his supervisors. This was an extraordinary feat considering he and Padma had started a family in Canberra, far from home. As a result of this baptism by fire, Brij was keenly aware of the vulnerabilities of PhD students, and always attentive

16. THE BOY FROM LABASA

to the mental wellbeing of his students. Yet he also treasured the ability to thrive in quiet solitude, allowing me the intellectual freedom to pursue my own research relatively unopposed.

Unlike the countless people whom I watched consult Brij for the latest opinion on Fiji, or politics, or career advice, my discussions with Brij centred on history. Brij was eager to talk about his love of the discipline, and pass on every pearl of wisdom he could. Brij was one of the last of his generation of Pacific historians in Coombs and I felt privileged to have been student of his. He was a wonderful history teacher, and an engaging and entertaining speaker. 'Make powerful points, not powerpoints!', he would often remark before giving a lecture, proudly showing me his single sheet of paper with handwritten notes. And of course, Brij always had one well-rehearsed comedic line to win over his audience, a joke that would have been tested beforehand on his unsuspecting PhD students.

Brij's scholarly contribution to Pacific history is impressive, not to mention his work on the Indian diaspora more broadly. His list of publications is incredibly long, and I would often walk into his office proud to have written 200 words in a day, only to leave dismayed that he had written 2,000. It was exciting to be able to discuss Pacific history with someone that had met, and worked with, its key founders and figures. We discussed the discipline's merits and its complications, reflecting on its past developments, and postulating on its fragile future in the corridors of ANU. In some ways Brij was nostalgic as he recalled the old days of his beloved Coombs building and bemoaned the loss of a sense of community. Yet his concerns also reflected a broader dissatisfaction amongst staff and students with the institutional changes being implemented in Australian academia (Lal 2011: 127–38). Amidst this uncertainty, many people would visit Brij for advice, one of the few people with the historical memory of ANU and Coombs, and someone who would always offer a friendly smile and a generous ear.

Yet the most important lessons I learnt from Brij were not about the nuances and debates within Pacific history. Rather, Brij inspired within me a love of writing, and a conviction in the importance of writing history. Brij loved reading anything and everything, from history to poetry, be it fiction, non-fiction, or 'faction' as he called it. I realised my literary education needed much improvement as Brij would regularly test my knowledge of authors and artists. The Brij I know enjoys writing more reflective and personal pieces, musing on important moments in his life, writing about stories of pain and struggle and happiness, stories that resonated with audiences beyond the academic world. This style of writing is a great pleasure to Brij, and his personal pieces found a captive audience, most evident in the success of *Mr Tulsi's Store* (Lal 2001) and *The Coombs: A House of Memories* (Lal and Ley 2006).

Under Brij's guidance, I found confidence in my own voice, and my writing improved considerably. He once asked me to write 300 words on the subject 'Why I write', a simple yet memorable task that provoked deep self-questioning. Brij's response to this same question was that he wrote to bear witness to his time and place. Brij was unusual in that he did not simply bear witness, but he also played an active role in shaping his nation's history and bringing to the fore voices previously unheard or ignored. His indefinite exile made his writing all the more significant. Brij told me he wrote books in the hope that they would stand the test of time, even if no one in Fiji ever read them. While at ANU, I enjoyed the emotional, personal and practical side of history that Brij showed to me, and the passion he has for both Fiji and for scholarship. Not only has his career helped to give a voice to Indian migrants in Fiji, but it has also helped connect transient people to their roots all over the world. I would often hear him answering phone calls from Indo-Fijians asking for help to trace their family origins. Brij was not one to sit in his ivory tower—history was as much about being socially engaged and responsible as it was about pursuing new and innovative research.

We discussed some of these historiographical and philosophical questions during the drive to and from Boort. Our conversations were influenced by the recent and much-anticipated national elections in Fiji, during which time news of the victory of Frank Bainimarama's 'Fiji First' party was dwarfed by other more dramatic events including the Scottish referendum, the Ebola virus outbreak in Africa, instability in the Middle East (including the ransom of Fijian troops captured whilst working for the UN in Syria), and police raids on alleged terrorist cells in Australia. Those few reports about the Fiji election pronounced it a success to the world, supported by official statements from independent observers and Australian officials who were relieved to see democracy restored. For someone unfamiliar with the long and turbulent history of Fiji it appeared a resounding victory, and a successful future for Fiji looked promising. Yet I was shocked how easily the past decade of violence, repression and military rule could be forgotten—a past that significantly shaped the outcome of the election, and would certainly influence the future.

16. THE BOY FROM LABASA

Although Brij did not visibly show it, I suspected his subdued demeanour following the election betrayed the anguish he felt at heart. It was unusual considering Brij was normally so positive and hopeful, despite the constant disappointment of broken promises, defamation from Fiji and abroad, and the consistent efforts of the Fijian military regime to restrict democratic processes. During our conversation in the car, Brij confessed he had initially decided to decline requests for interviews and commentary on the Fiji elections, until he was convinced otherwise by Padma who reminded him that there was no one else in his unique position with the authority or the conviction to speak out. It was then that I realised the importance of an historian's contribution to public debate. Brij's strength as an historian was evident in his cautious avoidance of the grand, sweeping generalisations and speculation of journalists and political commentators (dialogue that he termed 'paper fire' because it burned brightly, but was short-lived). Rather, Brij brought a measured, thoughtful and historical perspective to an otherwise uncritical debate. Whether or not you agreed with his position at that time, Brij was undoubtedly regarded an authority on Fiji, a position that was hard-earned through years of dedicated study in the academic profession. I also believe Brij is widely respected because he sticks to his guns. He was a constant in a rapidly changing and flippant political landscape in Fiji. Just as Hank had shown him, he also demonstrated to me the importance of being honest, upfront, consistent and, above all, strictly adhering to your principles and values.

I feel truly privileged to have been one of Brij's last students before his retirement. Shortly after our return from Boort on the 25 October, I was invited to a Diwali celebration at his home in Aranda. In many ways, this celebration reflected the shift in direction for Brij from a public and academic life to a private one. Rather than a sky full of lights and noises from the cacophony of fireworks and celebrations in Suva, we sat underneath a dark and silent Canberra sky, noticed only by the curious possums in the gum trees above. An unusual mix of cultures, ages and professions, Fiji friends, families, children, Rotarians, past and present students. A kava bowl in the corner, hot curries on the table, an esky full of beers and a good selection of Aussie wines, the occasional Island souvenir or picture hanging in the living room. In the darkness our faces were lit by the small, soft crackle of our sparklers. The most joyous and excited face belonged to Brij's first grandson, Jayan. Brij has often written and spoken about the love he had for his grandfather and the trials and tribulations he had faced in order to secure a better future for his family. Now Brij is in the same position to offer love and guidance to his own grandson. He has stocked his library full of his most precious books, ready for Jayan to read, keeping the memories of Fiji alive in his new Australian home.

References

Gammage, Bill, Brij V. Lal and Gavan Daws (eds). 2014. *The Boy from Boort: Remembering Hank Nelson*. Canberra: ANU Press. Online: press.anu.edu.au?p=286291 (accessed 17 January 2017).

Lal, Brij V. 2001. *Mr Tulsi's Store: A Fijian Journey*. Canberra: Pandanus Books.

———. 2011. *Intersections: History, Memory, Discipline*. Lautoka: Fiji Institute of Applied Studies and Sydney: Asia Pacific Publications.

Lal, Brij V. and Allison Ley (eds). 2006. *The Coombs: A House of Memories*. Canberra: Research School of Pacific and Asian Studies, The Australian National University.

Munro, Doug. 2009. *The Ivory Tower and Beyond: Participant Historians of the Pacific*. Newcastle-upon-Tyne: Cambridge Scholars Publishing.

17

My Fijian *Wantok*

Sam Alasia

I first met Brij Lal in 1982 when he was my lecturer in Pacific history at the University of the South Pacific (USP). Brij had been a student himself at the same university in the early 1970s and he told me once that some of his best friends were from the Solomons. He mentioned one in particular, Edward Masika from Malaita, who was a good soccer player. I cannot say whether Brij is a good soccer player or not. However, one skill and talent that he possesses, and to which all of us can attest, is his exceptional writing ability. It is this particular skill that I would like to dwell on here. In many respects, Brij played a major part in building up my confidence in English writing, though I still have a long way to go to reach his level.

I was in my final year of undergraduate studies at USP in 1982. Solomon Islands achieved Independence a few years earlier in 1978 and there were only 20 or so USP graduates from the Solomons by 1981. I was therefore under pressure from my government to successfully complete my studies and return home to assist in the civil service. I was also under considerable self-imposed pressure due to my involvement in numerous student activities on campus. It was the final semester, and we were told to undertake research on a topic of interest to us. There was no coursework, no assignments and there was no final exam. We were told to carry out our own research and present our findings in a final paper that was to be presented to Brij. It was a very interesting but challenging exercise.

The paper was due for submission on the Friday of the first week of November. Of the 25 or so students in the class, I was the only straggler. I went to see Brij that Friday to explain that I had not even started writing up my paper as I had been so tied up with student matters, and so requested an extension of time to Monday of the new week. Brij was visibly displeased but understood my situation and agreed to my request, warning that he would wait for me in his office on Monday. If I was late, then I was told not to bother handing in my paper, which meant that I had would fail the course and not graduate at the end of the year.

I worked my guts out over the weekend, and by Sunday night I was only midway through the piles of papers and sorting out my writings into a coherent approach. There were no computers, laptops and mobile phones back then and so all our essays were handwritten. I was quite worried but kept saying to myself 'it is now or never'. I must admit too that as a Christian I prayed for strength. I stayed up the whole night of Sunday without going to bed. With minutes to spare, I completed my paper, and had no time to read it through. Brij's office was a 15-minute walk from my accommodation so I ran as quickly as I could and managed to catch him at 9 am—just as he was walking out of his office, as he said he would do. I begged him to accept my paper, which he did with a becoming reluctance, telling me that I was the only one left.

Two weeks later, we went to class to receive the results. Brij handed out all the papers one by one and commented on each of them. I felt a lot of butterflies in my stomach when one after another student received their results, but not me. The suspense was unbearable. Finally, all the students got their papers, except myself. I held my breath but noticed that there was still one paper left on his table. He told the students that I was the last to hand in my assignment. I thought he was going to scold me. Instead, he informed the students that my paper was the best in the class. I smiled and felt satisfied with the result. Brij did not stop there. He encouraged me to polish up the paper and have it published. This paper was eventually published by USP's Institute of Pacific Studies (IPS).

After graduation in 1982, I was sent by Ron Crocombe (the Professor of Pacific Studies at USP) to the University of Melbourne to spend a few weeks with Professor Greg Denning. The main purpose of my time with Greg was to plan the writing of a history book on Solomon Islands that would provide 'insider' or indigenous perspectives. This book was published as *Ples Blong Iumi: Solomon Islands, the Past Four Thousand Years* (Alasia 1989). I am sure Brij had a hand in recommending me to Ron Crocombe.

I served in the civil service for six years before entering the Solomons' parliament in 1989, soon after *Ples Blong Iumi* was published. While still a Member of Parliament in 1997, I received an invitation and spent six weeks with a State, Society and Governance in Melanesia (SSGM) project at ANU. The SSGM had started a year earlier under the leadership of David Hegarty. I was one of the first Pacific Islanders to do a paper at the SSGM and Brij again had a hand in the invitation. I published a discussion paper with the SSGM on *Party Politics and Government in Solomon Islands* (Alasia 1997).

In 1999, I had asked Ron Crocombe for advice regarding my interest to pursue further studies at Master's degree level. Crocombe's advice to me was that in view of my publishing record, I can 'jump over' the Master's degree and instead pursue a PhD. This advice remained with me for about a decade.

In 2008, I had left parliament and was again invited to SSGM, during which time I had the opportunity to fully discuss with Brij my interest in pursuing doctoral studies at ANU. Without hesitation, Brij took me to see the head of the Department of History in the School of Culture, History and Language. After some discussions, I was given the green light.

Subsequently, in 2012, I resigned my post in the Prime Minister's office and fulfilled my long-term ambition to pursue doctoral studies at ANU in Canberra. Brij was there not only for me but for quite a number of Pacific Islanders whom he had supervised. As the chair of my supervisory panel, he was at times hard on me but I know that this was for my benefit. Incidentally, I was Brij's last PhD student. With his retirement and my own need to return to the Pacific Islands, I have applied to transfer my candidature to the University of the South Pacific. I am determined not to let him down.

I can testify that having been in employment for about 30 years and to become a student again is no easy task. It is at this juncture that I would like to sincerely thank Brij who has been a pillar of strength in my days at ANU. This was even made much more difficult because I was staying alone with no family members in Canberra. I shared many of my difficulties with Brij, who understood my situation very well because he is a Pacific Islander himself. He knows how we feel. He is patient, humble and simple. I could not have asked for a better supervisor and mentor than Brij. He ranks amongst the top supervisors of any university. Brij is my *wantok* and I shall cherish his many words of advice and encouragement. Enjoy your well-earned retirement with your family and *tagio tu mas*.

Glossary

Wantok we are from the same locality, country, or region. It is a form of identity.

Tagio tu mas a pidgin derivative for 'Thank you very much'.

References

Alasia, Sam L. 1988. 'Big man and party politics: The evolution of political parties in Solomon Islands'. *Pacific Perspective*, 8(2): 72–84.

Alasia, Sam. 1989. *Ples Blong Iumi: Solomon Islands, the Past Four Thousand Years*. Suva: Institute of Pacific Studies of the University of the South Pacific.

——. 1997. *Party, Politics and Government in Solomon Islands*. Canberra: Research School of Pacific Studies. State, Society and Governance in Melanesia Discussion Paper, 97/7. Canberra: The Australian National University.

——. 2008. 'Rainbows across the mountains: The first post-RAMSI general elections'. In *Politics and State Building in Solomon Islands*, edited by Stewart Firth and Sinclair Dinnen, pp. 119–47. Canberra: ANU E Press. Online: press-files.anu.edu.au/downloads/press/p78261/pdf/ch0565.pdf (accessed 23 January 2017).

Firth, Stewart and Sinclair Dinnen (eds). 2008. *Politics and State Building in Solomon Islands*. Canberra: ANU E Press. Online: press.anu.edu.au?p=78261 (accessed 17 January 2017).

He is the Very Model of a Pacific Historian

Robert Cribb

Read out at Brij Lal's farewell function at The Australian National University, 7 March 2016, and sung to the tune of 'I am the Very Model of a Modern Major-General' (with apologies to Messrs Gilbert and Sullivan).

He is the very model of a Pacific historian
He knows each island's governors right back to times Victorian
He's had a hand in every kind of matter constitutional
And we've also seen him take a role as leader institutional.
    Not everyone was terribly affectionate for CHL
    But under Brij we found the School was really doing very well
    With Fellowships, incentive funds, a bright new secretariat
    And student numbers climbing in the gentle care of Harriette.
In CAP Exec he fought for us against the dreaded Andrew twins
A thankless fight and we all know that no one ever truly wins
He battles bull where'er it's found just like a famous matador
But does he really have to wear those floral shirts he buys in Tulsi's store?
    His library's enormous and he must have written half of all
    The books on Fiji taking inspiration from that kava bowl
    In recent years his view has widened and we've seen he has for a [change]
    Begun to do some work on the great Indian diaspora.
And now he's going off to try his fortune as a Queenslander
With Padma by his side 'twill be at last a time for him and her.
We're going to miss him when he's gone; we don't know how we'll carry on
He's always been our shining star, he's going to be a Brij too far.

Glossary

CHL   School of Culture, History and Language, College of Asia and the Pacific, The Australian National University.

CAP   College of Asia and the Pacific, The Australian National University (of which CHL was a part).

Bibliography of Brij V. Lal's Academic Writings[1]

Compiled by Doug Munro

1977–78   'Exhaustion and persistence: Aspects of rural Indian society in Fiji'. *Quarterly Review of Historical Studies* (Calcutta), 17(2): 69–79.

1979   'The wreck of the *Syria*, 1884'. In *The Indo-Fijian Experience*, edited by Subramani, pp. 26–40. Brisbane: University of Queensland Press.

Republished

     2000   In ***Chalo Jahaji: On a Journey Through Indenture in Fiji***, Canberra: Division of Pacific & Asian History, The Australian National University, and Suva: Fiji Museum, pp. 153–65.

     2012   In ***Chalo Jahaji: On a Journey Through Indenture in Fiji***, Canberra: ANU E Press, pp. 153–65. Online: press-files.anu.edu.au/downloads/press/p212781/pdf/9.-The-Wreck-of-the-Syria-1884.pdf (accessed 7 March 2017).

1979   'Fiji girmitiyas: Background to banishment'. In *Rama's Banishment: A Centenary Tribute to the Fiji Indians*, edited by Vijay Mishra, pp. 12–39. Auckland and London: Heinemann Educational Books.

---

1   This listing is confined to Lal's academic writings, including review articles but not book reviews. His faction essays are not individually itemised but his faction/autobiographical volumes are. The titles of monographs, edited collections and special issues of journals appear in bold typeface.

1980 'Approaches to the study of Indian indentured emigration, with special reference to Fiji'. *Journal of Pacific History*, 15(1): 52–70. DOI: 10.1080/00223348008572387.

1980 'Political movement in the early East Indian community in Canada'. *Indian Journal of History*, 58: 193–220.

Republished

1981 In the *Journal of Intercultural Studies*, 2(1): 61–87. DOI: 10.1080/07256868.1981.9963169.

1980 'The elusive other India: A review article' [of *The Other India: The Overseas Indians and their Relationship – Proceedings of a Seminar*, edited by I.J. Bahadur Singh]. *Journal of Pacific Studies*, 6: 99–113.

1982 'An uncertain journey: The voyage of the *Leonidas*'. *Journal of Pacific Studies*, 8: 55–69.

Republished

2000 'The voyage of the *Leonidas*'. In *Chalo Jahaji*, pp. 143–51.

1982 'Canada: The tide of turbans'. In *Pacific Indians*, edited by Ron Crocombe, pp. 133–54. Suva: Institute of Pacific Studies of the University of the South Pacific.

1983 **Girmitiyas: The Origins of the Fiji Indians.** Canberra: The Journal of Pacific History. 2nd edition 2004, Lautoka: Fiji Institute of Applied Studies, with a foreword by Clem Seecharan, viii+190 pp.

Republished

2000 'A journey begins'. In *Chalo Jahaji*, pp. 67–98 [chapter 1 of *Girmitiyas*].

1983 'The Fiji General Elections of 1982: The tidal wave that never came'. *Journal of Pacific History*, 18(2): 134–57.

1983 'Indian indenture historiography: A note on problems, sources and methods'. *Journal of Pacific Studies*, 6(2): 33–50.

1983 'The 1982 national election and its aftermath'. *University of the South Pacific Sociological Bulletin*, 6: 3–17.

1984   ed. with John McGuire and Meredith Borthwick. *Problems of Method and Enquiry in South Asian History*. Perth: Centre for South and Southeast Asian Studies, Monograph 5.

1984   'Labouring men and nothing more: Some problems of Indian indenture in Fiji'. In *Indentured Labour in the British Empire, 1834–1920*, edited by Kay Saunders, pp. 126–54. London and Canberra: Croom Helm.

1985   'Kunti's cry: Indentured women on Fiji plantations'. *Indian Economic and Social History Review*, 22(1): 55–77.

Republished

        1989   In *Women in Colonial India: Essays on Survival, Work and the State*, edited by Jayasankar Krishnamurty, pp. 163–79. New Delhi and New York: Oxford University Press (a collection of articles originally published in the *Indian Economic and Social History Review*).

        2000   'Kunti's cry'. In *Chalo Jahaji*, pp. 195–214.

1985   'Veil of dishonour: Sexual jealousy and suicide on Fiji plantations'. *Journal of Pacific History*, 20(3–4): 135–55. DOI: 10.1080/00223348508572516.

Republished

        2000   'Veil of dishonour'. In *Chalo Jahaji*, pp. 215–38.

1986   ed. ***Politics in Fiji: Studies in Contemporary History***. Laie: Brigham Young University and Sydney: Allen & Unwin, xi+161 pp.

1986   'Politics since independence, 1970–1982'. In *Politics in Fiji*, pp. 74–106.

1986   'The emergence of the Fiji Labour Party'. In *Politics in Fiji*, pp. 139–57.

1986   'Murmurs of dissent: Non-resistance on Fiji plantations'. *Hawaiian Journal of History*, 20: 188–214.

Revised versions republished

1993   '"Nonresistance" on Fiji plantations: The Fiji Indian experience, 1879–1920'. In *Plantation Workers: Resistance and Accommodation*, edited by Brij V. Lal, Doug Munro and Edward D. Beechert, pp. 187–216. Honolulu: University of Hawaii Press, 1993.

2000   'Murmers of dissent'. In *Chalo Jahaji*, pp. 167–93.

2014   with Doug Munro. 'Nonresistance in Fiji'. In *Resistance and Indian Indenture Experience: Comparative Perspectives*, edited by Maurits S. Hassankhan, Brij V. Lal and Doug Munro, pp. 121–56. New Delhi: Manohar.

1986   ***Power and Prejudice: The Making of the Fiji Crisis***. Wellington: New Zealand Institute of International Affairs, vii+204 pp. Reprinted 1990.

1987   ed. ***Wansalawara: Soundings in Melanesian History***. Honolulu: Center for Pacific Islands Studies Occasional Paper. University of Hawaii at Mānoa.

1987   'Introduction'. In *Wansalawara*, pp. 1–12.

1988   'Before the storm: An analysis of the Fiji general election of 1987'. *Journal of Pacific Studies*, 12(1): 71–96.

1989   'Fiji Indians and the politics of disparity'. *Foreign Affairs Record* (New Delhi), 37: 95–105.

1989   'Rabuka's republic: a year on'. *Current Affairs Bulletin* (Sydney), 65(1): 4–14.

1990   ed. ***As the Dust Settles: Impact and Implications of the Fiji Coups***. Special Issue, *Contemporary Pacific: A Journal of Island Affairs*, 2(1): 1–230.

1990   'Introduction'. *Contemporary Pacific*, 2(1): 1–10.

1990   with Karen Peacock. 'Researching the Fiji coups'. *Contemporary Pacific*, 2(1): 183–95.

BIBLIOGRAPHY OF BRIJ V. LAL'S ACADEMIC WRITINGS

1990 'Islands of turmoil: Contemporary Fiji re-visited'. *Meanjin*, 49(4): 639–51.

1991 'Politics and society in post-coup Fiji'. *Cultural Survival Quarterly*, 15(2): 71–96.

1991 'For King and country: The Pacific War in Fiji'. In *Remembering the Pacific War*, edited by Geoffrey M. White, pp. 17–25. Honolulu: Center for Pacific Islands Studies, University of Hawaii.

1991 with Barry Shineberg. 'The story of the haunted line: Totaram Sanadhya recalls the labour lines in Fiji'. *Journal of Pacific History*, 26(1): 107–12.

Republished

2000 'The story of the haunted line'. In *Chalo Jahaji*, pp. 261–71.

1991 **Broken Waves: A History of the Fiji Islands in the Twentieth Century,** with a 'Preface' by Robert C. Kiste. Honolulu: University of Hawaii Press, xxii+404 pp.

1992 ed. ***Pacific Islands History: Journeys and Transformations***. 'Preface' by Donald Denoon. Canberra: The Journal of Pacific History, xiii+255 pp.

1992 'Introduction'. *Pacific Islands History*, pp. ix–xiii.

1992 'Rhetoric and reality: The dilemma of contemporary Fiji politics'. In *Culture and Democracy in the South Pacific*, edited by Ron Crocombe, Uentabo Neemia, Asesela Ravuvu and Werner vom Busch, pp. 97–116. Suva: Institute of Pacific Studies of the University of the South Pacific.

1992 'Plus ça change: Resources, politics and development in the South Pacific'. In *Resources, Development and Politics in the Pacific Islands*, edited by Stephen Henningham and Ron May, pp. 230–37. Bathurst, NSW: Crawford House Publishing.

1993 ed. with Doug Munro and Edward D. Beechert. **Plantation Workers: Resistance and Accommodation**. Honolulu: University of Hawaii Press, viii+342 pp.

1993 '"Nonresistance" on Fiji Plantations: The Fiji Indian experience, 1879–1920'. In *Plantation Workers*, pp. 187–216.

1993 'Chiefs and Indians: Elections and politics in contemporary Fiji'. *Contemporary Pacific*, 5(2): 275–301.

1993 'Melanesia in review, 1992: Fiji'. *Contemporary Pacific*, 5(2): 403–408.

1993 'Kenneth L. Gillion, 1929–1992: An appreciation'. *Journal of Pacific History*, 28(1): 93–96. DOI: 10.1080/00223349308572728.

1994 ed. with K.R. Howe and Robert D. Kiste. **Tides of History: The Pacific Islands in the Twentieth Century**. Honolulu: University of Hawaii Press, and Sydney: Allen & Unwin, xviii+475 pp.

1994 'The passage out'. In *Tides of History*, pp. 435–61.

1994 ed. with Yogendra Yadav. **Bhut Len Ki Katha: Totaram Sanadhya's Fiji**. New Delhi: Saraswati Press, (in Hindi), 171 pp.

1994 'Melanesia in review, 1993: Fiji'. *Contemporary Pacific*, 6(2): 438–43.

1994 Extended untitled review of *Pacific History: Papers from the 9th Pacific History Conference*, ed. Donald Rubinstein, in *Isla: A Journal of Micronesian Studies*, 2(1): 147–53.

1995 with Yogendra Yadav. 'Hinduism under indenture: Totaram Sanadhya's account of Fiji'. *Journal of Pacific History*, 30(1): 99–111.

1995 ed. with Hank Nelson. **Lines Across the Sea: Colonial Inheritance in the Post-Colonial Pacific**. Brisbane: Pacific History Association, xvi+320 pp.

1995 'Rabuka's republic: The Fiji snap elections of 1994'. *Pacific Studies*, 18(1): 44–77.

1996 with Paul Reeves and Tomasi Vakatora. **The Fiji Islands: Towards a United Future: Report of the Fiji Constitution Review Commission**. Suva: Parliamentary Paper no. 36, xix+719 pp.

1996 'The odyssey of indenture: Fragmentation and reconstitution in the Indian diaspora'. *Diaspora: A Journal of Transnational Studies*, 5(2): 167–88. DOI: 10.1353/dsp.1996.0012.

Republished

2000 'The odyssey of indenture'. In *Chalo Jahaji*, pp. 41–66.

1996 'From across the horizon: A sojourn in Hawaii'. *Journal of Pacific Studies*, 20: 224–37.

Republished

2001 'A sojourn in Hawai'i'. In *Mr Tulsi's Store: A Fijian Journey*. Canberra: PandanusBooks, pp. 111–26.

2013 *Mr Tulsi's Store: A Fijian Journey*. Canberra: ANU E Press. Online: press-files.anu.edu.au/downloads/press/p229551/pdf/ch07.pdf (accessed 24 January 2017).

1997 *A Vision for Change: AD Patel and the Politics of Fiji*. Canberra: National Centre for Development Studies, The Australian National University, xvii+282 pp.

Republished

2011 ed. *A Vision for Change: AD Patel and the Politics of Fiji*. Canberra: ANU E Press. Online: press.anu.edu.au/wp-content/uploads/2011/11/whole5.pdf (accessed 18 January 2017).

1997 with Paul Reeves and Tomasi Vakatora. **Huala'af ma vakaiof se ta av hugag'eseat ma teag'eseat : te ne komitit ne sakiroa constitution fup'aki.** (*Fiji Islands: towards a united future: Report of the Fiji Constitution Review Commission*, 1996, Rotuman Selections), Suva: Government Printer, 94 pp.

1997 ed. with Peter Larmour. **Electoral Systems in Divided Societies: the Fiji Constitution Review**. Canberra: National Centre for Development Studies and Stockholm: Institute for Democracy and Electoral Assistance, v+159 pp.

1997 'A new electoral system for Fiji: Recommendations of the Fiji Constitution Review Commission'. In *Electoral Systems in Divided Societies,* edited by Brij V. Lal and Peter Larmour, pp. 39–72. Canberra: National Centre for Development Studies, and Stockholm: Institute for Democracy and Electoral Assistance.

1997 with Paul Reeves and Tomasi Vakatora. **Research Papers of the Fiji Constitution Review Commission**. Vol. 1: *Fiji in Transition.* Suva: School of Social and Economic Development, University of the South Pacific, vii+312 pp.

1997 with Paul Reeves and Tomasi Vakatora. **Research Papers of the Fiji Constitution Review Commission**. Vol. II: *Fiji and the World.* Suva: School of Social and Economic Development, University of the South Pacific, vii+358 pp.

1997 'Towards a united future: *Report of the Fiji Constitution Review Commission'. Journal of Pacific History,* 32(1): 71–84. DOI: 10.1080/00223349708572828.

1997 'Brij V. Lal: Historian of indenture and of contemporary Fiji' [interview with Doug Munro], *Itinerario: European Journal of Overseas History,* 21(1): 16–27. DOI: 10.1017/S0165115300022671.

1997 'Submissions'. *Meanjin,* 56(2): 269–80.

Republished

1998 In *Another Way*, pp. 164–75.

2001 In *Mr Tulsi's Store*, pp. 153–68.

1997 'The decolonisation of Fiji: Debate on constitutional change, 1943–1963'. In *Emerging from Empire? Decolonisation in the Pacific,* edited by Donald Denoon, pp. 29–39. Canberra: Division of Pacific and Asian History, The Australian National University.

1997 'Coups in Fiji'. In *The Cambridge History of the Pacific Islanders,* edited by Donald Denoon, pp. 415–19. Cambridge: Cambridge University Press.

1997 'Ben's funeral'. In *Fiji: The Road Ahead.* National Federation Party, pp. 69–76. Suva: National Federation Party.

Republished

    2000   In *Chalo Jahaji*, pp. 377–88.

    2001   'Ben'. In *Mr Tulsi's Store*, pp. 139–52.

1998   ***Another Way: The Politics of Constitutional Reform in Post-Coup Fiji***. Canberra: Asia Pacific Press, xiv+223 pp.

1998   ed. ***Crossing the Kala Pani: A Documentary History of Indian Indenture in Fiji***. Canberra: Division of Pacific & Asian History, Research School of Pacific & Asian Studies, The Australian National University, and Suva: Fiji Museum, 328 pp.

1998   ed. with Lance Brennan. ***Across the Kala Pani: Indian Overseas Migration and Settlement.*** Special Issue, *South Asia: A Journal of South Asian Studies*, 21:(sup. 001): 1–237.

1998   'Understanding the Indian indenture experience'. *South Asia: A Journal of South Asian Studies*, 21:(sup. 001): 215–37. DOI: 10.1080/00856409808723356.

1998   'Bahraich'. In *Unfinished Journeys: India File from Canberra*, edited by Debjani Ganguly and Kavita Nandan, pp. 91–108. Adelaide: Centre for Research in the New Literatures in English, Flinders University.

Republished

    2000   'Return to Bahraich'. In *Chalo Jahaji*, pp. 25–39.

    2001   In *Mr Tulsi's Store*, pp. 25–44.

    2005   In *On the Other Side of Midnight*, pp. 34–52.

1999   'The voice of the people: Ethnic identity and nation building in Fiji'. *Journal of the Pacific Society*, 12(3–4): 1–12.

Republished

    2001   In *New Pacific Review*, 1(1): 127–44.

1999   'Bound for the colonies: A view of Indian indentured emigration in 1905'. *Journal of Pacific History*, 34(3): 307–09. DOI: 10.1080/00223349908572915.

Republished

    2000   'Bound for the colonies in 1905'. In *Chalo Jahaji*, pp. 137–42.

1999   ***A Time to Change: The Fiji General Elections of 1999.*** Canberra: Department of Political and Social Change Discussion Paper 23 in the Regime Change and Regime Maintenance Series, The Australian National University, 61 pp.

Republished in a revised and shortened form

    2000   In *Fiji Before the Storm*, ed. Lal, pp. 21–48.

2000   ***Chalo Jahaji: On a Journey Through Indenture in Fiji***, with a preface by Brinsley Samaroo. Canberra: Division of Pacific & Asian History, The Australian National University, and Suva: Fiji Museum, xviii+420 pp. Reprinted 2006 by the Fiji Hindu Society.

Republished

    2012   ***Chalo Jahaji: On a Journey Through Indenture in Fiji.*** Canberra: ANU E Press. Online: press.anu.edu.au/publications/chalo-jahaji (accessed 18 January 2017).

Including

Doug Munro, 'Of journeys and transformations: Brij V. Lal and the study of girmit', pp. 1–23. Online: press-files.anu.edu.au/downloads/press/p212781/pdf/1.-Of-Journeys-and-Transformations-Doug-Munro.pdf (accessed 24 January 2017).

and a sample of essays by Lal's Honours students:

    Glen Fowler. '"A want of care": Death and disease on Fiji plantations, 1890–1900'. Online: press-files.anu.edu.au/downloads/press/p212781/pdf/15.-A-Want-of-Care-Death-and-Disease-on-Fiji-Plantations-1800-1900-Glenn-Fowler.pdf (accessed 24 January 2017);

Nicole Duncan. 'Death on Fiji plantations, 1900–1909'. Online: press-files.anu.edu.au/downloads/press/p212781/pdf/16.-Death-On-Fiji-Plantations-1900-1909-Nicole-Duncan.pdf (accessed 24 January 2017);

Anthony Cole. 'Accidental deaths on Fiji plantations, 1879–1916'. Online: press-files.anu.edu.au/downloads/press/p212781/pdf/17.-Accidental-Deaths-on-Fiji-Plantations-1879-1916-Anthony-Cole.pdf (accessed 24 January 2017);

Jane Harvey. 'Naraini's story'. Online: press-files.anu.edu.au/downloads/press/p212781/pdf/18.-Narainis-Story-Jane-Harvey.pdf (accessed 24 January 2017);

Matthew Ryan. 'The Labasa strike, 1907'. Online: press-files.anu.edu.au/downloads/press/p212781/pdf/19.-The-Labasa-Strike-1907-Matthew-Ryan.pdf (accessed 24 January 2017).

2000 'A time to move'. In *Chalo Jahaji*, pp. 121–36 (published for the first time).

2000 'Mr Tulsi's store'. In *Chalo Jahaji*, pp. 367–76 (published for the first time).

2000 'Sunrise on the Ganga'. In *Chalo Jahaji*, pp. 389–98.

Republished

2005 In *On the Other Side of Midnight*, pp. 134–44.

2015 In *An Anthology of Writings on the Ganga: Goddess and River in History, Culture and Society*, edited by Assa Doron, Richard Barz, Barbara Nelson, pp. 122–31. New Delhi: Oxford University Press.

2000 ed. ***Fiji Before the Storm: Elections and the Dilemmas of Politics of Development***. Canberra: Asia Pacific Press, xii+205 pp.

Republished

2012   ed. ***Fiji Before the Storm: Elections and the Dilemmas of Politics of Development***. Canberra: ANU E Press. Online: press.anu.edu.au/wp-content/uploads/2012/12/whole13.pdf (accessed 18 January 2017).

2000   'The future of our past'. In *Fiji Before the Storm*, ed. Lal, pp. 1–6.

2000   'A time to change: The Fiji general elections of 1999'. In *Fiji Before the Storm*, ed. Lal, pp. 21–47.

2000   'Madness in May: George Speight and the unmaking of modern Fiji'. In *Fiji Before the Storm*, ed. Lal, pp. 175–94.

2000   ed. with Kate Fortune. ***The Pacific Islands: An Encyclopedia***. Honolulu: University of Hawaii Press, xxxvi+664 pp. Includes a CD-ROM version.

2000   with Kate Fortune. 'Preface' to *The Pacific Islands: An Encyclopedia*, ed. Lal and Fortune, pp. xv–xvi.

2000   'Suva'. In *The Pacific Islands: An Encyclopedia*, ed. Lal and Fortune, pp. 104–05.

2000   'Girmitiya'. In *The Pacific Islands: An Encyclopedia*, ed. Lal and Fortune, pp. 110–11.

2000   'A.D. Patel'. In *The Pacific Islands: An Encyclopedia*, ed. Lal and Fortune, pp. 280–81.

2000   'Colonial Sugar Refining Company'. In *The Pacific Islands: An Encyclopedia*, ed. Lal and Fortune, p. 355.

2000   'On the campaign trail'. *Conversations* (Canberra), 1: 20–34.

Republished

2001   In *Mr Tulsi's Store*, pp. 169–83.

2000   'Chiefs and thieves and other people besides: The making of George Speight's coup'. *The Journal of Pacific History*, 35(3): 281–93. DOI: 10.1080/00223340020010571.

2000	'Rabuka of Fiji: Coups, constitutions and confusion: Review and reflections'. *The Journal of Pacific History*, 35(3): 319–26.

Republished

	2015	In *Fijian Studies: A Journal of Contemporary Fiji*, 13(1): 85–97. Online: fijianstudies.net/wp-content/uploads/FS/13(1)/FS-13-1-Lal-Rabuka.pdf (accessed 24 January 2017).

2001	*Mr Tulsi's Store: A Fijian Journey*. Canberra: Pandanus Books, xi+209 pp.

Republished

	2013	*Mr Tulsi's Store: A Fijian Journey*. Canberra: ANU E Press. Online: press.anu.edu.au/wp-content/uploads/2013/03/whole3.pdf (accessed 18 January 2017).

2001	'Preface'. In *Mr Tulsi's Store*, pp. ix–xi.
2001	'Tabia'. In *Mr Tulsi's Store*, pp. 1–23.

Republished

	2005	In *On the Other Side of Midnight*, pp. 53–77.

2001	'From Labasa to Laucala Bay'. In *Mr Tulsi's Store*, pp. 81–103.

Republished as an altered version

	2004	'Laucala Bay'. In *Pacific Places, Pacific Histories*, ed. Lal, pp. 367–58.

2001	'The other side of midnight'. In *Mr Tulsi's Store*, pp. 105–09.
2001	with Michael Pretes. ***Coup: Reflections on the Political Crisis in Fiji***. Canberra: Pandanus Books, x+186 pp.

Republished

	2008	***Coup: Reflections on the Political Crisis in Fiji***. Canberra: ANU E Press. Online: press.anu.edu.au/wp-content/uploads/2011/06/whole_book7.pdf (accessed 18 January 2017).

2001   with Michael Pretes. 'Preface'. In *Coup,* Lal and Pretes, pp. ix–x.

2001   'Fijicoup.com'. In *Coup*, Lal and Pretes, pp. 1–7.

2001   'The sun set at noon today'. In *Coup*, Lal and Pretes, pp. 8–17.

2001   with Peter Hempenstall. **Pacific Places, Pacific Lives: Bursting Boundaries in Pacific History**. Canberra: The Journal of Pacific History, v+190 pp.

2001   'While the gun is still smoking: Witnessing participant history'. In *Pacific Places, Pacific Lives: Bursting Boundaries in Pacific History*, edited by Brij Lal and Peter Hempenstall, pp. 70–87. Canberra: The Journal of Pacific History.

Republished

     2011   In *Intersections: History, Memory, Discipline*, pp. 39–57.

2001   'Rewriting the social contract'. In *Perspectives on the Chinese Indonesians*, edited by Michael R. Godley and Grayson J. Lloyd, pp. 128–35. Adelaide: Crawford House Publishing.

2001   'Labasa secondary'. *Conversations*, 2(1): 96–118.

Republished

     2001   In *Mr Tulsi's Store*, pp. 59–80.

     2005   In *On the Other Side of Midnight*, pp. 110–33.

2001   'Siddiq Koya'. In *20th Century Fiji: People who Shaped this Nation*, edited by Stewart Firth and Daryl Tarte, pp. 49–50. Suva: USP Solutions. (There is an entry on Lal in this publication, by Stewart Firth, p. 208.)

2001   'A.D. Patel'. In *20th Century Fiji*, ed. Firth and Tarte, p. 51.

2001   'Totaram Sanadhya'. In *20th Century Fiji*, ed. Firth and Tarte, p. 73.

2001   'Sadhu Kuppuswami'. In *20th Century Fiji*, ed. Firth and Tarte, p. 86.

2001	'Vishnu Deo'. In *20th Century Fiji*, ed. Firth and Tarte, pp. 114–18.
2001	'Jai Ram Reddy'. In *20th Century Fiji*, ed. Firth and Tarte, pp. 119–24.
2001	'Kamla Prasad Mishra'. In *20th Century Fiji*, ed. Firth and Tarte, p. 131.
2001	'Apolosi Nawai'. In *20th Century Fiji*, ed. Firth and Tarte, p. 149.
2001	'Rusiate Nayacakalou'. In *20th Century Fiji*, ed. Firth and Tarte, pp. 203–04.
2002	'Making history, becoming history: Reflections on Fiji coups and constitutions'. *Contemporary Pacific*, 14(2): 148–67. DOI: 10.1353/cp.2002.0020.

Republished

> 2011   In *Intersections*, pp. 22–38.

2002	'From the sideline: Interview with Brij V Lal, historian and constitutional commissioner'. *Contemporary Pacific*, 14(2): 168–84.

Republished

> 2011   'From the sideline: An interview with Vilsoni Hereniko'. In *Intersections*, pp. 287–302.

2002	'In George Speight's shadow: Fiji elections of 2001'. *The Journal of Pacific History*, 37(1): 87–101.
2002	'Constitutional engineering in post-coup Fiji'. In *The Architecture of Democracy: Constitutional Design, Conflict Management, and Democracy*, edited by Andrew Reynolds, pp. 267–92. Oxford: Oxford University Press.
2002	'London link'. *Conversations*, 3(1): 78–83.

Republished

> 2011   'To London'. In *Intersections*, pp. 247–51.

2003 'In spite of Mr Speight: Fiji's road to the general elections'. In *Arc of Instability? Melanesia in the Early 2000s*, edited by R.J. May, pp. 55–61. Christchurch: Macmillan Brown Centre for Pacific Studies, and State, Society and Governance in Melanesia Project, Research School of Pacific and Asian Studies. Canberra: The Australian National University.

2003 'Debating Fiji's democratic future'. *Fijian Studies*, 1(1): 157–62.

2003 'Fiji's constitutional conundrum'. *The Round Table: The Commonwealth Journal of International Affairs*, 92(372): 671–85.

2003 'Heartbreak islands: Reflections on Fiji in transition'. *Asia Pacific Viewpoint*, 44(3): 335–50. DOI: 10.1111/j.1467-8373.2003.00218.x.

Republished

2004 In *Law and Empire in the Pacific: Fiji and Hawaii*, edited by Sally Engle Merry and Donald Brenneis, pp. 261–80. Santa Fe: School of American Research Press.

2011 In *Intersections*, pp. 8–21.

2003 'The road to Mr Tulsi's store'. *Meanjin* (Melbourne), 62(4): 42–48.

Republished

2008 In *Turnings*, pp. 1–12. Online: press-files.anu.edu.au/downloads/press/p230401/pdf/ch015.pdf (accessed 24 January 2017).

2003 'Afterword: The debris'. *Ethnographies of the May 2000 Fiji Coup*. Special issue of *Pacific Studies*, 25(4): 109–15.

2004 ed. **Pacific Places, Pacific Histories: Essays in Honor of Robert C. Kiste**. Honolulu: University of Hawai'i Press, vii+345 pp.

2004 'Place and person: an introduction'. In *Pacific Places*, ed. Lal, pp. 1–27.

2004	'Laucala Bay'. In *Pacific Places*, ed. Lal, pp. 237–58.
2004	ed. ***Bittersweet: The Indo-Fijian Experience***. Canberra: Pandanus Books, xiv+407 pp.
2004	'Greetings/Namaskar'. In *Bittersweet*, ed. Lal, pp. viii–ix.
2004	'Girmit, history, memory'. In *Bittersweet*, ed. Lal, pp. 1–29.
2004	'Primary texts'. In *Bittersweet*, ed. Lal, pp. 239–49.
2004	'Maarit' (in Fiji Hindi). In *Bittersweet*, ed. Lal, pp. 389–403.
2004	'People in between: Reflections from the Indian indentured diaspora'. In *Chinese and Indian Diasporas: Comparative Perspectives*, edited by Wong Siu-Lun, pp. 69–93. Hong Kong: University of Hong Kong: Centre of Asian Studies.

Republished

	2004	In *The Construction of an Indo-Caribbean Diaspora*, ed. Brinsley Samaroo and Ann Marie Bissessar, pp. 1–22. St Augustine: University of West Indies Press.
	2011	In *Intersections*, pp. 139–55.

2005	ed. ***The Defining Years: Pacific Islands, 1945–65***. Canberra: Division of Pacific and Asian History, The Australian National University, iv+153 pp.
2005	***On the Other Side of Midnight: A Fijian Journey***. New Delhi: National Book Trust, x+163 pp. Hindi version: *Fiji Yatra: Aadhi Raat Se Aage*.
2005	'Roots and routes'. In *On the Other Side of Midnight*, pp. 1–33.
2005	'Roots and routes, again'. In *On the Other Side of Midnight*, pp. 145–63.
2005	'Sairusi Nabogibogi'. *Fijian Studies*, 3(1): 131–37. Online: fijianstudies.net/wp-content/uploads/FS/3(1)/3-1-Lal.pdf (accessed 24 January 2017).

2005   '*Bahut Julum*: Reflections on the use of Fiji Hindi'. *Fijian Studies*, 3(1): 153–58. Online: fijianstudies. net/wp-content/uploads/FS/3(1)/3-1Lal-Talanoa.pdf (accessed 24 January 2017).

2006   **Islands of Turmoil: Elections and Politics in Fiji**. Canberra: Asia Pacific Press, and ANU E Press, xiii+282 pp. Online: press.anu.edu.au/publications/islands-turmoil/ download (accessed 6 March 2017).

2006   ed. with Peter Reeves and Rajesh Rai. **The Encyclopedia of the Indian Diaspora.** Singapore: Editions Didier Millet in association National University of Singapore, and Delhi: Oxford University Press; Honolulu: University of Hawai'i Press, vii+414 pp.

2006   'Introduction'. In *The Encyclopedia of the Indian Diaspora*, ed. Lal, Rai and Reeves, pp. 10–15.

2006   'The indenture system'. In *The Encyclopedia of the Indian Diaspora*, ed. Lal, Rai and Reeves, pp. 46–50.

2006   'Fiji'. In *The Encyclopedia of the Indian Diaspora*, ed. Lal, Rai and Reeves, pp. 370–82.

2006   ed. **British Documents on the End of Empire, Series B, Volume 10: Fiji**. London: The Stationery Office, xcviii+547 pp.

2006   'Introduction'. In *British Documents on the End of Empire, Series B, Volume 10: Fiji*, ed. Lal, pp. xxxiii–lxxxv.

2006   ed. with Doug Munro. **Texts and Contexts: Reflections in Pacific Islands Historiography**. Honolulu: University of Hawai'i Press, viii+264 pp.

2006   with Doug Munro. 'Introduction'. In *Texts and Contexts*, ed. Munro and Lal, pp. 1–16.

2006   'Passage across the sea: Indentured labour to Fiji and from the Solomons'. In *Texts and Contexts*, ed. Munro and Lal, pp. 166–77.

2006   ed. with Allison Ley. **The Coombs: A House of Memories**, with a foreword by William C. Clarke. Canberra: Research School of Pacific and Asian Studies, The Australian National University. xv+305 pp.

Republished

2014 *The Coombs: A House of Memories*. Canberra: ANU Press. Online: press-files.anu.edu.au/ downloads/press/n1669/pdf/book.pdf (accessed 30 June 2017).

2006 'The Coombs: journeys and transformations'. In *The Coombs*, ed. Lal and Ley, pp. 1–24.

2006 *A Time Bomb Lies Buried: Fiji's Road to Independence, 1960–1970*. State, Society and Governance in Melanesia Project, Research School of Pacific and Asian Studies, The Australian National University. Monograph no.1, ix+106 pp.

Republished

2008 *A Time Bomb Lies Buried: Fiji's Road to Independence, 1960–1970*. Canberra: ANU E Press. Online: press.anu.edu.au/wp-content/ uploads/2011/03/whole_book6.pdf (accessed 18 January 2017).

2007 'Kumkum: Maya's story'. *Cultural Dynamics*, 19(2–3): 309–27. Online: journals.sagepub.com/doi/abs/10.1177/ 0921374007080297 (accessed 6 March 2017).

2007 'Caught in the web: Public discourse in the age of electronic communication'. *Fijian Studies*, 5(1): 154–61.

Republished

2011 'Caught in the web'. In *Intersections*, pp. 279–86.

2007 'Anxiety, uncertainty, and fear in our land: Fiji's road to military coup, 2006'. *The Round Table: The Commonwealth Journal of International Affairs*, 96(389): 135–53. DOI: 10.1080/00358530701292447.

2007 'Three worlds: Inheritance and experience'. In *Translating Lives: Living with Two Languages and Cultures*, edited by Mary Besemeres and Anna Wierzbicka, pp. 26–44. Brisbane: University of Queensland Press.

Republished

2008 In *Turnings*, pp. 197–221.

2011   'One life, three worlds'. In *Intersections*, pp. 186–200.

2007   'Mr Arjun'. In *Stopover: A Story of Migration*, by Bruce Connew. Wellington: Victoria University Press, and Honolulu: University of Hawai'i Press, 28 pp. (unnumbered).

2007   ***This Process of Political Adjustment: Aftermath of the 2006 Fiji Coup***. State, Society and Governance in Melanesia Project, Research School of Pacific and Asian Studies, The Australian National University. Paper 2, 21 pp.

Republished

    2007   In *Fijian Studies*, 5(1): 89–124.

    2009   In *The 2006 Military Takeover in Fiji*, ed. Fraenkel, Firth and Lal, pp. 67–93.

2007   'Chance *hai*: From the campaign trail'. In *From Election to Coup. Fiji: The 2006 Campaign and its Aftermath*, edited by Jon Fraenkel and Stewart Firth, pp. 11–25. Canberra: Asia Pacific Press. Online: press-files.anu.edu.au/downloads/press/p54581/pdf/ch0211.pdf (accessed 26 June 2017).

2007   'Pacific history matters'. *Journal de la Société des Océanistes*, 125: 59–66. DOI: 10.4000/jso.894.

2007   'Caught in the web: Public discourse in an age of electronic communication'. *Fijian Studies*, 5(1): 156–63.

2008   ***Turnings: Fiji Factions***. Lautoka: Fiji Institute of Applied Studies, 224 pp.

Republished

    2013   ***Turnings: Fiji Factions***. Canberra: ANU E Press. Online: press.anu.edu.au/wp-content/uploads/2013/03/whole5.pdf (accessed 18 January 2017).

2008   'One life, three worlds'. In *Turnings*, pp. 197–221.

2008	ed. with Vicki Luker. ***Telling Pacific Lives: Prisms of Process***. Canberra: ANU E Press. xiv+299 pp. Online: press.anu.edu.au/wp-content/uploads/2011/03/whole_book7.pdf (accessed 18 January 2017).
2008	with Vicki Luker. 'Preface'. In *Telling Pacific Lives*, ed. Lal and Luker, pp. vii–xiv. Online: press-files.anu.edu.au/downloads/press/p22891/pdf/preface3.pdf (accessed 6 March 2017).
2008	'Telling the life of A.D. Patel'. In *Telling Pacific Lives*, ed. Lal and Luker, pp. 177–94. Online: press-files.anu.edu.au/downloads/press/p22891/pdf/ch132.pdf (accessed 6 March 2017).
2008	ed. with Ganesh Chand and Vijay Naidu. ***Fiji Coup: Twenty Years On***. Lautoka: Fiji Institute of Applied Studies, 230 pp.
2008	'The loss of innocence'. In *Fiji Coup*, ed. Lal, Chand and Naidu, pp. 1–23.
2009	ed. with William Safran and Ajaya Kumar Sahoo. ***Transnational Migrations: The Indian Diaspora***. London: Routledge, xxxv+174 pp.
2009	with William Safran and Ajaya Kumar Sahoo. 'Indian diaspora in transnational contexts: Introduction'. In *Transnational Migrations*, ed. Safran, Sahoo and Lal, pp. vii–xxxv.
2009	ed. with Jon Fraenkel and Stewart Firth. ***The 2006 Military Takeover in Fiji: A Coup to End All Coups?***. Canberra: ANU E Press, xiv+472 pp. Online: press.anu.edu.au/wp-content/uploads/2011/02/whole_book15.pdf (accessed 18 January 2017).
2009	'"Anxiety, uncertainty and fear in our land": Fiji's road to military coup, 2006' in *The 2006 Military Takeover in Fiji*, ed. Fraenkel, Firth and Lal, pp. 21–42.
2009	'"This process of political adjustment": The aftermath of the 2006 Fiji coup'. In *The 2006 Military Takeover in Fiji*, ed. Fraenkel, Firth and Lal, pp. 67–93.

2009 'One hand clapping: Reflections on the first anniversary of Fiji's 2006 coup'. In *The 2006 Military Takeover in Fiji*, ed. Fraenkel, Firth and Lal, pp. 425–47.

2009 'Reshmi'. In *Shifting Location: Indo-Fijian Writing from Australia*, edited by Subramani, pp. 119–34. Sydney: Casula Powerhouse.

Republished

2011 'Blurred lines'. In *Intersections*, pp. 208–19.

2009 'A well with no water'. *Contemporary Pacific*, 21(1): 73–89. DOI: 10.1353/cp.0.0032.

2009 'Indo-Fijians: Roots and routes'. In *The South Asian Diaspora: Transnational Networks and Changing Identities*, edited by Rajesh Rai and Peter Reeves, pp. 89–107. London: Routledge.

Republished

2011 'A hundred years in a lifetime'. In *Intersections*, pp. 165–85.

2009 'Promise postponed: A South African sojourn'. *Dreadlocks: The Literary Journal of the School of Language, Arts and Media*, 5: 4–17.

2009 'The Hague Immigration Lecture, 2008: Marking the 135th anniversary of the arrival of Indian people in Suriname'. *Fijian Studies*, 7(1): 145–54. Online: fijianstudies.net/wp-content/uploads/FS/7(1)/8-Lal.pdf (accessed 24 January 2017).

Republished

2013 In *Indian Diaspora*, ed. Amarjit Singh, pp. 285–92.

2010 ***In the Eye of the Storm: Jai Ram Reddy and the Politics of Postcolonial Fiji***. Canberra: ANU E Press. xxvi+735 pp. Online: press.anu.edu.au/wp-content/uploads/2011/03/whole3.pdf (accessed 18 January 2017).

2010 'Tuimacilai: A review essay'. *PacifiCurrents: eJournal of the Australian Association for the Advancement of Pacific Studies*, issues 1.2 & 2.1. Online: intersections.anu.edu.au/pacificurrents/lal_review.htm (accessed 18 January 2017).

Republished

    2015   'Making and unmaking of a Fijian colossus: A review essay of *Tuimacilai: A life of Ratu Sir Kamisese Mara*'. In *Fijian Studies*, 13(1): 31–41. Online: fijianstudies.net/wp-content/uploads/FS/13(1)/FS-13-1-Lal-Mara.pdf (accessed 24 January 2017).

2011   ***Intersections: History, Memory, Discipline***, with a 'Foreword' by Doug Munro, Lautoka: Fiji Institute of Applied Studies, and Sydney: Asia Pacific Publications, xi+321 pp.

Republished

    2012   ***Intersections: History, Memory, Discipline***. Canberra: ANU E Press. press.anu.edu.au/wp-content/uploads/2012/11/whole2.pdf (accessed 18 January 2017).

2011   'When it is over'. In *Intersections*, pp. 1–7.

2011   'Ungiven speech (2009)'. In *Intersections*, pp. 102–109.

2011   'The road from Laucala Bay'. In *Intersections*, pp. 11–26.

Republished

    2013   In *Ron Crocombe e Toa!: Pacific Writings to Celebrate his Life and Work*, ed. Linda Crowl, Marjorie Tuainekore Crocombe and Rod Dixon, pp. 316–31. Suva: University of the South Pacific Press.

2011   'Coombs 4240: A room of my own'. In *Intersections*, pp.127–38. Online: press-files.anu.edu.au/downloads/press/p209021/pdf/ch092.pdf (accessed 24 January 2017).

2011   ed. ***A Vision for Change: Speeches and Writings of AD Patel***. Canberra: ANU E Press, xxv+373 pp. Online: press.anu.edu.au/wp-content/uploads/2011/11/whole6.pdf (accessed 18 January 2017).

2011   'Introduction'. In *A Vision for Change: Speeches and Writings of AD Patel*, ed. Lal, pp. xi–xxv.

2011 'Where has all the music gone? Reflections on the fortieth anniversary of Fiji's independence'. *Contemporary Pacific*, 23(2): 412–36. DOI: 10.1353/cp.2011.0040.

Republished

> 2011 In *Intersections*, pp. 58–78. Online: press-files.anu.edu.au/downloads/press/p209021/pdf/ch053.pdf (accessed 24 January 2017).

2011 'Manuscript XXIII: Common roll and proportional representation: Submission of the National Federation Party to the Street Royal Commission, 6 August 1975'. *Journal of Pacific History*, 46(1): 89–101. Online: dx.doi.org/10.1080/00223344.2011.573638 (accessed 6 March 2017).

2011 ***Common Roll, Communal Roll, Proportional Representation: Historical Documents Relating to the Search for a Suitable Electoral System for Fiji.*** State, Society and Governance in Melanesia Project, Working Paper 1/2011. Research School of Pacific and Asian Studies. Canberra: The Australian National University, 67 pp.

2012 ed. with Ashutosh Kumar and Yogendra Yadav. ***Bhut Len ki Katha: Girmit ke Anubhav. By Totaram Sanadhya*** (The story of the haunted line: The experience of Girmit by Totaram Sanadhya). New Delhi: Rajkamal Prakashan, 143 pp.

2012 ed. ***Fiji and the Coup Syndrome***. Special issue of *The Round Table: The Commonwealth Journal of International Affairs*, 101(6): 489–601.

2012 'Editorial: Fiji's coup conundrum'. *The Round Table: The Commonwealth Journal of International Affairs*, 101(6): 489–97. URL: dx.doi.org/10.1080/00358533.2012.749097 (accessed 7 March 2017).

2012 'Girmit: A journey through Indian indenture historiography'. *Man In India*, 92(2): 215–24.

2012 'Trajectories of transformation: Fiji Indians from common roll to consociationalism'. *Diaspora Studies: Journal of the Organisation for Diaspora Initiatives*, 5(2): 147–69. DOI: 10.1080/09739572.2013.807545.

2012   'Fiji: the autocratic style of Ratu Mara'. *Archifacts: Journal of the Archives and Records Association of New Zealand*, October 2012: 74–85.

2013   'In search of the "children of the wind": A journey to Chattisgarh'. *South Asia: Journal of South Asian Studies*, 36(2): 297–307.

2013   'Manuscript XXVI: The implications of Fijian independence'. *Journal of Pacific History*, 48(1): 78–94. DOI: 10.1080/00223344.2012.755747.

2013   'Fiji: Sailing in uncharted seas'. *The Round Table: The Commonwealth Journal of International Affairs*, 102(5): 481–82. DOI: 10.1080/00358533.2013.834174.

2013   'The Hague immigration lecture'. In *Indian Diaspora: Voices of Grandparents and Grandparenting*, edited by Amarjit Singh, pp. 285–92. Rotterdam: Sense Publishers.

2013   'Indian indenture: Experiment and experience'. In *Routledge Handbook of the South Asian Diaspora*, edited by Joya Chatterji and David Washbrook, pp. 79–95. London: Routledge.

2013   'The strange career of Commodore Frank Bainimarama's Fiji 2006 coup'. State, Society and Governance in Melanesia Project, Discussion Paper 9/2013. Research School of Pacific and Asian Studies. Canberra: The Australian National University, 19 pp.

2013   'Darrell Tryon (1942–2013): a personal tribute'. *Outrigger: Blog of the Pacific Institute*, 17 May. Online: pacificinstitute.anu.edu.au/outrigger/2013/05/17/darrell-tryon-1942-2013-a-personal-tribute/ (accessed 18 January 2017).

2014   ed. with Maurits S. Hasankhan and Doug Munro. **Resistance and Indian Indenture Experience: Comparative Perspectives**. New Delhi: Manohar, 315 pp.

2014   with Maurits S. Hasankhan. 'Introduction'. In *Resistance and Indian Indenture Experience: Comparative Perspectives*, ed. Hasankhan, Lal and Munro, pp. 9–18.

2014	with Doug Munro. 'Non-resistance in Fiji'. In *Resistance and Indian Indenture Experience: Comparative Perspectives*, ed. Hasankhan, Lal and Munro, pp. 121–56.
2014	ed. with Bill Gammage and Gavan Daws. ***The Boy from Boort: Remembering Hank Nelson***. Canberra: ANU Press, ix+224 pp. Online: press.anu.edu.au/wp-content/uploads/2014/07/whole011.pdf (accessed 18 January 2017).
2014	with Bill Gammage and Gavan Daws. 'Preface'. In *The Boy from Boort: Remembering Hank Nelson*, ed. Gammage, Lal and Daws, pp. vii–viii. Online: press-files.anu.edu.au/downloads/press/p286291/pdf/preface.pdf (accessed 7 March 2017).
2014	'Hank of Coombs'. In *The Boy from Boort: Remembering Hank Nelson*, ed. Gammage, Lal and Daws, pp. 75–88. Online: press-files.anu.edu.au/downloads/press/p286291/pdf/ch101.pdf (accessed 7 March 2017).
2014	'In Frank Bainimarama's shadow: Fiji, elections and the future'. *Journal of Pacific History* 49(4): 457–68. DOI: 10.1080/00223344.2014.977518.
2014	'Nandu's shadow'. *Fijian Studies*, 12(1–2): 73–83. Online: fijianstudies.net/2014-21/ (accessed 11 March 2017).
2015	ed. with Jack Corbett. ***Political Life Writing in the Pacific: Reflections on Practice***. Canberra: ANU Press, xi+167 pp. Online: press.anu.edu.au/wp-content/uploads/2015/07/whole4.pdf (accessed 18 January 2017).
2015	with Jack Corbett. 'Preface'. In *Political Life Writing in the Pacific*, ed. Corbett and Lal, pp. ix–x. Online: press-files.anu.edu.au/downloads/press/p319171/pdf/preface2.pdf (7 March 2017).
2015	'End of a phase of history: Writing the life of a reluctant Fiji politician'. In *Political Life Writing in the Pacific*, ed. Corbett and Lal, pp. 59–74. Online: press-files.anu.edu.au/downloads/press/p319171/pdf/ch053.pdf (accessed 12 December 2016).

2015 '"The world becomes stranger, the pattern more complicated": Culture, identity and the Indo-Fijian experience'. In *Indian Diaspora: Socio-cultural and Religious Worlds*, edited by P. Pratap Kumar, pp. 52–72. Leiden: Brill.

2015 'Avatars of Fiji's girmit narrative'. In *Narrative and Identity Construction in the Pacific Islands*, edited by Farzana Gounder, pp. 177–93. Amsterdam and Philadelphia: Benjamins Publishing.

2015 with Knut Jacobsen. 'Dispersals, migrations, diversity of communities and the notion of an Indian diaspora'. In *Routledge Handbook of Contemporary India*, edited by Knut Jacobsen, pp. 159–71. London: Routledge.

2015 'Pratap Chand's *A Fijian Memoir: Footprints of a Girmitiya's Grandson*'. *Fijian Studies*, 13(1): 135–38. Online: fijianstudies.net/wp-content/uploads/FS/13(1)/FS-13-1-Lal-Pratap.pdf (accessed 24 January 2017). Address delivered at the launch of Pratap Chand's memoir in Canberra.

2016 **Historical Dictionary of Fiji**. New York: Rowman & Littlefield, xlix+293 pp.

2016 'Of journals and journeys: Reflections'. *Fijian Studies*, 14(1): 5–22. Online: fijianstudies.net/2016-vol-14-no-1/ (accessed 16 February 2017).

2016 'The tamarind tree: Vignettes from a plantation frontier in Fiji'. *Fijian Studies*, 14(1): 35–49. Online: fijianstudies.net/2016-vol-14-no-1/ (accessed 11 March 2017).

2016 'The journey of Girmit'. *Islands Business*, January: 12–13.

2016 'Faction: I am leaving now'. *Fijian Studies*, 14(2): 58–66. Online: fijianstudies.net/14-2/ (accessed 11 March 2017).

2016 'Exile and a land of memory: C.K. Chen in conversation with Brij V. Lal, scholar, activist'. *Fijian Studies*, 14(2): 143–59. Online: fijianstudies.net/14-2/ (accessed 29 June 2017).

2017 'Girmit', *South Asia* (special section on 'Keywords', edited by Meera Ashar, Trent Brown, Assa Doron, Craig Jeffrey), 40(2): 313–15. DOI: 10.1080/00856401.2017.1294233 (accessed 26 June 2017).

Made in the USA
Middletown, DE
09 October 2020